AF166662

Lecture Notes
in Business Information Processing   556

LNBIP reports state-of-the-art results in areas related to business information systems and industrial application software development – timely, at a high level, and in both printed and electronic form.

The type of material published includes

- Proceedings (published in time for the respective event)
- Postproceedings (consisting of thoroughly revised and/or extended final papers)
- Other edited monographs (such as, for example, project reports or invited volumes)
- Tutorials (coherently integrated collections of lectures given at advanced courses, seminars, schools, etc.)
- Award-winning or exceptional theses

LNBIP is abstracted/indexed in DBLP, EI and Scopus. LNBIP volumes are also submitted for the inclusion in ISI Proceedings.

Jānis Grabis · Yves Wautelet
Editors

Advanced Information Systems Engineering Workshops

CAiSE 2025 Workshops
Vienna, Austria, June 16–20, 2025
Proceedings

 Springer

Editors
Jānis Grabis 🆔
Riga Technical University
Riga, Latvia

Yves Wautelet 🆔
KU Leuven
Brussels, Belgium

ISSN 1865-1348   ISSN 1865-1356 (electronic)
Lecture Notes in Business Information Processing
ISBN 978-3-031-94930-2   ISBN 978-3-031-94931-9 (eBook)
https://doi.org/10.1007/978-3-031-94931-9

This Springer imprint is published by the registered company Springer Nature Switzerland AG
The registered company address is: Gewerbestrasse 11, 6330 Cham, Switzerland

If disposing of this product, please recycle the paper.

Preface

Over its 37 editions, the Conference on Advanced Information Systems Engineering (CAiSE) has been established as a leading venue for information systems engineering research on innovative topics with rigorous scientific theories. This year the CAiSE conference was dedicated to the Bridging Silos theme to invite contributions addressing information systems engineering in a coherent manner encompassing human, organizational, economic, societal, and technological aspects. CAiSE 2025 was held in Vienna, Austria on 16–20 June, 2025.

Every year, CAiSE is accompanied by a significant number of high-quality workshops. Their aim is to address specific emerging challenges in the field, to facilitate interaction between stakeholders and researchers, to discuss innovative ideas, and to present new approaches and tools.

Seven workshops were held at the conference this year and three out of those workshops were joint workshops:

- 3rd Workshop on Knowledge Graphs for Semantics-Driven Systems Engineering (KG4SDSE)
- 3rd International Workshop on Hybrid Artificial Intelligence and Enterprise Modelling for Intelligent Information Systems (HybridAIMS)
- Joint Workshop on Blockchain for Information Systems Engineering (B4ISE) and Workshop on Information Systems and AI for Life Sciences (iSAILS)
- 3rd Workshop on Modelling and Implementation of Digital Twins for Complex Systems (MIDas4CS)
- Joint Process Mining with Unstructured Data workshop (PMUD) and International Workshop on Multimodal Process Mining (MMPM)
- Joint Workshop on Large Language Models in Service-Oriented Architectures and Systems Design: Innovations and Applications (LLM-SOA) and Generation of Synthetic Datasets for Information Systems (GENSYN)
- 1st Workshop on Compliance in the Era of Artificial Intelligence (CAI).

The workshops collectively attracted 59 submissions. Three submissions were desk rejected as out of scope. 56 submissions entered the review process, and out of these submissions 24 were accepted for publication as full papers and 5 as short ones. The selection was based on the scrutiny of three reviewers per paper from the program committee of each workshop following a single-blind scheme. Besides contributed research, several workshops also featured keynote presentation and discussion papers.

We would like to thank the organizers of the workshops for their excellent job. We also express our gratitude to the reviewers for their timely and constructive work, as well as the publicity chairs for their activities that helped to attract submissions. We thank the Proceedings Chair, Marianne Schnellmann, and Springer for their swift communication and support of the proceedings production process. Finally, we warmly thank General

Co-chairs Gerti Kappel and Hend*erik* A. Proper and Organization Chair Dominik Bork as well as the whole CAiSE organization team for their great support.

April 2025

Jānis Grabis
Yves Wautelet

Organization

Workshop Chairs

Jānis Grabis	Riga Technical University, Latvia
Yves Wautelet	KU Leuven, Belgium

Contents

**Joint Process Mining with Unstructured Data workshop (PMUD) and
International Workshop on Multimodal Process Mining (MMPM)**

**Joint Workshop on Large Language Models in Service-Oriented
Architectures Design: Innovations and Applications (LLM-SOA) and
Generation of Synthetic Datasets for Information Systems (GENSYN)**

1st Workshop on Compliance in the Era of Artificial Intelligence (CAI)

3rd Workshop on Knowledge Graphs for Semantics-Driven Systems Engineering (KG4SDSE)

3rd Workshop on Knowledge Graphs for Semantics-Driven Systems Engineering (KG4SDSE 2025)

The 3rd Workshop on **Knowledge Graphs for Semantics-Driven Systems Engineering** (KG4SDSE)[1] followed the successful workshops held in 2023 and 2024 at CAiSE, with a desire to create a focal point for the information systems engineering community and research groups that are working with Knowledge Graphs in a systems engineering context.

The workshop aimed to highlight the role of semantics in information systems engineering and the integration patterns that can streamline semantics between Semantic Web technologies, Conceptual Modeling methods and, more recently, Large Language Models or other flavors of Generative AI. Knowledge engineering is expected to contribute as a paradigm for novel knowledge flows and knowledge-based systems where new research questions and engineering challenges are emerging. The workshop was a timely event aiming to stimulate discussions on these questions and challenges, accepting both early-stage results and regular research papers.

This year the workshop received 13 submissions in total, with authors from 7 countries. Based on three constructive (single-blind) evaluations per paper from the Program Committee, we accepted 5 papers that we found interesting for the workshop community, covering diverse research approaches – both empirical experimentation and conceptual design-oriented work:

- Steven Alter revisits the Work Systems Framework by applying Large Language Models to produce situational knowledge graphs of work systems descriptions;
- Bara, Meseşan and Silaghi report on experiments with Retrieval-Augmented Generation for Entity Alignment tasks;
- Popoviciu and Ghiran develop a domain-specific modeling language for the tourism sector and leverage the ADOxx capabilities for model-driven RDF graph production;
- Völz, Amlashi and Song make a proposition that closes the knowledge transfer loop between ADOxx metamodeling platform and RDF semantic graphs;
- The short paper of Mosolygó et al. investigates graph querying complexity patterns to improve the support for knowledge graphs query benchmarking.

We are thankful to the authors of submitted papers who helped turn this workshop into a recurring event, and we are grateful to the CAiSE conference committee and workshop chairs for hosting it again, during the Pre-conference Days of CAiSE 2025.

---

[1] https://www.omilab.org/activities/events/caise2025_kg4sdse/.

This event was supported by OMiLAB NPO, Germany, and FORTH-ICS, Greece, and facilitated by the dedicated efforts of our Web presence chair, Iulia Vaidian (OMiLAB).

April 2025

Robert Andrei Buchmann
Dimitris Karagiannis
Dimitris Plexousakis

Organization

Workshop Chairs

Robert Buchmann   Babeş-Bolyai University, Romania
Dimitris Karagiannis   University of Vienna, Austria
Dimitris Plexousakis   Institute of Computer Science, FORTH and University of Crete, Greece

Web Chair

Iulia Vaidian   OMiLAB NPO, Germany

Program Committee

Amin Anjomshoaa	Vienna University of Economics and Business, Austria
Nick Bassiliades	Aristotle University of Thessaloniki, Greece
Michael Fellmann	University of Rostock, Germany
Hans-Georg Fill	University of Fribourg, Switzerland
Anne Füßl	Technische Universität Ilmenau, Germany
Aurona Gerber	University of the Western Cape, South Africa
Ana-Maria Ghiran	Babeş-Bolyai University, Romania
Adrian Groza	Technical University of Cluj-Napoca, Romania
Paul Johannesson	Stockholm University, Sweden
Marite Kirikova	Riga Technical University, Latvia
Manolis Koubarakis	National and Kapodistrian University of Athens, Greece
Jose Emilio Labra Gayo	Universidad de Oviedo, Chile
Ana León	Universitat Politècnica de València, Spain
Massimo Mecella	Sapienza Università di Roma, Italy
Andreas Opdahl	University of Bergen, Norway
Andrea Polini	University of Camerino, Italy
Achim Reiz	University of Rostock, Germany
Ben Roelens	Open University, The Netherlands
Anisa Rula	University of Brescia, Italy
Maribel Yasmina Santos	University of Minho, Portugal

Using an LLM to Create Situation-Specific Knowledge Graphs Based on a Domain Knowledge Graph: Practical Possibilities and Semantic Challenges

Steven Alter[(✉)] [iD]

University of San Francisco, 2130 Fulton St., San Francisco 94117, USA
`alter@ufca.edu`

Abstract. This paper demonstrates possibilities and challenges in using an LLM to create a domain knowledge graph (DKG) for the work system domain and then converting it to a situation-specific knowledge graph (SSKG) for a specific system. It starts by summarizing existing ideas about work systems and a taxonomy of knowledge objects that have been presented previously. It uses an LLM to create a DKG based on parts of the work system perspective and highlights semantic challenges in that process. It uses an LLM to apply that DKG in creating SSKGs for two case study examples, one about ride hailing and one about medical care. It uses the LLM to identify parts of the DKG that were not the involved in links to nodes containing information from each case. It uses an LLM to prune those unnecessary nodes from the SSKG but also asks the LLM to identify parts of the DKG that might be relevant even though they were not included in a pruned SSKG. The conclusion stresses both practical possibilities and semantic challenges revealed in this research and discusses next steps related to use of LLMs in conjunction with DKGs and SSKGs in systems engineering.

Keywords: Knowledge graph · work system perspective · domain knowledge graph · situation-specific knowledge graph · large language model · knowledge object · taxonomy of knowledge objects

1 Pursuing a Challenge for Semantics-Driven Systems Engineering

The CFP of the KG4SDSE workshop before CAISE 2025 notes that knowledge graphs (KGs) have been primarily investigated as engineered artifacts by themselves with emphasis on formalisms, enabling technologies such as RDF, knowledge management, and so on. The CFP aims to "shift focus from what KGs are or how they can be built toward how they can be relevant to IS engineering", with particular interest in the interplay between KGs and LLMs. This paper pursues that aspiration by demonstrating possibilities and challenges encountered when using an LLM to create a domain knowledge graph (DKG) for the domain *work system* and converting it to a situation-specific knowledge graph (SSKG) supporting IS engineering for a specific current or future system while attending to constraints, issues, and challenges for that system.

J. Grabis and Y. Wautelet (Eds.): CAiSE 2025 Workshops, LNBIP 556, pp. 5–17, 2025.
https://doi.org/10.1007/978-3-031-94931-9_1

Assumptions. This paper's approach to possibilities and challenges in using KGs for semantics-driven systems engineering is based on a set of assumptions.

- General knowledge about sociotechnical (with human participants) and totally automated work systems also applies to information systems, a special case of work system, whose activities are devoted to processing information.
- Work system theory (Fig. 1) and its extensions in the broader work system perspective can serve as a scaffolding for organizing much of the domain knowledge about IS and linking it to information about specific situations being analyzed.
- Knowledge objects (KOs) are individual instances of knowledge. A taxonomy of KOs (Fig. 3) divides KOs into five large categories (concepts, data, interpretations, generalizations, methods) and KO types within those categories (Fig. 3)
- Information about specific information systems can be linked to nodes in a domain knowledge graph (a DKG) containing knowledge from the work system perspective.
- An LLM can use a DKG for work systems as a scaffolding for constructing a situation-specific knowledge graph (an SSKG). That SSKG can be used to analyze a specific information system and organize additional information about that system.
- DKGs and SSKGs produced by using LLMs may generate positive net value for system engineering despite requiring human attention due to the token- and probability-based internal operation of LLMs and the resulting imprecision and inaccuracy in DKGs and SSKGs that might be produced.

Goal. This paper shows how an LLM can support initial steps in IS engineering by: 1) creating a DKG based on the work system perspective, 2) using that DKG to create an initial SSKG for a specific work system (which may be an information system), 3) pruning the SSKG to eliminate parts of the DKG that seem extraneous for the analysis at hand, 4) using and possibly extending the SSKG as part of the analysis.

Organization. This paper proceeds as follows: First it summarizes the work system perspective, which has evolved over several decades and has been presented many times. Next it explains the latest version of a taxonomy of KOs. It demonstrates the process of using an LLM to create an initial DKG, based on the core of the work system perspective and several of the categories in the taxonomy of KOs. It shows results of using an LLM to convert the initial DKG into an SSKG for each of two published case studies, one about ride hailing (RDH403) and one about problematic use of an electronic medical records system while providing medical care (EMR558). The resulting SSKGs are designated RDH-01 and EMR-01. Those SSKGs are pruned to eliminate parts of the DKG that have no links other aspects of the situations in the respective SSKGs. The pruned SSKGs are RDH-02 and EMR-02. An additional step asks the LLM to identify parts of the DKG that were not reflected in RDH-02 or EMR-02 but that might be relevant (as might happen when a documented analysis fails to mention factors that might matter). The conclusion explains implications and next steps related to use of LLMs in conjunction with KGs in IS systems engineering.

Caveat. This paper builds directly on the author's stream of research during the last 20+ years, as summarized most recently in [1]. Due to KG4SDSE's length limitation, this paper does not include references linking its ideas and approach parts of the IS engineering literature that are cited in many papers referenced in [1–4]. Also, it does not repeat many citations in a 2024 panel report about SDSE [5].

Acronyms. SDSE (semantics-driven systems engineering) KG (knowledge graph), DKG (domain KG), SSKG (situation-specific KG), KO (knowledge object), LLM (large language model), DKG-01, DKG-02 (two versions of a domain KG for IS), WST (work system theory).

2   Work System Theory and the Work System Perspective

Work system theory (WST) [2] and its extensions in the work system perspective [1] provide a scaffolding for organizing domain knowledge that can be used in the analysis and design of specific information systems in specific situations.

Work. Work is viewed as the application of human, informational, physical, and other resources to produce product/services for internal or external customers. Work occurs in homes, businesses, governments, and other situations where purposeful use of resources aims to produce outcomes.

Work System. Work system is defined in Fig. 1. The first *and/or* in the definition says that a work system may be a sociotechnical system whose human participants perform some of the work activities or it may be a totally automated system. Work in work systems may or may not be repeatable and may be structured to varying degrees, e.g., unstructured (designing a unique advertisement), semi-structured (diagnosing a complex medical condition), workflows involving some discretion (processing invoice payments), or highly structured (manufacturing semiconductors). A key question in designing or analyzing a work system is whether activities or processes are stated as requirements that must be followed or as guidelines that encourage exercise of judgment in dealing with special cases or exceptions.

Work System View of an Enterprise. A very small enterprise might be viewed as a single work system, although it is typically more useful to say that enterprises operate and serve their customers through multiple work systems and their interactions. Typically, the operation and interaction of work systems maintain the enterprise, obtain and apply resources, and produce product/services for customers and economic results.

Information Systems and Projects as Work Systems. An IS is a work system whose activities are devoted to capturing, transmitting, storing, retrieving, deleting, manipu-lating, and/or displaying information. Projects such as software development are work systems designed to produce specific product/services and then go out of existence. Thus, work system ideas apply to projects even though detailed description of large projects requires project-specific ideas such as work-breakdown-structures and planned start and end dates of tasks. Digital agents and automated IT services fit the definition of work system and therefore can be viewed as (encapsulated) work systems.

Work System Theory. The three parts of WST [2] are shown in Fig. 1. The work system framework identifies nine elements of a basic understanding of a work system's form, function, and environment during a period when it is stable enough to retain its identity even though incremental changes may occur, such as minor personnel substitutions or technology upgrades. *Processes and activities, participants, information,* and *technologies* are completely within the work system. The term *processes and activities* is used instead of *business process* because many work systems involving activities such as teaching, diagnosis, and consulting are guided by skills, experience, and judgment of participants rather than by pre-defined work flows that require conformance. *Customers* and *product/services* may be partially inside and partially outside because customers often participate in activities within a work system and because product/services take shape within a work system. *Product/services* is used instead of products and services because many things viewed as products bring features associated with services (such as customization) and many things viewed as services bring features associated with products (such as repetitive production). *Infrastructure* refers to human, informational, and technical resources shared by multiple work systems and not associated primarily with one work system. *Environment* includes factors and forces in the organizational, cultural, competitive, technical, regulatory, and demographic context that are relevant because they affect the work system's effectiveness and efficiency. *Strategies* may exist at the enterprise, department, and work system levels. The work system life cycle model (WSLC - not used here) describes how work systems evolve through iterations of planned change through projects and unplanned change through adaptations and workarounds.

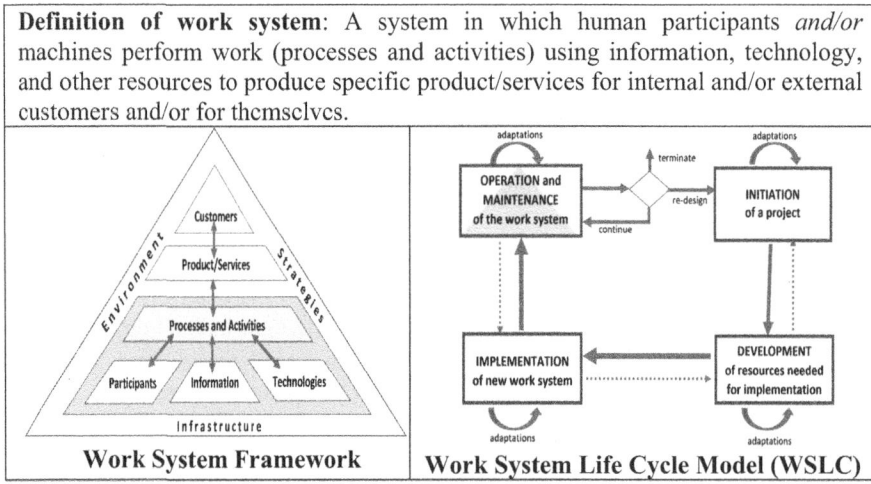

Fig. 1. Three components of work system theory [2]

Facets of Work and Facets of Work Systems. The work system framework (Fig. 1) says nothing about topics such as making decisions, communicating, processing information, coordinating, controlling execution, and so on. The idea of "facet" is analogous to a facet of a cut gem. It is not a separate component, but rather a face or aspect that can be observed or analyzed. This paper's use of facet differs from the approach to facet modeling in computer science.

Table 1 identifies 18 "facets of work", i.e., facets of *processes and activities* in Fig. 1, that were identified through an iterative process that used specific criteria for deciding whether an aspect of work or activity might qualify as a facet of work [3]. Each facet brings many ideas that should not be overlooked when considering work systems carefully. To qualify, an aspect of work must be easily understood, widely applicable, and associated with concepts and other knowledge, evaluation criteria, and design trade-offs that are useful for analyzing work systems and information systems; it must have sub-facets that can be discussed; it must bring open-ended questions for starting conversations (see details in [3, pp. 323–331, 346–353]). The various facets of work often are not independent in operational systems. For example, making decisions often involves communicating, learning, and thinking.

Table 1. 18 Facets of work

Making decisions	Applying knowledge	Performing support work
Communicating	Planning	Interacting socially
Processing information	Controlling execution	Providing service
Thinking	Improvising	Creating value
Representing reality	Coordinating	Co-creating value
Providing information	Performing physical work	Maintaining security

Figure 2 [3, p. 335] uses inward facing arrows to extend the idea of facets of work beyond Table 1 by identifying facets of work systems as a whole and facets of each element of the work system framework (not just *processes and activities*). Most of the facets in Fig. 2 satisfy most of the criteria mentioned earlier. The idea of facets provides

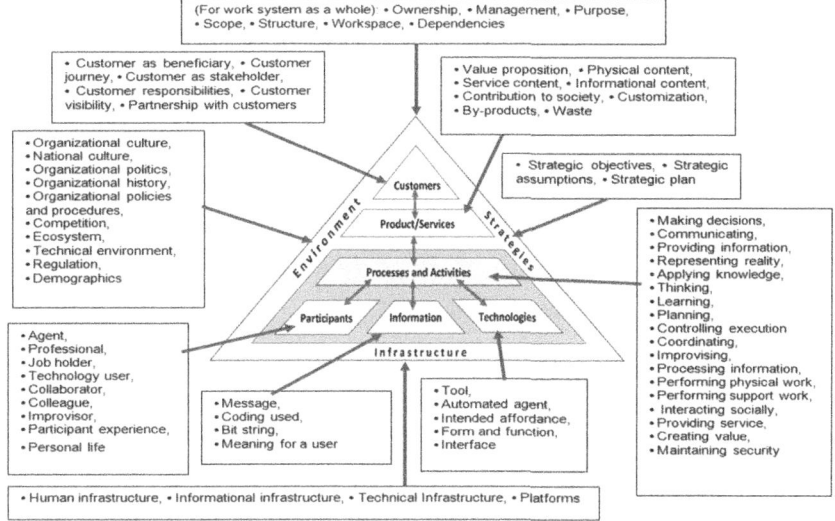

Fig. 2. Facets of work systems and work system elements

part of a path for identifying requirements and issues that otherwise might be overlooked, as demonstrated using two case study examples presented later.

Work System Perspective. WST is the core of a broader work system perspective that includes many additional topics such as a service value chain framework, theory of workarounds, system interaction theory, work system principles, service system axioms, IS usage theory, facets of work, agent responsibility framework, and so on. The taxonomy of knowledge objects Fig. 3 identifies many types of knowledge that might be included in a DKG that builds on the work system framework.

3   A Taxonomy of Knowledge Objects

This paper assumes that knowledge exists in the form of "knowledge objects" (KOs) and that the categories and types of KOs in Fig. 3 are relevant to IS engineering. That taxonomy of KOs evolved from assuming that science is the creation, evaluation, accumulation, dissemination, synthesis, and prioritization of KOs, including the re-evaluation, improvement, or replacement of existing KOs by other KOs that are more effective for understanding important aspects of the relevant domain [4, p. 9]. Tacit knowledge is not included because instances of tacit knowledge are not defined clearly enough to be evaluated, accumulated, synthesized, etc. Non-tacit knowledge is not restricted to abstractions since data and information can be viewed as KOs.

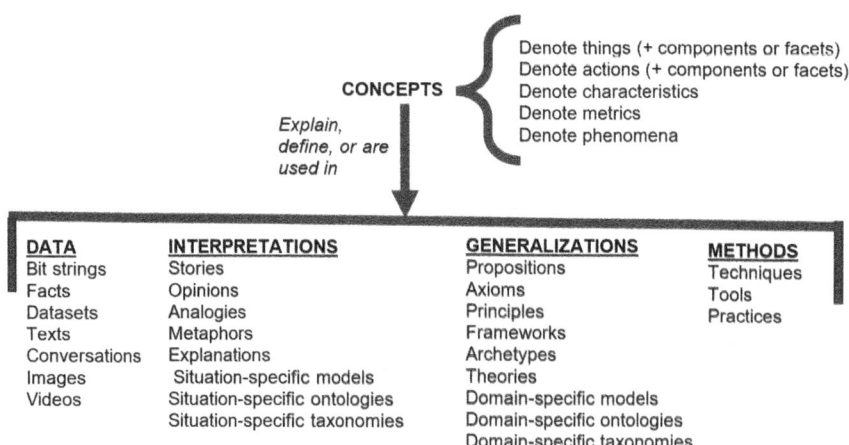

Fig. 3. Taxonomy of knowledge objects [4, updated slightly]

Figure 3 starts with five categories of conceptual artifacts that are concepts (related to things, actions, characteristics, metrics, and phenomena). Concepts and other conceptual artifacts including interpretations, generalizations, and methods are "discussable ideas, ranging from theories, designs and plans down to concepts, like unemployment and gravity." [6, p. 65]. The arrow in Fig. 3 says that concepts are used to define, explain, or express other KOs that can be organized in four broad categories: data and three types of conceptual artifacts: interpretations, generalizations, and methods. Figure 1 says that the non-abstract KO category of data includes facts, datasets, texts, conversations, images, and videos. Understanding and applying data of each of those types requires the use of concepts. The same can be said about interpretations and generalizations. Likewise, concepts are essential for defining and explaining the techniques, tools, and practices that are constituents of methods.

4   Creating a Relevant Domain Knowledge Graph

4.1   Producing an Initial Domain Knowledge Graph – DKG-01

The LLM ChatGPT-03-mini was used to convert the definition of work system (Fig. 1) and a mostly RDF-like summary of the work system framework (Fig. 1) into initial version of a domain KG for the domain of work systems. The following prompt was used:

Produce a knowledge graph that represents the ideas in the following: A work system is a system in which human participants and/or machines perform work (processes and activities) using information, technology, and other resources to produce specific product/services for internal and/or external customers (or for themselves). A basic understanding of a work system can be organized around the nine elements of the work system framework [and] the work system. • The nine elements of a work system include customers, product/services, processes and activities, participants, information, technologies, environment, infrastructure, and strategies. • A work system produces (one or more) product/services. • A work system's product/services are directed toward (one or more) customers. • A work system's customers receive, use, or otherwise benefit directly from its product/services. • A work system operates through (one or more) activities. • Activities produce (one or more) product/services. • Processes produce (one or more) product/services. • Processes consist of groups of related activities with an initial activity and a final activity. • Participants are people who perform (one or more) of a work system's activities. • A work system produces, updates, or uses information. • A work system uses technologies. • A work system's environment affects one or more of the work system's elements. • Infrastructure is human, informational, and technical resources that are used by the work system but are managed outside of it and are shared with other work systems. • Strategies are a type of information

The DKG produced by the LLM is designated as DKG-01. It is condensed into three columns of Table 2 to identify the nodes and edges that the LLM produced in mermaid format [7]. Using mermaid format helps here because displaying DKG-01 graphically would require an illegibly tiny font. Adding other types of KOs from Fig. 3 will produce DKG-02 (next).

Table 2. DKG-01 produced by an LLM based on the prompt above.

graph LR	%% Relationships among	E -->|affects| WS
%% Main node for the work	elements	E -->|affects| PS
system	WS -->|produces| PS	E -->|affects| P
WS[Work System]	PS -->|directed toward| C	E -->|affects| A
%% Core elements (nodes)	C -->|receives/uses| PS	E -->|affects| PT
PS[Product/Services]	WS -->|operates through| A	E -->|affects| I
C[Customers]	A -->|produces| PS	E -->|affects| T
P[Processes]	P -->|consists of| A	E -->|affects| S
A[Activities]	A -- "initial/final activities"	Inf-->|used by (but managed
PT[Participants]	--> P	externally)| WS
I[Information]	WS -->|involves| PT	S -->|is a type of| I
T[Technologies]	PT -->|performs| A	
E[Environment]	WS	
Inf[Infrastructure]	-->|produces/updates/uses| I	
S[Strategies]	WS -->|uses| T	

4.2 Producing a More Complete Domain Knowledge Graph – DKG-02

The taxonomy of KOs (Fig. 3) points to many types of KOs that do not appear in DKG-01. The three prompts below instruct ChatGPT-4o to expand DKG-01 to include three other types of knowledge that exist in the work system perspective: facets of work systems [3], work system principles [8] and obstacles and risks (unpublished diagram in a format similar to Fig. 3). Those three types of KOs suffice as illustrations for showing how DKGs might include KOs of every type in Fig. 3. Each prompt includes items related to work systems as a whole and the nine elements of the work system framework. The use of "…." indicates that only the beginning of each prompt is shown.

Expand the knowledge graph by adding facets to its nodes based on the following: A work system as a whole and each work system element has facets, as listed next. Facets of work system as a whole include: • Ownership, • Management, • Purpose, • Scope, • Structure, • Workspace, • Dependencies. Facets of customers include: • Customer as beneficiary, • Customer journey, • Customer as stakeholder, • Customer responsibilities, ……

Expand the knowledge graph by adding principles to its nodes based on the following: Principles related to work system as a whole include: • Maintain compatibility and coordination with other work systems. • Incorporate goals, measurement, evaluation, and feedback. • Minimize unnecessary risks. • Maintain balance between work system elements. ….

Add the following obstacles and risk factors to the knowledge graph: Obstacles and risk factors for work system as a whole include: • Inadequate management • Inadequate security • Inadequate measurement of success. Obstacles and risk factors for customers include: • Unrealistic expectations • Unmet customer needs or concerns • Customer segments with contradictory requirements or needs • Unsatisfying customer experience ….

DKG-02 adds nodes for facets, principles, and obstacles for the 10 entity types in DKG-01 (work system as a whole and nine work system elements). The entirety of DKG-02 would cover nine pages of this paper if shown in full. As a representative example, Table 3 shows a subset of the KOs that were added to DKG-01 for the work system element *processes and activities* (abbreviated PA in Table 3). Thus, PA_F1 says that the facet F1 (making decisions) is linked to the node PA (*processes and activities*).

Table 3. Small subset of LLM extensions of DKG-01 that appear in DKG-02

%% Facets for PA	%% Principles for PA	%% Obstacles for PA
PA_F1[Making Decisions]	PA_P1[Match process flexibility with product variability]	PA_O1[Inadequate resources]
PA_F2[Communicating]		PA_O2[Inadequate quality controls]
PA_F3[Providing Information]	PA_P2[Perform the work efficiently]	PA_O3[Uncertainty about work methods]
PA_F4[Representing Reality]	PA_P3[Encourage appropriate use of judgment]	PA_O4[Excessive variability in work practices]
PA_F5[Applying Knowledge]	PA_P4[Control problems at their source]	PA_O5[Over-structured work practices]
PA_F6[Thinking]		
PA_F7[Learning]		PA_O6[Excessive interruptions]
PA_F8[Planning]	PA_P5[Monitor quality & timing of inputs/outputs]	
PA_F9[Controlling Execution]	PA_P6[Boundaries between steps .....]	PA_O7[Excessive ......]

5   Producing Situation-Specific KGs for Two Case Studies

This section demonstrates the application of DKG-02 to produce an SSKG for each of two case studies: RDH403 (3,385 words) was extracted from an *Organization Science* article [9] that explored resistance versus control in ride hailing and gig work. EMR558 (9,248 words) is the entirety of a famous surgeon's article "Why Doctors Hate Their Computers." [10]. It discusses benefits and challenges of using an electronic medical records system while providing medical care. The lengthy prompt for each case starts by saying "this is the first step in a multi-stage prompt that will create a new knowledge graph that describes the situation concerning [the specific case]." Each prompt in this stage includes four steps that build cumulatively on DKG-02 as illustrated below:

Step 1. The core of the SSKG is the core of DKG-02, i.e., 10 domain nodes (entire WS and nine elements of the work system framework). The LLM identifies aspects of the specific work system (RDH403 or EMR558) that are instances of core elements. Each instance is a new node linked to a core node by an edge labeled "WS element."

Table 4 is a small subset of the nodes that step 1 produced in mermaid format for RDH. For example, the first line says that drivers are participants. The third line reflects possible semantic confusion (a topic mentioned again later) by saying that the ride hail platform is a participant rather than part of the technology in the work system.

Table 4. Small illustrative subset of "WS element" nodes for an SSKG for the RDH case

WS element: Participants	*Drivers* → "WS element" → Participants *Customers (Riders)* → "WS element" → Participants *RideHail Platform (as Algorithmic Controller)* → "WS element" → Participants
WS element: Processes and activities	*Algorithmic Ride Matching* → "WS element" → Processes & Activities *Customer Rating System* → "WS element" → Processes & Activities *Driver Performance Monitoring* → "WS element" → Processes & Activities
WS element: Information	*Driver Ratings & Feedback* → "WS element" → Information *Ride Acceptance & Cancellation Data* → "WS element" → Information *Customer Complaints & Reviews* → "WS element" → Information

Step 2. Expand the SSKG by identifying aspects of the specific work system that are instances of work system facets (Fig. 3) in DKG-02. Each instance is a new node linked to a core node by an edge labeled "facet." Table 5 reveals a semantic confusion where the LLM categorizes medical scribes (human doctors in India) as automated agents.

Table 5. Small illustrative subset of "facet" nodes for an SSKG for the EMR case

WS element Participants	*Doctors as Improvisors in Managing Digital Workflows* → "facet " → PT_F7 (Improvisor) *Burnout Due to EMR Documentation Load* → "facet " → PT_F8 (Participant Experience)
WS element Information	*Lack of Consistency in Patient Records* → "facet " → I_F4 (Meaning for a User) *Poorly Structured Problem Lists in EHRs* → "facet " → I_F2 (Coding Used)
WS element Technologies	*Doctors Struggle with EMR UI* Complexity → "facet " → T_F5 (Interface) *Medical Scribes Used as Workaround for EMR Inefficiency* → "facet " → T_F2 (Automated Agent)

Step 3. Continue expanding the SSKG by identifying aspects of the specific work system that might be governed by 24 WS principles [8] in DKG-02. A sentence summarizing each instance is linked to a core node by an edge labeled "principle" (Table 6).

Step 4. Continue expanding the SSKG by identifying aspects of the specific work system that are described by one of the obstacles or risks included in DKG-02. Each instance is a new node linked to a core node by an edge labeled "obstacle" (Table 7).

The resulting SSKG after just the above four steps could be used (carefully) for IS engineering because it organizes a view of the situation that includes work system

Table 6. Small illustrative subset of "principle" (*) nodes for an SSKG for the EMR case

WS as a whole	*WS_P2 (Incorporate goals, measurement, evaluation, & feedback) *Physicians' EMR usage is measured but lacks efficiency evaluations.* → "principle" → WS_P2
Processes & activities	*PA_P5 (Monitor quality & timing of inputs/outputs) *Doctors spend excessive time entering data rather than interacting with patients.* → "principle" → PA_P5
Customers	*C_P2 (Balance priorities of different customers) *The system is designed for both doctors and administrators, leading to usability conflicts.* → "principle" → C_P2

Table 7. Small illustrative subset of "obstacle" (*) nodes for an SSKG for the EMR case

WS as a whole	*WS_O3 (Inadequate measurement of success) *EMR effectiveness is measured by usage, not efficiency or usability.* → "obstacle " → WS_O3
Participants	*PA_O7 (Excessive complexity) *Basic medical tasks require too many clicks and steps in the system.* → "obstacle " → PA_O7
Customers	*C_O1 (Unrealistic expectations) *Doctors are expected to manage both medical care and complex EMR documentation.* → "obstacle" → C_O1

elements, facets, principles, and obstacles relevant to the specific situation. KOs of the other KO types (Fig. 3) could be added using steps similar to those above.

6 Pruning the SSKGs to Eliminate Unnecessary Nodes

Identifying and eliminating nodes in DKG-02 that are not linked to any node related to the specific situation would make the size of SSKGs produced by the LLM less overwhelming (e.g., by removing some of the 18 facets and 24 principles in DKG-02). The LLM expressed the unnecessary nature of some facet nodes as follows:

- PA_F2 (Communicating) – General communication issues are not a central concern.
- PA_F4 (Representing Reality) – EMR558 does not discuss how the system represents real-world patient data in a digital format.
- PA_F5 (Applying Knowledge) – There is no focus on medical professionals using knowledge.

7 Reconsidering Possibly Relevant Nodes that Were Pruned

All three of the pruned facets mentioned above actually were relevant in the case. Communication (F2) was important even if it was not named as *communication*. There were several situations where EMR558 did not represent reality (F4) effectively. Medical professionals obviously applied knowledge (F5) while practicing medicine. An additional prompt asked the LLM to read the cases again to identify nodes that might be relevant even though they had been pruned. A relevant instance for F10 was "EMR systems must coordinate information across multiple departments."

8 Conclusion

Following the KG4SDSE CFP, this paper focused on how KGs "can be relevant to IS engineering," with particular interest in the interplay between KGs and LLMs. An LLM created two versions of a domain KG. DKG-01 expressed the core ideas in WST (Sect. 4.1). DKG-02 added three other types of KOs: facets, principles, and obstacles (Sect. 4.2). The taxonomy of KOs (Sect. 3) identified other KO types that might have been included (but not in 12-pages). The LLM used DKG-02 to summarize two case studies as situation-specific KGs (SSKGs) (Sect. 5). Even those limited summaries could be useful in requirements analysis for IS engineering, as was implied by applications of an LLM to three cases in [11]. Examples in Sects. 5, 6, and 7 highlight the fundamental LLM limitation that statistical proximity of words in texts does not constitute "understanding" of the words or the context in which they are used.

A Fundamental Problem. Semantic clarity for IS and systems engineering is challenged by polysemy, multiple meanings for the same word, such as system, information, information system, IS project, service, user, implementation, etc. E.g., some readers of EMR558 might see the relevant system as a system of providing medical care and others might see it as an electronic medical records system.

An Opportunity and Challenge for Systems Engineering. Extensive KGs produced in this research (but not shown in detail) might support early stages of systems engineering where LLMs can help analysts gather and organize information from different sources based on clear conceptual frameworks. However, even when the KGs are based on a carefully articulated theoretical approach (WST in this research), analysts will need to inspect LLM outputs carefully to assure that the types of semantic confusions noted in Sects. 5, 6, and 7 are identified and eliminated.

8.1 Implied Paths Forward for Semantic-Driven Systems Engineering

1) **Use systems analysis outlines based on domain KGs**. During 2003–2017 many hundreds of MBA and EMBA students produced management briefings using systems analysis outlines based on ideas like those in DKG-01 and DKG-02 [1, p. 348]. Their system summaries covered some of the same topics as the SSKGs discussed here. A DKG for work systems could be the basis of SDSE (semantics-driven software engineering) outlines presented to analysts or users through online questionnaires,

chatbots, or a combination of those approaches. The results for individual respondents or groups of respondents could be organized and compiled using an LLM or LLM-based tool (e.g., Google's NotebookLM).

2) **Greatly extend DKG-01 and DKG-02 to include non-obvious nuances.** The spirit of SDSE calls for recognizing and addressing polysemy when producing DKGs and SSKGs. E.g., Sect. 2's distinctions and nuances about *customers, product/services,* and *processes and activities* were not reflected fully in DKG-01. The complexity of the sixth of a series of metamodels that tried to express a more detailed approach to WST (see [1, p. 355]) only hints at the level of detail that would be needed in DKGs that minimize semantic confusion due to polysemy, domain nuances, and other issues. That metamodel's complexity implies that producing those DKGs would be an enormous task even if LLMs gathered and filtered knowledge from the scientific literature.

3) **Develop tools that reflect realistic limits of KGs and LLMs**. It is easy to say that SDSE users of KGs and LLMs should exercise the utmost caution in using their outputs. Beyond that, tool-building research might produce SDSE tools and methods that minimize problems due to the limits of KGs and LLMs.

4) **Test ideas and methods related to DKGs and SSKGs**. Published case studies were used to illustrate a possible approach to SDSE based on DKGs and SSKGs. Going deeper calls for further development and real-world application of these ideas.

Disclosure of Interests.   The author has no competing interests.

References

1. Alter, S.: Steps toward articulating a work system perspective that addresses a grand challenge for the is discipline. In: Strecker, S., Jung, J. (eds.) Informing Possible Future Worlds: Essays in Honour of Ulrich Frank, Logos Verlag Berlin, pp. 343–367 (2024). https://library.oapen.org/bitstream/handle/20.500.12657/90739/external_content.pdf?sequence=1#page=359. Accessed 27 Feb 2025
2. Alter, S.: Work system theory: overview of core concepts, extensions, and challenges for the future. J. Assoc. Inf. Syst. **14**(2), 72–121 (2013)
3. Alter, S.: Facets of work: enriching the description, analysis, design, and evaluation of systems in organizations. Commun. Assoc. Inf. Syst. **49**(13), 321–354 (2021)
4. Alter, S.: Making cyber-human systems smarter. Inf. Syst. **127**, 1–12, 102428 (2025)
5. Buchmann, R., et al.: Large language models: expectations for semantics-driven systems engineering. Data Knowl. Eng. **152**, 102324 (2024)
6. Bereiter, C.: Education and Mind in the Knowledge Age. Routledge, New York (2005)
7. Sveidqvist, K., Jain, A.: The Official Guide to Mermaid.js: Create Complex Diagrams and Beautiful Flowcharts Easily Using Text and Code. Packt Publishing (2021)
8. Alter, S., Wright, R.: Validating work system principles for use in systems analysis and design. In: Proceedings of ICIS (2010)
9. Cameron, L.D., Rahman, H.: Expanding the locus of resistance: understanding the co-constitution of control and resistance in the gig economy. Organ. Sci. **33**(1), 38–58 (2022)
10. Gawande, A.: Why Do Doctors Hate Their Computers? The New Yorker (2018)
11. Alter, S.: Could a large language model contribute significantly to requirements analysis?. In: Proceedings of EMMSAD (2024)

Dynamic Adaption of Metamodels Based on Knowledge Graphs

Danial M. Amlashi[1]([✉]) [iD], Alexander Voelz[1] [iD], and Junsup Song[2] [iD]

[1] Doctoral School Computer Science, University of Vienna, Vienna, Austria
{danial.mohammadi.amlashi,alexander.voelz}@univie.ac.at
[2] Department of Computer Science and Engineering, Jeonbuk National University,
Jeonju-si, Republic of Korea
junsup@jbnu.ac.kr

Abstract. In this work, we report on recent developments regarding the dynamic adaption of metamodels at runtime. This new approach is complemented by *AdoPy*, a Python-based wrapper for metamodel adaption procedures that also facilitates RDF-driven modifications and extensions. The conceptualization and implementation of the approach leverage knowledge graphs to extract relevant classes, relationships, and attributes, enabling the dynamic adaption of modeling method libraries. By integrating these capabilities into ADOxx, the proposed solution links metamodeling and knowledge graphs with systems engineering.

Keywords: Knowledge Graph · Metamodeling · Method Engineering · Semantics-Driven Systems Engineering · AdoPy · ADOxx

1 Introduction

In the field of conceptual modeling and systems engineering, the ability to adapt metamodels dynamically is becoming increasingly relevant for responding to evolving domain-specific requirements. Traditional metamodeling approaches rely on static definitions, hindering flexibility and adaptability during iterative method engineering processes. Knowledge graphs have emerged as a promising solution, offering reasoning capabilities as well as flexible data representation and integration. Associated advancements regarding the integration of semantic data sources focus on enriching and contextualizing modeling-related activities. However, comparable metamodeling-related activities remain an unexplored research field with considerable potential for semantics-driven systems engineering.

To address these challenges, we present the conceptualization and implementation of a dynamic metamodel adaptation approach, which is complemented by *AdoPy*, a Python-based wrapper that facilitates RDF-driven modeling method modifications. This approach leverages knowledge graphs to extract relevant classes, relationships, and attributes, enabling the automated modification of modeling methods through RDF sources. By integrating these capabilities into the ADOxx platform, we validate the proposed solution that aims to bridge knowledge graphs and semantics-driven modeling method engineering.

J. Grabis and Y. Wautelet (Eds.): CAiSE 2025 Workshops, LNBIP 556, pp. 18–29, 2025.
https://doi.org/10.1007/978-3-031-94931-9_2

The remainder of this contribution is structured as follows: Sect. 2 provides a brief theoretical background by summarizing key characteristics of metamodeling, method engineering, knowledge graphs, and related works. In Sect. 3, the design problem of this research is formulated. Subsequently, the envisioned integration of knowledge graphs for dynamic modeling method modification and extension within the ADOxx metamodeling platform is outlined in Sect. 4. Finally, Sect. 5 discusses our approach's strengths, limitations, and potential future directions before the summarizing conclusion.

2   Theoretical Background

The theoretical foundations of conceptual modeling and knowledge graphs have been covered in previous contributions [30–32]. Therefore, this section provides a brief recap of the most relevant aspects, focusing on metamodeling, modeling method engineering, and knowledge graphs. Moreover, related works regarding the integration of knowledge graphs with conceptual modeling and their combined utilization in semantics-driven systems engineering are covered.

2.1   Metamodeling and Modeling Method Engineering

Metamodeling plays a central role in conceptual modeling, aiming to reduce complexity through abstraction and formal representation [25]. Modeling languages provide a structured way to represent systems using well-defined syntax, notation, and semantics, which are governed by metamodels [19]. These metamodels ensure that model instances adhere to a common architecture and enable automatic processing and analysis [22]. According to the Generic Modeling Method Framework (GMMF) [19], a modeling method consists of three key components: the *modeling language*, which specifies how a system is represented with regards to syntax, notation, and semantics; the *modeling procedure*, which guides the practical application of the language; *mechanisms and algorithms*, which enable advanced functionalities, such as model-based code generation.

In case modeling methods are customized for specific application domains, so-called *Domain-Specific Modeling Methods* (DSMMs) are utilized (cf. [20, 21]). These methods adapt general modeling concepts to specific domains, providing tailored functionalities that meet the unique requirements of those domains [16]. Moreover, Agile Modeling Method Engineering (AMME) [12] offers a structured framework to develop and refine modeling methods iteratively, ensuring continuous improvement through its life cycle phases: Create, Design, Formalize, Develop, and Deploy. Finally, metamodeling platforms like ADOxx[1] provide the necessary infrastructure for developing, customizing, and deploying DSMMs.

2.2   Knowledge Graphs and Related Works

Knowledge graphs have emerged as a powerful means of representing structured knowledge by explicitly capturing concepts, entities, and their relationships in a

---

[1] Available at: https://adoxx.org.

graph-based format [9]. Although the term lacks an established definition and is often used synonymously with related terms like *Ontology* or *Knowledge Base* [8], it gained widespread recognition after Google introduced its knowledge graph in 2012. In the context of the Semantic Web, knowledge graphs are typically implemented using the Resource Description Framework (RDF), which enables machine-readable, linked representations of data [33]. RDF provides a foundation for Linked Open Data (LOD), facilitating interoperability and seamless data integration across different sources. Beyond static representations, knowledge graphs incorporate reasoning engines that utilize inference for deriving implicit knowledge from explicitly defined relationships [8].

Knowledge Graphs and Conceptual Modeling. An increasing effort has recently been invested in leveraging conceptual modeling through knowledge graph-based capabilities. Before the term knowledge graph was popularized, methods from the ontology field were utilized to enhance traditional conceptual modeling. Initial contributions on *Ontology-Driven Conceptual Modeling* (ODCM) highlight the role of foundational ontologies in addressing semantic interoperability challenges [10]. More recent publications apply ODCM principles to microservice architectures for improved system modularity [24]. Also, the classification of conceptual modeling elements has been automated according to foundational ontology categories through Graph Neural Networks [1]. Moreover, an ontology-based meta-modeling approach following the OCDM principles has been proposed, which integrates human- and machine-interpretable models for the purpose of ensuring consistency and adaptability in domain-specific modeling [11].

Another area of research concerns the seamless transformation of conceptual models into knowledge graphs, for which several approaches exist. Early works introduced an RDF serialization functionality in the context of ADOxx [6], which since then has been realized as an extension for direct integration within ADOxx-based modeling methods [3] and utilized for model-driven enterprise data fabric approaches [18]. Following a similar approach, a diagrammatic modeling tool was proposed that enables users to construct RDF graphs visually and generate machine-readable N-triples using metamodeling principles [7]. Considering more platform-agnostic solutions, CM2KG^{cloud} presents a web-based implementation that transforms conceptual models from different metamodeling platforms (e.g., EMF, ADOxx, Papyrus) into knowledge graphs, supporting formats such as RDF, GraphML, and OWL [27].

Building on the principle of LOD, Linked Open Models (LOM) extend this paradigm by integrating conceptual model information into linked data systems. The resulting LOM approach enables conceptual models to act as structured, human-readable, and semantically rich knowledge representations that enhance the interoperability and query capabilities [14]. Furthermore, the integration of domain-specific models with linked data has been explored to enrich existing linked datasets with additional semantic constraints derived from conceptual modeling [3]. A practical application of LOM is presented in [30], showcasing how conceptual models can be aligned with external knowledge graphs to realize more meaningful knowledge structures through semantic enrichment.

Semantics-Driven Systems Engineering. Knowledge graphs have emerged as key enablers in systems engineering by structuring domain knowledge in a machine-processable format, which enables advanced querying, semantic integration, and reasoning. Early examples include a knowledge-centric management framework that integrates conceptual modeling and knowledge graphs to support service-oriented systems engineering [5] and an interoperability mechanism between ADOxx and GraphDB that enables reasoning over semantic-rich conceptual models [15]. In this context, the notion of *Semantics-Driven Systems Engineering* (SDSE) has recently emerged, emphasizing the transition from traditional model-driven engineering to a knowledge representation-centric approach [2]. An example of applying SDSE principles is provided in the context of smart building management, where an ontology-based metamodeling approach enables engineers to create and maintain domain knowledge through visual models [23]. Moreover, the individual steps underlying SDSE are structured as a repeatable process in [4] that is subdivided into five stages: (i) DSMM conceptualization and realization cycle, (ii) DSMM utilization for knowledge capturing, (iii) knowledge graph generation for various DSMM components, (iv) semantics-driven feature parameterization, and (v) feedback loops for propagating required changes.

3   Problem Statement

The iterative development of DSMMs requires continuous metamodel adaptions to reflect changing domain requirements. Traditionally, metamodeling platforms rely on static metamodel definitions. Consequently, integrating domain-specific changes into modeling method libraries often demands time-intensive manual effort, thus reducing agility. While existing research primarily investigates how conceptual models can enrich or inform knowledge graphs, there remains an unexplored potential in reversing this knowledge flow. Specifically, leveraging RDF-based knowledge graphs to dynamically enrich DSMM metamodels at runtime represents an intriguing direction to address the aforementioned limitations.

This contribution follows the principles of Design Science Research (DSR), focusing on the design, development, and demonstration of a design artifact that addresses a formulated problem statement [34]. Within the DSR methodology, such a problem is systematically defined by clearly distinguishing the artifact, its basic requirements, and associated goals. The core artifact of this research is a dynamic metamodel adaptation approach that integrates RDF-driven knowledge graph modifications into metamodeling environments.

The underlying goal of this contribution is summarized by formulating the design problem according to the DSR template [34]:

Improve the iterative development of DSMMs (**problem context**)
... by introducing a dynamic metamodel adaption approach (**artifact**)
... that provides RDF-based information extraction mechanisms as well as integration with a given metamodeling platform (**requirements**)
... to facilitate metamodel modifications and extensions at runtime. (**goal**)

4   Dynamic Metamodel Adaption

Metamodels must dynamically adapt to evolving requirements and domain-specific constraints to fully leverage the potential of knowledge graphs in systems engineering. This section introduces an approach for dynamic metamodel adaption, enabling runtime refinements of modeling methods.

4.1   Conceptualization: Dynamic Metamodel Adaption Approach

The process of modeling method development usually requires change requests to be implemented within the next life cycle iteration. While such an approach ensures consistency, it introduces additional effort when frequent modifications, in the sense of rapid prototyping (cf. [28]), are required. To address this issue, we present a conceptualization of the dynamic metamodel adaption approach that is contextualized within Fig. 1 as an extension to both the AMME life cycle [13] and the high-level view on the repeatable SDSE process [4], respectively.

The AMME life cycle, as depicted in Fig. 1a, structures the development of DSMMs through five sequential iteration phases. As mentioned previously, adaptions of modeling methods require a complete cycle, incorporating both micro-iterations within phases and inter-iteration evaluations for broader method refinement. The dynamic metamodel adaption approach extends the AMME life cycle by integrating the possibility of knowledge graph-based refinements within the deployment phase, thus not necessitating a new iteration cycle. This mechanism allows structured change requests derived from applying the deployed DSMM in real-world contexts to inform metamodel adaptions dynamically and accelerate method evaluation by reducing manual effort.

Building upon the AMME life cycle extension, Fig. 1b contextualizes the dynamic metamodel adaption approach within the broader SDSE process. More precisely, the first two stages of the SDSE process (cf. Sect. 2.2) are depicted in Fig. 1b while also considering the fifth stage of propagating required change requests through feedback loops. Subsequently, we assume that the evaluation results associated with the fifth stage can be structured in the form of a *Change Request Knowledge Graph*. Instead of requiring manual adjustments, this graph-based representation enables automated reasoning and structured updates to the metamodel, as described in the previous paragraph. By integrating this knowledge graph-driven feedback loop, the dynamic adaption approach allows for continuous method evolution without necessitating a complete AMME iteration.

Both conceptual perspectives of the dynamic metamodel adaption approach require a dedicated environment to test, validate, and refine developed solutions. The OMiLAB (Open Model Initiative Laboratory) ecosystem provides such an infrastructure, offering a collaborative space for DSMM development and evaluation [17]. With its physical and digital resources, OMiLAB supports the practical application of metamodeling frameworks, enabling researchers and practitioners to experiment with conceptual modeling-based techniques [29]. As our approach relies on structured feedback and dynamic modifications, OMiLAB presents an ideal environment for real-world experimentation and further validation.

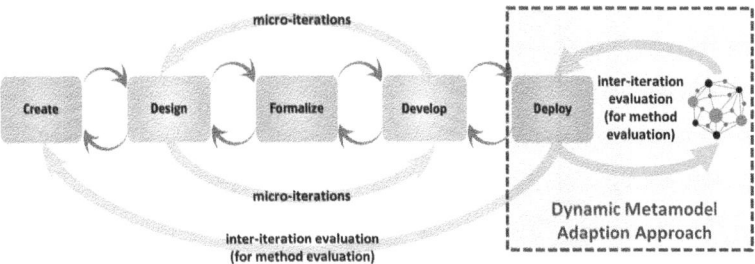

(a) Dynamic metamodel adaption within AMME (adapted from [13])

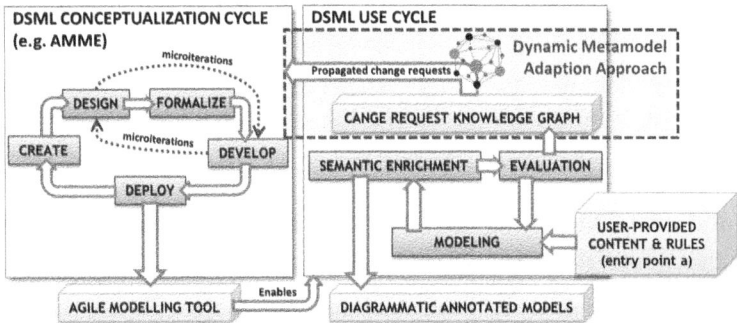

(b) Dynamic metamodel adaption within SDSE (adapted from [4])

Fig. 1. Conceptualization of the dynamic metamodel adaption approach contextualized as an extension within (a) the AMME life cycle and (b) the SDSE process

4.2   Implementation: Dynamic Metamodel Adaptions Using *AdoPy*

To realize the conceptual approach outlined in Sect. 4.1, we implemented *AdoPy*[2], a Python-based wrapper that enables metamodel adaptions for the ADOxx metamodeling platform. A central feature of the *AdoPy* library is the `transform_to_modeltype` function available for the `class KnowledgeGraph`. This function parses a knowledge graph (e.g., in Turtle format) using the `rdflib` library to extract OWL classes (`owl:Class`), their hierarchical relationships (via `rdfs:subClassOf`), object properties (`owl:ObjectProperty`), and datatype properties (`owl:DatatypeProperty`). These are transformed into fitting ADOxx meta^{2}model components such as class instances, their superclasses, relation instances, and attribute instances, with the class hierarchy maintaining inheritance and `_D-construct_` serving as the default root. Moreover, generic graphical notations are included in the transformation process. Finally, the resulting components are exported as ADOxx map (i.e., export.leo) and integrated at runtime as a new model type using the `ASC_GlobalProcedures_MetaModelAtRuntime` script, which provides global

---

[2] Available at: https://adoxx.org/modules/details/?id=487.

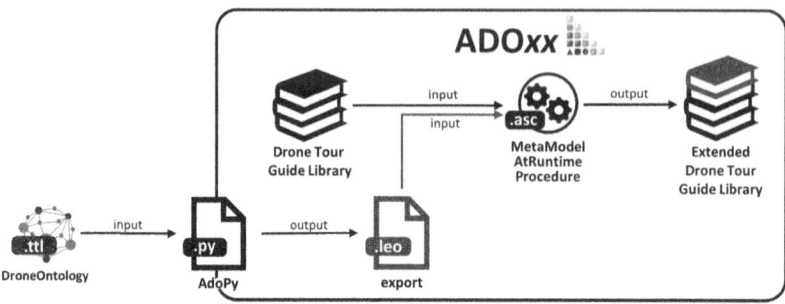

Fig. 2. Dynamic metamodel adaption approach instance: An ADOxx implementation

procedures for retrieving library information and dynamically extending it with new classes, attributes, and relationships.

4.3   Validation: Modeling Method Library Configuration in ADOxx

For the validation of the dynamic metamodel adaptation approach, we extend an existing ADOxx-based modeling method that is associated with the drone tour guide scenario presented in [30]. In the contribution, semantic matching was utilized to enrich city tour models of a DSMM with LOD from DBpedia and Wikidata. To validate the conceptualization and implementation of our proposed approach, we assume that the DSMM has been deployed, tested, and evaluated. Moreover, it is implicd that the resulting change requests include the integration of a new model type named *Drone Specification*, which provides the possibility to detail each drone based on its components and associated requirements. Lastly, the model type specification is assumed to be available in form of a Turtle file, which we derived from the Dronetology[3] by manually extracting suitable elements. Based on these assumptions, Fig. 2 displays an instance of the dynamic metamodel adaption approach implemented in the context of ADOxx.

The exemplary validation process in Fig. 2 starts by providing the extracted *Drone Ontology*, which is subsequently displayed in Fig. 3a, as an input to *AdoPy*. Next, the `transform_to_modeltype` function is utilized to transform relevant classes and properties into corresponding meta^{2}model components, which are compiled in a model type and exported as ADOxx-specific map (cf. Sect. 4.2). Finally, the *export* file is used to extend the existing modeling method library via *MetaModelAtRuntime* procedures. The resulting extensions are highlighted in Fig. 3b, which displays the class hierarchy of the extended library.

The integrated *Drone Specification* model type enables users to create drone models within the ADOxx environment that are dedicated to capturing relevant components and requirements. More specifically, drone instances can be linked to selected components and requirements through corresponding relations. In addition, a given component can also be associated with certain requirements to

---

[3] Available at: https://www.dronetology.net/dronetology/index-en.html.

(a) DroneOntology.ttl file   (b) Extended drone tour guide library

Fig. 3. Comparison of (a) the Turtle-based input file and (b) the resulting extension to the class hierarchy of the drone tour guide library in ADOxx (cf. Fig. 2)

express that it satisfies these requirements. In this way, the semantic structure and hierarchy of the *DroneOntology* are preserved, as detailed in the displayed comparison between the Turtle-based input file and the resulting extension to the class hierarchy of the drone tour guide library (cf. Fig. 3).

This validation example showcases that *AdoPy* effectively extends modeling methods at runtime for the purpose of modeling drones and their requirements, thus demonstrating its potential for broader applications in the SDSE context.

5   Discussion

This research introduces a metamodel adaption approach that enhances SDSE by leveraging knowledge graph-based feedback to dynamically modify and extend already deployed modeling methods. While the proposed approach enables a more flexible way of addressing change requests that result from the evaluation phase, several limitations must be discussed to ensure its broader applicability.

In the context of the applied DSR methodology (cf. Sect. 3), OMiLAB has served as an experimentation environment that provides the necessary infrastructure for testing and validating developed artifacts, especially within the demonstration phase. However, current limitations have motivated a reiteration back to the *Design and Development* phase (cf. [26]) to enhance mechanisms of the `ASC_GlobalProcedures_MetaModelAtRuntime` extension[4], which underpin the core capabilities of our approach. Future research will focus on a broader integration within SDSE processes by addressing current limitations. Such limitations and related prospects are outlined in the remainder of the discussion.

---

[4] Ongoing developments are available at: https://adoxx.org/modules/details/?id=188.

A primary constraint of our approach is the manual steps currently required to extend a modeling method library. As a reference, each transformation step illustrated in Fig. 2 must be manually executed. This includes the initial import of the *DroneOntology* within *AdoPy*, the subsequent execution of the `transform_to_modeltype` function, and the concluding utilization of the *MetaModelAtRuntime* procedure, which takes the generated *export* file and the existing library as inputs to output the extended library. In addition, the DSMM deployment, testing, and evaluation are prerequisites, meaning that a modeling method library must already exist before it can be dynamically refined. This further implies that the dynamic adaptation process is not fully automated, as human intervention is necessary for developing the DSMM in the first place and at multiple subsequent stages. Achieving higher levels of automation remains a critical area of improvement for the future.

Another limitation relates to the platform dependency of our approach. The current implementation is tightly coupled with ADOxx, as it relies on *AdoPy* for processing knowledge graph-driven metamodel extensions and on procedures provided by the `ASC_GlobalProcedures_MetaModelAtRuntime` script. While ADOxx offers robust support for metamodeling, extending this approach to other platforms requires additional effort. Moreover, the assumption that derived change requests can be automatically structured into a knowledge graph poses challenges, as feedback data from real-world modeling tool applications is often unstructured and heterogeneous. Transforming this feedback into a structured knowledge graph representation usually remains a human effort that demands more sophisticated semantic processing techniques.

Despite these limitations, the proposed approach for dynamic metamodel adaptions represents a meaningful step toward flexible and efficient modeling method development in the sense of rapid prototyping. By continuously evolving metamodels based on structured feedback and reasoning, this work contributes to the ongoing evolution of SDSE. Beyond dynamic refinements, our approach also opens up opportunities for automated library initialization, enabling the creation of an initial DSMM structure directly from knowledge graphs. This could significantly reduce the manual effort required for early-stage DSMM development, thereby addressing one limitation of the current approach. By extending this mechanism, future work will explore how entire modeling environments can be dynamically instantiated and evolved, further reinforcing the role of rapid, knowledge-driven prototyping within SDSE. In this context, OMiLAB provides the ecosystem to support these advancements, ensuring a practical foundation for implementing and refining both current and upcoming developments.

Moreover, this research contributes to the scientific field by reversing the traditional knowledge-flow direction between DSMMs and knowledge graphs. Whereas prior research primarily investigates how metamodel-based designs can enhance knowledge graphs (cf. Sect. 2.2), this approach leverages RDF-based inputs to dynamically adapt metamodels at runtime. This reverse flow represents a promising new perspective, expanding the capabilities and agility of SDSE.

6   Conclusion

In the field of conceptual modeling and SDSE, the ability to adapt metamodels dynamically offers considerable advantages for responding to constantly evolving requirements. This work introduces an approach to metamodel adaptations at runtime, leveraging knowledge graphs to enable the dynamic extension of deployed modeling methods. The proposed approach utilizes *AdoPy*, which allows for RDF-driven modification and extension of ADOxx libraries. Such procedures are especially relevant within SDSE process stages, where feedback mechanisms guide the evaluation of DSMMs. Instead of treating generated feedback as static input for the next AMME iteration cycle, we assume a knowledge graph-based specification of change requests that can be leveraged to enhance agility and reduce manual effort in iterative DSMM development by utilizing the dynamic metamodel adaption approach proposed in this work. The corresponding validation demonstrates our proposed approach's feasibility and practical utility in the context of a drone tour guide case. This establishes a new perspective in SDSE, where modeling methods continuously evolve through structured, semantics-driven feedback rather than discrete iteration cycles. Future works will focus on refining the metamodel adaption approach, for example, by automating the modeling method extension process with the help of LOD-based suggestions, and on addressing the remaining limitations discussed in this work.

References

1. Ali, S.J., Guizzardi, G., Bork, D.: Enabling representation learning in ontology-driven conceptual modeling using graph neural networks. In: Advanced Information Systems Engineering, pp. 278–294. Springer, Cham (2023). https://doi.org/10.1007/978-3-031-34560-9_17
2. Buchmann, R., et al.: Large language models: expectations for semantics-driven systems engineering. Data Knowl. Eng. **152**, 102324 (2024). https://doi.org/10.1016/j.datak.2024.102324
3. Buchmann, R.A., Karagiannis, D.: Enriching linked data with semantics from domain-specific diagrammatic models. Bus. Inf. Syst. Eng. **58**(5), 341–353 (2016). https://doi.org/10.1007/s12599-016-0445-1
4. Buchmann, R.A.: Semantics-driven systems engineering: requirements and prerequisites for a new flavor of model-driven engineering. In: Metamodeling: Applications and Trajectories to the Future, pp. 19–34. Springer, Cham (2024). https://doi.org/10.1007/978-3-031-56862-6_2
5. Buchmann, R.A., Ghiran, A.-M.: Serviceology-as-a-service: a knowledge-centric interpretation. In: ICServ 2017. LNCS, vol. 10371, pp. 190–201. Springer, Cham (2017). https://doi.org/10.1007/978-3-319-61240-9_18
6. Buchmann, R.A., Karagiannis, D.: Agile modelling method engineering: lessons learned in the comvantage research project. In: Ralyté, J., España, S., Pastor, Ó. (eds.) PoEM 2015. LNBIP, vol. 235, pp. 356–373. Springer, Cham (2015). https://doi.org/10.1007/978-3-319-25897-3_23
7. Chis, A., Buchmann, R.A., Ghiran, A.M.: Towards a modeling method for low-code knowledge graph building. In: Proceedings of the 16th IFIP WG 8.1 Working Conference on the Practice of Enterprise Modeling and the 13th Enterprise Design and

Engineering Working Conference (PoEM & EDEWC - Companion 2023). CEUR-WS (2023). https://ceur-ws.org/Vol-3645/forum4.pdf

8. Ehrlinger, L., Wöß, W.: Towards a definition of knowledge graphs. In: Martin, M., Cuquet, M., Folmer, E. (eds.) Joint Proceedings of the 1st International Workshop on Semantic Change & Evolving Semantics (SuCCESS'16) co-located with the 12th International Conference on Semantic Systems (SEMANTiCS 2016), vol. 1695. CEUR-WS.org (2016). https://ceur-ws.org/Vol-1695/paper4.pdf

9. Flasiński, M.: Symbolic artificial intelligence. In: Introduction to Artificial Intelligence, pp. 15–22. Springer, Cham (2016). https://doi.org/10.1007/978-3-319-40022-8_2

10. Guizzardi, G.: The role of foundational ontologies for conceptual modeling and domain ontology representation. In: 2006 7th International Baltic Conference on Databases and Information Systems, pp. 17–25. IEEE (2006). https://doi.org/10.1109/dbis.2006.1678468

11. Hinkelmann, K., Laurenzi, E., Martin, A., Thönssen, B.: Ontology-based meta-modeling. In: Dornberger, R. (ed.) Business Information Systems and Technology 4.0. SSDC, vol. 141, pp. 177–194. Springer, Cham (2018). https://doi.org/10.1007/978-3-319-74322-6_12

12. Karagiannis, D.: Agile modeling method engineering. In: Karanikolas, N., Akoumianakis, D., Nikolaidou, M., Vergados, D., Xeno, M. (eds.) Proceedings of the 19th Panhellenic Conference on Informatics, pp. 5–10. Association for Computing Machinery, New York (2015). https://doi.org/10.1145/2801948.2802040

13. Karagiannis, D.: Conceptual modelling methods: the amme agile engineering approach. In: Karagiannis, D., Lee, M., Hinkelmann, K., Utz, W. (eds.) Domain-Specific Conceptual Modeling: Concepts, Methods and ADOxx Tools, pp. 3–21. Springer, Cham (2022). https://doi.org/10.1007/978-3-030-93547-4_1

14. Karagiannis, D., Buchmann, R.A.: Linked open models: extending linked open data with conceptual model information. Inf. Syst. **56**, 174–197 (2016). https://doi.org/10.1016/j.is.2015.10.001

15. Karagiannis, D., Buchmann, R.A.: A proposal for deploying hybrid knowledge bases: the adoxx-to-graphdb interoperability case. In: Proceedings of the 51st Hawaii International Conference on System Sciences, pp. 4055–4064 (2018). https://doi.org/10.10125/50399

16. Karagiannis, D., Buchmann, R.A., Burzynski, P., Reimer, U., Walch, M.: Fundamental conceptual modeling languages in OMiLAB. In: Domain-Specific Conceptual Modeling, pp. 3–30. Springer, Cham (2016). https://doi.org/10.1007/978-3-319-39417-6_1

17. Karagiannis, D., Buchmann, R.A., Utz, W.: The omilab digital innovation environment: Agile conceptual models to bridge business value with digital and physical twins for product-service systems development. Comput. Ind. **138**, 103631 (2022). https://doi.org/10.1016/j.compind.2022.103631

18. Karagiannis, D., Burzynski, P., Utz, W., Buchmann, R.A.: A metamodeling approach to support the engineering of modeling method requirements. In: 2019 IEEE 27th International Requirements Engineering Conference (RE), pp. 199–210. IEEE (2019). https://doi.org/10.1109/re.2019.00030

19. Karagiannis, D., Kühn, H.: Metamodelling platforms. In: Bauknecht, K., Tjoa, A.M., Quirchmayr, G. (eds.) EC-Web 2002. LNCS, vol. 2455, pp. 182–182. Springer, Heidelberg (2002). https://doi.org/10.1007/3-540-45705-4_19

20. Karagiannis, D., Lee, M., Hinkelmann, K., Utz, W. (eds.): Domain-Specific Conceptual Modeling: Concepts, Methods and ADOxx Tools, 1st edn. Springer, Cham (2022). https://doi.org/10.1007/978-3-030-93547-4

21. Karagiannis, D., Mayr, H.C., Mylopoulos, J. (eds.): Domain-Specific Conceptual Modeling: Concepts, Methods and Tools, 1 edn. Springer, Cham (2016). https://doi.org/10.1007/978-3-319-39417-6

22. Kühn, H., Junginger, S., Karagiannis, D., Petersen, C.: Metamodellierung im geschäftsprozeßmanagement: Konzepte, erfahrungen und potentiale. In: Desel, J., Pohl, K., Schürr, A. (eds.) Teubner Reihe Wirtschaftsinformatik, vol. 12923, pp. 75–90. Vieweg+Teubner Verlag, Wiesbaden (1999). https://doi.org/10.1007/978-3-322-93104-7_5

23. Laurenzi, E., Allan, J., Campos, N., Stoller, S.: An ontology-based meta-modelling approach for semantic-driven building management systems. In: Advanced Information Systems Engineering Workshops, pp. 200–211. Springer, Cham (2024). https://doi.org/10.1007/978-3-031-61003-5_18

24. Morais, G., Bork, D., Adda, M.: Towards an ontology-driven approach to model and analyze microservices architectures. In: Proceedings of the 13th International Conference on Management of Digital EcoSystems, MEDES 2021, pp. 79–86. ACM (2021). https://doi.org/10.1145/3444757.3485108

25. Mylopoulos, J.: Conceptual modelling and telos. In: Conceptual Modelling, Databases, and CASE: An Integrated View of Information System Development, pp. 49–68. Wiley, New York (1992)

26. Peffers, K., Tuunanen, T., Rothenberger, M.A., Chatterjee, S.: A design science research methodology for information systems research. J. Manag. Inf. Syst. **24**(3), 45–77 (2007). https://doi.org/10.2753/mis0742-1222240302

27. Smajevic, M., Ali, S.J., Bork, D.: Cm2kgcloud - an open web-based platform to transform conceptual models into knowledge graphs. Sci. Comput. Program. **231**, 103007 (2024). https://doi.org/10.1016/j.scico.2023.103007

28. Tripp, S.D., Bichelmeyer, B.: Rapid prototyping: an alternative instructional design strategy. Educ. Tech. Res. Dev. **38**(1), 31–44 (1990). https://doi.org/10.1007/bf02298246

29. Vaidian, I., Jurczuk, A., Misiak, Z., Neidow, M., Petry, M., Nemetz, M.: Challenging digital innovation through the omilab community of practice. In: Karagiannis, D., Lee, M., Hinkelmann, K., Utz, W. (eds.) Domain-Specific Conceptual Modeling: Concepts, Methods and ADOxx Tools, pp. 41–64. Springer, Cham (2022). https://doi.org/10.1007/978-3-030-93547-4_3

30. Voelz, A., Amlashi, D.M., Lee, M.: Semantic matching through knowledge graphs: a smart city case. In: Ruiz, M., Soffer, P. (eds.) Advanced Information Systems Engineering Workshops, pp. 92–104. Springer, Cham (2023). https://doi.org/10.1007/978-3-031-34985-0_10

31. Völz, A., Amlashi, D.M., Burzynski, P., Utz, W.: Adoxx: Eine low-code-plattform für die entwicklung von modellierungswerkzeugen. HMD Praxis der Wirtschaftsinformatik **61**(5), 1295–1316 (2024). https://doi.org/10.1365/s40702-024-01096-x

32. Völz, A., Vaidian, I.: Digital transformation through conceptual modeling: the nemo summer school use case. In: Modellierung 2024, pp. 139–156. Gesellschaft für Informatik e.V., Bonn (2024). https://doi.org/10.18420/modellierung2024_014

33. W3C: RDF - resource description framework (2014). https://www.w3.org/RDF/. Accessed 20 Feb 2025

34. Wieringa, R.J.: Design Science Methodology for Information Systems and Software Engineering. Springer, Heidelberg (2014). https://doi.org/10.1007/978-3-662-43839-8

Benchmarking Knowledge Graph Question Answering via Complexity-Aware Queries

Balázs Mosolygó[1]([✉])[iD], Andreas L. Opdahl[1][iD], Guohui Xiao[2][iD],
Jiaoyan Chen[3][iD], and Ana Ozaki[4][iD]

[1] University of Bergen, Bergen, Norway
{balazs.mosolyo,andreas.opdahl}@uib.no
[2] Southeast University, Nanjing, China
[3] University of Manchester, Manchester, UK
[4] University of Oslo, Oslo, Norway

Abstract. This paper presents our progress towards creating an end-to-end query generation approach. The resulting pairs of NL and executable queries can be used for setting up KGQA datasets and benchmarking LLMs. The usage of a rigorous theoretical background will ensure that queries are generated with predeterminable complexities.

Keywords: Knowledge Graphs · Graph Theory · LLMs

1 Introduction

Several recent studies have investigated synergies between Large Language Models (LLMs) and Knowledge Graphs (KGs) [9,10]. LLMs benefit greatly from KGs due to their well-structured nature and provide an opportunity for KG technologies to gain more ground. Their capabilities in generating queries based on natural language questions (NLQs) may help overcome the initial learning overhead associated with the adoption of new database technologies. Knowledge graph question answering (KGQA) [7,15] aims to generate equivalent queries to NLQs to ease the usage of KG technologies for non-expert users. While efforts such as QALD [13] to create large high-quality datasets for these tasks are ongoing, current approaches have several limitations. They often rely on crowd-sourcing or pattern-based query generation with no explicit control over the final queries' structure, leading to sets of queries that are not necessarily representative of either practical query sets or NLQs potentially posed against KGs. Additionally, they often focus on either DBpedia [8] or Wikidata [14], which may not generalize to KGs with different schema complexity or typing systems.

Another setting where the structured nature of KGs has been used to progress our understanding of LLMs is LLM benchmarking [6]. A pressing issue in this community is the potential for newer LLMs to memorize static benchmarks, thus making them obsolete. Recent works such as NPHardEval [4] and SCYLLA [11] aim to overcome these issues by automatically generating benchmarks based on mathematical problems from different complexity classes. While

© The Author(s), under exclusive license to Springer Nature Switzerland AG 2025
J. Grabis and Y. Wautelet (Eds.): CAiSE 2025 Workshops, LNBIP 556, pp. 30–37, 2025.
https://doi.org/10.1007/978-3-031-94931-9_3

these approaches negate the possibility of memorization, they rely on numerical problems such as finding a certain number in a list or providing a solution to the traveling salesman problem, which places unnecessary focus on the different models' ability to correctly parse and understand numbers, introducing a point of failure beside the models' ability to reason.

This paper describes our results towards generating a dataset for KGQA and LLM benchmarking tasks by automatically creating NLQ-practical query pairs, where members of the pairs express the same query relating to an underlying KG. This dataset will fill gaps both within the KGQA context by granting access to large sets of non-trivial queries for lesser-known KGs without the need to crowd-source information, and in the LLM benchmarking context by allowing for the creation of a dynamic benchmark based on NLQs of different complexities with computable answers.

In Sect. 2, we describe treewidth and hyperedge replacement grammars and their connection to query answering as preliminaries. In Sect. 3, we describe our theoretical goals in detail and provide our current results, and finally in Sect. 4, we describe future work both in the theoretical development of the query generation algorithm and its relation to the larger project in general.

2   Preliminaries

2.1   Boolean Conjunctive Queries

We use bold letters such as $\mathbf{t}$ for tuples $\langle t_1, ..., t_i \rangle$ of corresponding elements. Let Δ_c and Δ_v be countably infinite sets of *constants* and *variables* respectively, and let Σ be a finite set of relation symbols, where $ar(R)$ is the *arity* of $R \in \Sigma$. $t \in \Delta_c \cup \Delta_v$ is a *term* and $R(\mathbf{t})$ is an *atom*, where $R \in \Sigma$ and $|\mathbf{t}| = ar(R)$. Boolean conjunctive queries (BCQs) [1] form a class of first order queries of the form: $\exists \mathbf{y}.\varphi[\mathbf{y}]$, where φ is a conjunction of atoms (for conciseness we may omit the existential quantifier). BCQs can be thought of as graphs as shown in Fig. 1.

2.2   Treewidth

To define treewidth [2, 12] we define tree decompositions first. Let $G = (V, E)$ be an undirected, unlabeled graph where V is a set of vertices and E is a family of subsets of V, $E = \{\{v_i, ..., v_j\} \mid v_i, ..., v_j \in V\}$. A graph where the size of each subset in E is exactly two will be referred to as normal graphs or just graphs, whereas graphs without this restriction will be referred to as hypergraphs. Let $G = (V, E)$ be a normal graph, then a sequence of $n \geq 3$ distinct vertices $v_0, ..., v_n$ is cycle in G if $\{v_i, v_{i+1}\} \in E$ for all $0 \leq i < n$, and $\{v_n, v_0\} \in E$. A tree is a connected undirected acyclic graph.

Definition 1. *Let the pair $\langle T, \chi \rangle$ be a tree decomposition of a normal graph G where $T = (N, F)$ is a tree and $\chi : N \to 2^V$ is a labeling function adhering to the following rules:*

1. *for each vertex v of G, there exists $p \in N$ such that $v \in \chi(p)$;*
2. *for each edge $e = \{v_i, v_j\}$ in E, there exists $p \in N$ such that $e \subseteq \chi(p)$ (for edge e $e \in 2^V$, due to the way we defined edges earlier);*
3. *for each vertex v of G, the set $\{p \in N \mid v \in \chi(p)\}$ induces a connected sub-tree of T.*

The width of a tree decomposition $\langle T, \chi \rangle$ is defined as $max_{p \in N} |\chi(p)| - 1$. The treewidth of a graph G is the width of its smallest tree decomposition.

Treewidth describes the degree of cyclicity present in a graph. A graph with a treewidth of 1 is a tree, and a graph with a treewidth of 3 contains the four clique K_4 as its minor, where a k clique is a normal graph with k vertices that contains every possible edge. Graph minors are defined in Definition 2. Figure 1 shows an example of two graphs and some of their respective tree decompositions. The above connection between treewidth and graph complexity connects treewidth to BCQs as well, meaning that treewidth may be used as a metric to describe their complexity [5].

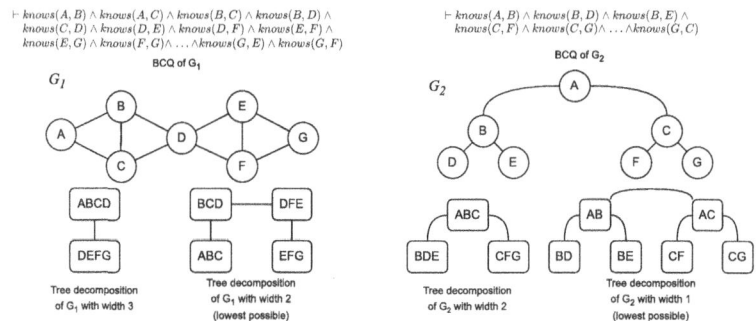

Fig. 1. Examples of calculating the treewidth of two graphs which correspond to two BCQs assuming that each edge is labeled with "knows".

Definition 2. *A graph $G = (V, E)$ is a minor of $H = (W, F)$ if G may be obtained from H by a series of vertex deletions, edge deletions and edge contractions. An edge contraction is an operation replacing vertices v_i and v_j by w, where the neighborhood of w is $N(w) = N(v_i) \cup N(v_j)$.*

In general, for a value of treewidth k there is a set of forbidden graph minors $\mathcal{H}_f$ so that no graph with a treewidth of k may have any $H_f \in \mathcal{H}_f$ as its minor.

2.3   Hyperedge Replacement Grammars

Our definitions here follow [3] with the omission of definitions for attachment nodes and external nodes of hypergraphs for the sake of conciseness.

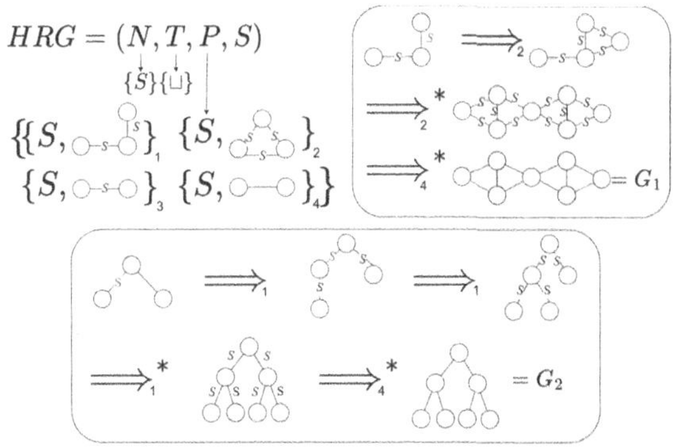

Fig. 2. Example of an HRG and 2 derivations. The terminal label for the grammar is the empty character. During each direct derivation the replaced edge is highlighted.

Let C be an arbitrary but fixed set of labels. Let $H = (W, F, lab)$ be a hypergraph, where W is a set of vertices, $F = \{f_i \mid f_i \subseteq W\}$ is a set of hyperedges and lab a labeling function $lab : F \to C$.

Definition 3. *A hyperedge replacement grammar is a system $HRG = (N, T, P, S)$ where N is a set of nonterminal labels $N \subseteq C$, T is a set of terminal labels with $T \subseteq C$ and $N \cap T = \emptyset$, P is a finite set of productions over N and $S \in N$ is the start symbol.*

Nonterminal labels are used to select which hyperedges may be replaced by applying a production $p \in P$ to a given hypergraph. Terminal labels mark edges as completed, meaning that no production may replace them during later derivations. The start symbol serves as the starting point on any derivation using an HRG.

A hyperedge replacement grammar generates hypergraph languages $L(HRG)$ by applying production rules arbitrarily to hypergraphs by removing edges with nonterminal labels and replacing them with hypergraphs. Once all edges with nonterminal labels have been replaced by graphs whose every edge is terminally labeled a derivation ends and a hypergraph generated by the grammar is created. A production $p \in P$ is a pair (A, R) where $A \in N$ and R is a hypergraph. A is called the *left-hand side* of p and is denoted by $lhs(p)$, while R is the *right-hand side* of p and is denoted by $rhs(p)$. The width of a hyperedge replacement grammar HRG is $max_{p \in P}|rhs(p)| - 1$ where the width of a hypergraph is defined as its number of vertices.

H directly derives denoted by $H \Longrightarrow_P H'$ or $H \Longrightarrow H'$ if P is clear from the context. A sequence of direct derivations $H \Longrightarrow ... \Longrightarrow H'$ is called a derivation of length l and is denoted by $H \Longrightarrow_P^* H'$. In cases where the exact derivation rule used matters, we will use $H \Longrightarrow_i H'$ for direct derivations and $H \Longrightarrow_i^* H'$ for a sequence of derivations using p_i, where $p_i \in P$.

An example of an HRG and two derivations is shown in Fig. 2.

The following theorem establishes a key connection between hyperedge replacement grammars and treewidth.

Theorem 1 ([2]). *(1.) Every graph generated by a hyperedge replacement grammar of width k has treewidth at most k.*

(2.) For every k, there exists a hyperedge replacement grammar of width k that generates exactly the directed graphs with treewidth at most k.

3   Methodology and Results

3.1   Problem Setup

Our project's overarching aim is to create an end-to-end method for generating high-quality datasets for KGQA and LLM benchmarking. Figure 3 presents an overview of the project. This paper contains the theoretical background and our progress so far towards the completion of the basic query generation phase. The query realization phase the queries will be transformed into practical query languages. The most likely target is SPARQL since it is currently the most used query language in the KGQA context, during this step additional complexity introduced by language features will be accounted for. The last phase of the project will rely on LLMs to transform our practical queries into realistic NLQs. Assuming the context of the semantic web, our final dataset will consist of NLQ-SPARQL pairs, where SPARQL queries will have tags describing their complexity. The task of KGQA is to transform NLQs to queries, therefore answers to NLQs must be the same as the results of their respective SPARQL pairs, assuming that the underlying KG is consistent.

We assume limited access to the KG in question, focusing on the relevant ontology and statistics assumed to be provided instead to account for practical concerns such as data privacy. The information that will be accounted for is the following will be the classes and relations present in the KG, the domain and range classes of each relation and information about subclass relations and disjointness.

Our goal is to generate queries that do not contain patterns whose presence would contradict the information provided about the underlying KG, which we will refer to as fulfilling the semantic requirements. Additionally, queries should be varied in complexity, for which we will use treewidth as a guide.

3.2   Progress Towards Graph Generation

Due to the correspondence between graphs and BCQs, this problem is equivalent to generating graphs with vertex and edge labels. Vertex labels are necessary to represent class information in semantic knowledge graphs, which presents our first challenge, as HRGs do not explicitly support assigning labels to vertices. We will overcome this by assigning hyperedges with an arity of one to vertices and using them as stand-ins for vertex labels. This poses practical problems as it requires the generation of an intricate, and possibly large set of productions

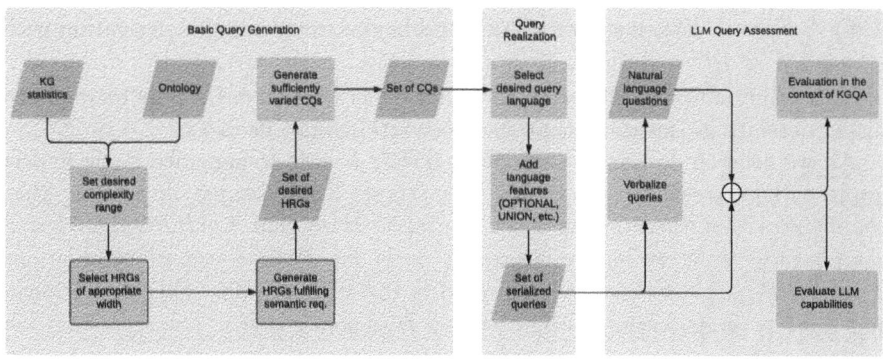

Fig. 3. A high-level overview of our project plan. Processes with a red highlight require Proposition 1 to hold. Note that CQs refer to conjunctive queries, which are functionally the same as BCQs in our case. (Color figure online)

after which we would need to decide whether the generated HRG is capable of producing a terminal graph or not. This is considered future work.

It is necessary to sharpen the contents of Theorem 1 as only setting an upper bound is insufficient due to our need for specific treewidth values. Below, we show that adding a lower bound is plausible in a way that does not eliminate any graph that we would be interested in generating.

Definition 4. *Let $HRG = (N, T, P, S)$ be a hyperedge replacement grammar and $H = (W, F, lab)$ a hypergraph so that $\exists f \in F, lab(f) \in N$. A production $p \in P$ is considered to be path preserving iff there is a path between w_i and w_j, where $w_i, w_j \in W$ in $H = (W, F)$, then if $H \Longrightarrow_p^* H'$ then there is a path between w_i and w_j in $H' = (W', F')$. Note that since a derivation using any hyperedge replacement grammar does not remove nodes, we know that if $w_i, w_j \in W$ then $w_i, w_j \in W'$.*

The existence of a hyperedge replacement grammar of width k that generates every hypergraph with treewidth at most k is stated in Theorem 1. To prove Proposition 1, we need to show the existence of a hyperedge replacement grammar HRG_k that generates exactly hypergraphs with a treewidth of k.

Proposition 1. *There is a hyperedge replacement grammar that exactly generates every graph of width k.*

Proof. Constructing HRG_k is done by first generating a set of productions P_S where for each $p_S \in P_S$, $lhs(p_S) = S$, $rhs(p_S) \in \mathcal{H}_f^{k-1}$ and $(\bigcup_{p_S \in P_S} rhs(p_S)) = \mathcal{H}_f^{k-1}$, where $\mathcal{H}_f^{k-1}$ is the set of forbidden minors for treewidth $k - 1$. Adding every possible unique path preserving production P_{pres}, see Definition 4, where $\forall p_{pres} \in P_{pres}$ $lhs(p_{pres}) \neq S, rhs(|p_{pres}|) < k)$ completes our set of production rules $P_{HRG_k} = P_S \cup P_{pres}$. Note that the requirement for not having S as the lhs of any production rule in P_{pres} forces every derivation to start with an element of $\mathcal{H}_f^{k-1}$. Since HRG_k has a width of k and begins every possible derivation with an element of $\mathcal{H}_f^{k-1}$, it can only generate graphs with a treewidth of exactly k due to a combination of Theorem 1.1 and the fact that no paths may be removed during derivations, meaning that the treewidth cannot decrease.

All we need to do now is show that HRG_k is able to generate every hypergraph with a treewidth of k and only those. Lets assume it cannot, that would mean that there exists a set of graphs $\widehat{\mathcal{H}}$ so that $L_S(HRG_k) \cap \widehat{\mathcal{H}} = \emptyset$ where every $\widehat{H} \in \widehat{\mathcal{H}}$ has a treewidth of k, let R be a set of productions $R = \{p \in P_{HRG_k} \mid lhs(p) = S\}$, where S is the start symbol. This would mean that there is no derivation so that $r \Longrightarrow_P^* \widehat{H}$, where $r \in R$.

Due to the way we construct P_S we know that for every hypergraph with a treewidth of k, it must have at least one of $rhs(p_S)$ as its minor, meaning that $rhs(p_S)$ must be obtainable from $\widehat{H}$ with a series of vertex removals, edge removals and edge contractions. Let the chain of hypergraphs generated during this process be $H_0...H_n$ where $H_0 = \widehat{H}$ and $H_n = rhs(p_S^t)$ where p_S^t is the rule whose right hand side is a minor of $\widehat{H}$, and let $\widehat{H}$ be a hypergraph from $\widehat{\mathcal{H}}$ that requires only one path removal to be generated. Since we assumed that $\widehat{H}$ needs a path to be removed during it's generation, that implies the existence of a graph in its generation chain that has a treewidth of less then k, as otherwise it would be generated by HRG_k. Consequently there has to be a graph in $H_0...H_n$ called H_i that has a treewidth of less than k, as otherwise we could choose to recreate this process using HRG_k to generate $\widehat{H}$. However, H_i cannot exist, since to have a treewidth of less than k, it must not have $rhs(p_S^t)$ as its minor, while we know that both H_{i+j} and H_{i-l}, have $rhs(p_S^t)$ as their minor as H_0 and H_n both have a treewidth of k. Executing graph minor operations on a graph $\overline{H}$, that does not have $\overline{G}$ as minor, cannot lead to a graph $\overline{H}'$ that does have $\overline{G}$ as its minor. Due to the definition of graph minors in Definition 2 if $\overline{H}$ does not have $\overline{G}$ as its minor, that means that $\overline{G}$ is not obtainable from $\overline{H}$ via graph minor operations. For $\overline{H}'$ to exist, it must be obtainable from $\overline{H}$ and $\overline{G}$ must be obtainable from $\overline{H}'$ via graph minor operations. This would mean that $\overline{G}$ is also obtainable from $\overline{H}$ leading to a contradiction caused by the existence of $\overline{H}'$. Therefore, H_i cannot exist, meaning that assuming the existence of $\widehat{H}$ and by extension $\widehat{\mathcal{H}}$ leads to a contradiction.

4 Conclusion and Future Work

In this short paper, we presented our progress toward creating a theoretical framework for generating boolean conjunctive queries that have predictable complexity and fulfill semantic requirements imposed by statistics over knowledge graphs. We have shown that HRGs are sufficient for generating labeled graphs with predetermined treewidth. Completing the query generation algorithm still requires the definition of methods to generate HRG productions that simulate every potential semantic requirement we might have.

As future work, beyond the construction of our method, we plan to evaluate LLMs in the setting of KGQA, reasoning, and complexity approximation. The method allows for the automatic construction of both KGQA datasets (question-query pairs) and QA datasets (question-answer pairs) since, in this setting, we can execute the queries generated by our method to attain answers for the generated NLQs. We will also have access to complexity measures for different questions, allowing us to evaluate the LLMs' ability to forecast the resource requirements of practical queries. To do this, we will evaluate if our complexity measure correlates with query execution times in practice.

References

1. Baader, F., Nutt, W.: Basic description logics. In: The Description Logic Handbook: Theory, Implementation, and Applications, pp. 43–95 (2003)
2. Bodlaender, H.L.: A partial k-arboretum of graphs with bounded treewidth. Theor. Comput. Sci. **209**(1–2), 1–45 (1998)
3. Drewes, F., Kreowski, H.J., Habel, A.: Hyperedge replacement graph grammars. In: Handbook of Graph Grammars and Computing by Graph Transformation: Volume 1: Foundations, pp. 95–162. World Scientific (1997)
4. Fan, L., Hua, W., Li, L., Ling, H., Zhang, Y.: Nphardeval: dynamic benchmark on reasoning ability of large language models via complexity classes. arXiv preprint arXiv:2312.14890 (2023)
5. Gyssens, M., Paredaens, J.: A Decomposition Methodology for Cyclic Databases. Springer, Cham (1984)
6. Ibrahim, N., Aboulela, S., Ibrahim, A., Kashef, R.: A survey on augmenting knowledge graphs (KGs) with large language models (LLMs): models, evaluation metrics, benchmarks, and challenges. Discover Artif. Intell. **4**(1), 76 (2024)
7. Lan, Y., He, G., Jiang, J., Jiang, J., Zhao, W.X., Wen, J.R.: Complex knowledge base question answering: a survey. IEEE Trans. Knowl. Data Eng. **35**(11), 11196–11215 (2022)
8. Lehmann, J., et al.: DBpedia-a large-scale, multilingual knowledge base extracted from Wikipedia. Semant. Web **6**(2), 167–195 (2015)
9. Pan, J.Z., et al.: Large language models and knowledge graphs: opportunities and challenges. Trans. Graph Data Knowl. **1**(1), 1–38 (2023)
10. Pan, S., Luo, L., Wang, Y., Chen, C., Wang, J., Wu, X.: Unifying large language models and knowledge graphs: a roadmap. IEEE Trans. Knowl. Data Eng. (2024)
11. Qi, Z., et al.: Quantifying generalization complexity for large language models. arXiv preprint arXiv:2410.01769 (2024)
12. Robertson, N., Seymour, P.D.: Graph minors. II. Algorithmic aspects of tree-width. J. Algorithms **7**(3), 309–322 (1986)
13. Usbeck, R., et al.: QALD-10-the 10th challenge on question answering over linked data: shifting from DBpedia to Wikidata as a KG for KGQA. Semant. Web **15**(6), 2193–2207 (2024)
14. Vrandečić, D., Krötzsch, M.: Wikidata: a free collaborative knowledgebase. Commun. ACM **57**(10), 78–85 (2014)
15. Yani, M., Krisnadhi, A.A.: Challenges, techniques, and trends of simple knowledge graph question answering: a survey. Information **12**(7), 271 (2021)

Towards Industry 5.0 in Tourism Sector Through Conceptual Modeling and Semantic Technology for Personalized Travel Itineraries

Andreea Popoviciu and Ana-Maria Ghiran$^{(\boxtimes)}$ ⓘ

Faculty of Economics and Business Administration, Babeş-Bolyai University,
Cluj-Napoca, Romania
andreea.popoviciu@stud.ubbcluj.ro,
anamaria.ghiran@econ.ubbcluj.ro

Abstract. While the last two decades were dominated by the so called Fourth Industrial Revolution or Industry 4.0 with rapid technological advancements, we are now facing a new shift in the industry, where the primary focus should no longer be on increasing efficiency or business profits but emphasizing the role of a company in promoting the well-being of the society. Although this is largely recognized, how to achieve it is still a relatively ambiguous desideratum. In the dynamic and competitive tourism industry, managing and designing personalized travel itineraries in an effective way is essential for ensuring customer satisfaction and operational efficiency. In this paper, we aim to contribute to improving this process by providing a solution that involves the creation of a conceptual modeling language. The language can be used for two model types: one for creating the actual itineraries, and another one for representing the resources needed for certain tourist attractions, such as necessary equipment. Additionally, we will store information from the created models in a graph database using RDF serialization, benefiting of the Linked Data capabilities that enable connecting with information that resides outside the modeling environment (e.g. about each tourist). Using a graph-based structure enables data analysis and easier identification of connections and patterns between elements.

Keywords: Conceptual modeling · Graph representation · Travel itinerary

1 Introduction

Industry 4.0 emphasized automation and smart technologies, and this translated, in many cases, into an innovation requirement for businesses in order to remain competitive and keep customers. Companies invested in cyber-physical systems, IoT solutions, automated processes [1]. However, the rapid pace of technological advancements and their adoption soon raised some concerns about their long-term benefits considering their impact on the environment and societal level.

Industry 5.0 [2] transforms the existing Industry 4.0 approach through a sustainable development – both environmental sustainability and social responsibility. It considers

J. Grabis and Y. Wautelet (Eds.): CAiSE 2025 Workshops, LNBIP 556, pp. 38–49, 2025.
https://doi.org/10.1007/978-3-031-94931-9_4

the social implications of technological advancements (like worker displacements) and the effects on the community (what relationships or interactions are created between individuals and groups) and it promotes the idea that technology augments human capabilities rather than replacing them. Collaboration between humans and machines becomes a key element in the Industry 5.0. [3].

Industry of the Future (aka. industry 5.0) is an approach that must be assumed by all current companies that aim to continue their activity in the time ahead (i.e. modern organizations must be increasingly adaptive and respond to the stimuli of the environment they operate in) [4]. Yet, there are very few studies that advise on concrete ways, what small and medium-sized companies (SMEs) need to do.

Through this paper, our goal is to help SMEs to identify some concrete solutions that could help them in their transition to the Industry 5.0. We advocate for two key ingredients that enable this changeover:

1) a domain-specific modeling language to capture in high fidelity the customer needs (i.e. enhancing customer satisfaction) and, in the same time, in an easier way (i.e. enhancing worker satisfaction) – this will contribute in supporting the human centric aspect of the Industry 5.0.
2) generating a machine-readable interpretation of the knowledge that can be linked to other processable information – this will contribute to an enhanced human-machine collaboration; it can augment human insights (by allowing multiple data sources to be connected and processed at a high speed) and enabling more informed decisions. Our recommended approach is to employ semantic technologies, like RDF [5] and its associated query language, SPARQL [6], to obtain such machine-readable descriptions.

To demonstrate our proposal, we appeal to a fictitious travel agency that can act as an adequate candidate in showcasing how SMEs can adhere to the Industry 5.0 principles. The travel sector is an exemplary industry that has been affected by technological advancements, increased demand and more sophisticated requirements from customers. As tourists seek unique and well-coordinated experiences, travel agencies must adapt by leveraging advanced tools to streamline and enhance their service offerings. Therefore, a travel agency represents an appropriate example to showcase our proposal.

The remainder of this paper is structured as follows: Sect. 2 describes the enabling technologies (e.g. conceptual modeling and semantic technologies), Sect. 3 presents the Design Science Research (DSR) methodology and details our proposal structured according to the employed methodology and last section contains the conclusions and directions for future developments.

2 Background on Enabling Technologies

The primary purpose of a conceptual model is to ensure transparent communication among stakeholders and to provide a comprehensive specification for systems' development (in model-driven development) or for simulations (in analyzing complex problems which are costly to be tested in real situations) [7]. From a general point of view, without a conceptual model, projects face risks such as unclear goals, inadequate granularity decisions, and misalignment with stakeholder expectations. Conceptual modeling has been commonly perceived as being based on standards, however, literature on modeling pragmatics [8] pointed out that there is an increased need for domain specificity or situational customization of the modeling languages and tools. Having a domain-specific modeling language, customized to the organizational needs, will fit better to the company's particular application area. In the tourism industry, modeling languages like UML, BPMN were employed to model business processes, customer interactions, managing itineraries [9, 10], however, these approaches missed specific concepts (like new types of activities), new attributes (e.g. interests' scores) or new constraints required (e.g. the order of specific concepts).

Our modeling tool aims to improve the itinerary planning process, ensuring that all aspects of a trip are meticulously organized and easily customizable. By integrating resource representation, travel agencies can better prepare for the specific needs of each tourist attraction, enhancing the overall travel experience.

RDF provides a graph-based data representation to various sources of information. It also enables the federation of enterprise data, acting as a common layer for information resources. RDF's capability to link heterogeneous data sources enables more comprehensive insights and better decision-making. RDF [5] has been adopted as an information model that conceptualizes a domain (i.e. defines an ontology), allowing both a machine processable description as well as a human intelligible content. RDF has been employed as the underlying technology in developing recommender systems [11] to provide personalized recommendations for Point of Interests based on the tourists' preferences, personality traits and other contextual factors. Nevertheless, building ontologies and graphs requires some expertise (e.g. regarding RDF serialization formats) which hindered the adoption of RDF at citizen-level [12]. Despite the research regarding visualizations of knowledge graphs and ontologies, they miss the flexibility of conceptual models that can adaptively support various abstraction levels or selection of various active perspectives. For this reason, we advocate for the use of a modeling tool with a domain-specific modeling language that empowers employees with a graphical and straightforward means for inventorying and easily configuration of their clients' travel itineraries.

3   Methodology

In this section, we will describe the methodology used for the development of our proposed solution. We employed Design Science Research (DSR) Methodology [13], as the methodology that is particularly suited for information systems (IS) science. IS is considered an "applied research discipline" [14] in the sense it applies theory from other disciplines to solve problems related to IT and organizations. DSR supports developing a practical solution that addresses complex, real-world problems. Adopting Industry 5.0 principles requires devising a new artefact that enhances both productivity and worker satisfaction. According to DSR methodology, we structured our research into six phases – problem identification, objectives definition, design and development, demonstration, evaluation and communication.

3.1 Problem Identification

First, we familiarized ourselves with the definitions of the prevalent notions and concepts employed in the tourism industry, particularly by travel agencies.

A travel agency is an individual, firm, or corporation that assembles and coordinates travel goods and services to facilitate travel arrangements (i.e. it creates packages and facilitates access to selected travel attractions, amenities, and ancillary services of a destination, presenting them to tourists). A travel itinerary is a detailed plan outlining the origin, destination, and all stopping points in a traveler's tour. Travel agencies prepare itineraries for tour packages, ensuring all travel details.

Building customer experience proved to be a more effective way in attracting and keeping customers rather than other forms of marketing campaigns [15]. In many cases in the tourism industry, it is a common and a well-known practice to combine multiple services into a bundle and provide it as a distinguished offer, which companies can present to increase their advantage over competitors. Clearly, bundle packages must be very closely adapted to suit customers' needs, otherwise they might not provide the required ratio "price per added value". Ideally, these bundles should be created personalized for each customer.

We analyzed the current market and the activities of travel agencies to identify the elements involved in creating a travel itinerary. We determined that an itinerary requires the representation of the trip's start and end events, along with the inclusion of tourist attractions and breaks for relaxation or meals between the periods of visiting tourist attractions. Additionally, it is necessary to specify the resources required for tourist attractions.

3.2 Objectives Definition

We aim to create a highly personalized itinerary using a domain-specific modeling language, for which we will calculate an interest score to present to tourists the value of visiting a particular attraction based on their preferences. Furthermore, we will store information from the created models in a graph database using RDF serialization. This database also includes information about each individual tourist (clients of the travel agency). Utilizing a graph-based structure enables a comprehensive data analysis (both on the content from the models and from other data sources) and facilitates an easy identification of connections and patterns between elements.

3.3 Design and Development

Figure 1 provides an overview of the metamodel for the proposed modeling language. Our modeling language should facilitate the creation of two distinct model types: one that will describe the flow of activities and another one that will describe the employed resources required for specific tourist attractions, such as necessary equipment and different supplies. Accordingly, the class diagram illustrates that our modeling language supports this distinction, as the Travel Itineraries model is separated from the Travel Resources model. Within the Travel Itineraries model, a link is established for the TouristAttraction concept to access elements of type TravelSupply and TravelClothingItem.

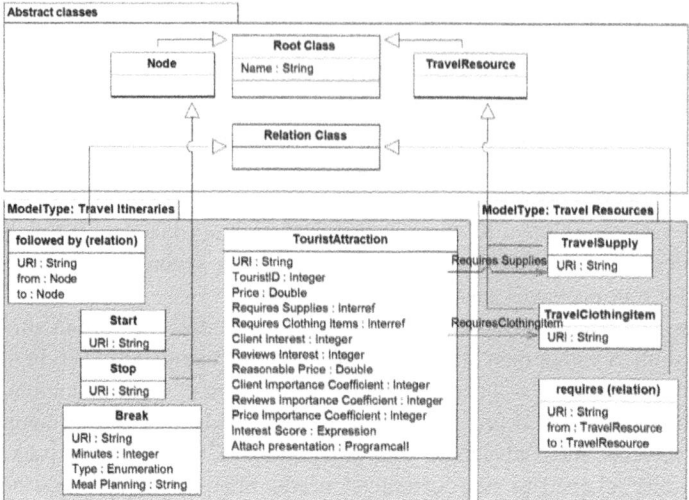

Fig. 1. Metamodel for the proposed modeling language

The section on abstract classes comprises four classes that serve as general concepts, allowing specific attributes to be inherited by child classes. These four classes will not be visually represented in the diagrams. There are two primary concepts, Node and Travel Resource, which are inherited by other concepts from the two models. Abstract classes can also be used to express relationships between concepts on a broad scope: e.g., the "followed by" relationship can originate from a Node element (either a Start, Stop, TouristAttraction or Break) and point to another Node element, whereas the "requires" relationship can link a Travel Resource element to another element.

Concepts in <u>Travel Itineraries</u> models are:

- Start/Stop: the former marks the beginning of the journey, named according to the destination to be visited, while the latter marks the end of the itinerary. The concepts have the following attributes:

  - Name: Specifies the itinerary destination.
  - TouristID: Specifies the ID of the tourist for whom the itinerary is created.
  - URI: unique identifier to overwrite the generated identifier by the modeling environment.

- TouristAttraction: Represents tourist attractions, containing descriptions, the importance score, and possibly an external object such as a presentation video. Attributes for this concept include:

  - Name: Specifies the name of the tourist attraction.
  - TouristID: Specifies the ID of the tourist for whom the itinerary is created.
  - TouristDestination: Specifies the tourist's destination.
  - Price: Specifies the price for visiting the attraction.

- Requires Supplies: Links the tourist attraction to necessary resources that are not clothing items.
- Requires Clothing Items: Links to the clothing items needed for visiting the attraction.
- URI: unique identifier to overwrite the generated identifier by the modeling environment.
- Client Interest: Specifies the client's interest in visiting the attraction, with values ranging from 0 to 10.
- Reviews Interest: Indicates interest from tourists who have already visited the attraction, with values ranging from 0 to 10.
- Reasonable Price: The maximum price the client considers reasonable for visiting an attraction.
- Client Importance Coefficient: Specifies the importance of the client's interest level, with values from 0 to 10.
- Reviews Importance Coefficient: Specifies the importance of interest based on reviews, with values from 0 to 10.
- Price Importance Coefficient: Indicates the importance of the attraction's visit price to the client, with values from 0 to 10.
- Interest Score: An EXPRESSION attribute calculating a score to determine the worthiness of visiting an attraction. It considers client interest, review-based interest, reasonable price, and the three importance coefficients.
- Attach presentation: A PROGRAMCALL attribute for associating a video or document with the attraction.

• Break: Represents breaks within the itinerary, which could be meal or relaxation breaks. It has the following attributes:

- Name: Specifies a representative name for each break.
- TouristID: Specifies the ID of the tourist for whom the itinerary is created.
- TouristDestination: Specifies the destination for the tourist's itinerary.
- Minutes: Specifies the duration of the break in minutes. If the break is 60 min or less, "Short Break" is displayed above the Break object; for breaks longer than 60 min, "Long Break" is displayed.
- Type: Specifies whether the tourist will relax or eat during the break.
- Meal planning: An attribute that becomes active and modifiable only when the Break object is of type Eating. It allows for entering meal planning details for the tourist.
- URI: Unique identifier to overwrite the generated identifier by the modeling environment.

The concepts in the Travel Itineraries model will be interconnected through a "followed by" relationship.

We ensure that the model adheres to certain constraints: there could be only one Start element and one Stop element; no element could originate from a Stop element, nor could any element lead directly to a Start element. These constraints were established to maintain the integrity and logical flow of the itinerary model.

The second model type, Travel Resources, specifies the resources required for visiting an attraction. Concepts in this model include:

- TravelClothingItem: Represents necessary clothing items for a tourist attraction, such as comfortable shoes for walking tours or swimwear for beach visits.
- TravelSupply: Represents non-clothing items needed for visiting an attraction, such as maps, tickets, or cameras
- ComplexEquipment: A container object, grouping TravelClothingItem and Travel-Supply concepts (e.g. backpacks, bags).

All concepts contain the attributes Name and URI.

If an element in a Travel Resources model requires another element, they can be connected using the "requires" relationship.

We implemented the modeling language using the ADOxx Development Toolkit [16]. We defined the notation, syntax, and semantics for each concept, along with the relationships connecting these concepts. Based on this formalism, ADOxx platform generates a modeling tool that supports the intuitive creation of models.

The Travel Itineraries models describe graphical travel itineraries for destinations. This gives a clear and easy-to-follow visual representation.

The clients provide information to be used within the two types of models. When they engage with the tourism services, they will receive an overview of the tourist attractions at their desired destination, as recommended by the agency. In the same time, they also provide information to be used in computing the relevance for visiting an attraction for each tourist (a formula to calculate the importance score). The importance score will be a weighted sum, incorporating the client's interest level in visiting an attraction, the attraction's rating based on reviews from various tourists, and the cost of visiting the attraction. The travel agent tests multiple variants until obtains the most relevant interest score for the client.

The client will be asked to specify their interest level (I_{Client}) in visiting each tourist attraction and a maximum price (P_{Max}) they consider reasonable for visiting an attraction. Additionally, the client will provide three coefficients representing the weights needed to calculate the importance score:

CI_{Client} - The weight of the client's interest level.
$CI_{Reviews}$ - The weight of the interest level based on reviews from other tourists.
$CP_{Attraction}$ - The weight of the price of visiting an attraction for the client.

The coefficients and interest levels will range from 0 to 10.

$I_{Reviews}$ represents the interest level derived from reviews by multiple tourists, which can be obtained from various review sites. P denotes the price of visiting the attraction. Normalization of these values ensures a consistent scale. The client's interest level and review interest level are divided by 10, while the attraction price is divided by the maximum reasonable price set by the client.

The importance score will range from 0 to 1, where 0 signifies low importance and 1 indicates high importance.

To calculate the importance score (I_{Score}) for visiting a tourist attraction, the following formula will be applied:

$$I_{Score} = (CI_{Client}/10) * (I_{Client}/10) + (CI_{Reviews}/10) * (I_{Reviews}/10) + (CP_{Attraction}/10) * (P/P_{Max})$$

The interest score is an EXPRESSION attribute that will be automatically displayed in ADOxx Modelling Toolkit. The formula is presented in Fig. 2.

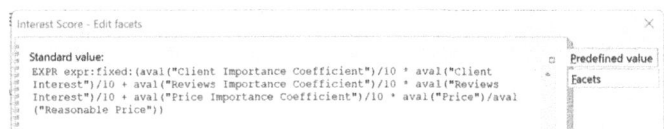

Fig. 2. Formula used to calculate interest score

Figure 3 presents the graphical notation for the concepts and relationships used in the Travel Itineraries model (left) and Travel Resources model (right).

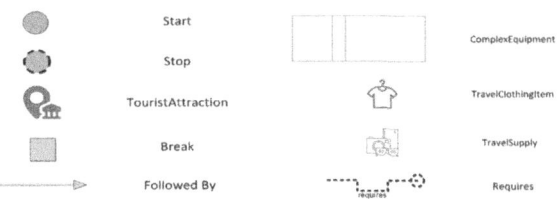

Fig. 3. Graphical notation for concepts in Travel Itineraries (left) and Travel Resources (right)

3.4 Demonstration

The visual representation of these models aids travel agents in planning and communicating travel plans effectively. Moreover, the flexibility of the ADOxx environment allows for easy modifications and updates to models. Figure 4 exemplifies a Travel Itineraries model (left) and resources using the Travel Resources model type (right). The objects in the tourist attractions diagrams can be linked to resources. Figure 5 shows how the interest score for visiting a tourist attraction is calculated. The travel agency's employee will input the client's level of interest, the level of interest based on reviews from other tourists, the maximum price the tourist considers reasonable for visiting an attraction, and the importance coefficients for the three indicators. The Interest Score is an EXPRESSION attribute that was presented in Fig. 2.

Connecting Information Described in the Models with Other External Information
Importing the language library and models' content into a graph based structure (e.g. GraphDB [17]) supports enhanced data querying and analysis capabilities.

Semantic querying capabilities enable travel agencies to extract meaningful insights from models. This integration supports customization of itinerary planning, allowing

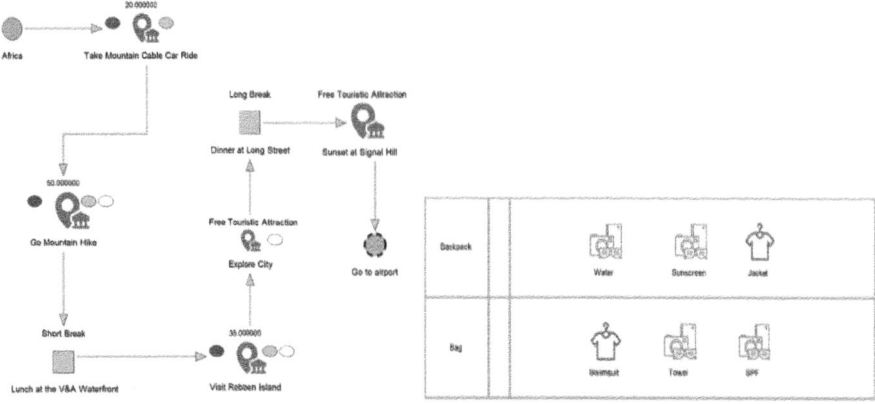

Fig. 4. Modelling a travel itinerary for Africa (left) and traveling resources (right)

Fig. 5. Visual representation of calculating the Interest Score

agencies to quickly generate and modify travel plans based on a wide range of criteria. Additionally, the ability to analyze historical travel data provides agencies with valuable trends and patterns, driving innovation in travel services.

Because we use unique URIs, we can connect objects from the models with information from external sources. (e.g. information about tourists who have used services of the travel agency). This information can be found in a table similar to the one in Fig. 6. To map data from this table, we can use the Ontotext Refine [18], which allows us to map data from a tabular format to RDF format and then to upload the mapped data directly into GraphDB.

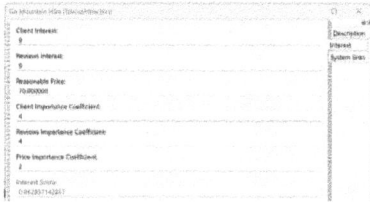

Fig. 6. Example of external source data and mapping in Ontorefine

3.5   Evaluation

After transforming data using Ontorefine, we import information from models and meta-model (modeling language) into GraphDB. Extracting the graph structure from models created on the ADOxx platform has been described in [19] while transformation patterns to guide the implementation were presented in [20]. Having all the information in a single repository, we can begin querying the data to identify connections and patterns. To start, we can extract the name of the tourist attraction and the interest score for each tourist. The query is shown on the left side of Fig. 7, while the results are displayed on the right side.

Fig. 7. Query Tourist Attraction Name and Interest Score

We can also generate a new relationship based on a chain of existing relationships. An example of such a query is shown in Fig. 8. Here we generate the relationships 'has-TouristAttraction' and 'needs.' The 'hasTouristAttraction' relationship is established between tourists (information from sources external to the modeling environment), and tourist attractions (extracted from created models), while the 'needs' relationship is established between tourists and the resources required to visit a tourist attraction. The result of this query can be seen on the right side of the Fig. 8.

Fig. 8. CONSTRUCT query to generate relationships hasTouristAttraction and needs

3.6   Communication

The communication phase of the DSR methodology is important for disseminating the results. This paper communicates the results of the first DSR iteration and how we achieved them. We summarize here the main contributions:

We developed a conceptual modeling language in the ADOxx development toolkit for the travel industry that enables the detailed modeling of travel plans through two types of models: Travel Itineraries and Travel Resources. By explicitly modeling the sequence and relationships between these elements, travel planners can design itineraries that are both logical and user-friendly. The Travel Resources model allows travel agencies to systematically manage and suggest appropriate resources for various types of tourist attractions, enhancing the preparedness and comfort of travelers. By addressing both the workers' needs and the travelers' requirements, the models align with the human-centric goals of the Industry 5.0.

To support the evolving needs and expectations of the travelers, the information regarding the travel itineraries should be connected to other data sources and should be made amenable to machine processing, hence semantic technologies play an essential role. RDF provides a standardized method for data interchange not only on the web, as it was initially conceived, but in any domain. In Industry 5.0 context, where collaboration between humans and machines as well as between different organizations is very important, RDF can be particularly beneficial by supporting data linking and sharing across the value chain network. We demonstrated how information extracted from models can be connected to information from other sources and how new relationships can be constructed between different entities.

4   Conclusion

The development of a conceptual modeling language tailored for the travel industry represents a significant advancement in streamlining and enhancing travel itinerary and resource management. Utilizing the ADOxx Development Toolkit, we defined a language for modeling travel itineraries and associated resources. This language was subsequently used to create models within the ADOxx Modelling Toolkit, translating complex travel plans into structured, manageable data models.

By leveraging semantic technologies and a structured modeling approach, travel agencies can manage vast amounts of travel-related data more efficiently. This not only reduces the time and effort required for itinerary planning and resource allocation but also enhances the accuracy and customization of travel services offered to clients.

The conceptual modeling language and its implementation offer substantial benefits for travel agencies. Its ease of use, featuring an intuitive design and user-friendly interface, reduces the need for extensive training and facilitates smooth integration into existing workflows. Additionally, it significantly boosts efficiency in itinerary planning by reducing the time and manual effort required, thus ensuring timely and accurate travel plans. Advanced querying and analysis capabilities offer data-driven insights for informed decision-making and service improvement. Detailed models enable the customization of travel plans tailored to individual preferences, further enhancing customer satisfaction.

In conclusion, the developed conceptual modeling language and its implementation within ADOxx and GraphDB provide a powerful framework for modernizing travel agency operations. This approach not only addresses current operational challenges but also positions travel agencies to meet the evolving demands of the market and deliver exceptional travel experiences.

Nevertheless, it is important to emphasize that the proposed approach is not limited to the tourism sector. The employed technologies (the combination of domain-specific modeling methods and semantic technologies) can be applied to a wide range of domains where businesses seek to become more effective (both customer/employee oriented, and technologically empowered), aligning with the goals of Industry 5.0.

References

1. Calp, M.H., Bütüner, R.: Society 5.0: effective technology for a smart society. In: Artificial Intelligence and Industry 4.0, pp. 175–194. Academic Press (2022)
2. Leng, J., et al.: Industry 5.0: prospect and retrospect. J. Manuf. Syst. **65**, 279–295 (2022)
3. European Commission (2024): Industry 5.0. https://research-and-innovation.ec.europa.eu/res earch-area/industrial-research-and-innovation/industry-50_en. Accessed 13 July 2024
4. Koutsopoulos, G., Andersson, A., Stirna, J., Henkel, M.: Application and evaluation of interlinked approaches for modeling changing capabilities. Softw. Syst. Model. 1–30 (2024)
5. W3C Recommendation (2014): RDF Resource Description Framework 1.1 Concepts and Abstract Syntax. https://www.w3.org/TR/rdf11-concepts/. Accessed 01 July 2024
6. W3C Recommendation (2013): SPARQL 1.1 Query Language. https://www.w3.org/TR/spa rql11-query/. Accessed 01 July 2024
7. Robinson, S., Arbez, G., Birta, L.G., Tolk, A., Wagner, G.: Conceptual modeling: definition, purpose and benefits. In: 2015 Winter Simulation Conference (WSC), pp. 2812–2826. IEEE (2015)
8. Bjeković, M., Proper, H.A., Sottet, J.S.: Embracing pragmatics. In: Conceptual Modeling: 33rd International Conference, ER 2014, Atlanta, GA, USA, 27–29 October 2014. Proceedings 33, pp. 431–444. Springer, Cham (2014)
9. Vranić, V., Lang, J., Nores, M.L., Arias, J.J.P., Solano, J., Laseca, G.: Use case modeling in a research setting of developing an innovative pilgrimage support system. Univ. Access Inf. Soc. 1–18 (2023)
10. Rueda Caicedo, L.J., Bermón Angarita, L., López Trujillo, M.: Framework for the generation of tourist experiences. J. Inf. Knowl. Manag. 2450031 (2024)
11. Silva, D.L.C.D.: Development of an ontology of tourist attractions for recommending points of interest in a group recommender system for tourism. Doctoral dissertation (2023). https:// recipp.ipp.pt/bitstream/10400.22/24146/1/Tese_5143.pdf. Accessed 01 July 2024
12. Chiş, A., Buchmann, R.A., Ghiran, A.M.: Towards a modeling method for low-code knowledge graph building. In: Proceedings of PoEM Forum, Vienna, Austria (2023)
13. Wieringa, R.J.: Design Science Methodology for Information Systems and Software Engineering. Springer, Cham (2014)
14. Peffers, K., et al.: Design science research process: a model for producing and presenting information systems research arXiv preprint arXiv:2006.02763 (2020)
15. Lawless, M.W.: Commodity bundling for competitive advantage: strategic implications. J. Manag. Stud. **28**(3), 267–280 (1991)
16. BOC Group (2024): The ADOxx Metamodeling platform. https://www.adoxx.org/live/home. Accessed 01 July 2024
17. Ontotext. GraphDB Platform (2024). https://graphdb.ontotext.com/. Accessed 01 July 2024
18. Ontotext. Ontorefine (2024). https://www.ontotext.com/products/ontotext-refine/. Accessed 01 July 2024
19. Buchmann, R.A., Karagiannis, D.: Enriching linked data with semantics from domain-specific diagrammatic models. Bus. Inf. Syst. Eng. **58**, 341–353 (2016)
20. Buchmann, R.A., Karagiannis, D.: Pattern-based transformation of diagrammatic conceptual models for semantic enrichment in the Web of Data. Procedia Comput. Sci. **60**, 150–159 (2015)

Retrieval-Augmented Generation for Entity Alignment in Knowledge Graphs: An Incipient Experiment

Davide Mario Ricardo Bara, Daria Maria Mesesan,
and Gheorghe Cosmin Silaghi$^{(\boxtimes)}$ (iD)

Business Informatics Research Center, Babeş Bolyai University,
Cluj-Napoca, Romania
gheorghe.silaghi@ubbcluj.ro

Abstract. With the rapid expansion of artificial intelligence applications, traditional entity alignment methods in knowledge graphs often face challenges in scalability and robustness, particularly when dealing with large and heterogeneous datasets. In this paper we propose EA-RAG, a novel Retrieval-Augmented Generation approach for entity alignment, combining retrieval mechanisms with large language models to explore generative solutions. Using the DBP15k dataset, we compare EA-RAG with several embedding-based models from the literature. Our results demonstrate significant potential for EA-RAG as a generative alternative to embedding-based methods in entity alignment tasks.

Keywords: Entity Alignment · Knowledge Graphs · Embedding · Retrieval-Augmented Generation · Large Language Model

1 Introduction

Nowadays, companies build and maintain knowledge graphs (KG) as a flexible way to represent, store and use their internal data as knowledge, empowering various production processes within their information systems (IS). On the other side, large language models (LLM), seen by many as being a powerful expression of artificial intelligence (AI), help those companies automate tasks and increase productivity. However, not all companies own enough computational resources to train and run their own LLM with their private data. This situation creates a dependency on external suppliers for AI solutions, with organizations typically interacting with LLMs via APIs—dynamically sending task-relevant data and integrating the returned responses into their information systems.

LLMs are huge deep learning models with billions of parameters trained on large amounts of publicly available data. They exhibit a strong performance on answering questions and solving tasks that rely on their training data. But, in general, they fail to properly adapt to private and sensitive information not seen within their training schedule. Therefore, to integrate an LLM within a

© The Author(s), under exclusive license to Springer Nature Switzerland AG 2025
J. Grabis and Y. Wautelet (Eds.): CAiSE 2025 Workshops, LNBIP 556, pp. 50–62, 2025.
https://doi.org/10.1007/978-3-031-94931-9_5

company specific process or IS, one needs to either fine-tune the LLM with the private information or to transmit small pieces of sensible information with each request in a pipeline, described as retrieval-augmented generation (RAG). In this scenario, KGs become a key asset due to their proven ability to integrate well with LLMs, enhancing their operation and overall performance [5].

Entity alignment (EA) is a foundational task in KG research, focusing on identifying and aligning entities that represent the same real-world object across different KGs [9,11,12]. KGs organize information as triples in the form of *(subject → predicate → object)*, each piece of data in the KG being described by an Uniform Resource Identifier (URI). In the context of integrating an LLM within the production processes of a company, proper alignment of the company specific KG with the public knowledge used by the LLM becomes essential. A RAG-based approach will benefit from the alignment between the private and the public knowledge, enhancing the performance of the LLM.

EA is a specific case of a broader challenge in data integration, studied under various terms such as *entity resolution*, *record linkage*, and *deduplication* [12]. Traditional methods for EA rely heavily on heuristic rules, string similarity metrics, and attribute matching. While interpretable and computationally efficient, these approaches fail to scale for large, complex KGs and often achieve suboptimal performance [9,12]. Moreover, they assume a closed-world setting, where missing data implies absence. In contrast, KGs generally operate under the Open-World Assumption, where unobserved data may still exist, further complicating alignment tasks [12].

Recent advances involve the usage of deep learning models - including LLMs, in solving the EA task, modeled as a classification problem. Embedding-based techniques were developed to learn low-dimensional vector representations of entities and relationships in a shared embedding space. Methods like *BootEA* [7], *GCN-Align* [8], or *MTransE* [2] leverage these embeddings in order to align entities based on similarity calculations. Although these methods show promising results on benchmark datasets like DBP15K [6] or DWY-NB [11], they often achieve Hits@1 scores of around 0.5, leaving room for significant improvements.

In this study we approach the EA problem with the help of a Retrieval-Augmented Generation (RAG) pipeline [4]. RAG emerged as a promising alternative for addressing tasks with sparse or noisy information. It combines a retrieval mechanisms and LLMs to dynamically retrieve and generate alignment predictions. We integrate external knowledge extracted from the private KG during the alignment process, aiming to handle incomplete attributes and semantic variability. However, this introduces challenges such as computational complexity and reliance on high-quality data. We will explore whether RAG techniques could be effectively employed to reliable solve the EA task, and how the RAG alternative compares with traditional EA algorithms in terms of performance, scalability, or accuracy.

We will contribute by designing EA-RAG: a RAG pipeline for solving the EA task with the help of an LLM, enhancing the performance of embedding-based approaches. Our results are relevant from both a research and business perspective. Initial results show that the achieved performance is superior to several other approaches, thus enabling more precise data integration, driving better operation in LLM-enhanced business processes.

This paper evolves as following. In Sect. 2 we introduce the EA task and review several relevant solutions found in the literature. Section 3 describes the DBP15k dataset and the EA-RAG approach. Section 4 presents and discusses the results obtained by solving the EA task with the considered methods. The last section concludes the paper.

2 Background Definitions and Related Work

This section reviews the main categories of entity alignment (EA) methods analysed in this study, focusing on semantic matching models (MTransE, BootEA), graph neural network-based approaches (GCN-Align), and the potential of RAG for EA.

2.1 Problem Definition

As indicated in Zhao et al. [12], a KG is a graph $G = (E, R, T)$ consisting of a set of entities E, a set of relations R and a set of triples T, where $T \subseteq E \times R \times E$ represents directed edges in the graph. A single triple $(h, r, t) \in T$ represents a relationship between a head entity h and a tail entity t through a specific relation r. Each entity in the graph is identified by a unique identifier.

Entity alignment (EA) is a crucial step needed in order to combine knowledge across multiple KGs. Given a source graph $G_1 = (E_1, R_1, T_1)$ and a target graph $G_2 = (E_2, R_2, T_2)$, the EA task discovers equivalent entity pairs in the source and the target graphs, i.e. the set $S = \{(u, v) \mid u \in E_1, \ v \in E_2, \ u \leftrightarrow v\}$, where $\leftrightarrow$ represents the equivalence relationship, which means that u and v refer to the same real-world object.

EA could be seen as a supervised learning task if a training dataset with matched pairs (u, v) is available, and a model learns to match the remaining unmatched entities, or as a unsupervised learning task if the training dataset is missing.

Several solutions are available to solve the EA task, as presented below. We direct the reader to consult the comprehensive surveys of Zhang et al. [11], Zeng et al. [9] and the book of Zhao et al. [12] for a more detailed discussion about EA in KGs.

2.2 Models for Solving the EA Task

Semantic matching models start by representing the entities and their relationships as numerical vectors in a shared space. These models rely on the idea that similar entities, such as two entries for the same football club, should have similar vector representations [12].

The foundational model in this category is **TransE** [1]. TransE treats relationships as translations between entities. It learns embeddings such that adding the relationship vector to the head entity vector results in a vector which is close to the tail entity vector. While TransE performs well for simple relationships, it struggles with complex ones, such as one-to-many or many-to-many relationships [12]. Building upon TransE, **MTransE** was designed to handle multilingual KGs by transforming entities from different languages into a shared vector space [2]. However, MTransE struggles with sparsity and noisy data, particularly in datasets lacking sufficient attributes or relationships. Another method from this category demonstrating good results is **BootEA** [7], which employs a semi-supervised, iterative approach to refine entity alignments by combining relation and attribute triples.

Graph Neural Network-based models (GNN) use the graph structure to learn better representations for entities. Instead of treating each entity individually, these models aggregate information from the entity's neighbours [12]. **GCN-Align** [8] is a popular GNN-based model. It uses graph convolutional networks (GCNs) to learn embeddings that capture both local (direct neighbors) and global (overall graph structure) information. By combining structural and attribute information, GCN-Align can create more accurate representations for entities, especially in datasets with dense relationships. However, GCN-Align requires significant computational resources and struggles with sparsely connected entities, where there are few or no meaningful neighbours to aggregate information from [9].

2.3   Entity Alignment Toolkit

The **Entity Alignment Toolkit**[1] [9] (**EAkit**) is an open-source framework designed to evaluate and implement a variety of EA methods. Built using PyTorch, EAkit provides a modular and extensible platform for researchers to experiment with embedding and graph-based alignment techniques. The toolkit includes preconfigured scripts for running state-of-the-art models, such as **MTransE**, **BootEA**, and **GCN-Align**, and supports benchmark datasets like DBP15K.

EAkit organizes its architecture into separate components for data preprocessing, embedding generation, and alignment evaluation. Encoders and decoders form the core of the system, allowing models to process inputs like entity relationships and attributes, while optimizing embeddings for alignment. Additionally, EAkit integrates visualization tools like TensorBoard to monitor metrics such as loss, accuracy, and alignment quality during training and testing.

EAkit uses well-established metrics, including **Hits@1**, **Hits@10** and **MRR**. Hits@1 evaluates the proportion of instances where the correct answer is ranked first, providing a strict measure of top-rank accuracy. In contrast, Mean Reciprocal Rank (MRR) and Hits@10 assess the model's ability to rank the correct answer within the top positions, with MRR considering the inverse of the rank

---

[1] EAkit is publicly available at https://github.com/THU-KEG/EAkit.

of the first correct answer across all queries, and Hits@10 measuring the frequency of correct answers appearing within the top 10 results. For our incipient experiment we will use only Hits@1, as we are concerned about a strict accuracy measure.

EAkit and the methods it implements represent a significant step toward standardizing the evaluation of EA techniques. By providing comprehensive metrics, preconfigured models, and integration with widely used datasets, EAkit ensures that researchers can effectively compare methods across diverse scenarios. We will use EAkit to run several models in the literature on our selected dataset, in order to enable a comparison between EA-RAG and the other alternatives.

2.4   Retrieval Augmented Generation for EA

Retrieval Augumented Generation (RAG) [4] combines retrieval mechanisms with LLMs to dynamically retrieve and generate alignment predictions. Unlike embedding-based methods, which rely solely on learned embeddings, RAG incorporates external knowledge during the alignment process. For example, if the alignment between two entities is unclear, RAG can retrieve additional information to improve the prediction confidence.

In general, RAG offers several advantages. It dynamically retrieves additional knowledge, making it effective for sparse or noisy datasets [9]. Additionally, it incorporates contextually relevant information from external sources, which enhances accuracy for challenging alignments [12].

However, RAG also faces significant challenges [4]. It requires considerable computational resources due to its reliance on both retrieval mechanisms and LLMs. Moreover, high-quality retrieval systems are essential to ensure alignment accuracy and minimize noise in the retrieved data [9].

While RAG has shown promise in related tasks such as question answering [4], its application to EA remains an emerging area of study. This research aims to benchmark RAG against embedding-based methods to assess its scalability and accuracy for EA tasks. To the best of our knowledge, no prior work has specifically applied RAG for EA. Instead, previous studies have primarily incorporated LLMs within broader EA frameworks, as demonstrated in the works of Jiang et al. [3] and Zhang et al. [10].

3   Methodology

In this section we present our methodology. We introduce the dataset used in our experiments and the architectural components of EA-RAG.

3.1   Dataset

This study utilizes the **DBP15K** dataset[2] [6], a widely recognized benchmark for evaluating EA methods. Specifically, we use the `fr_en` subset to align entities between the French and English knowledge graphs extracted from DBpedia. The dataset's multilingual nature and structural diversity present challenging scenarios for evaluating the robustness and scalability of EA methods.

The `fr_en` subset is comprised of a series of files. It includes **entities** that represent real-world objects such as "Eiffel_Tower" or "Paris_FC", **relation triples**, which describe relationships between entities (e.g. "Paris_FC plays_in France"), and **attribute triples**, which specify properties of entities (e.g. "Paris_FC has_nickname PFC"). Finally, it includes **links** between entities, with 15,000 standard alignments between entities in the French and English knowledge graphs. The dataset structure is illustrated in Fig. 1. Statistics regarding the overall structure of the fr_en subset are illustrated in Table 1, highlighting its complexity and robustness.

```
DBP15K/
|-- zh_en/
|-- ja_en/
|-- fr_en/
    |-- en_att_triples    # Attribute triples from the English KG
    |-- en_rel_triples    # Relation triples from the English KG
    |-- ent_ids_1         # Entity IDs from the French KG
    |-- ent_ids_2         # Entity IDs from the English KG
    |-- ill_ent_ids       # Ground-truth entity alignments
    |-- fr_att_triples    # Attribute triples from the French KG
    |-- fr_rel_triples    # Relation triples from the French KG
    |-- triples_1         # All triples from the French KG
    `-- triples_2         # All triples from the English KG
```

Fig. 1. Directory structure of the DBP15K dataset.

Table 1. Statistics for fr_en subset of the DBP15K dataset.

Sub-dataset	#Entity	#Relation	#Relation Triple	#Attribute Triple
French	66,858	1,379	192,191	528,665
English	105,889	2,209	278,590	576,543

---

[2] The DBP15K dataset is available at https://github.com/nju-websoft/JAPE. Papers utilizing the dataset are reported at https://paperswithcode.com/dataset/dbp15k.

3.2 EA-RAG - Retrieval-Augmented Generation for Entity Alignment

We build our RAG pipeline inspired by the work of Zhang et al. [11], who proposed a general embedding-based framework for EA. Our EA-RAG model uses the `text-embedding-3-small`[3] pre-trained model from OpenAI to create vector representations for each graph node, Pinecone[4] for vector storage and retrieval, and the `gpt-4o-mini` pre-trained LLM to predict the aligned entities.

The structure of the EA-RAG framework is illustrated in Fig. 2 and includes three key modules. The dataset is first processed by the *Embedding Module*, which transforms entities into vector embeddings and stores them in the vector store. The *Alignment Module* queries the vector store using cosine similarity to retrieve the top 5 most similar entities and forwards them to the LLM, along with the name of the source entity. Finally, the *Inference Module* compares the predicted entities with the ground truth, measuring the model's performance using the Hits@1 score.

Since LLMs are best suited for responding queries in natural language, we first convert the graph node information into natural language sentences which are then input into the Embedding Module. These sentences were derived from the RDF graph generated after processing the datasets. Triples converted into a textual format are treated as documents containing contextual infor-

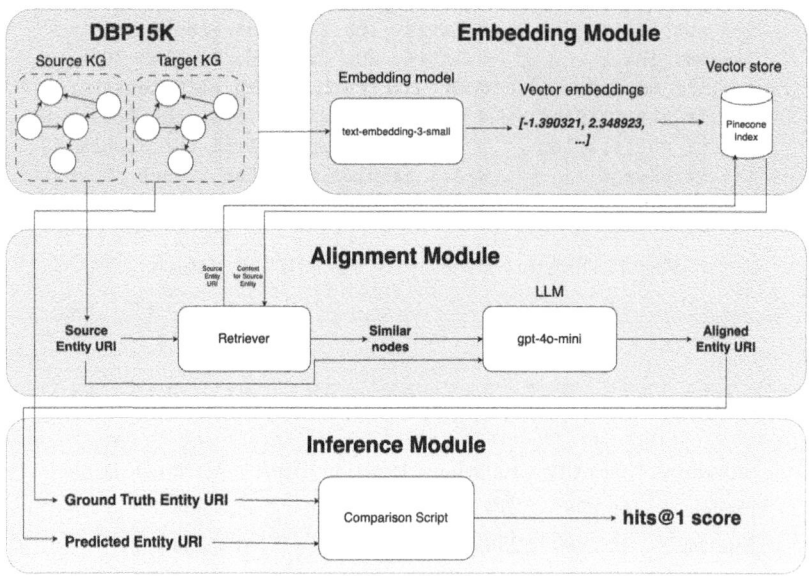

Fig. 2. The architecture of the EA-RAG model.

---
[3] https://openai.com/index/new-embedding-models-and-api-updates/.
[4] https://www.pinecone.io/.

mation about entities. To process them using a RAG approach, this data is split into 2000-character chunks with a 10% overlap for contextual continuity. These node descriptions are then converted into embeddings using the `text-embedding-3-small` model via the OpenAI API and stored in a Pinecone index. Each embedding vector has a length of 1536.

3.3   The Data Processing Pipeline

Since we do not need to fine-tuned models in our EA-RAG processing pipeline, we can treat the entire dataset as a test set. EA-RAG is tasked with predicting the corresponding entity from the French dataset (with URIs starting with http://fr.dbpedia.org/resource/) for each entity in the English dataset (with URIs starting with http://dbpedia.org/resource/).

To have reference results for comparison, we implemented MTransE, BootEA and GCN-Align in the EAkit for DBP15k benchmark. The validation strategy across all reference methods tested in sec. 4 involves splitting 20% of the dataset for validation, ensuring robust performance evaluation on unseen data.

The following parameters were selected for MTransE: the embedding dimension was set to 100, sufficient for capturing multilingual features efficiently, the learning rate was set 0.002, and a margin of 1.5 was applied, providing flexibility in distinguishing positive and negative samples.

The parameters for GCN-Align were set as follows: the number of GCN layers was configured to 2, balancing local and global feature aggregation, the embedding dimension was set to 200, optimized for relationally dense datasets, the learning rate was set to 0.005 to facilitate rapid convergence without causing instability, and a dropout rate of 0.3 was applied to reduce overfitting.

BootEA was run with the embedding dimension set to 300, learning rate set to 0.001, the batch size was configured to 128, and we used a margin of 1.0 to effectively separate positive and negative samples.

We will monitor Hits@1 and Mean Reciprocal Rank (MRR) metrics during training. To minimize overfitting, for BootEA and MTransE we use early stopping criteria based on Hits@1 improvements.

4   Results and Discussion

This section presents the results obtained experimenting with MTransE, GCN-Align, BootEA and EA-RAG on the DBP15K (`fr_en`) subset. Beside the quantitative results, we include visual insights from the learning curves of tested models. The evaluation reports the Hits@1 metric. Moreover, the computational efficiency of each method is discussed. The source files of our system can be accessed at https://github.com/DariMe20/Entity-Alignment-KG.

The experiments implemented in EAkit were conducted on a Lenovo Yoga Slim 7 Pro Laptop with 16GB of RAM that operates on a x64-based processor architecture. Code was written in Python version 3.9. Metrics visualization and performance evaluation were conducted using TensorBoard, which tracks key metrics such as loss, accuracy, and overall alignment quality.

EA-RAG was implemented in Python 3.11 environment and executed on an M1 MacBook Air with 16 GB of RAM. The method uses APIs for generating embeddings, storing them in a vector database, and aligning entities using an LLM, making it compatible with most modern laptops. Its modular structure and reliance on widely available tools rather than computing power ensure that it can be easily reproduced, implemented, and extended by other researchers for further experimentation and development.

Table 2 summarizes the final performance metrics for each method. Figure 3 presents the learning curves for Hits@1 over training epochs for BootEA, GCN-Align, and MTransE.

Table 2. Performance of Methods on DBP15K (`fr_en`).

Method	Hits@1	Processing Time
BootEA	0.5148	11h 53 m
GCN-Align	0.4303	25 m 37 s
MTransE	0.4073	11 m 29 s
EA-RAG	**0.6465**	**60 m 59 s**

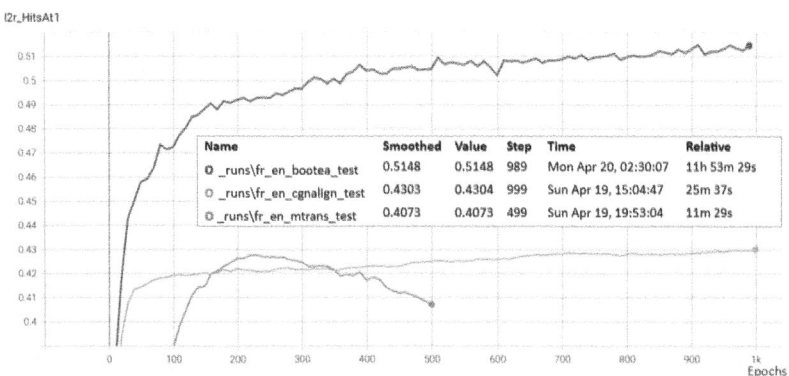

Fig. 3. Learning curves showing Hits@1 progression during training for BootEA, GCN-Align, and MTransE.

BootEA achieved the highest Hits@1 score (0.5148) among the EAkit evaluated methods. The iterative refinement mechanism, which progressively incorporates new alignments during training, contributed significantly to its strong performance. However, the high computational cost (approximately 12 h) poses a scalability limitation for larger datasets. BootEA proved to be particularly effective for handling noisy and sparse datasets. **GCN-Align** outperformed MTransE with a Hits@1 score of 0.4303. Its convolutional network architecture managed to capture both local and global graph structures, making it particularly effective for relationally dense entities. However, GCN-Align struggles with sparsely connected entities, leading to its lower overall performance compared to BootEA. **MTransE** demonstrated the lowest Hits@1 score (0.4073) but was the most computationally efficient, requiring only approximately 11 min of processing time. Its simplicity and reliance on translational embeddings limited its ability to model complex relationships, particularly in sparse or noisy datasets.

For the **EA-RAG** model, we conducted experiments on three datasets:

- **Small:** A subset with 150 entities, representing 1% of the DBP15K dataset.
- **Medium:** A subset with 1500 entities, representing 10% of the DBP15K dataset.
- **Large:** The entire DBP15K dataset, containing 15000 entities.

While running our first experiment on the small dataset, we observed the entire process took about 5 min and we decided to parallelize the execution. We introduced blocking primitives (a semaphore and locks) when calling the LLM, which ensured the script rotates between 5 API Keys in order to prevent the system from hitting the rate limit imposed by OpenAI[5]. Furthermore, the LLM was configured with a temperature of 0.4 for controlled randomness in response generation.

At the same time, after performing a qualitative analysis of the results, we realized that many entities were correctly aligned, but not identified as such due to naming inconsistencies. To address this issue we implemented a normalization script within the Inference Module, that handles cases like abbreviations and the use of special characters.

Table 3. EA-RAG experiment results on different dataset sizes.

Dataset Size	Hits@1 Score	Number of Entities	Time Taken
Small Dataset	0.6667	150	28.5 s
Medium Dataset	0.6421	1,500	6 m 44.1 s
Large Dataset	0.6465	15,000	60 m 59 s

Table 3 summarizes the experiment results across the three datasets. Completion times scaled proportionally with the dataset size: Small (150 entities) in 28.5 s, Medium (1,500 entities) in 6 min 44.1 s, and Large (15,000 entities) in 61 min. This linear increase was expected due to dataset growth and the necessity for multiple API calls during entity alignment. Hits@1 scores were consistent across the three datasets. The slight performance decrease with larger

---

[5] https://platform.openai.com/docs/guides/rate-limits.

datasets might be due to increased entity complexity, whereas Hits@1 scores for the Medium and Large datasets are in the same confidence interval.

We notice EA-RAG achieved the highest Hits@1 score (0.6465) while completing the task in 61 min, outperforming the embedding-based methods in both accuracy and efficiency.

4.1 Limitations and Future Directions

The methods implemented using EAKit have a series of limitations. BootEA is characterized by a high computational cost, which restricts its scalability to larger datasets. GCN-Align is limited by its dependency on graph connectivity, making it less generalizable to datasets that are sparse. Finally, MTransE's main drawback lies in the fact that it employs a simplistic modeling approach, which results in a reduced accuracy when dealing with complex relationships or noisy attributes.

Regarding EA-RAG, the rate limits imposed by OpenAI on their API constituted a major roadblock that we managed to overcome by rotating between 5 API Keys. As the original dataset was quite large and required more API calls than we expected, we only managed to run the EA-RAG full experiment once. We believe the system can be further improved through more experiments, potentially by tweaking parameters like temperature and number of documents retrieved. At the same time, we believe the context can be improved by enhancing graph data using a smaller pre-trained language model. This would make potentially ambiguous triples easier to process, by replacing vague labels with more descriptive words.

5   Conclusion

This paper evaluates the effectiveness of Retrieval-Augmented Generation (RAG) for entity alignment (EA), compared to traditional embedding-based models such as BootEA, GCN-Align, and MTransE, using the DBP15K (fr_en) dataset. EA-RAG achieved the highest Hits@1 score (0.6465), outperforming all other tested methods, including BootEA (0.5148), GCN-Align (0.4303), and MTransE (0.4073). Its ability to combine the predictive power of an LLM with the increased accuracy of vector search contributed to superior alignment accuracy.

In terms of efficiency, EA-RAG also demonstrated better scalability, completing the dataset in 61 min, compared to BootEA's 12-h runtime, while maintaining superior accuracy. However, the rate limits and API costs associated with LLM highlight the need for further optimization for large-scale applications.

Future work needs to validate this RAG-based approach on additional datasets, such as DWY-NB [11], DBP-FB [13] or DWY100K [7], also considering other evaluation metrics like MRR or Hits@10. We should perform ablation studies to isolate the effectiveness of the individual components in our processing pipeline and an independent human evaluation for assessing the retrieval quality.

To further improve the model's performance and enhance the transparency in the LLM reasoning we could try other techniques recommended in practice such as fine-tuning[6], model distillation[7] or prompt engineering[8].

Acknowledgments. D.M.R. Bara thanks Babeş-Bolyai University for granting him the special scholarship for scientific activity during the academic year 2024–2025.

References

1. Bordes, A., Usunier, N., García-Durán, A., Weston, J., Yakhnenko, O.: Translating embeddings for modeling multi-relational data. In: Advances in Neural Information Processing Systems 26: 27th Annual Conf. on Neural Information Processing Systems 2013, Lake Tahoe, United States, pp. 2787–2795 (2013). https://proceedings.neurips.cc/paper/2013/hash/1cecc7a77928ca8133fa24680a88d2f9-Abstract.html

2. Chen, M., Tian, Y., Yang, M., Zaniolo, C.: Multilingual knowledge graph embeddings for cross-lingual knowledge alignment. In: Proceedings of the 26th International Joint Conference on Artificial Intelligence, IJCAI 2017, Melbourne, Australia, pp. 1511–1517. ijcai.org (2017). https://doi.org/10.24963/IJCAI.2017/209

3. Jiang, X., et al.: Unlocking the power of large language models for entity alignment. In: Proceedings of the 62nd Annual Meeting of the Association for Computational Linguistics (Vol. 1: Long Papers), Bangkok, Thailand, pp. 7566–7583. Association for Computational Linguistics (2024). https://doi.org/10.18653/V1/2024.ACL-LONG.408

4. Lewis, P.S.H., et al.: Retrieval-augmented generation for knowledge-intensive NLP tasks. In: Advances in Neural Information Processing Systems 33: Annual Conference on Neural Information Processing Systems 2020, NeurIPS 2020, Virtual (2020). https://proceedings.neurips.cc/paper/2020/hash/6b493230205f780e1bc26945df7481e5-Abstract.html

5. Pan, S., Luo, L., Wang, Y., Chen, C., Wang, J., Wu, X.: Unifying large language models and knowledge graphs: a roadmap. IEEE Trans. Knowl. Data Eng. **36**(7), 3580–3599 (2024). https://doi.org/10.1109/TKDE.2024.3352100

6. Sun, Z., Hu, W., Li, C.: Cross-lingual entity alignment via joint attribute-preserving embedding. In: d'Amato, C., et al. (eds.) ISWC 2017. LNCS, vol. 10587, pp. 628–644. Springer, Cham (2017). https://doi.org/10.1007/978-3-319-68288-4_37

7. Sun, Z., Hu, W., Zhang, Q., Qu, Y.: Bootstrapping entity alignment with knowledge graph embedding. In: Proceedings of the 27th International Joint Conference on Artificial Intelligence, IJCAI 2018, Stockholm, Sweden, pp. 4396–4402. ijcai.org (2018). https://doi.org/10.24963/IJCAI.2018/611

8. Wang, Z., Lv, Q., Lan, X., Zhang, Y.: Cross-lingual knowledge graph alignment via graph convolutional networks. In: Proceedings of the 2018 Conference on Empirical Methods in Natural Language Processing, Brussels, Belgium, pp. 349–357. Association for Computational Linguistics (2018). https://doi.org/10.18653/V1/D18-1032

---

[6] https://platform.openai.com/docs/guides/fine-tuning.

[7] https://platform.openai.com/docs/guides/distillation.

[8] https://platform.openai.com/docs/guides/prompt-engineering.

9. Zeng, K., Li, C., Hou, L., Li, J., Feng, L.: A comprehensive survey of entity alignment for knowledge graphs. AI Open **2**, 1–13 (2021). https://doi.org/10.1016/J.AIOPEN.2021.02.002

10. Zhang, R., et al.: AutoAlign: fully automatic and effective knowledge graph alignment enabled by large language models. IEEE Trans. Knowl. Data Eng. **36**(6), 2357–2371 (2024). https://doi.org/10.1109/TKDE.2023.3325484

11. Zhang, R., Trisedya, B.D., Li, M., Jiang, Y., Qi, J.: A benchmark and comprehensive survey on knowledge graph entity alignment via representation learning. VLDB J. **31**(6), 1143–1168 (2022). https://doi.org/10.1007/s00778-022-00747-z

12. Zhao, X., Zeng, W., Tang, J.: Entity Alignment - Concepts, Recent Advances and Novel Approaches. Springer (2023). https://doi.org/10.1007/978-981-99-4250-3

13. Zhao, X., Zeng, W., Tang, J., Wang, W., Suchanek, F.M.: An experimental study of state-of-the-art entity alignment approaches. IEEE Trans. Knowl. Data Eng. **34**(6), 2610–2625 (2022). https://doi.org/10.1109/TKDE.2020.3018741

3rd International Workshop on Hybrid Artificial Intelligence and Enterprise Modelling for Intelligent Information Systems (HybridAIMS)

3rd International Workshop on Hybrid Artificial Intelligence and Enterprise Modelling for Intelligent Information Systems (HybridAIMS 2025)

Hybrid Artificial Intelligence represents an increasingly emerging research domain that merges two significant branches of artificial intelligence: sub-symbolic AI (e.g., machine learning techniques such as Neural Networks, Large Language Models, or Generative AI) and symbolic AI (e.g., ontologies and Knowledge Graphs, Rule-Based Systems, or Fuzzy Logic). These two paradigms possess complementary strengths, enabling the development of Intelligent Information Systems. For instance, while neural networks excel at identifying patterns in extensive datasets, symbolic approaches leverage domain-specific knowledge to facilitate logical reasoning, enforce constraints, and enhance the interpretability of conclusions.

Typically, AI solutions are integrated within applications that supply the necessary data for analysis and utilize the outcomes of these analyses for subsequent processes. Consequently, constructing such intelligent information systems demands high expertise in both sub-symbolic and symbolic AI approaches, alongside a deep understanding of the application domain and associated IT requirements. Engaging domain experts early in the development process is advantageous, as it enhances the quality of the resulting system. However, this early collaboration can be challenging due to the differing perspectives and terminologies used by the various stakeholders from business, specific application domains, IT, and AI.

Enterprise Modeling (EM), as a scientific discipline, offers a solution to this challenge by facilitating alignment between the business and IT worlds. It provides solid theories for the conceptual representation, design, implementation, and analysis of information systems. The use of graphical notations in enterprise models enhances their interpretability, improving communication and decision-making among the diverse stakeholders.

In this context, integrating Hybrid Artificial Intelligence with Enterprise Modeling has the potential to significantly advance the design and implementation of Intelligent Information Systems, combining the strengths of both fields to deliver systems of high value and utility.

The International Workshop on Hybrid Artificial Intelligence and Enterprise Modelling for Intelligent Information Systems (HybridAIMS) brings together researchers and practitioners from Knowledge Representation and Reasoning (including Semantic Web technologies), Machine Learning (including Generative AI), and Enterprise Modeling. The goal is to explore how the integration of these three fields can advance the engineering of intelligent information systems across various application domains.

HybridAIMS 2025 received eight high-quality international submissions. Each paper underwent a single-blind review by three to five members of the Program Committee. The top four manuscripts were accepted for publication as full papers in the Springer

LNBIP series, while four were accepted as short papers to be published in a CEUR volume affiliated with CAiSE. All the papers were presented on June 16, 2025.

Dominik Bork delivered the invited talk to open the workshop with a presentation titled "Conceptual Modeling and Machine Learning: Opportunities, Challenges, and Lessons Learned". The talk explored the integration of Conceptual Modeling and Machine Learning. Dominik first provided a state-of-the-art overview and then highlighted both the opportunities and challenges in this hybrid research field. He then presented his recent research, sharing insights on: a) transforming conceptual models into structures that facilitate the application of Machine Learning, and b) utilizing Large Language Models, Knowledge Graphs, and Graph Neural Networks to enable AI-assisted conceptual modeling. The talk concluded with a synthesis of lessons learned and a proposal for future research directions.

Full Papers

Andreas Martin *et al.* presented a Hybrid Intelligence approach that integrates long-context large language models (LLMs), human expertise, and hybrid clustering mechanisms to address inconsistencies in technical documents that arise from contradictory statements and omissions. A corpus of up to 300 technical documents from the Swiss National Cooperative for the Disposal of Radioactive Waste (Nagra) was used as a case study.

Daniel Henselmann *et al.* explored the impact of Knowledge Graph representations on question answering (KGQA) with Large Language Models. The authors considered three dimensions of representation: (i) subsets, (ii) modeling, and (iii) annotations, and hypothesized that different variations impact the F1 scores of KGQA systems.

Liubov Kovriguina *et al.* presented the MATRIX ontology (Multi-Agent Experience Transfer, Reasoning and Interaction eXchange), a conceptualization behind the shared memory layer that can serve as a memory, decision, and experience model for heterogeneous agentic teams, and show its applications in a policy transfer use case.

Cristiana Nemtoc and Ana-Maria Ghiran compared two approaches–the RAG retrieval method and GraphRAG–that leverage the current capabilities of Large Language Models to facilitate natural language querying on invoice data.

Short Papers

Adam Aron Rynkiewicz *et al.* introduced FELA–Flexible Entity Linking Architecture–a framework designed for seamless entity linking across multiple knowledge bases. The approach uses two knowledge bases–Wikidata and Agrovoc–and leverages fine-tuned Large Language Models, a generic embedding model, and a Large Language Model-based reranking module to enhance entity disambiguation.

Maja Spahic-Bogdanovic *et al.* presented iModuleBuddy, an AI-driven academic planning approach for students that combines course recommendations with structured study planning. The authors suggested a multiagent AI system that uses both a retrieval-augmented generation (RAG) and a job-ranking algorithm to generate study plans.

Rene Dorsch *et al.* presented COMPASS, a methodology for prompt optimization projects that systematically applies process mining techniques to discover and guide agent behavior. The authors proposed five phases: to plan the project, extract data from the LLM, transform data into event logs, explore and analyze LLM-based agent behavior, and provide guidelines for prompt refinement.

Georgios Koutsopoulos *et al.* presented CLAIM, a prototype legal analysis tool that combines Model-Driven Development with Large Language Model functionalities to support the interpretation of Intellectual Property (IP) case decisions in complex and extensive legal documents.

We thank the authors for their noteworthy contributions and the members of the Program Committee for their invaluable help in the reviewing and discussion phases. We hope that the reader will benefit from reading these papers to learn more about the latest advances in research about the convergence of hybrid artificial intelligence and enterprise modeling.

April 2025

Emanuele Laurenzi
Hans Friederisch Witschel
Peter Haase
Marco Montali

Organization

Workshop Chairs

Emanuele Laurenzi	FHNW, Switzerland
Hans-Friedrich Witschel	FHNW, Switzerland
Peter Haase	Metaphacts, Germany
Marco Montali	Free University of Bozen-Bolzano, Italy

Program Committee

Kurt Sandkuhl	University of Rostock, Germany
Heiko Maus	German Research Center for Artificial Intelligence, Germany
Pascal Hitzler	Kansas State University, USA
Steven Alter	University of San Francisco, USA
Oscar Pastor	Polytechnic University of Valencia, Spain
Robert Andrei Buchmann	Babeş-Bolyai University of Cluj Napoca, Romania
Henderik A. Proper	TU Wien, Austria
Dominic Bork	TU Wien, Austria
Stefano Borgo	CNR-ISTC, Italy
Maria Luisa Sapino	University of Turin, Italy
Jānis Grabis	Riga Technical University, Latvia
Raimundas Matulevičius	University of Tartu, Estonia
Andreas Martin	FHNW, Switzerland
Manuel Renold	FHNW, Switzerland
Michela Quadrini	University of Camerino, Italy
Massimo Callisto De Donato	University of Camerino, Italy
Charuta Pande	FHNW, Switzerland

Natural Language Querying of Invoice Data Using RAG and GraphRAG: Leveraging LLMs for Financial Document Insights

Teodora Cristiana Nemtoc and Ana-Maria Ghiran$^{(\boxtimes)}$

Faculty of Economics and Business Administration, Babeş-Bolyai University,
Cluj-Napoca, Romania
{cristiana.nemtoc,anamaria.ghiran}@econ.ubbcluj.ro

Abstract. Various organizations' stakeholders often base their decisions on insights extracted from financial documents such as invoices. Most of the time, these are non-technical stakeholders, thus requiring a translation into a structured database query. This paper explores two approaches that leverage the current capabilities of LLMs (Large Language Models) and facilitate natural language querying applied on factual data. We compared the established RAG retrieval method with its extension, GraphRAG, as both of these methods empower decision makers to quickly address natural language queries at their convenience to obtain actionable insights from invoices, reducing reliance on specialized personnel for database interrogation.

Keywords: Invoice processing · RAG · GraphRAG · Information Extraction

1 Introduction

A company's prosperity is affected by its managers' capacity to base their decisions on data to optimize areas like liquidity assurance, selection of suppliers, enhancing sale strategies or designing targeted marketing campaigns. This kind of information is often available in simple financial documents such as invoices, and managers should benefit from it without any intermediaries for translating their business-level needs into technical queries to extract insights from invoices.

We address this challenge with an AI-driven approach that enables natural language querying of invoice data, eliminating the need for technical expertise. The use of AI applications to support employees' work has been blooming lately: from simple chat bots designed to improve customer support to complex platforms meant to deliver AI digital assistants for various roles within an enterprise (e.g. desksense.ai, sintra.ai). Tools like Google Document AI, Acrobat AI Assistant have specialized in document processing, enabling businesses to automate data entry, OCR, named entity recognition, and to analyze various documents including invoices. Our aim is not to deliver just another tool that could be used for human-like question-answering on invoice data but rather to contribute in identifying the most appropriate method for this.

© The Author(s), under exclusive license to Springer Nature Switzerland AG 2025
J. Grabis and Y. Wautelet (Eds.): CAiSE 2025 Workshops, LNBIP 556, pp. 69–80, 2025.
https://doi.org/10.1007/978-3-031-94931-9_6

The proposed solution leverages: a) Generative AI models, more specifically LLMs (Large Language Models) to process and generate human-like text for dealing with interactions with non-technical persons, b) RAG (Retrieval Augmented Generation) techniques as retrieval methods for factual information, and c) knowledge graphs (KGs) for enhanced reasoning and as truth validators. These are modern AI capabilities that each business must adopt not just as an advantage but as a necessity for long-term innovation and sustainability.

The structure of the paper is as follows: the paper begins by detailing the problem statement and motivation for our work and sets some clearly defined objectives; Sect. 2 analysis related works, while Sect. 3 outlines the research methodology; Sect. 4 details the two implemented approaches and Sect. 5 discusses the results by comparing the two techniques; finally, Sect. 6 concludes by summarizing the findings and outlining potential directions for future research.

1.1 Context Problem and Motivation

Various stakeholders involved in the decision process of a company must consider different pieces of information that can be found in invoices to make data-driven decisions that align with their functional responsibilities. For example, a General Manager can evaluate the average delivery time or payments by aggregating data regarding the Due date and Fulfilment date. She can further re-negotiate better terms or consider diversifying suppliers. A Financial Manager can be interested in identifying customers with high due amounts and adjusting the payment schedules to maintain liquidity. A Salesperson might be concerned in analyzing the type of products that are bought together and could identify patterns in customer preferences. She can propose complementary items to a potential customer, increasing sales revenues. Similarly, a Chief Marketing Officer can analyze purchase patterns and can design targeted marketing campaigns such as promotions or discounts to encourage purchases from similar customer segments.

This kind of stakeholders usually lack the technical expertise to interact directly with data. It was always a discrepancy between the way managers formulate their questions and the language required to query that information. This is due to the fundamental difference in their perspectives: managers often communicate in high-level operational needs while data analysts must think in terms of specific data structures. Most of the time, managers relied on intermediaries to translate their business needs into the necessary technical queries, which can lead to a delayed process and even loss of meaning as the managers' intent might be misunderstood.

Extracting information from invoices in natural language enables managers to access actionable insights to support their operational and strategic decision-making process without requiring any technical expertise. In this way, a broader range of business stakeholders can benefit from insights taken from business data, ultimately enhancing efficiency and accuracy in the business process.

We aim to lay the groundwork for advanced retrieval systems, replacing the standard structured query language with natural language inputs. This advancement enhances usability for the end-users, broadens the range of applications that can use insights from invoice data. Furthermore, the manual analysis of financial documents is significantly reduced, simplifying the process of managing and operating such documents. This implies that the need for specialized personnel proficient in specific query languages and database operations is eliminated, as the proposed solution is designed to be accessible to any user, providing stakeholders with direct access to the invoice querying system.

1.2 Solution Overview and Research Objective

Each company is faced with the requirement to switch from the cumbersome process of manually handling financial data, which is prevalent in most companies, to AI-driven solutions for automation, optimization and acceleration of workloads and business tasks. Large Language Models (LLMs) cannot accurately answer questions about particular invoice data simply because such information is typically outside the training sources. In this case, RAG (Retrieval Augmented Generation) – driven LLMs [1], which retrieve relevant data from external sources in real time and use it to generate more appropriate and meaningful responses, have proven to be highly effective [2]. By integrating real-time query mechanisms, RAG-driven LLMs can access invoice-specific data, ensuring that responses are given based on updated information rather than relying solely on pre-trained data.

Our solution investigates RAG and its new branch, Graph RAG [3], to replace traditional information extraction procedures.

The accuracy and efficiency of RAG depend on the quality of the information it is able to provide as context. In answering complex queries that involve relationships between concepts or require mechanisms of reasoning and logical deduction, standard RAG can face significant challenges – if the question to be answered stretches across several sections of the document (several rows of the dataset in our case), critical information can be omitted, as the retrieval only selects top k results.

A more structured data framework, governed by predefined rules and schemas that define the relationships between concepts, can address these limitations.

This can be achieved with GraphRAG which, as reflected in its name, retains the main properties of RAG while using a Knowledge Graph for improving the quality of LLM responses [3].

The main advantage of GraphRAG lies in the structured nature of the graph. By identifying the key entities and their relationships, it supports the retrieval process, as clear paths within the graph can be traversed regardless of the distance between nodes or the number of hops required.

The current paper will explore both RAG and Graph RAG approaches – a) using data from textual documents and b) leveraging the potential of constructing a graph at data indexing phase. These techniques are evaluated comparing their results with those given by querying the local knowledge graph, which is the most precise method for retrieving the required information (the ground truth).

The objective of our approach can be formulated as follows: to compare various techniques that allow natural language querying of invoice data and assess the effectiveness of these techniques, (e.g. how each technique supports accurate and efficient information retrieval).

With the stated objective, the proposed solution aims to overcome limitations related to volume, time, labor, and personnel that typically arise in handling financial documents such as invoices. The ultimate goal is to analyze the strengths and weaknesses of each methodology, providing guidance on their application, identifying the best alternative for handling invoices, and determining suitable use cases for application.

2 Literature Review

While applying RAG over text documents (unstructured data sources such as pdf files) is a well-explored technique, combining KGs and LLMs is still an exploratory stage [4]. Initial research that integrates both KGs and LLMs was done to answer complex questions that required reliable results, sustained by factual knowledge, hence mitigating the hallucination problems.

Supplementing LLMs with non-parametric knowledge when interacting with LLM through prompt interface has been analyzed by [5] who compared the effectiveness of prompting LLMs with textual fragments and KGs, concluding on the superiority of KGs over other passages.

Other possible implementations of the joint use of KGs with LLMs provide a structured data context for LLMs in the form of graphs. This involved retrieving triples from KGs as knowledge context and further use LLMs to generate responses [6, 7]. This enables LLMs to treat KGs as repositories of factual information, repositories that can act as a data fabric layer over multiple knowledge sources (text based, serializable diagrammatic representations or structured and semi-structured information). Leveraging existing KGs as a source of context or factual information [8–10] is just one possible interpretation of the GraphRAG.

Lan and Jiang [11] employed LLMs and proposed a query graph generation method to handle questions with constraints and questions for multiple hops of relations.

In many cases, GraphRAG means improving the performance of question-answering tasks in LLMs in conjunction with RAG technique, by using the LLM to create a KG based on a private dataset [12]. This is the original meaning for the GraphRAG in the Microsoft approach [13]. In their proposal, the unstructured input is sent to an LLM for structuring the data into a graph format, where nodes (information chunks) represent entities and edges capture relationships between these entities. A community detection algorithm identifies nodes close to each other and community summaries are generated. Each community will be responsible for providing responses to specific queries, the results being then combined into a map-reduce fashion in order to obtain a general answer for those questions that require synthesized information across entire corpus.

This approach transitions from the conventional RAG methodology, where documents are treated as standalone units, to a perspective that considers them as generators of potential connections and relationships. This is the interpretation of the GraphRAG that we are considering in this current paper. We plan to investigate the other GraphRAG manifestations in future iterations of our study.

3 Methodology

As the current work reports results pertaining to applicative research, we required a methodology that could systematically address the problem and develop a practical solution. The appropriate methodology in this case is Design Science Research (DSR) [14] which focuses on creating and evaluating artifacts designed to solve real-world problems. Applying DSR, our study follows a rigorous approach to the development and demonstration of innovative techniques for extracting information from invoices in natural language.

The recommended phases in DSR are: problem identification and motivation, objectives definition, design and development, demonstration, evaluation and communication [14]. First, we identified as a problem, the challenges that business stakeholders face in extracting insights from invoice data in natural language. Then we defined clear research objectives and devised a DSR artifact as an efficient method to process invoices and answer business questions in natural language.

The flow of the activities performed to identify the optimal approach is depicted in Fig. 1.

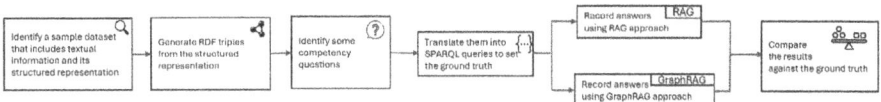

Fig. 1. Design process of the proposed solution

3.1 Identification of a Sample Dataset

Invoices serve as valuable sample datasets to exemplify our scenario that compare RAG and GraphRAG as different information extraction methodologies. As textual documents, they uncover relevant information in raw format. Simultaneously, many of them also provide information in a semi-structured format due to the legal requirements often associated with them. Hence, they can be used to compare AI capabilities in natural language question-answering applied to text or structured information.

The utilized dataset is publicly available at Huggingface[1] and comprises 538 invoice documents both in raw format, as well as in a structured format, as JSON. The chosen dataset is suitable for NLP tasks as it easily allows Named Entity Recognition and Information Retrieval. Additionally, it has a relatively well-defined structure, which facilitates Knowledge Graph construction.

---

[1] https://huggingface.co/datasets/lokaspire/invoice_dataset.

3.2 Generate RDF Triples

The dataset includes two columns: one with the unstructured textual content of the invoices and the other column in JSON format, which contains fields encountered in most invoices.

An example of an invoice is provided in Fig. 2, followed by the structured representation in JSON format.

Invoice no: 61356291 Date of issue: 09/06/2012 Seller: Client: Chapman, Kim and Green Rodriguez-Stevens 64731 James Branch 2280 Angela Plain Smithmouth, NC 26872 Hortonshire, MS 93248 Tax Id: 949-84-9105 Tax Id: 939-98-8477 IBAN:GB50ACIE59715038217063 ITEMS Qty No. Description UM Net price Net worth VAT [%] Gross worth Wine Glasses Goblets Pair Clear 5,00 each 12,00 60,00 10% 66,00 1. Glass 28,08 With Hooks Stemware Storage 4,00 each 112,32 10% 123,55 2. Multiple Uses Iron Wine Rack Hanging Glass Replacement Corkscrew Parts 1,00 each 7,50 7,50 10% 8,25 3. Spiral Worm Wine Opener Bottle Houdini HOME ESSENTIALS GRADIENT 1,00 each 12,99 12,99 10% 14,29 4 STEMLESS WINE GLASSES SET OF 4 20 FL OZ (591 ml) NEW SUMMARY VAT [%] Net worth VAT Gross worth 10% 192,81 19,28 212,09 Total $ 192,81 $ 19,28 $ 212,09


```
{
  "InvoiceDetails": {
    "InvoiceNumber": "61356291",
    "InvoiceDate": "09/06/2012",
    "InvoiceDueDate": ""
  },
  "SellerDetails": {
    "SellerName": "Chapman, Kim and Green",
    "SellerAddress": "64731 James Branch\nSmithmouth, NC 26872",
    "SellerTaxNumber": "Tax Id: 949-84-9105",
    "SellerContactNumber": "",
    "SellerEmail": ""
  },
  "BuyerDetails": {
    "ClientName": "Rodriguez-Stevens",
    "ClientAddress": "2280 Angela Plain\nHortonshire, MS 93248",
    "ClientTaxNumber": "Tax Id: 939-98-8477",
    "ClientContactNumber": "",
    "ClientEmail": ""
  },
  "ItemDetails": [
    {
      "Description": "Wine Glasses Goblets Pair Clear Glass",
      "Qty": "5.00",
      "UnitOfMeasure": "each",
      "NetPrice": "12.00",
      "Tax": "10%",
      "Total_for_each_item": "66.00"
    },
    {
      "Description": "With Hooks Stemware Storage Multiple Uses Iron Wine Rack Hanging Glass",
      "Qty": "4.00",
      "UnitOfMeasure": "each",
      "NetPrice": "112.32",
      "Tax": "10%",
      "Total_for_each_item": "123.55"
    },
    {
      "Description": "Replacement Corkscrew Parts Spiral Worm Wine Opener Bottle Houdini",
      "Qty": "1.00",
      "UnitOfMeasure": "each",
      "NetPrice": "7.50",
      "Tax": "10%",
      "Total_for_each_item": "8.25"
    },
    {
      "Description": "HOME ESSENTIALS GRADIENT STEMLESS WINE GLASSES SET OF 4 20 FL OZ (591 ml) NEW",
      "Qty": "1.00",
      "UnitOfMeasure": "each",
      "NetPrice": "12.99",
      "Tax": "10%",
      "Total_for_each_item": "14.29"
    }
  ],
  "BankDetails": {
    "IBAN": "GB50ACIE59715038217063",
    "AccountNumber": "",
    "IFSC": ""
  },
  "InvoiceSummary": {
    "TotalTaxableAmount": "192.81",
    "TotalTaxesAmount": "19.28",
    "FinalTotal": "212.09"
  }
}
```


Fig. 2. Sample invoice data

Based on the identified fields in the JSON data, we defined an ontology, shown in Fig. 3. The visual representation was done in GraphXX, a prototype graph modelling tool described in [15].

This ontology was followed in converting the JSON invoice data into RDF triples. On average, 52 triples resulted for each invoice. Figure 4 shows an example of the resulted triples (left side) and corresponding graph representation (right side) for one invoice, the same one that was previously shown in Fig. 1.

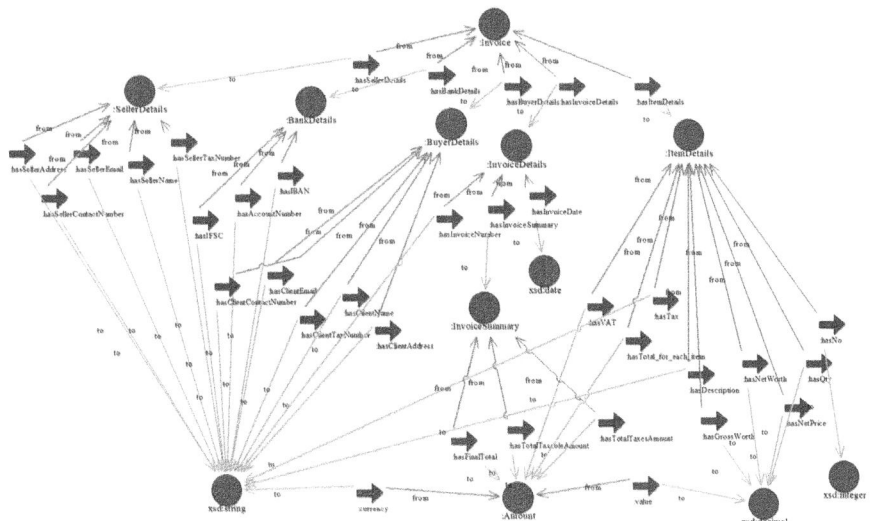

Fig. 3. Invoice data ontology

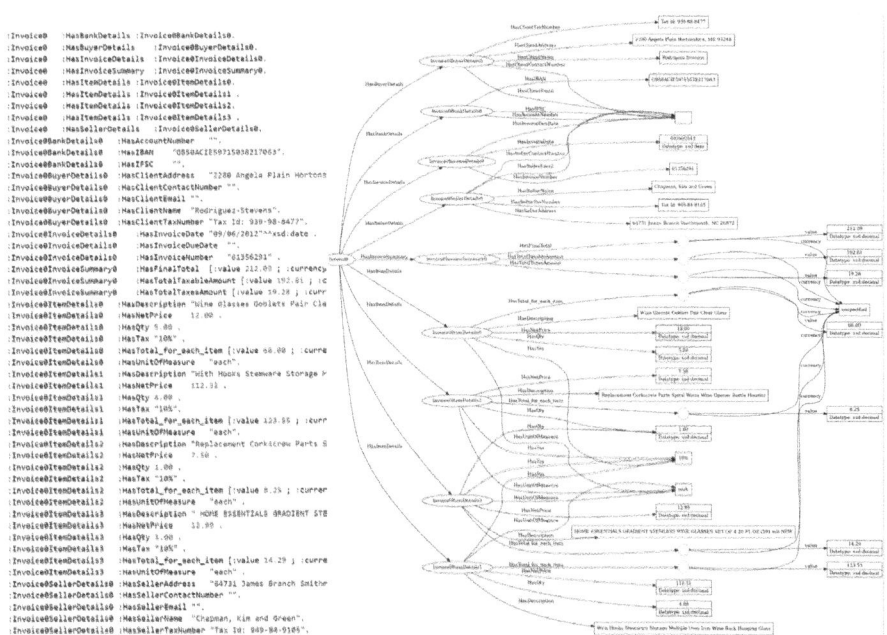

Fig. 4. Generated RDF triples and their visual representation in RDFGrapher [18]

3.3 Identify Sample Competency Questions and Generate Ground Truth

We selected a few representative questions that real-world business stakeholders may pose when analyzing invoice data. This is not a comprehensive list but rather just an exemplification of the variety of possible types of inquiries that may be of interest, ensuring consistency with the categorization introduced at the beginning of the paper (Table 1).

Table 1. Sample business questions and their SPARQL representation

Business Stakeholder	Sample question	SPARQL query

General Manager	What could be a breakdown of purchases by supplier?	`SELECT ?sellerName (GROUP_CONCAT(?product; separator=", ") AS ?products)`
		`WHERE {`
		`    ?invoice :HasItemDetails ?details.`
		`    ?details :HasDescription ?product.`
		`    ?invoice :HasSellerDetails ?sellerDetails.`
		`    ?sellerDetails :HasSellerName ?sellerName}`
		`GROUP BY ?sellerName`

	Which suppliers have the longest fulfillment times?	`PREFIX ofn:<http://www.ontotext.com/sparql/functions/>`
		`SELECT ?supplierName (MAX(?fulfillmentTime) AS ?maxFulfillmentTime)`
		`WHERE {`
		`    ?invoice :HasSellerDetails ?seller.`
		`    ?seller :HasSellerName ?supplierName.`
		`    ?invoice :HasInvoiceDetails ?details.`
		`    ?details :HasInvoiceDate ?invoiceDate.`
		`    ?details :HasInvoiceDueDate ?dueDate.`
		`    BIND(ofn:days-from-duration(xsd:date(?dueDate) -`
		`xsd:date(?invoiceDate)) AS ?fulfillmentTime)}`
		`GROUP BY ?supplierName`
		`ORDER BY DESC(?maxFulfillmentTime)`

Financial Manager	Calculate the total amount for the items listed in the invoice with number 61356291	`SELECT (SUM(?totalValue) AS ?totalSum)`
		`WHERE{`
		`    ?invoice :HasItemDetails ?details.`
		`    ?details :HasTotal_for_each_item ?total.`
		`    ?total :value ?totalValue.`
		`    ?invoice :HasInvoiceDetails ?invoiceDetails.`
		`    ?invoiceDetails :HasInvoiceNumber "61356291"}`

	Which customers have the highest outstanding due amounts?	`SELECT ?clientName (SUM(?total) AS ?totalDueAmount)`
		`WHERE {`
		`    ?invoice :HasBuyerDetails ?buyer.`
		`    ?buyer :HasClientName ?clientName.`
		`    ?invoice :HasInvoiceSummary ?summary.`
		`    ?summary :HasFinalTotal [ :value ?total ].}`
		`GROUP BY ?clientName`
		`ORDER BY DESC(?totalDueAmount)`
		`Limit 5`

Sales Manager	Which products are frequently bought together?	`SELECT ?product1 ?product2 (COUNT(*) AS ?frequency)`
		`WHERE {`
		`    ?invoice :HasItemDetails ?item1.`
		`    ?item1 :HasDescription ?product1.`
		`    ?invoice :HasItemDetails ?item2.`
		`    ?item2 :HasDescription ?product2.`
		`    FILTER(?item1 != ?item2)  }`
		`GROUP BY ?product1 ?product2`
		`ORDER BY DESC(?frequency)`

	What is the invoice number where Crawford, Acosta, and Solomon are involved as sellers?	`SELECT    ?invoiceNumber WHERE{`
		`    ?invoice :HasSellerDetails ?seller.`
		`    ?seller :HasSellerName "Crawford, Acosta and Solomon".`
		`    ?invoice :HasInvoiceDetails ?details.`
		`    ?details :HasInvoiceNumber ?invoiceNumber }`

Chief Marketing Officer	What are the highest spending customers?	`SELECT ?clientName (SUM(?totalValue) AS ?totalSpent)`
		`WHERE {`
		`    ?invoice :HasBuyerDetails ?buyer.`
		`    ?buyer :HasClientName ?clientName.`
		`    ?invoice :HasInvoiceSummary ?summary.`
		`    ?summary :HasFinalTotal ?total.`
		`    ?total :value ?totalValue.}`
		`GROUP BY ?clientName`
		`ORDER BY DESC(?totalSpent)`

	What is the highest quantity bought for each product?	`SELECT ?product (MAX(?quantity) as ?highestqty)`
		`WHERE {`
		`    ?invoice rag:HasItemDetails ?item.`
		`    ?item rag:HasDescription ?product.`
		`    ?item rag:HasQty ?quantity.     }`
		`GROUP BY ?product`

These questions serve as benchmarks for comparing the performance of RAG and GraphRAG frameworks in providing accurate responses to business stakeholders.

4   Solution Development

The paper aims to investigate the practical applicability of the RAG and Graph RAG, exploiting the capabilities of LlamaIndex.

While some LLM providers have started introducing RAG components into their APIs (e.g. OpenAI's Assistants feature), using a standalone framework such as LlamaIndex provides many more customization options.

LlamaIndex [16] is a data framework that connects various datasets and an LLM, effectively working with both unstructured and structured typology of the invoices. After ingesting data, it must be structured and organized in a way to efficiently enable its retrieval and querying. LlamaIndex supports different types of indexing strategies which organize data chunks into a specific data structure, each with its strengths and trade-offs. The indexing processes will organize the invoices' information into Document objects which will further undergo parsing and embedding phases, preparing the data for the retrieval stage.

In this study, we tested two of the indexing methods: VectorStoreIndex and KnowledgeGraphIndex.

While Vector Databases focus on similarity between concepts [17], the Knowledge Graphs come with a structure that shifts the focus to explicit relationships between these elements. A vector database identifies the similarity between two constructs without understanding the direct or indirect relationship formed between them. Knowledge Graphs include not only the entities as standalone units but also associated information through connections formed and hierarchical structures.

The KnowledgeGraphIndex, extracts entities and relationships from the ingested text and constructs a KG. This index is useful when various facts must be connected in a network of data. We expected it to be particularly relevant when the formulated questions need to traverse multiple entities to reach a target in order to retrieve its associated value. Moreover, the KnowledgeGraphIndex provides a more efficient way to handle updates compared to vector based approaches (which impose reindexing when modifying data), thus it can prove to be more suitable in case of invoice data.

The OpenAI library was employed for defining the LLM, following the configurations recommended by LlamaIndex, with GPT-3.5-turbo selected as the designated model. For the embeddings step, we used the library's default settings, utilizing the text-embedding-ada-00 model, which provides a good balance between quality, performance, and cost. We did not find it particularly useful to select a different, local, embedding model for the moment, as we did not have concerns for privacy of the data (the employed dataset is a public one, selected just for the current study investigation purposes).

4.1   Extracting Insights Using RAG Approach

In the first scenario, we test the RAG workflow in LlamaIndex, as depicted in Fig. 5. It begins by ingesting the invoices, in raw text format, undergoing a chunking process. The default RAG process in LlamaIndex involves the usage of Vector Stores.

As invoice documents are parsed, compacted chunks are detected and encapsulated into Node objects. LlamaIndex encompasses a methodology for constructing a Vector-StoreIndex directly from a collection of documents, which, in this case, will consist of invoices. The final data will be stored as high-dimensional vectors that will simplify the querying process. LlamaIndex allows for the creation of query engines based on existing vector stores indexes. A query engine exposes an interface that allows the user to pose questions in natural language, returning answers in the targeted format, based on the specified initial settings. Relevant nodes identified from the query are mapped with the corresponding instances stored during the indexing phase. Subsequently, the appointed LLM generates an appropriate response considering the constructed context.

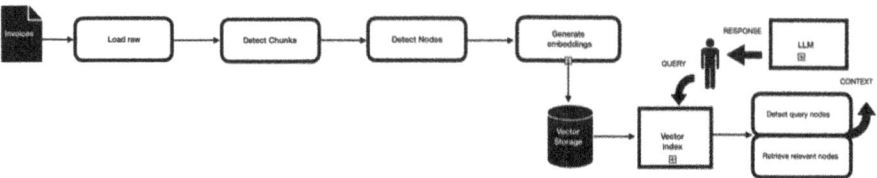

Fig. 5. Processing steps in RAG approach

4.2 Extracting Insights Using GraphRAG Approach

In the second scenario, the same input goes through some additional processing steps - entity recognition techniques are employed to identify entities and relationships between them. The workflow starts with the transformation of the raw input into multiple Document objects, which then undergo text extraction procedures. In the entity extraction process, depending on the desired level of flexibility and customization, a higher degree of specificity can be achieved by explicitly stating the required entities and relationships, along with a graph schema that incorporates rules for the constituent concepts. The retrieval will select the chunks based on their relations. The final context is sent to an LLM, which processes the input and returns the output to the user in natural language.

The returned results are improved, compared to the vector-based approach, as they include not only the relevant entities for the question, but also reveal a chain of potential connections. These associations enable more accurate and detailed answers by uncovering indirect relationships that cannot be obtained exclusively through direct methods (Fig. 6).

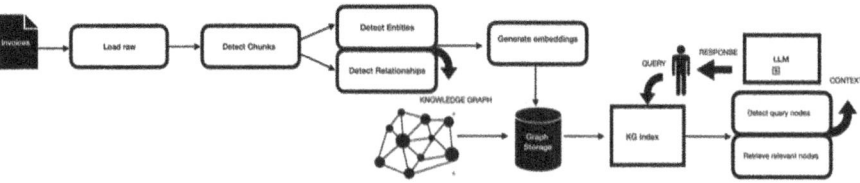

Fig. 6. Processing steps in GraphRAG approach

5 Results and Analysis

The performance of RAG and GraphRAG approaches depends on the query formulation, its complexity and whether additional operations such as aggregations or sorting must be performed, which require traversing the entire dataset for answering queries. Although both techniques can support non-technical stakeholders, employing them instead of established querying mechanisms might omit critical information or generate false positive results.

In general, both RAG and GraphRAG perform well when questions are formulated to identify an entity based on a specific property, as in the case of extracting the invoice number when the seller of an invoice is mentioned.

However, limitations arise when questions are formulated in a summary-oriented manner, and the expected output should provide a synthesized overview, where both approaches provide only partial results. As a result, questions such as "What could be a breakdown of purchases by supplier?", "Who are the highest-spending customers?", and "What is the highest quantity bought for each product?" yield partial summaries, with each technique returning different items. Other limitations can be observed with operations such as aggregations, filtering, computing values, sorting, etc. Although GraphRAG failed to correctly order the customers by their spending amounts, it successfully retrieved entities from invoices with the correct seller role.

6 Conclusion

This study explored the effectiveness of RAG and GraphRAG methodologies for extracting insights from invoice data using natural language. The invoice dataset was chosen precisely because of its simplistic and clear structure, which facilitated the parallel exploration of RAG and GraphRAG technologies – it allowed that the evaluation process to be easily established by comparing the results of SPARQL queries with those returned by an LLM. Our comparative evaluation assessed that GraphRAG improves the precision and interpretability of the retrieved information.

Considering the relevance and growing interest in GraphRAG, several technology providers have tackled this concept with their own conceptualizations and individual understandings of it. For this reason, it would be worthwhile to extend the comparison to include various libraries and examine the results achieved with different technologies. In doing so, a thorough analysis could be conducted, resulting in a detailed set of guidelines for effectively utilizing GraphRAG in diverse scenarios. This would provide a clearer understanding of how different implementations influence performance and applicability, helping to identify the most suitable tools and approaches for specific use cases.

References

1. Lewis, P., et al.: Retrieval-augmented generation for knowledge-intensive NLP tasks. Adv. Neural. Inf. Process. Syst. **33**, 9459–9474 (2020)

2. Gao, Y., et al.: Retrieval-augmented generation for large language models: a survey. arXiv preprint arXiv:2312.10997 (2023)
3. Han, H., et al.: Retrieval-augmented generation with graphs (graphRAG). arXiv preprint arXiv:2501.00309 (2024)
4. Zhao, P., et al.: Retrieval-augmented generation for AI-generated content: a survey. arXiv preprint arXiv:2402.19473 (2024)
5. Huang, W., Zhou, G., Lapata, M., Vougiouklis, P., Montella, S., Pan, J.Z.: Prompting large language models with knowledge graphs for question answering involving long-tail facts. arXiv preprint arXiv:2405.06524 (2024)
6. Li, S., et al.: Graph reasoning for question answering with triplet retrieval. arXiv preprint arXiv:2305.18742 (2023)
7. Jiang, J., Zhou, K., Zhao, W.X., Li, Y., Wen, J.R.: ReasoningLM: enabling structural subgraph reasoning in pre-trained language models for question answering over knowledge graph. arXiv preprint arXiv:2401.00158 (2023)
8. Llamaindex: Knowledge Graph RAG Query Engine (2025). https://docs.llamaindex.ai/en/stable/examples/query_engine/knowledge_graph_rag_query_engine.html. Accessed 31 Feb 2025
9. GraphDB Knowledge Hub, What is Graph RAG? (2025). https://www.ontotext.com/knowledgehub/fundamentals/what-is-graph-rag/. Accessed 31 Feb 2025
10. Data Science Central, Understanding GraphRAG – addressing the limitations of RAG (2025). https://www.datasciencecentral.com/understanding-graphrag-2-addressing-the-limitations-of-rag/. Accessed 31 Feb 2025
11. Lan, Y., Jiang, J.: Query graph generation for answering multi-hop complex questions from knowledge bases. Association for Computational Linguistics (2020)
12. Larson J., Truitt S.: GraphRAG: unlocking LLM discovery on narrative private data (2024). https://www.microsoft.com/en-us/research/blog/graphrag-unlocking-llm-discovery-on-narrative-private-data/. Accessed 31 Feb 2025
13. Edge, D., et al.: From local to global: a graph rag approach to query-focused summarization. arXiv preprint arXiv:2404.16130 (2024)
14. Wieringa, R.J.: Design Science Methodology for Information Systems and Software Engineering. Springer (2014)
15. Chiş, A., Buchmann, R.A., Ghiran, A.M.: Towards a modeling method for low-code knowledge graph building. In: PoEM Forum @ PoEM2023, Vienna, Austria (2023)
16. Llamaindex: Official Documentation (2025). https://docs.llamaindex.ai/en/stable/understanding/. Accessed 31 Feb 2025
17. Taipalus, T.: Vector database management systems: fundamental concepts, use-cases, and current challenges. Cogn. Syst. Res. **85**, 101216 (2024)
18. Living Laboratory Data Service for the Semantic Web, RDFGrapher (2025). https://www.ldf.fi/service/rdf-grapher. Accessed 31 Feb 2025

Impact of Knowledge Graph Representations on Question Answering with Language Models

Daniel Henselmann[1]([✉])[iD], Rene Dorsch[1][iD], and Andreas Harth[1,2][iD]

[1] Fraunhofer IIS, Nuremberg, Germany
{daniel.henselmann,rene.dorsch,andreas.harth}@iis.fraunhofer.de
[2] Friedrich-Alexander-Universität Erlangen-Nürnberg, Nuremberg, Germany

Abstract. The emergence of Large Language Models (LLMs) brought new approaches to Knowledge Graph Question Answering (KGQA), chasing the vision of querying structured data using natural language. While existing work focuses on improving KGQA approaches, this paper explores the impact of different knowledge graph representations. We consider three dimensions of representation: (i) subsets, (ii) modeling, and (iii) annotations, hypothesizing that different variations impact the F_1 scores of KGQA systems. We conduct experiments on a custom knowledge graph featuring integrated data and n-ary relations. Results demonstrate an improvement in the F_1 score from 17.6% to 44.5% between the default and best variant, confirming the hypothesis.

Keywords: Question answering · Knowledge graphs · Large language models · Knowledge representation

1 Introduction

Knowledge Graph Question Answering (KGQA) pursues the vision that users ask questions in natural language that are answered based on factual data. While KGQA is still a hard task to solve, the emergence of Large Language Models (LLMs) has led to new possibilities [3,12]. Research on LLM-augmented KGQA focuses on improving the approaches but assumes a KG with a given fixed representation.

We consider a different angle and evaluate different representations of KGs with the same KGQA approach. Specifically, we represent the same knowledge in different ways, varying in explicit information. Our hypothesis is the following: *Different representations of KGs impact the F_1 score of LLM-augmented KGQA.*

We identify at least three major dimensions of KG representations:

- **Subsets.** Most KGs are too large to be entirely added to the LLM prompt. Therefore, approaches to KGQA obtain relevant subgraphs to discover and understand the KG.

J. Grabis and Y. Wautelet (Eds.): CAiSE 2025 Workshops, LNBIP 556, pp. 81–92, 2025.
https://doi.org/10.1007/978-3-031-94931-9_7

- **Modeling.** Modeling options for ontologies in KGs are numerous. Different modeling options vary in expressiveness and explicitness of the information used to describe the same knowledge.
- **Annotations.** Annotations do not "contribute to the 'logical' knowledge" [9, Section 8] in a KG but provide additional information as text.

The dimensions have considerable depth and warrant dedicated research. We focus on selected subdimensions, which we quantitatively evaluate through experiments to test our hypothesis.

The experiments are conducted on a custom KG (see Sect. 5.3) and use Graf von Data (GvD) (see Sect. 5.1), a KGQA agent similar to the state-of-the-art (SPINACH [13]) that is KG-agnostic. The results show an increase in the F_1 score from 17.6% for the default variant to a maximum of 44.5%, an improvement of 26.9pp/153%, confirming the hypotheses.

Our contributions are (i) a KG unknown to LLMs, including integrated data and n-ary relations, and (ii) a quantitative performance evaluation of selected KG representations for KGQA.

The remainder of the paper is structured as follows. Section 2 positions the paper w.r.t. related work. Section 3 introduces an example. Section 4 discusses considered variants. Section 5 explains the experimental setup. Section 6 describes the conducted experiments and discusses the results. Section 7 concludes the paper and outlines future work.

2   Related Work

Multiple fundamental approaches to LLM-augmented KGQA have emerged using different interfaces through which the LLM obtains KG data. In fine-tuning approaches, LLMs are specifically trained on a KG [22] and answer questions directly. Workflow approaches execute a fixed sequence of actions to add information from the KG to the prompt before calling the LLM to answer the question. Added information may include example question-answer-pairs [17,24], ontology terms [10], a subgraph [1,11,17], and/or URIs [24]. In agent approaches, an agent iteratively alternates between consulting the LLM and obtaining information from the KG through actions [23] to build a SPARQL query that, when executed, retrieves the answer from the KG. The core actions are searching entities (Search) [13,21], retrieving entities (Describe) [13,20,21], and executing SPARQL queries (Query) [13,21]. Some agents also include searching paths between two entities [20] and retrieving usage examples of properties [13].

While the approaches differ, all obtain information that changes with KG representation. The SPINACH agent [13] achieves state-of-the-art results on Wikidata. Consequently, we focus on agent approaches.

3   Example

In the following, we explore how varying KG representations might impact the agent's result for the natural language question: "companies in Germany". Our

KG (see Sect. 5.3) describes enterprises in the semiconductor industry. The KG contains a *Geo* pattern (Fig. 1a), in which terms from the Organization Ontology [18] and GeoNames' ontology[1] express in which regions an organization has sites. The hierarchical regions are connected with the transitive `gn:parentFeature` property. For prefixes, we refer to the repository linked in the KG description in Sect. 5.3.

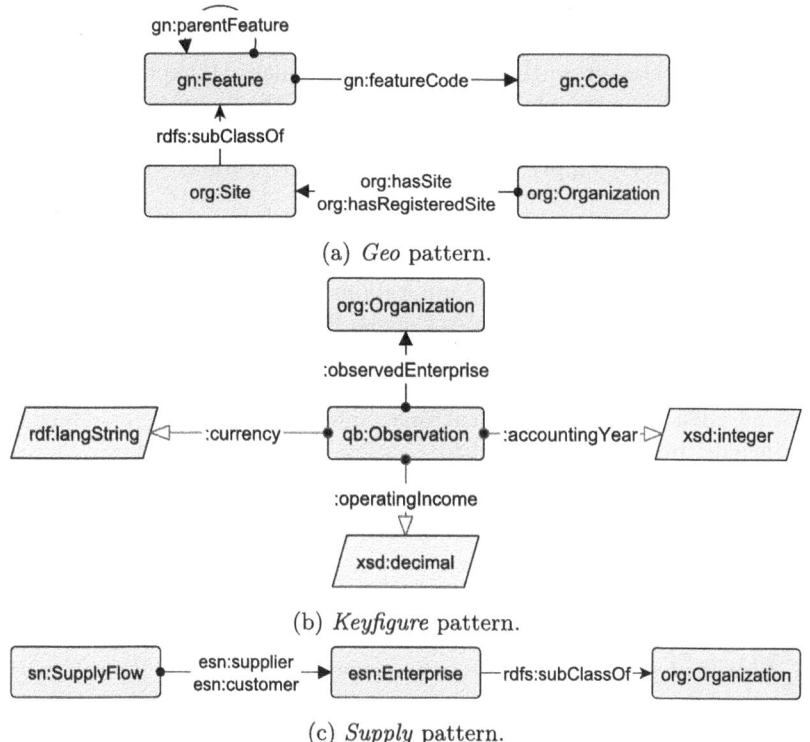

(a) *Geo* pattern.

(b) *Keyfigure* pattern.

(c) *Supply* pattern.

Fig. 1. Important patterns in our ontology visualized in Graffoo [6] notation.

The required SPARQL query to retrieve companies in Germany uses the Geo pattern and requires the URI of Germany:

```
PREFIX org: <https://www.w3.org/ns/org#>
PREFIX gn: <http://www.geonames.org/ontology#>
PREFIX : <https://solid.iis.fraunhofer.de/e-40200/2024/10/
          velektronik-graph-clean/region/wdQ183.ttl#>
SELECT ?x WHERE {
    ?x org:hasRegisteredSite _:y .
    _:y gn:parentFeature+ :this . }
```

---

[1] See http://www.geonames.org/ontology/documentation.html.

Discovering the required relation in the KG is easier if (i) the Describe action on Germany returns incoming triples to detect subordinate regions linked from an `org:Organization` and (ii) the Describe action on `gn:Feature` returns the subclass alignment with `org:Site`. Adding the property `gn:locatedIn` could link Germany directly from an organization. To find the class `org:Organization` and understand that a company is an organization, a comment for the class could add the description.

Other important patterns in the KG are *Keyfigure* and *Supply*, both of which represent n-ary relations. In the Keyfigure pattern (Fig. 1b), the `qb:Observation` class from the Data Cube Vocabulary [4] expresses key figures (operating income as example) of organizations. In the Supply pattern (Fig. 1c), the `sn:SupplyFlow` class from the Abstraction Independent Supply Network Ontology[2] expresses a supply relation between organizations.

4   Considered Representation Variants

We identify subsets, modeling, and annotations as dimensions of KG representations. As the foundation, we consider Concise Bounded Descriptions (CBD) [19] for **subsets**, the RDFS/OWL [2,9] features class, object and datatype property, subclass, subproperty, and property characteristics besides 'inverse' for **modeling**, and `rdfs:label` for **annotations**. Subdimensions that introduce alterations include, but are not limited to:

- **Subsets**
  - *Entity boundaries* like CBD define the triples returned when describing or dereferencing an entity.
  - **Domain subsets** include triples that belong to a certain domain.
- **Modeling**
  - *Inverse properties* link two entities in opposing direction.
  - *Shortcut properties* represent a property path to directly link two entities.
  - **Ontology Design Patterns** are distinguishable patterns independent of an ontology that express an established relation.
  - **Ontology reuse and alignment** focus on combining terms from several ontologies in one KG while maintaining semantics.
  - **Upper ontologies** introduce classes on a high abstraction to support applied ontologies with fundamental semantics.
  - **SKOS concepts** offer a hierarchical classification different from classes.
  - **Shapes** express ontologies alternatively or supplementary to OWL.
- **Annotations**
  - *Comments* are human-readable descriptions of an entity.
  - **Alternative labels** express synonyms or abbreviations.
  - **Examples** show example uses.

This paper focuses on the four subdimensions highlighted in italics, for which we discuss possible variants in the Sects. 4.1, 4.2, 4.3 and 4.4 and conduct experiments to test our hypothesis.

---

[2] See https://purl.org/supply-network/onto#.

4.1   Entity Boundaries

Entity boundaries refer to a method of extracting a limited set of triples about a specific entity within the KG. Several ways exist: The CBD algorithm [19] includes the outgoing triples of an entity while recursively including the outgoing triples of encountered blank nodes. Alternatively, all neighboring triples of an entity can be retrieved [20], potentially selected by semantic relevance [21]. Wikidata's Linked Data Interface[3] returns outgoing triples of an entity with additional statements according to Wikidata's data model and property information. The returned triples are verbose but may be filtered using the LLM and a dedicated prompt [13].

Variants. *Outgoing* triples of a subject are the default variant for our experiments, which aligns with CBD because we do not consider blank nodes.

We retrieve the entire *neighborhood* as another variant by adding incoming triples. The consideration of encountered (potentially nested) blank nodes when retrieving the neighborhood is an open question out of the scope of this paper.

Furthermore, we introduce *specific* class and object property boundaries. Besides outgoing triples, the specific boundaries[4] include selected triples regarding subclasses/subproperties, domain, and range. The motivation is (i) to reduce the number of returned triples without losing valuable information and (ii) to add valuable information (classes in domain and range, types, and labels) outside of the neighborhood.

Examples. When describing a `gn:Feature` instance (e.g., Germany) in the geo pattern, the returned triples do not contain the backwards traversable links to discover a related `org:Organization` instance. To find the link, the agent must describe the `org:Organization` to follow the outgoing triples.

The classes `qb:Observation` and `sn:SupplyFlow` express n-ary relations. The choice of outgoing triples for an n-ary relation without any single individual standing out as the subject of the relation follows a W3C Working Group Note [16]. Consequently, instances of these classes can never be discovered with default entity boundaries.

Describing the class `gn:Feature` returns no information on the `org:Site` subclass nor on the properties that have `gn:Feature` as domain or range.

4.2   Inverse Properties

An inverse property inverts the relation of a property and links two entities in the opposing direction [9]. The information represented by two properties inverse of each other is redundant [15]. Yet, materializing both triples adds explicit information, potentially making it easier for an LLM to grasp a pattern.

---

[3] See https://www.wikidata.org/wiki/Wikidata:Data_access.

[4] SPARQL queries available at https://github.com/Quarkse/kg-rep-llm-qa/tree/main/entity-boundaries.

The addition of inverse properties also covers some of the effects that extended (i.e., neighborhood or specific) entity boundaries have because either an inverse property or incoming triples add a reverse link to retrieved data.

But unlike entity boundaries, properties are present in all KGQA agent actions: The Search action has more options to match the keyword, the Describe action returns more triples that can be understood, and the Query action has two inverse alternatives for each triple pattern.

Variants. For the experiments, we assume no inverse properties as the default. As an alternative variant, we define inverse properties for all object properties in the ontology, which is a baseline approach. We leave sophisticated variants with selected inverse properties to future work. Table 1 shows the inverse properties for the highlighted patterns.

Examples. In the highlighted patterns, inverse properties ensure that all information is reachable when traversing the data with Describe actions.

Table 1. Inverse properties for the three patterns from Fig. 1.

Inverse property	Default property
org:siteOf	org:hasSite
:registeredSiteOf	org:hasRegisteredSite
:childFeature	gn:parentFeature
:featureCodeOf	gn:featureCode
:enterpriseObservation	:observedEnterprise
:outgoingSupplyFlow	esn:supplier
:incomingSupplyFlow	esn:customer

4.3   Shortcut Properties

A shortcut property is a single property that represents a property path [7,14].

Relations between entities that are not linked directly are less obvious to discover and understand. N-ary relations relate multiple entities through a dedicated entity [16]. As a consequence, two entities that are part of the n-ary relation are not directly linked. An additional shortcut property that links the two directly expresses their binary relation more explicitly.

Similarly, a shortcut property can explicitly express the relation to a specific entity in a chain of transitive properties. For this scenario, OWL supports the definition of a property through a property chain [9]. However, property chains are a list of properties with fixed length and no reverse properties. Property paths in SPARQL [8] support both and more.

Shortcut properties reduce the number of entities the agent needs to discover and understand because a shortcut property allows to skip some of the modeling if the skipped details are not required to answer the given question. Like inverse properties, shortcut properties impact all KGQA agent actions.

Variants. For the experiments, we assume no shortcut properties as the default. As an alternative variant, we add shortcut properties where they shorten reoccurring property paths required in answers. The naive approach of adding all possible shortcut properties is not sensible because it leads to properties expressing extensive relations with dubious meaning. Table 2 shows the shortcut properties for the highlighted patterns.

Examples. In the Geo pattern, the shortcut property gn:parentCountry skips a path of transitive gn:parentFeature properties. Thus, the agent does not have to grasp the transitivity. Additionally, the agent may understand that gn:parentCountry points to a country and thus does not have to identify a country by label or by the gn:featureCode. The shortcut property gn:locatedIn additionally takes the discovery and understanding that the location of an organization comes from its registered site out of the equation.

The shortcut properties :hasSupplier and :hasCustomer for the Supply pattern abbreviate the path through the n-ary relation by directly linking suppliers and customers. Thus, the agent does not have to understand sn:SupplyFlow.

Table 2. All shortcut properties.

Shortcut property	Default property path (SPARQL syntax)
gn:parentCountry	gn:parentFeature+
gn:locatedIn	org:hasRegisteredSite/gn:parentFeature+
:hasSupplier	^esn:customer/esn:supplier
:hasCustomer	^esn:supplier/esn:customer

4.4 Comments

The rdfs:comment property expresses a human-readable description of an entity to clarify the meaning [2]. The usage includes "prose documentation, examples, test cases" [2, Section 3.7], making rdfs:comment a versatile property. Consequently, the application of rdfs:comment greatly differs between ontologies.

Additional comments on classes and properties help to reduce the ambiguity of the chosen terms. Comments can also increase the likelihood of matches when searching entities. Therefore, the Search action of the agent includes both the rdfs:label and rdfs:comment into the vector compared to the searched term.

Variants. For the experiments, we assume no comments as the default. As an alternative variant, we add a rdfs:comment literal to all classes, properties, and individuals in the ontology. For newly defined terms in the ontology, we write a comment that describes the term in the context of the ontology. If a reused term has a comment in the original ontology, we use that comment regardless of how well the comment fits the use case and selection of ontology terms. All comments (and labels) are in English only.

Examples. In the highlighted patterns, comments might reduce ambiguity for the KGQA agent. For example, the meaning of the class `gn:Code` is not clear without a description. The direction of the properties `esn:supplier` and `esn:customer` is ambiguous as they lack a suffix ("hasSupplier" or "supplierOf").

5   Experimental Setup

5.1   Agent

We use an LLM-based agent called Graf von Data (GvD)[5] that has three actions at its disposal, which return information from the knowledge graph: a list of URIs for a keyword (Search), a subgraph for a URI (Describe), and a SPARQL result set for a SPARQL query (Query). GvD and the state-of-the-art SPINACH share their agent architecture and require no prior knowledge of the KG. Contrary to SPINACH, GvD is knowledge graph-agnostic and supports integrated data.

5.2   Language Model

We conduct all experiments with Llama 3.3 70B[6] because it is open source and performs well[7] in instruction following, which is required for agent approaches. Our empirical comparison of several LLMs for GvD confirms Llama 3.3 as a strong choice. For our experiments, we set the temperature to 0 and top_p to 1. All experiments were conducted with the Llama 3.3 hosted at Chat AI [5] without any fine-tuning.

5.3   Knowledge Graph

We evaluate variants of KG representation with a custom KG[8]. The KG describes enterprises in the semiconductor industry, their sites, and the supply relations between them. The KG integrates data from the Welektonik[9] Wikibase, Wikidata, DBLP, and Library of Congress. We modeled the data with a custom ontology that reuses established design patterns and ontology terms but also defines new terms when required. The KG contains 32,276 to 48,117 triples, depending on the variant.

The KG differs from other KGs for KGQA evaluation (i) because it is unknown to LLMs, (ii) in the integration of multiple data sources and ontologies, and (iii) in the modeling, which includes n-ary relations.

---

[5] Prompt and screenshot available at https://github.com/Quarkse/kg-rep-llm-qa/tree/main/agent.

[6] See https://huggingface.co/meta-llama/Llama-3.3-70B-Instruct.

[7] See https://github.com/meta-llama/llama-models/blob/main/models/llama3_3/MODEL_CARD.md and https://t.co/6oQ7b3Yuzc.

[8] Available at https://github.com/Quarkse/kg-rep-llm-qa/tree/main/knowledgegraph.

[9] See https://welektronik.iis.fraunhofer.de/wiki/Main_Page.

5.4   Corpus

Our evaluation corpus[10] consists of 58 handcrafted question-query-pairs. Of those, 14 contain the Geo pattern, 15 the Keyfigure pattern, and 11 the Supply pattern. The remaining 18 contain none of the three patterns.

Each question-query-pair consists of a question in natural language and one to four triple patterns of a (gold standard) SPARQL query expressing the correct answer in the KG. Each question requires one variable, which is always a URI. Focusing on URIs allows the agent (i) to retrieve found results to questions to represent them with added context and (ii) removes the problem of whether attributes (the currency of the operating income) or dimensions (the accounting year of the operating income) shall be included in the answers. Even though future work should evaluate questions requiring more complex queries, our results still indicate the ballpark of the impact on F_1 scores.

5.5   Evaluation Metrics

As evaluation metrics, we use the Exact Match (EM) and F_1 scores to compare the SPARQL result sets for our corpus. The EM metric checks whether the result of the generated query completely matches the result of the gold standard query in the corpus. The F_1 metric considers both how many entities in the results are also in the gold standard result and how many of the entities in the gold standard result are in the results. We adopt the generalization to not penalize additional variables retrieved by the queries [13]. We run all experiments five times and give the mean values.

6   Results and Discussion

Table 3 shows the 13 conducted experiments[11] with EM and F_1 scores for the entire corpus and for the questions covering the three patterns from Fig. 1.

Across the **Entire Corpus**, the neighborhood as entity boundaries considerably improves the scores (experiments 2 vs. 1 and 4 vs. 3). Extending class and property boundaries with specific information improves the scores a little (3 and 4 vs. 1 and 2). The combination of neighborhood triples for individuals and specific information for classes and properties achieves the best scores.

For the following experiments (5 to 13), we consider the default (outgoing/outgoing) and the best (neighborhood/specific) entity boundaries.

Adding inverse properties to the modeling considerably improves the scores for default boundaries (5) but decreases scores for the extended boundaries (6). Shortcut properties considerably improve the scores for both boundary variants (7 and 8). The combination of inverse and shortcut properties further improves scores (9 and 10), especially in combination with extended boundaries (10). The

---

[10] Available at https://github.com/Quarkse/kg-rep-llm-qa/tree/main/corpus.

[11] Available at https://github.com/Quarkse/kg-rep-llm-qa/tree/main/experiments.

Table 3. Experiment results. The highest scores are marked in bold.

	Entity Boundaries		Inverse Properties	Shortcut Properties	Comments	Entire Corpus		Geo Pattern		Keyfigure Pattern		Supply Pattern	
No.	Individuals	Classes/Properties				EM	F_1	EM	F_1	EM	F_1	EM	F_1
1	outgoing	outgoing	–	–	–	13.5	17.6	4.3	7.1	**6.7**	**6.9**	5.5	5.9
2	neighborh.	neighborh.	–	–	–	24.1	28.4	17.4	24.7	4.0	4.1	0.0	2.7
3	outgoing	specific	–	–	–	16.9	22.3	8.5	14.9	4.0	4.0	1.8	11.4
4	neighborh.	specific	–	–	–	27.3	31.7	21.4	29.5	5.4	5.4	1.8	3.6
5	outgoing	outgoing	✓	–	–	20.1	25.3	17.2	19.3	5.3	6.1	9.1	9.4
6	neighborh.	specific	✓	–	–	23.1	25.3	8.6	10.7	2.7	3.7	1.8	2.9
7	outgoing	outgoing	–	✓	–	24.8	31.8	30.0	39.6	4.0	4.5	27.3	31.8
8	neighborh.	specific	–	✓	–	32.8	40.2	45.7	**59.4**	4.0	4.2	16.4	25.9
9	outgoing	outgoing	✓	✓	–	26.0	32.3	27.2	39.1	0.0	0.2	23.7	26.0
10	neighborh.	specific	✓	✓	–	**38.3**	**44.5**	**50.0**	58.3	2.7	3.6	**34.6**	**39.2**
11	outgoing	outgoing	–	–	✓	13.4	17.6	2.9	5.9	1.3	3.9	1.8	3.0
12	neighborh.	specific	–	–	✓	20.4	24.8	21.4	25.6	0.0	1.9	1.8	7.9
13	neighborh.	specific	✓	✓	✓	34.1	40.9	40.0	53.4	4.0	4.0	23.7	33.5

latter achieves the highest EM (38.3%) and F_1 (44.5%) scores on the entire corpus. Thus, changing the KG representation for KGQA achieved an improvement from the default's EM score of 13.5% by 24.8pp/184% and the default's F_1 score of 17.6% by 26.9pp/153%.

Adding comments to the default variant has no impact on the scores (11), and to other variants (12 and including the best in 13) lowers the scores.

Potential reasons for decreasing scores despite adding information to the KG representation are (i) a longer prompt, (ii) the inclusion of more irrelevant information, and (iii) the Search action being congested by the comments. All three could lead to the LLM having a harder time identifying the relevant information.

Results for the (transitive) **Geo** pattern follow the trends of the entire corpus but specifically profit from shortcut properties (7 to 10). The highest F_1 score of 59.4% is achieved with shortcut but without inverse properties, improving on the default by 52.3pp/739%, outperforming the entire corpus (8).

Results for the (n-ary) **Keyfigure** pattern show no improvement in any variant, and the scores remain on a low level or decrease. Seemingly, the LLM fails to understand the pattern across all considered variants.

Results for the (n-ary) **Supply** pattern show scores mostly improving with shortcut properties (7 to 10). The best variant aligns with the entire corpus with an F_1 score of 39.2%, improving on the default by 33.3pp/567% (10).

The results indicate that LLM-augmented KGQA struggles with n-ary relations in comparison to binary relations.

7 Conclusion

The paper provides insight into LLM-augmented KGQA, for which we formulated the hypothesis that different KG representations impact the F_1 score. The experiments on several variants of KG representation confirm the hypotheses. Adding inverse and shortcut properties in combination with extended entity boundaries improved the F_1 score by 26.9pp/153% to 44.5%.

Future work may consider (i) more variants, (ii) additional subdimensions, (iii) questions requiring multiple variables, (iv) other KGQA approaches, and (v) different LLMs. Additionally, a comparison of runtimes, numbers of tokens, and, consequently, costs of LLM reasoning could uncover drawbacks of different KG representations.

Acknowledgments. The authors gratefully acknowledge the scientific support and HPC resources provided by the Erlangen National High Performance Computing Center (NHR@FAU). The hardware is funded by the German Research Foundation (DFG).

Disclosure of Interests. The authors have no competing interests to declare that are relevant to the content of this article.

References

1. Avila, C.V.S., Casanova, M.A., Vidal, V.M.P.: A framework for question answering on knowledge graphs using large language models. In: Meroño Peñuela, A., et al. (eds.) The Semantic Web: ESWC 2024 Satellite Events, vol. 15344, pp. 168–172. Springer, Cham (2025). https://doi.org/10.1007/978-3-031-78952-6_20

2. Brickley, D., Guha, R.: RDF Schema 1.1 (2014). https://www.w3.org/TR/rdf-schema/. Accessed 06 Oct 2021

3. Chakraborty, N., Lukovnikov, D., Maheshwari, G., Trivedi, P., Lehmann, J., Fischer, A.: Introduction to neural network-based question answering over knowledge graphs. WIREs Data Min. Knowl. Discov. **11**(3), e1389 (2021). https://doi.org/10.1002/widm.1389

4. Cyganiak, R., Reynolds, D.: The RDF data cube vocabulary (2014). https://www.w3.org/TR/vocab-data-cube/. Accessed 11 Dec 2024

5. Doosthosseini, A., Decker, J., Nolte, H., Kunkel, J.M.: Chat AI: a seamless slurm-native solution for HPC-based services (2024). https://doi.org/10.48550/arXiv.2407.00110

6. Falco, R., Gangemi, A., Peroni, S., Shotton, D., Vitali, F.: Modelling OWL ontologies with Graffoo. In: Presutti, V., Blomqvist, E., Troncy, R., Sack, H., Papadakis, I., Tordai, A. (eds.) ESWC 2014. LNCS, vol. 8798, pp. 320–325. Springer, Cham (2014). https://doi.org/10.1007/978-3-319-11955-7_42

7. Fichtner, M., Ribaud, V.: Paths and shortcuts in an event-oriented ontology. In: Dodero, J.M., Palomo-Duarte, M., Karampiperis, P. (eds.) MTSR 2012. CCIS, vol. 343, pp. 214–226. Springer, Heidelberg (2012). https://doi.org/10.1007/978-3-642-35233-1_22

8. Harris, S., Seaborne, A.: SPARQL 1.1 Query Language (2013). https://www.w3.org/TR/sparql11-query/. Accessed 03 Sept 2023

9. Hitzler, P., Krötzsch, M., Parsia, B., Petel-Schneider, P., Rudolph, S.: OWL 2 Web Ontology Language Primer, 2nd edn. (2012). https://www.w3.org/TR/owl2-primer/. Accessed 06 Oct 2021

10. Jiang, L., Yan, X., Usbeck, R.: A structure and content prompt-based method for knowledge graph question answering over scholarly data. In: Joint Proceedings of

Scholarly QALD 2023 and SemREC 2023 Co-Located with ISWC 2023, vol. 3592. CEUR-WS, Athens (2023)

11. Kovriguina, L., Teucher, R., Radyush, D., Mouromtsev, D.: SPARQLGEN: one-shot prompt-based approach for SPARQL query generation. In: Proceedings of the Posters and Demo Track of the 19th International Conference on Semantic Systems (SEMANTiCS 2023), vol. Vol-3526. CEUR, Leipzig (2023)

12. Lehmann, J., Gattogi, P., Bhandiwad, D., Ferré, S., Vahdati, S.: Language models as controlled natural language semantic parsers for knowledge graph question answering. In: Frontiers in Artificial Intelligence and Applications. IOS Press (2023). https://doi.org/10.3233/FAIA230411

13. Liu, S., Semnani, S.J., Triedman, H., Xu, J., Zhao, I.D., Lam, M.S.: SPINACH : SPARQL-based information navigation for challenging real-world questions. In: Findings of the Association for Computational Linguistics: EMNLP 2024, pp. 15977–16001. Association for Computational Linguistics (2024). https://doi.org/10.18653/v1/2024.findings-emnlp.938

14. Mungall, C., Ruttenberg, A., Osumi-Sutherland, D.: Taking shortcuts with OWL using safe macros. Nat. Precedings (2010). https://doi.org/10.1038/npre.2010.5292.1

15. Noy, N.F., McGuinness, D.L.: Ontology development 101: a guide to creating your first ontology. Technical report, Stanford University, Stanford (2001)

16. Noy, N., Rector, A.: Defining N-ary relations on the semantic web (2006). https://www.w3.org/TR/swbp-n-aryRelations/. Accessed 19 Dec 2024

17. Piao, G., Mountantonakis, M., Papadakos, P., Sonawane, P., OMahony, A.: Toward exploring knowledge graphs with LLMs. In: Joint Proceedings of Posters, Demos, Workshops, and Tutorials of the 20th International Conference on Semantic Systems (SEMANTiCS 2024), vol. Vol-3759. CEUR-WS, Amsterdam (2024)

18. Reynolds, D.: The organization ontology (2014). https://www.w3.org/TR/vocab-org/. Accessed 27 Jan 2025

19. Stickler, P.: CBD - concise bounded description (2005). https://www.w3.org/Submission/CBD/. Accessed 01 Oct 2021

20. Sun, L., Tao, Z., Li, Y., Arakawa, H.: ODA: observation-driven agent for integrating LLMs and knowledge graphs (2024). https://doi.org/10.48550/arXiv.2404.07677

21. Xiong, G., Bao, J., Zhao, W.: Interactive- KBQA: multi-turn interactions for knowledge base question answering with large language models (2024). https://doi.org/10.48550/arXiv.2402.15131

22. Xu, S., et al.: Fine-tuned LLMs know more , hallucinate less with few-shot sequence-to-sequence semantic parsing over wikidata. In: Proceedings of the 2023 Conference on Empirical Methods in Natural Language Processing, pp. 5778–5791. Association for Computational Linguistics (2023). https://doi.org/10.18653/v1/2023.emnlp-main.353

23. Yao, S., et al.: ReAct: synergizing reasoning and acting in language models. In: The Eleventh International Conference on Learning Representations ICLR 2023. Kigali, Rwanda (2023). https://doi.org/10.48550/arXiv.2210.03629

24. Zahera, H.M., Ali, M., Sherif, M.A., Moussallem, D., Ngonga Ngomo, A.C.: Generating SPARQL from natural language using chain-of-thoughts prompting. In: Knowledge Graphs in the Age of Language Models and Neuro-Symbolic AI. Studies on the Semantic Web, vol. 60, pp. 353–368. IOS Press, Amsterdam (2024). https://doi.org/10.3233/SSW240028

The MATRIX Ontology - Semantic Memory for Multi-agent Experience Transfer, Reasoning and and Interaction eXchange

Liubov Kovriguina[1]([✉]) [iD], Dmitry Mouromtsev[2] [iD], and Peter Haase[1] [iD]

[1] metaphacts GmbH, Walldorf, Germany
{lk,ph}@metaphacts.com
[2] Omni Audio, Helsinki, Finland
d.mouromtsev@gmail.com

Abstract. Multi-agent collaboration has a long established record in reinforcement learning, and has gained momentum in the recent years with the breakthroughs in language-based intelligence. At the same time, there has been demonstrated a significant potential of joining LLM and RL agents in a single pipeline. Memory is the central component of multi-agent pipelines, both in learning and inference: it stores long-term experience, agents' transactions in the working memory, other learning artifacts. However, given a plethora of protocols, environments, and experience representations, the challenge is to implement interpretable decision-making between RL agents (neural layer), and LLM agents (symbolic) in working memory, and experience transfer in the long run. Driven by the idea that agents should be able to collaborate autonomously, and learn how to use, transfer, and synthesize new knowledge and processes, we propose a graph-based memory model, which can be shared and reused by both RL and LLM agentic teams on any representation level. This memory model is a collection of RDF graphs, allowing for neural and symbolic representations at the same time, and providing interoperability and explainability of knowledge graphs. In the current paper, we introduce the MATRIX ontology (Multi-Agent Experience Transfer, Reasoning and Interaction eXchange), a conceptualization behind the shared memory layer, that can serve as a memory, decision, and experience model for heterogeneous agentic teams, and show its applications in different use cases.

Keywords: ontology for multi-agent experience transfer · semantic memory for multi-agent teams · multi-agent reinforcement learning · knowledge graphs for shared memory representation · experience transfer between neuro-symbolic agents

L. Kovriguina and D. Mouromtsev—These authors contributed equally to this work.

J. Grabis and Y. Wautelet (Eds.): CAiSE 2025 Workshops, LNBIP 556, pp. 93–104, 2025.
https://doi.org/10.1007/978-3-031-94931-9_8

1   Introduction

AI agents—whether LLM-based or trained via reinforcement learning (RL)—are widely used to incrementally improve on setting the task, proposing solutions, planning the execution, and making insights. Currently, in the generative AI community, the understanding of an "agent" becomes continuously diffused via building agents of arbitrary granularity and functionality and often disregarding the presence of an environment with its feedback. In contrast, notions of "agent" and "multi-agent" have a well-established theoretical foundations in RL, especially its MARL (multi-agent) part [1]. Recent research shows the benefits of joint multi-agent setups [6] that combine LLM agents (operating on symbolic and sub-symbolic level) and RL agents (operating in vector spaces). Moreover, both produce valuable artifacts of the learning process, which can be interchangeably reused. Despite these advances, a major bottleneck remains: LLMs work on symbolic and sub-symbolic level, and RL agents operate almost exclusively in vector space. In complex open environments, agents often expected to reason under uncertainty, justify and explain their decisions to others, and reuse knowledge from past interactions. These tasks require shared, interpretable memory of learned artifacts that allows for reasoning and knowledge transfer and reuse.

To address this, we propose a shared semantic memory model structured as a knowledge graph, governed by the MATRIX Ontology (Multi-Agent Experience Transfer, Reasoning, and Interaction eXchange, see Sect. 4). This memory framework stores artifacts generated by humans, LLMs, and RL agents and supports explanation, experience reuse, and facilitate agents' ability to share knowledge, adapt, and collaborate during decision-making.

Our **contributions** are therefore summarized as follows:

- A shared memory model for multi-agent teams to store and exchange tasks, decisions, and learning processes (see Sects. 3, 4);
- MATRIX Ontology as a unified schema for neuro-symbolic agents' experience representation and reasoning (see Sect. 4);
- Mechanisms for policy reuse, experience sampling, and artifact sharing to accelerate learning (see Sect. 5.1);
- A symbolic representation that enables both semantic reasoning and integration with neural models for adaptive behavior (see Sect. 4.1).

This shared memory approach directly addresses the challenges of cross-agent knowledge sharing and coordinated decision-making, providing a foundation for explainable and adaptive collaboration in mixed teams of AI and human agents.

2   Related Work

The development of agentic memory and multi-agent interaction models has recently gained significant attention [1]. Burtsev et al. [9] propose a hierarchical memory framework that allows LLM-based agents to accumulate and structure experiences for more autonomous behavior. Complementing this, RDF-based memory for LLM agents [8] introduces graph-based knowledge storage, enabling agents to organize and retrieve relational information effectively. In the area of agent communication and collaboration, Sumers et al. [10] review cognitive architectures for language agents, discussing how agents handle reasoning, memory, and interaction. However, their work does not offer a formal ontological framework to support heterogeneous agent collaboration. The taxonomy of multi-agent collaboration by Microsoft [6] directly addresses the problem of experience transfer between diverse teams, highlighting key challenges such as role specialization and agent heterogeneity. Further, recent advances in LLM-driven multi-agent systems (Salakhutdinov et al. [7,12]) explore how agents can reason, plan, and act jointly, often relying on large language models.

3 Methodological Approach for Ontology Development

The MATRIX ontology has been developed using the LOT methodology, which offers industry-oriented best practices for ontology development, publication, and maintenance [5]. It defines iterations over a basic workflow, which comprises four major steps (1) Ontology requirements specification; (2) Ontology implementation; (3) Ontology publication; and (4) Ontology maintenance.

Ontology requirements specification included the use case specification, the purpose and scope of the ontology and the requirements proposal (Sect. 3.1). Defining the purpose, scope and requirements took several iterations including a conceptual modeling step leveraging the BFO ontology (see Sect. 3.2), and fast prototyping for the refining of competency questions. Moreover, requirements were derived from the results obtained by the authors in the previous experiments on knowledge graphs injection in RL agent's learning process [11].

Ontology implementation started with conceptualization of the learning process in multi-agent teams with a focus on aligning LLM and RL teams whenever possible, that instances of both teams could reuse experience of other agents stored in the semantic memory, backed by the MATRIX ontology. Classes, relations and attributes are described in Sect. 4.

Publication of the ontology has been accomplished following the guidelines implemented in the metaphactory platform, with a review process. **Maintenance of the ontology** will be done via the metaphactory platform on the metaphacts GmbH Ontology Repository[1].

The primary objectives of this model include:

- **Standardized representation** of learning artifacts at an abstract level for multi-agent decision-making.
- **Facilitation of semantic queries**, allowing efficient retrieval and reuse of past experiences.
- **Learning process and experience sharing:** The ontology enables multi-agent teams to document, retrieve, and share learning experiences effectively.

---

[1] https://ontologies.metaphacts.com/matrix/.

By structuring past interactions, decision pathways, and environment observations, it allows agents to benefit from prior experiences rather than learning
from scratch in each new scenario.

- **Improving decision-making in multi-agent and mixed LLM-RL
teams:** By structuring knowledge representation in a graph-based format,
the ontology allows for enhanced decision-making by providing contextualized past experiences, best practices, and failure scenarios. This is particularly useful in mixed teams where LLMs and RL agents must collaborate, as
it offers a structured approach to decision-making alignment.
- **Experience retrieval and transfer learning:** The ontology supports
efficient retrieval of relevant past experiences based on contextual similarity, agent type, or environmental factors. This enables agents to quickly
access useful prior experiences, facilitating adaptive learning and reducing
the exploration-exploitation dilemma.

3.1   Ontology Requirements: Learning Process and Experience Exchange in Multi-Agent RL and LLM Teams

When designing the MATRIX ontology, we assumed it to serve as a memory
and experience model for different types of agentic teams. This has posed several
questions to clarify:

- *What are the learning strategies in MARL, and how do agents share experience and communicate?*
- *What artifacts do the agents learn in LLM and RL teams?*
- *Which learning and interaction artifacts should be stored in the memory to
allow further experience transfer and memory operations (compression, inference, forgetting, etc.)?*
- *What are decision-making strategies in multi-agent teams?*
- *What roles do the agents have in multi-agent teams and what are the known
principles for agents' teaming?*

The analysis of existing approaches in multi-agent reinforcement learning,
and of the structure in LLM-based agentic workflows has resulted in the careful
selection of concepts (both occurants and endurants), that were settled as the
core of the multi-agent memory. Depending on the actual team setup (LLM, RL,
or mixed) this core can be augmented with more specific classes and properties,
which would be at the same time reusable by the team of a different structure.
To define the scope and requirements of our ontology, we formulate the following
competency questions:

1. **Task and agent classification:** What types of tasks require an environment,
and which agent types are suitable for them?
2. **Environment configuration:** How are different environments structured,
and what setup parameters define them?
3. **Performance metrics:** Which environmental conditions yield the best and
worst performance, and under what circumstances?

4. **Task-specific team performance:** How do performance metrics vary across tasks, learning strategies, and team configurations? (See Sect. 5.2)
5. **Action-to-reward mapping:** Given a set of observations, what actions did agents take, and what were their resulting rewards?
6. **Experience reuse:** How can new teams leverage prior experiences to optimize learning and execution strategies? (See Sect. 5.1)
7. **Decision-making process tracking:** How do agents record, analyze, and refine their decision-making pathways?
8. **Inter-agent communication:** How do agents share observations and knowledge, and how does this impact team performance?

3.2 BFO Ontology as Conceptual Modeling Framework

Our ontology design is based on well-established ontological perspectives on processes and objects. Specifically, we adopt the distinctions outlined by Heller and Herre [3], who differentiate between endurants (continuants) and processes based on their relationship to time:

– **Endurants** are individuals without temporal parts or phases, existing within a fixed time frame. They can be indexed by temporal boundaries.
– Processes, classified as **occurrents**, have temporal parts and cannot exist at a singular time boundary. A typical process consists of a sequence of planned steps; however, in dynamic environments, the feasibility of each step depends on external conditions and observations.

Transitions between states shape the knowledge graph in the agent's memory, mapping historical data to current states and potential future actions. A similar modeling approach has been applied in work on the Basic Formal Ontologie [2]. To resolve conflicts between representing processes as pre-planned sequences and their dependence on dynamic environmental conditions, we draw on Zemach's [13] dichotomy between **continuant** and **occurrent** ontologies, a distinction also implemented in **BFO 2** [4].

4 The MATRIX Ontology

The MATRIX Ontology provides a structured way to represent and organize learning processes, decisions, observations, and policies, enabling agents to share, reuse, and adapt experiences across tasks and domains. The ontology integrates both symbolic and sub-symbolic artifacts, making it suitable for mixed teams and diverse architectures. The ontology is represented in Fig. 1. The MATRIX Ontology is grounded in foundational distinctions between processes and objects, following the formal separation of occurrents (processes and endurants (entities) as defined in BFO. This dual view allows MATRIX to model time-dependent learning and interaction processes alongside static configurations and roles of agents.

Fig. 1. The Multi-Agent Experience Transfer, Reasoning and eXchange (MATRIX) Ontology Model

Processes are temporal entities composed of evolving, interdependent steps. These classes are designed to represent both learning and decision processes, essential for reconstructing and analyzing agent experiences:

- **Episode**: A bounded sequence of agent-environment interactions with outcomes (rewards, observations).
- **Trial**: A specific learning or inference run, defined by unique parameters and configurations.
- **LearningProcess**: A complete learning or fine-tuning trajectory, often spanning multiple episodes or trials.

- **Checkpoint**: A saved state of an agent or team that can be restored for continued learning or analysis.
- **Task**: A goal-oriented activity that agents seek to solve; includes environmental context and constraints.
- **DecisionStep**: A discrete step in which an agent or team makes a decision based on available external resources and internal models.
- **LearningStep**: A part of learning pipeline, such as policy update for RL agents or prompt update for LLM agents, enabling experience acquisition and adaptation.

Endurants are time-independent entities that exist as individuals during and across processes. These classes encode agents' roles, capabilities, and the context for action:

- **Action**: A specific operation an agent can perform within an environment; may include parameters and interpretations (e.g., LLM prompts, control commands).
- **Policy**: A strategy or mapping from observations to actions, represented as symbolic rules, neural networks, or LLM-based plans.
- **AgentRole**: The role or specialization of an agent within a team (e.g., teammate or learner), supporting heterogeneous cooperation.
- **Team**: A group of agents that collaborate on a task, characterized by structure and division of roles.
- **Agent**: An individual entity capable of autonomous behavior; described by type (RL, LLM, Human), capabilities, and roles.
- **ActionSpace**: The set of all possible actions available to an agent in a given environment.
- **EnvironmentResponse**: Feedback from the environment, including observations and rewards, that guides agent adaptation.
- **AgentInput**: The information or planned actions provided by the team members and available within a decision step before taking a next decided action, which may include observations, inter-agent communications, and resources (e.g., external tools, human input).

Several modeling principles shaped the design of MATRIX Ontology to meet the unique demands of multi-agent learning and reasoning:

1. **Explicit Representation of Decision and Learning Steps:** The inclusion of DecisionStep and LearningStep classes allows detailed capture of how decisions are made, what knowledge is used, and how learning occurs, making it possible to analyze, explain, and optimize agent behaviors.
2. **Role-based Agent Modeling:** Through AgentRole and Team, MATRIX supports flexible team configurations, where agents with different capabilities (RL agents, LLMs, humans) collaborate. This role-based design encourages specialization and coordination, essential for scalable multi-agent systems.
3. **Focus on Experience Transfer and Reuse:** By capturing rich contextual information around actions, decisions, and outcomes, MATRIX facilitates retrieval of past experiences and supports transfer learning. New agents

or teams can sample relevant past cases, analyze decision pathways, and adapt previous knowledge to new tasks.

4. **Support for Inter-Agent Communication and Interaction:** MATRIX models `AgentInput` and `EnvironmentResponse` to capture not only environmental dynamics but also inter-agent communications, essential for collaborative decision-making in mixed teams.

4.1 Decision Model

One of the most complex and variable aspects of ontological modeling in MATRIX is the representation of decision-making model within a team of agents. The architecture and specificity of these processes can vary widely: from trivial models, where an action proposed by an agent is directly accepted as a decision without any modification, to complex iterative models that require applying sophisticated theories and computational models such as game theory, neural networks, Kalman filters, graph-based reasoning or LLM-based agents. Additionally, decision-making may involve external resources and tools, including human assistance, making the process even more elaborate.

Figure 2 illustrates a generalized scheme of a multi-agent decision-making model (left) and provides a detailed view of how heterogeneous inputs from diverse agents can be represented as a set of vectors (right).

In the development of MATRIX Ontology, we intentionally avoided creating numerous specific classes to represent every possible variation of decision-making models, as this would lead to a large and overly complicated set of classes, significantly increasing the complexity of agents' semantic memory structure. Instead, we opt for a single abstract class that serves as a generic representation of any decision-making model, regardless of its internal mechanics, and a class `Decision step` that represents iterations made by agents during their communications. The specific characteristics and mechanisms of each model are captured through a set of object and data properties, including:

- `communication` (exchange of information among agents),
- `constraints` (limitations or rules affecting the decision),
- `interpretator` (mechanism for interpreting agent inputs),
- `processor` (component for processing inputs or options),
- `resource` (external tools or human inputs used during decision-making),
- `hasDecidedAction` (final selected action),
- `hasPredictedAction` (anticipated or forecasted action).

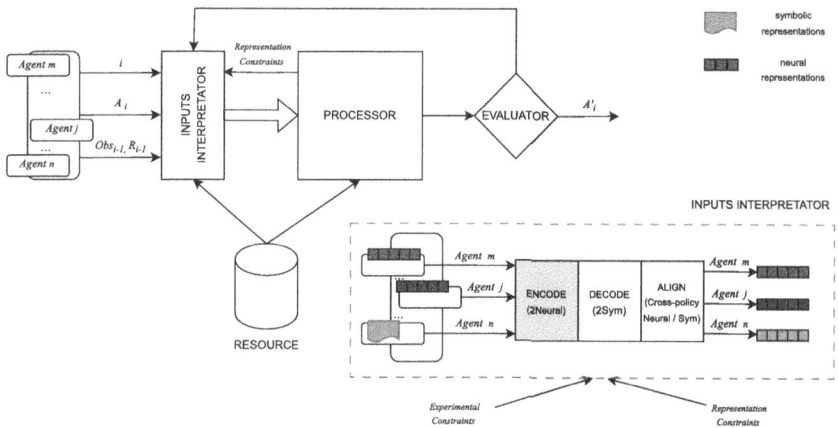

Fig. 2. Decision Model Structure and its Artifacts in the MATRIX Ontology Model. *The example shows agents' input sharing in the vector space.*

5   Ontology Validation and Usage

We validate the ontology for two types of teams (a team consisting of only RL agents, and a team of only LLM agents) with particular use cases focusing on the reusability of semantic memory artifacts and experience transfer. An important aspect of the validation was to showcase applicability of the ontology model for capturing multi-agent learning scenarios, which were previously challenging to bring together.

5.1   MATRIX Ontology as Semantic Memory for Reinforcement Learning Teams: Policy Transfer Use Case

In multi-agent reinforcement learning (MARL), "agents learn optimal decision policies by trying actions and receiving rewards, with the goal of choosing actions to maximize the sum of received rewards over time. While in single-agent RL the focus is on learning an optimal policy for a single agent, in MARL the focus is on learning optimal policies for multiple agents and the unique challenges that arise in this learning process" [1]. One of the research lines in improving RL efficiency is policy transfer, when another team of agents starts learning from already achieved results. Given a plethora of neural architectures and optimizing algorithms, choosing and applying an appropriate policy becomes challenging. To demonstrate the usability of the MATRIX ontology to improve MARL learning, we have implemented experiments with MARLLib[2] in Multi Particle Environments (MPE). MPE are a set of communication oriented environment where particle agents can (sometimes) move, communicate, see each other, push each other around, and interact with fixed landmarks[3].

---

[2] https://marllib.readthedocs.io/en/latest/index.html.
[3] https://pettingzoo.farama.org/environments/mpe/.

Fig. 3. SPARQL Query and Diagram Fragment illustrating MATRIX Ontology Validation for Policy Transfer between MARL Teams. Natural language request: *Find checkpoints of policies optimized with multi-agent PPO algorithm learned by a team of RL agents in the MPE (multi-particle) environment*

We have populated memorable objects with the team setup, learning process and artifacts for the **simple spread** scenario, and were able to validate most of the competency questions and decision model on it. In **simple spread**, an RLTeam consists of 3 **Agents** in a discrete **Action Space**, and **Learning Process** is organized in **Episodes** and **Learning Steps**. Each **Learning Step** consolidates **Agent Input**, caused **Environment Response**, and **Decision Step**. At the end of an **Episode** a **Checkpoint** with intermediate **Policy** parameters is produced. Based on the modeled **MemorableObjects**, it is possible to retrieve **Checkpoints** trained with particular **Algorithm** parameters and under given **Environment** configuration. Figure 3 shows a relevant ontology fragment (1), a SPARQL query (2) to retrieve policy checkpoints learned in a particular environment and optimized with a particular algorithm (3).

5.2 MATRIX Ontology as Semantic Memory for LLM Teams: Multi-agent SPARQL Query Generation

To validate the ontology for the LLM teams, we have modeled SPARQL query generation task in a multi-agent setup, and populated memorable objects for two teams. One of the teams was built of **SPARQLTranslation** (LLM) and **Reflection** (LLM) agents, and another team joined **SPARQLTranslation** (LLM), **Retriever** (LLM+Tool) and **ProbabilisticInference** (RL) agents. In both teams, **SPARQLTranslation** agent was the **Learner**, and other agent helped him as **Teammates**. The team works in an **Environment**, consisting of a knowledge graph, F1-score as a reward function, and retrieved results as observations. An **Action** of the infinite **Action Space** is the SPARQL query, generated by the team and executed by the **SPARQLTranslation** agent. **Decision Step** was defined as a conversation between team members, trying to improve their prompts with obtained `Observations` and `Rewards`. Each attempt to generate or improve the query was considered as a `Learning Step`, and learning artifacts were logged in a `Dataset` for further LLM fine-tuning at the end of each episode.

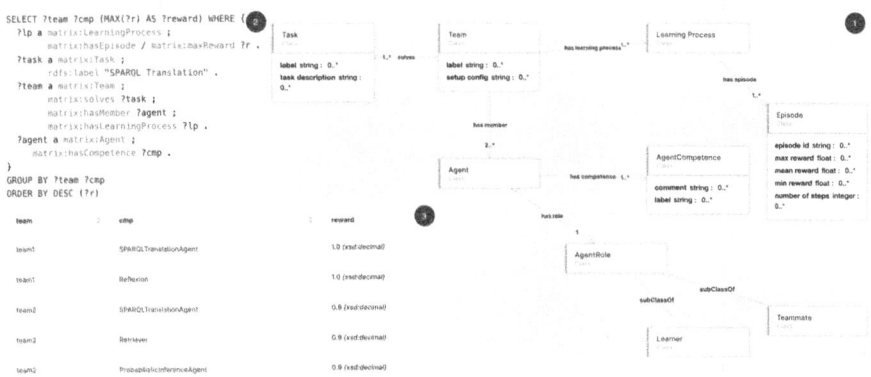

Fig. 4. SPARQL Query and Diagram Fragment illustrating MATRIX Ontology Validation for Experience Transfer across Multi-Agent LLM Teams. Natural language request: *What was the structure of multi-agent teams working on SPARQL query generation task which learning resulted in high rewards?*

Agents accumulate learning artifacts, retrieve positive and negative samples for LLM fine-tuning and summarize the input. The image 4 shows a relevant ontology fragment (1), a SPARQL query (2) to learn about the structure of the teams, which got the highest rewards (3).

6 Future Work

Multiple studies of multi-agent interaction and learning show the central role of experience transfer for agents' decision-making, and some existing approaches already represent working memory as a graph. With introducing the MATRIX ontology, we provide heterogeneous agentic teams an instrument operating both on neural and symbolic levels. Thus, agents can get inspiration from the decision making process across other teams and develop a common language. In future, we aspire to proof the value of the MATRIX ontology as a cognitive layer, focusing on the questions *How can agents extract, generalize, and adapt knowledge from past experiences to novel situations?* and *How do agents decide when to explore novel strategies versus relying on proven approaches?* (exploration vs. exploitation balance), and improve neuro-symbolic multi-agent learning.

References

1. Albrecht, S.V., Christianos, F., Schäfer, L.: Multi-agent Reinforcement Learning: Foundations and Modern Approaches. MIT Press (2024)
2. Arp, R., Smith, B., Spear, A.D.: Building ontologies with basic formal ontology (2015)
3. Heller, B., Herre, H.: Ontological categories in GOL. Axiomathes **14**(1–3), 57–76 (2004)
4. Otte, J.N., Beverley, J., Ruttenberg, A.: BFO: basic formal ontology. Appl. Ontol. **17**(1), 17–43 (2022)
5. Poveda-Villalón, M., Fernández-Izquierdo, A., Fernández-López, M., García-Castro, R.: LOT: an industrial oriented ontology engineering framework. Eng. Appl. Artif. Intell. **111**, 104755 (2022)
6. Pternea, M., et al.: The RL/LLM taxonomy tree: reviewing synergies between reinforcement learning and large language models. J. Artif. Intell. Res. **80**, 1525–1573 (2024)
7. Putta, P., et al.: Agent Q: advanced reasoning and learning for autonomous AI agents (2024). https://arxiv.org/abs/2408.07199
8. Rasmussen, P., Paliychuk, P., Beauvais, T., Ryan, J., Chalef, D.: Zep: a temporal knowledge graph architecture for agent memory. arXiv preprint arXiv:2501.13956 (2025)
9. Sagirova, A., Kuratov, Y., Burtsev, M.: SRMT: shared memory for multi-agent lifelong pathfinding. arXiv preprint arXiv:2501.13200 (2025)
10. Sumers, T., Yao, S., Narasimhan, K., Griffiths, T.: Cognitive architectures for language agents. Trans. Mach. Learn. Res. (2023)
11. Wardenga, R., et al.: Knowledge graph injection for reinforcement learning. In: CEUR Workshop Proceedings, vol. 3559, pp. 1–14. RWTH Aachen, Aachen (2023)
12. Wu, Y., et al.: AgentKit: structured LLM reasoning with dynamic graphs. arXiv preprint arXiv:2404.11483 (2024)
13. Zemach, E.M.: Four ontologies. In: Mass Terms: Some Philosophical Problems, pp. 63–80 (1979)

Discovering Inconsistencies in Documents with Long-Context LLMs

Andreas Martin[1]([✉])(iD), Hans Friedrich Witschel[1]([✉])(iD), Mona Stockhecke[2](iD), Patrick Nydegger[1], and Kyrylo Buga[1](iD)

[1] School of Business, FHNW University of Applied Sciences and Arts Northwestern Switzerland, Riggenbachstrasse 16, 4600 Olten, Switzerland
{andreas.martin,hansfriedrich.witschel,kyrylo.buga}@fhnw.ch,
patrick.nydegger@students.fhnw.ch
[2] Nagra, Hardstrasse 73, 5430 Wettingen, Switzerland
mona.stockhecke@nagra.ch

Abstract. The increasing complexity and scale of technical document corpora present challenges for consistency verification, particularly in politically sensitive or high-stakes contexts. This paper proposes an iterative approach that integrates long-context large language models (LLMs), human expertise, and hybrid clustering mechanisms to address these challenges. The approach focuses on two types of inconsistencies: real inconsistencies, such as contradictory statements or omissions, and fabricated inconsistencies, which are plausible yet artificially introduced.

This paper uses the Swiss National Cooperative for the Disposal of Radioactive Waste (Nagra) and its corpus of up to 300 technical documents as a case study. Experimental results suggest that targeted structuring of document contexts improves recall in inconsistency detection. The findings highlight the potential of combining structured human input with LLM-based reasoning for improving document integrity and trustworthiness. Future work will focus on refining the approach, including automated clustering strategies and optimization of prompt engineering.

Keywords: Hybrid Human-AI Inconsistency Detection · Long-Context Large Language Models · Document Consistency Verification

1 Introduction

In politically sensitive or high-stakes contexts, the ability to uncover and address both real and fabricated inconsistencies in text is critical for maintaining trust and ensuring the reliability of public documentation.

The ongoing advancements in artificial intelligence (AI) and natural language processing (NLP) are transforming the analysis of complex information, particularly within large-scale, multimodal datasets. While the integration of long-context large language models (LLMs) holds the hypothetical potential to

J. Grabis and Y. Wautelet (Eds.): CAiSE 2025 Workshops, LNBIP 556, pp. 105–116, 2025.
https://doi.org/10.1007/978-3-031-94931-9_9

enhance document verification in extensive document collections, certain challenges are still preventing the research communities from fully realizing these potentials, e.g. the issue of effectively directing the attention of LLMs to the relevant parts of a very long context [16]. For some downstream tasks, the use of long context windows can simply be replaced or combined with an effective retrieval component to overcome such problems [18].

However, when considering the task of finding inconsistencies in a large document corpus, retrieval is not an adequate replacement of long context windows: since it is not previously known which portions of the corpus may contain inconsistent (e.g. contradictory) content it is not possible to formulate a query that will pre-select text chunks that are likely to contain inconsistencies. However, since inconsistencies can usually only appear in text portions that are semantically related [6], human knowledge about semantic relations between documents in a corpus may be used to guide automated approaches.

Previous work has already identified the difficulty of detecting inconsistencies across potentially wide spans of intermediate text. For instance, Li et al. [12] found that LLMs struggle substantially more when contradictory statements are not contained in neighboring sentences, but at larger distances within a document. The goal of this paper is to extend these investigations to corpora of related documents – such that inconsistent content may not be found *within* one document, but in two or more. Furthermore, we also suggest widening the focus from *contradictions* (as emphasised in previous work [6,12]) to *inconsistencies*, spanning a larger range of problematic phenomena. Finally, to make this endeavour feasible, we suggest incorporating human knowledge in the process, where human experts provide some guidance that helps an LLM to focus on portions of a large context that is more likely to contain inconsistencies.

A compelling case exemplifying these challenges is the Swiss National Cooperative for the Disposal of Radioactive Waste (Nagra), tasked with ensuring consistency across a vast corpus of close to 300 technical documents, comprising approximately 30,000 pages. These documents, integral to Nagra's operations, include not only textual narratives but also multimodal elements such as graphical representations and technical diagrams.

For Nagra, full consistency and correctness of their documents are of utmost importance because of the high stakes involved in deep geological repositories for nuclear waste and the need to meet the strict legislativ and regulativ criteria of surveillance by authorities. Furthermore, public documentation like Nagra's is increasingly subject to diverse interpretations in society, alternative analyses, and potential misuse – fueled by the accessibility of LLMs.

2 Related Work

The problem of inconsistencies appearing within larger document corpora has been studied in several domains, e.g. for regulatory documents [15], but also for the documentation of e.g. libraries in programming [13] or cybersecurity reports [8].

Before applying various kinds of solutions to detect inconsistencies, it is common to perform some kind of pre-selection of text passages. For instance, one may try to select only text passages that discuss a certain topic such as a certain article of a specific regulation [4] or one may apply supervised machine learning to identify passages of a certain type (e.g. norms within a contract, see [2]).

The pre-selection of passages can then be followed by pairing or grouping passages that exhibit a high semantic similarity (as we will also discuss for our scenario later), as determined via e.g. the comparison of embeddings [10] or by determining that they contain the same kinds of entities, e.g. contract parties in [3]. Paired text chunks or sentences can then be passed through e.g. a Natural Language Inference check, testing whether the assertions made in them imply each other logically or not [9].

The rapid evolution of large language models (LLMs) has significantly influenced natural language processing, particularly in managing extensive and complex document corpora. Thus, applying LLMs for inconcistency checking is being taken up by researchers (see e.g. [12,14]) as an alternative to traditional NLP approaches [6,9].

Traditional LLMs were constrained by limited context windows, significantly restricting their ability to process extensive texts. Recent innovations have expanded these capabilities, enabling models to handle considerably larger contexts. For instance, Google's Gemini 1.5 series exemplifies this progress, offering a 1-million-token context window with the Flash variant and extending up to 2 million tokens with the Pro variant[1]. These enhancements enable the processing of large documents and complex datasets, broadening the range of tasks that LLMs can undertake.

Despite these advancements, challenges persist. As [7] highlight, retrieval-augmented generation (RAG) methods in long-context LLMs face performance degradation as the number of retrieved passages increases. While larger retrieval sets improve recall by including more relevant information, they often introduce "hard negatives" – irrelevant or misleading information that degrades the quality of generated outputs. Other authors have confirmed the difficulties that LLMs have when confronted with tasks that involve long-context dependencies, even if these dependencies fit into the context window of modern models [11,12].

Thus, effectively integrating the capabilities that long-context reasoning may enable remains a challenge. Models must maintain reliable performance across varying context lengths while addressing issues such as retrieval quality, reasoning precision, and scalability. Furthermore, as [1] demonstrate, multilingual and low-resource settings present additional hurdles, with performance gaps becoming more pronounced in such contexts. To fully realize the potential of long-context LLMs, future efforts must focus on addressing these challenges, including optimizing methods for retrieval and chunk pre-selection, refining model fine-tuning, and improving adaptability across diverse languages and datasets. These advancements are essential to ensure that LLMs can deliver robust and reliable results in high-stakes, large-scale document analysis tasks.

---

[1] Google's Gemini input token limit: https://ai.google.dev/gemini-api/docs/models/gemini.

3   Approach

This section outlines our proposed iterative approach for verifying document consistency in large, multimodal datasets. The approach integrates long-context large language models (LLMs) with human-in-the-loop expertise to improve inconsistency detection. Our methodology follows four key phases: (1) LLM pipeline and user interface development, (2) data ingestion and symbolic knowledge structuring, (3) long-in-context reasoning with structured focus, and (4) data collection and AI optimization

3.1   Preliminaries: Definition of Inconsistencies

Previous work has focused the discussion of inconsistencies on immediate contradictions between statements in text [6,12]. We will take up the definitions made therein and extend them with formal inconsistencies related to e.g. references between documents. Similar to [6], we adopt a notion of contradictions that deviates from strict logical reasoning: while the two statements "Sally sold a boat to John" and "John sold a boat to Sally" can be true at the same time, we choose to treat them as inconsistent since it is highly *unlikely* that they are. As opposed to the early work of [6], we nowadays have the advantage that LLMs may be capable of uncovering such unlikely scenarios rather well. Table 1 shows the types of inconsistencies that we focused on.

3.2   Semi-automated Consistency Checking Phases

Our approach for semi-automated consistency checking in document corpora is structured into four key phases:

1. **LLM Pipeline and User Interface Development**: includes selecting and integrating long-context LLMs and construction or selection of a simple user interface (UI) for uploading document corpora. At first, this UI will rely on conversational instructions to the LLM for e.g. modeling dependencies between document parts. Later, this may be designed in a graphical way, using e.g. drag and drop functions to arrange document parts by semantic similarity.
2. **Data Ingestion and Prompt Engineering:** involves preparing the document corpus and optimizing the LLM's behavior through prompt engineering. In most cases, no sophisticated document preprocessing may be needed besides conversion to plain text. Prompts are tailored by domain experts to address specific types of inconsistencies, see Table 1.
3. **Long-In-Context Reasoning:** utilizes the long-context reasoning capabilities of LLMs to analyze the document corpus. By leveraging extended context windows, the LLM can theoretically process multiple interrelated documents simultaneously, identifying patterns and inconsistencies that span across sections or even entire corpora. In practice, this step usually needs iteration

Table 1. Different types of inconsistencies, including contradictions (with types above the double horizontal line based on [6,12]) and examples from the domain of the Nagra corpus

Type	Description	Domain example
Antonym		"was realized in the *early* phases..."
		"was realized in the *late* phases..."
Negation		"was realized in the early phases..."
		"was *not* realized in the early phases..."
Numeric (Number)	different numbers are used to quantify	"The repository will be monitored for *50* years"
		"The repository will be monitored for *10* years"
Numeric (Unit)	different units are used to quantify	"The repository will be monitored for 50 *years*"
		"The repository will be monitored for 50 *months*"
Factive	Stated facts are incompatible	"The Eastern border of the project perimeter follows *Zweidlenstrasse* with a distance of 50 m"
		"The Eastern border of the project perimeter follows *Schlossallee* with a distance of 50 m"
Structure	Sequence of events or periods is exchanged	"*operation* of the central area ... (*phase 1*)"
		"The highest utilisation intensities are to be expected during *construction* activities (*phases 1*, 3 and 5) and ..."
Cross-references	Cross-reference to another document part promises content that is not contained therein	"the correspoding justification can be found in Chapters 6 and 7 of (Nagra 2025a)"
		"Chapter 6: Maps project perimeter areas"
Tables/Figures	Wrong captions or multiple figures with same number	"Fig. 4–5: Layers of Fig. 4–5: Main techniques for..."

to reduce the size of context windows if the rate of identified inconsistencies (recall) proves to be low. As we will see in our experiments below, we observed, consistent with the findings of [12], a low recall of results when LLMs had no directions in terms of which parts of a document collection to focus on. When document similarities are modeled in advance, LLMs can be prompted to direct their attention to the more closely related parts. As stated in [6]: "For texts to be contradictory, they must involve the same event" – which we can generalize by saying that text chunks can only be inconsistent among each other if they are semantically related.

4. **Data Collection and Analysis:** focuses on evaluating the system's effectiveness in terms of precision and – more importantly – recall and on identifying areas for improvement via collection of qualitative and quantitative data. We focus on recall because the costs of handling some false positive alerts are much lower than those of a false negative, i.e. a missed identification of a true inconsistency. Options for improvement derived from qualitative analysis comprise above all the possibility to decrease the size of context windows by prompting the LLM with human-modeled semantic interrelationships of document parts. A systematic variations of different LLMs and their parameters (such as temperature) leads to quantitative results that allow to find the best LLM configuration.

3.3   Proposed Hybrid Document Processing

The proposed hybrid processing approach, as illustrated in Fig. 1, combines structured document organization with long-context LLM-based analysis to detect inconsistencies in large document corpora. The approach integrates human expertise in defining document relationships with automated text processing, supporting the identification of both real and fabricated inconsistencies. This structured workflow is particularly relevant in contexts where ensuring document consistency and clarity is critical.

The process begins with a technical document corpus, which consists of multiple related documents that may contain inconsistencies. These inconsistencies could be contradictions, omissions, or ambiguities, either arising naturally from errors or introduced deliberately or inadvertently. Given the size and complexity of such corpora, structuring the documents before analysis can improve the efficiency and reliability of inconsistency detection.

To address this, domain experts define relationships between document sections, manually pre-clustering semantically related sections before further processing. This structured organization ensures that documents are analyzed in contextually meaningful groupings rather than as isolated fragments. Once this structure is defined, and clustering mechanisms are applied, combining semantic similarity-based grouping with keyword-based retrieval. This allows for a more targeted analysis, reducing noise and improving recall.

Following clustering, prompt engineering is employed to refine the LLM's focus. The model is designed to leverage structured output, which specifies both the type of inconsistency and its exact location within the text. Experts design

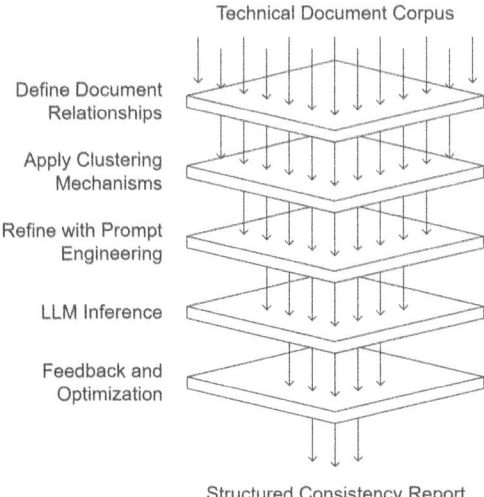

Technical Document Corpus

Define Document
Relationships

Apply Clustering
Mechanisms

Refine with Prompt
Engineering

LLM Inference

Feedback and
Optimization

Structured Consistency Report

Fig. 1. Proposed hybrid processing steps for document consistency checking, combining human expertise and LLM analysis

structured prompts that instruct the model to concentrate on specific types of inconsistencies, such as contradictions or inconsistencies in numerical values or cross-references. By refining how the model interacts with the corpus, prompt engineering helps improve the relevance and accuracy of the results.

After structuring and prompt refinement, the long-context LLM inference phase is initiated. The pre-clustered document segments are processed within the LLM's extended context window, enabling the model to assess relationships across multiple sections and identify potentially inconsistent text passages. This approach aims to improve the detection of inconsistencies that may span across documents or different sections of the same document.

To further enhance reliability, the system incorporates a feedback and optimization loop. Human experts review the detected inconsistencies, validate their accuracy, and refine the clustering strategies and prompts based on the outcomes. If necessary, adjustments to the LLM parameters are made to improve precision and recall. This iterative refinement process enables continuous improvements in consistency detection.

Finally, a structured consistency report is generated, consolidating the findings and highlighting both real and fabricated inconsistencies. This report serves as a basis for further expert review and clarification, ensuring that potential inconsistencies are addressed systematically. By combining structured document organization with LLM-based processing, this approach provides a method for verifying the consistency of large document collections while incorporating expert oversight to maintain accuracy and reliability.

4   Experiments

We now describe a simple and experimental instantiation of our approach. The four phases were implemented as follows:

1. LLM Pipeline: We tested our approach with several versions of Gemini (which offers very long context windows), namely Gemini 2.0 Pro Experimental, Gemini 2.0 Flash Experimental, Gemini 2.0 Flash Thinking Experimental, 1.5 Pro, 1.5 Flash and 1.5 Flash 8b. For interaction between human experts and these LLMs we relied directly on their conversational interfaces.
2. Data Ingestion and Prompt Engineering: in our experiments, this step involved not only the selection of documents, but also the creation of some artificial inconsistencies within the chosen corpus. In fact, we chose a corpus of only two documents that have a certain semantic overlap in some chapters. We found statements about the same or very similar events or aspects in these documents, which we observed to be consistent with each other. We then manually destroyed this consistency by inserting several instances of the inconsistencies listed in Table 1. We then simply concatenated the two documents to form a giant new document.

   Our prompt to the LLM was initially simple, just asking it to identify inconsistencies in general, and later became more sophisticated, providing it with the aforementioned categories of inconsistencies and corresponding examples. The prompt also included an example of the desired output of the consistency check, using two given sentences containing inconsistencies (a form of one-shot learning).

   We finally submitted the prompt to the LLM (via its conversational interface) followed by a plain-text version of the concatenated giant document with the artificially created inconsistencies. This approach allowed us to measure not only the precision of the consistency check, but also its recall.
3. Long-In-Context Reasoning: here, we experimented with various context lengths, comprising a) entire documents, b) chapters and c) sub-chapters. For sub-document levels, we used our knowledge about specific sections into which we had introduced inconsistencies for aligning chapters, or (sub-)sub-chapters (see Sect. 5 for ideas how to automate this step in future work). Obviously, we had introduced the inconsistencies into semantically related units of text. We then filled only the aligned items into the context window. As an example of sub-chapter alignment, we concatenated Sects. 4.1 and 4.4 from the first document with Sects. 3.2, 3.3 and 3.6 from the second document – where all these items revolved around the geographical location of the deep geological repository and its transport accessibility. Overall, the giant concatenated document consists of just over 163,000 tokens, the 5 sections from the sub-chapter level mentioned above make up 9,950 tokens.
4. Data Collection and Analysis: Overall, we had introduced 46 inconsistencies into our giant concatenated documents, with 21 in the tested chapter unit and 13 in the mentioned sub-chapter unit. We were thus able to produce a mini-statistic of precision and recall for each of a large number of

combinations of LLMs, temperature and analysis unit (document, chapter, (sub-)sub-chapter), in order to get some first impressions of what works and what does not.

Figure 2 shows our experimental results. From the figure, it can be seen how our parameter search became finer when moving to the sub-chapter level, based on early insights that the coarser units did not deliver satisfactory results.

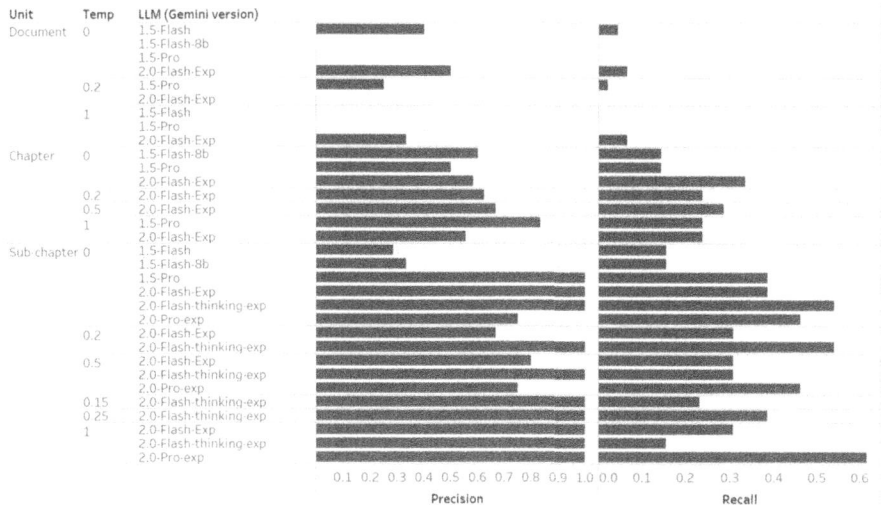

Fig. 2. Results of experimenting with various document units, temperatures and LLMs, in terms of precision (left) and recall (right)

In fact, we can see that the best results are obtained with Gemini 2.0 Pro Experimental on sub-chapter level, using a temperature of 1. The finding regarding the temperature is not a consistent one (i.e. there is no clear trend towards higher temperatures showing better results), but it is surely interesting and deserves further investigation.

Overall, the best level of recall we reach is slightly above 60%, with precision being less of a problem.

5   Discussion

In general, our findings from experiments can be summarised as follows: there is no clear winner in terms of the different LLM versions that we tried – however, Gemini 2.0 versions tended to score better than Gemini 1.5 versions in comparative settings. As stated above, there was no systematic dependence of performance on the LLM's temperature, in particular we could not observe that this task benefits from lower temperatures. The clearest trend can be observed with respect to the unit of analysis: not very surprisingly, and in line with the findings of [12], smaller units lead to better performance, i.e. it is beneficial to draw the LLMs attention more closely to document regions where contradictions may occur.

Based on the insight that contradictions, and also other inconsistencies, can only occur in semantically closely related portions of text we have developed a strategy for automating such "pre-processing" that shall be explored in future work. It shall work along the following lines:

– We first invite experts to perform a "pre-clustering" of documents, i.e. to identify groups of documents that are semantically related.
– Hierarchical chunking [17] is applied to each document, resulting in small chunks that are organised in a tree structure, where the numbers and head-lines of (sub-)chapters containing a chunk are kept as metadata. Then, the formatting of the documents can be discarded and the plain text is mapped into an embedding space.
– A fuzzy clustering algorithm capable of determining an optimal number of clusters (e.g. Gaussian Mixture Models, see [5]) is applied to the chunk embeddings, resulting in semantically coherent clusters that will serve as "contexts" for the LLM. As a validation step, we suggest that domain experts shall review a few clusters. Because the origin of chunks in terms of source document and (sub-)chapter is known via their metadata, it may suffice for experts to review only those source data (i.e. numbers and headlines), especially if they are familiar with the corpus.
– Finally, we pass each cluster to the LLM as a context, together with a prompt that asks it to identify inconsistencies within that context, comprising few-shot examples.

The iterative and interactive nature of this approach ensures adaptability and scalability, allowing domain experts to refine outcomes over time, without demanding too much of their time. In this context, a more advanced user interface will play a crucial role in making advanced AI capabilities accessible to non-technical users.

Despite these advantages, the approach also presents challenges. The success of the system depends on the quality of the prompts, the effectiveness of the hybrid clustering approach, and the ability of the LLM to maintain performance across varying document complexities. Additionally, significant domain expertise and resources are required to implement and refine the approach effectively.

6   Conclusion

This paper presents an iterative approach for verifying document consistency using long-context LLMs and human-in-the-loop oversight that helps the LLM to focus its attention to document parts where inconsistencies may occur.

The approach is particularly well-suited for large, multimodal datasets, such as the 300-document corpus used by Nagra. Our first experimental results show that well-targeted reduction of context window size greatly helps to increase recall of consistency checks. While further automation will be subject to future work (see previous section), we believe that human inputs will remain helpful, both via oversight/feedback and modeling of document dependencies in advance.

Future work will also include optimizing prompt engineering, and addressing challenges in handling extensive multimodal content. By building on the findings of this research, the proposed approach has the potential to advance the field of document consistency verification, for reliability and trust in large-scale documentation.

Acknowledgments. This work has been funded by the Nagra, National Cooperative for the Disposal of Radioactive Waste.

References

1. Agrawal, A., Dang, A., Bagheri Nezhad, S., Pokharel, R., Scheinberg, R.: Evaluating multilingual long-context models for retrieval and reasoning. In: Sälevä, J., Owodunni, A. (eds.) Proceedings of the Fourth Workshop on Multilingual Representation Learning (MRL 2024), pp. 216–231. Association for Computational Linguistics, Miami (2024). https://doi.org/10.18653/v1/2024.mrl-1.18. https://aclanthology.org/2024.mrl-1.18/

2. Aires, J.P., Meneguzzi, F.: Norm conflict identification using a convolutional neural network. In: Aler Tubella, A., Cranefield, S., Frantz, C., Meneguzzi, F., Vasconcelos, W. (eds.) COIN/COINE 2017/2020. LNCS (LNAI), vol. 12298, pp. 3–19. Springer, Cham (2021). https://doi.org/10.1007/978-3-030-72376-7_1

3. Aires, J.P., Pinheiro, D., Lima, V.S., Meneguzzi, F.: Norm conflict identification in contracts. Artif. Intell. Law **25**(4), 397–428 (2017). https://doi.org/10.1007/s10506-017-9205-x

4. Alshamsan, A.R., Chaudhry, S.A.: Detecting privacy policies violations using natural language inference (nli). In: 2022 IEEE Asia-Pacific Conference on Computer Science and Data Engineering (CSDE), pp. 1–6. IEEE (2022)

5. Cozzolino, I., Ferraro, M.B.: Document clustering. Wiley Interdisc. Rev. Comput. Stat. **14**(6), e1588 (2022)

6. De Marneffe, M.C., Rafferty, A.N., Manning, C.D.: Finding contradictions in text. In: Proceedings of ACL-08: HLT, pp. 1039–1047 (2008)

7. Jin, B., Yoon, J., Han, J., Arik, S.O.: Long-context LLMs meet RAG: overcoming challenges for long inputs in RAG (2024). http://arxiv.org/abs/2410.05983. arXiv:2410.05983 [cs]

8. Jo, H., Kim, J., Porras, P., Yegneswaran, V., Shin, S.: Gapfinder: finding inconsistency of security information from unstructured text. IEEE Trans. Inf. Forensics Secur. **16**, 86–99 (2020)

9. Lattimer, B.M., Chen, P., Zhang, X., Yang, Y.: Fast and accurate factual inconsistency detection over long documents. arXiv preprint arXiv:2310.13189 (2023)

10. van Leijenhorst, L., de Vries, A.P., Habben Jansen, T., Wertheim, H.: Sopalign: a tool for automatic estimation of compliance with medical guidelines. In: European Conference on Information Retrieval, pp. 307–312. Springer, Heidelberg (2023). https://doi.org/10.1007/978-3-031-28241-6_31

11. Li, J., Wang, M., Zheng, Z., Zhang, M.: Loogle: can long-context language models understand long contexts? arXiv preprint arXiv:2311.04939 (2023)
12. Li, J., Raheja, V., Kumar, D.: Contradoc: understanding self-contradictions in documents with large language models. arXiv preprint arXiv:2311.09182 (2023)
13. Li, R., Yang, Y., Liu, J., Hu, P., Meng, G.: The inconsistency of documentation: a study of online c standard library documents. Cybersecurity **5**(1), 14 (2022)
14. Luo, Z., Xie, Q., Ananiadou, S.: Chatgpt as a factual inconsistency evaluator for text summarization. arXiv preprint arXiv:2303.15621 (2023)
15. Schumann, G., Gómex, J.M.: Detection of conflicts, contradictions and inconsistencies in regulatory documents: a literature review. In: 2024 Fifth International Conference on Intelligent Data Science Technologies and Applications (IDSTA), pp. 81–88. IEEE (2024)
16. Tworkowski, S., Staniszewski, K., Pacek, M., Wu, Y., Michalewski, H., Miłoś, P.: Focused transformer: contrastive training for context scaling. Adv. Neural. Inf. Process. Syst. **36**, 42661–42688 (2023)
17. Verma, P.: S2 chunking: a hybrid framework for document segmentation through integrated spatial and semantic analysis. arXiv preprint arXiv:2501.05485 (2025)
18. Xu, P., et al.: Retrieval meets long context large language models. In: The Twelfth International Conference on Learning Representations (2023)

Joint Workshop on Blockchain for Information Systems Engineering (B4ISE) and Workshop on Information Systems and AI for Life Sciences (iSAILS)

Workshop on Blockchain for Information Systems Engineering (B4ISE) and Information Systems and AI for Life Sciences (iSAILS)

Information systems are evolving rapidly, driven by the emergence of novel technologies and increasing demands for intelligent, secure, and adaptable digital infrastructures. This is particularly evident in the rise of artificial intelligence, data science, and decentralized technologies such as blockchain. These developments are not just supporting existing domains, but they significantly redefine how systems are conceived, built, and deployed. Blockchain, in particular, introduces new paradigms for trust, transparency, and verifiable automation, challenging traditional models of information systems. At the same time, the exponential growth of data in sectors such as healthcare and life sciences is opening new dimensions of what information systems must process, learn from, and deliver.

These technological shifts raise fundamental questions about how we design, model, and evolve information systems. Challenges such as integration, scalability, and verification demand new conceptual and technical approaches. This workshop focused on these questions, exploring how cutting-edge technologies can shape the next generation of information systems and how those systems, in turn, can drive innovation across application domains. We aimed to uncover new methods and frameworks for advancing the theory and practice of information systems, addressing both internal complexities and their broader impact on society and industry.

This year, we joined the workshops "Blockchain for Information Systems Engineering (B4ISE)" and "Information Systems and AI for Life Sciences (iSAILS)", given the synergy between the two programs. Following thorough reviews (≤ 2 reviewers, ≤ 3 PC members each), the joint event accepted 3 full and 1 short paper from 6 submissions, in line with Springer's 50% rate. Setting the stage for these papers, we had the opportunity to host a keynote by Hans-Georg Fill, who explored our topics, B4ISE and iSAILS, from a shared perspective. The program was continued with four paper presentations as well as four journal-first presentations by invited authors. We thank all contributing authors, our journal-first speakers — Andrea Morichetta, Mark C. Ballandies, and Raimundas Matulevičius — our keynote speaker, Hans-Georg Fill, and our program committee members for their valuable contributions to the workshop.

Alessandro Marcelletti
Sarah Bouraga
Felix Härer
Alberto García S.
Anna Bernasconi
César Henrique Bernabé

Organization

B4ISE Workshop Co-chairs

Alessandro Marcelletti	University of Camerino, Italy
Sarah Bouraga	EM Normandie Business School, France
Felix Härer	FHNW University of Applied Sciences and Arts, Switzerland

B4ISE Workshop Program Committee

Victor Amaral de Sousa	University of Namur, Belgium
Marco Comuzzi	Ulsan National Institute of Science and Technology, South Korea
Claudio Di Ciccio	University of Utrecht, The Netherlands
Nicolas Herbaut	Paris 1 Panthéon-Sorbonne University, France
Julius Köpke	University of Klagenfurt, Austria
Wim Laurier	UCLouvain Saint-Louis Brussels, Belgium
Yue Liu	Data61, CSIRO, Australia
Edoardo Marangone	Sapienza University of Rome, Italy
Giovanni Meroni	Technical University of Denmark
Andrea Morichetta	University of Camerino, Italy
Georgios Palaiokrassas	Yale University, USA
Pierluigi Plebani	Polytechnic University of Milan, Italy
Johannes Sedlmeir	University of Luxembourg, Luxembourg
Monique Snoeck	KU Leuven, Belgium
Francesco Tiezzi	University of Florence, Italy

iSAILS Workshop Co-chairs

Alberto García S.	Universitat Politècnica de València, Spain
Anna Bernasconi	Politecnico di Milano, Italy
César Henrique Bernabé	Leiden University Medical Center, The Netherlands

iSAILS Workshop Program Committee

Nelly Barret	Politecnico di Milano, Italy
Mireia Costa	Universitat Politècnica de València, Spain
Johann Eder	University of Klagenfurt, Austria

A Blockchain-Based Model for Fungible Assets and Secure Transformation Processes Traceability

Nicolas Herbaut$^{(\boxtimes)}$, Eddy Kiomba Kambilo , and Yuntian Ding

Centre de Recherche en Informatique, Université Paris 1 Panthéon-Sorbonne, 75013 Paris, France
{nicolas.herbaut,eddy.kambilo,yuntian.ding}@univ-paris1.fr

Abstract. Blockchain has been proposed to support supply chain use cases due to its numerous properties, such as transparency, immutability, and auditability. For simple scenarios, such as asset ownership transfer, these solutions work well. However, in cases where exchanged components are further used in manufacturing processes to produce refined items, which then serve as the basis for other products, maintaining traceability while enforcing specific business rules becomes a challenge. Tracking and transforming physical goods also present trust issues regarding the actual existence of the goods and the conditions of the transformation processes, such as temperature or precise location. In this paper, we present BC24, a smart supply chain model that leverages blockchain and RFID to support asset, process, and environmental traceability. We validate our model through a real industrial use case in an agro-food supply chain specializing in meat processing.

Keywords: blockchain · supply chain · IoT · ERC-1155 · Agro-food

1 Introduction

Supply chain (SC) traceability is crucial for fostering consumer trust, particularly for products impacting health, such as medicine, safety equipment, or food [5]. It also holds economic significance by supporting claims regarding product quality, safety, and social responsibility—especially in light of consumers' increasing preference for environmentally friendly products.

However, current centralized frameworks are vulnerable to fraud, corruption, data falsification, and single points of failure because of the lack of transparency, monopolistic control, and asymmetric information distribution [8].

Blockchain has been widely explored for enhancing the logistics and transportation functions of the supply chain [1], particularly for its capabilities in improving data integrity—through security, immutability, and tamper resistance—and data auditability via decentralization, transparency, and disintermediation. However, the validation of physical entries cannot be ensured

J. Grabis and Y. Wautelet (Eds.): CAiSE 2025 Workshops, LNBIP 556, pp. 121–128, 2025.
https://doi.org/10.1007/978-3-031-94931-9_10

solely by blockchain integrations. This reveals two crucial challenges in supply chains even with blockchain: (1) coordination between on-chain information and manufacturing standards; (2) a reliable cyber-physical link between real-world states and the corresponding on-chain ones.

In this paper, we present **BC24** to address the current limitations. In BC24, resources are represented using an extended token smart contract that builds upon ERC-1155 to support supply chain traceability. This smart contract incorporates a configurable state machine engine that enforces critical business rules related to asset creation, production, and transfer. BC24 introduces a device that links blockchain cyber resources to physical resources, enabling joint lifecycle management. Additionally, we integrate sensor measurements into the traceability information and enforce specific business rules defined within the state machine through a dedicated state machine specification. We validate our model through a real-world implementation for an agro-food startup.

We follow the four steps of the **Design Science Research (DSR) methodology** cycle [11]:

- **Identify a Problem**: In Sect. 3, we present the challenges in SC traceability that this paper aims to resolve, based on an analysis of current solutions in Sect. 2.
- **Define Objectives of the Solution**: In Sect. 4, we derive requirements for BC24.
- **Design and Development**: In Sect. 5, we specify our BC24 model and provide insights into its design choices and inner workings.
- **Validation**: In Sect. 6, we discuss the requirements mapping using a scenario from a real industrial use case, and in Sect. 7, we discuss the limitations of our approach before concluding.

2   Related Work

The perceived benefits of blockchain in supply chain management have been extensively covered in the literature through numerous review [2]. Numerous studies have proposed blockchain-based traceability frameworks that aim to increase transparency, prevent fraud, and improve accountability [10]. These frameworks rely on the immutability of blockchain to ensure once data is recorded, it cannot be altered retroactively. However, they often fall short in addressing two critical dimensions required for trust in high-risk sectors like agri-food: data management (the processing flexibility challenge) and security (the traceability of data integrity and cyber-physical continuity challenges) - the focus of our work.

Cyber-physical continuity highlights the gap between the digital representation of processes and the actual physical operation. Several authors have proposed Internet of Things (IoT) using QR codes or NFC tags to enable end consumers to retrieve traceability information on the final product [9]. This approach benefits consumers by allowing them to verify product origin and ensuring that packaging claims align with reality, thereby increasing trust in the product. However, these devices can be bypassed or spoofed, especially in loosely controlled environments (QR/RFID tags can be copied). Blockchain alone does not guarantee that physical processes (such as the actual quantity of meat delivered) match the digital records.

Traceability of data integrity refers to the problem of falsified or manipulated data being recorded on-chain. To ensure data integrity, some researchers have proposed using state machines to prevent illegal transactions based on predefined business rules [7]. This approach helps supply chain managers block invalid data from entering the blockchain. However, the current mechanisms are declarative and lack connection to physical product measurements, making them inadequate for enforcing real-world constraints like location or temperature regulations in the agri-food sector.

Finally, for on-chain data processing, researchers often rely on ad hoc smart contracts [2], which lack standardization and can be costly. To improve this, **TokenTrail**, based on ERC-1155 was proposed by [6] as a flexible solution for managing traceability tokens. Its use in the agri-food sector has shown that ERC-1155 can effectively capture both unique and quantitative data. However, combining ERC-1155 with proactive data integrity measures could offer not only traceability but also greater control over processing steps in the supply chain.

3   Research Problems Analysis

Malpractice remains a major customer concern in the food supply chain. For instance, the agromafia's influence in Italy is estimated to generate €25 billion in annual revenue [3]. To reduce malpractice in the food supply chain, the European Union has introduced new "food integrity" measures, but these measures still only go so far as to trace the issues backward in case of a problem and to identify the responsible parties when malpractice is detected. This cat-and-mouse approach struggles to fully reassure consumers, who may reasonably fear that fraud is going undetected. Therefore, it is crucial to ensure the traceability of data integrity. Blockchain technology is known to provide a platform that ensures data integrity. However, as we indicated in our related work on limitation, even with the use of blockchain to enhance data integrity and traceability, two fundamental gaps remain a true challenge for blockchain-integrated supply chains:

- **Traceability of Data Integrity**: the potential falsification of traceability data and processes, as it can be tampered with. In the Horsegate case, Spanghero relabeled horse meat as beef.
- **Cyber-physical continuity**: the lack of continuity between the cyber and physical worlds, where traceability data is not directly linked to the real product in production processes. In the Horsegate case, Spanghero produced more beef ground meat by mass than it received from suppliers, which should not have been possible.

These aspects lead to the series of requirements we will discuss next.

Table 1. Goals and Requirements for Supply-Chain Traceability.

	Goal	Requirement
R1	Data Integrity	Information artifacts must be permanent
R2		Information artifacts must be non-repudiable
R3		Information artifacts for process inputs must be propagated to outputs
R4		Processes themselves must be traced and prevent abuse
R5	Cyber-physical continuity	Material cannot be processed without a physical token
R6		Processes must generate a new physical token attached to their output
R7	Processing flexibility	Processes must support using only a fraction of a certified input
R8		Selected inputs for processes can be non-certified

4 Requirements of BC24

Our model aims to address the two identified gaps: Traceability of Data Integrity and cyber-physical continuity. Additionally, in practical deployment of supply chain traceability, only specific artifacts (e.g., meat in our example) need to be tracked, while others may not be traceable or may be economically or legally unfeasible to track. Therefore, the system should also support **flexibility in processing**. Table 1 shows the mapping of the goals and requirements.

All information added to the record must ensure integrity and non-repudiability, preventing falsification or tampering (**R1** and **R2**). Upstream traceability of certified raw materials should be automatically propagated during processing and attached to the resulting certified product, including details like the responsible manufacturer's details (**R3**). Thresholds and safeguards should be applied to ensure processes follow specifications (**R4**) (e.g., a batch cannot yield more output than input). This prevents stakeholders from injecting unsourced material.

Raw materials must correspond to certified inputs to confirm their presence (**R5**). The output of the process should be attached to a new certified input, which is initialized from the application of a given certified process to the original input (**R6**). (Physical tokens are used to represent these inputs and facilitate traceability.) Physical materials may be entirely or partially used in a certified process, depending on the parameters (**R7**). Any remaining certified material after certified processing could be used in another certified process.

Process execution should support using base materials that do not require any certification (**R8**). For example, if only certain ingredients are certified, the process would prevent manufacturing more than the allowable quantity.

5 BC24 Solution

In this section, we present the BC24 model, which consists of three main components: The **BC24 Network** (Hyperledger Besu), which supports the entire traceability solution and allows different actors to interact with the overall system; several **Field Nodes**, deployed on stakeholder premises, that support physical token management, process interaction, and also participate in the consensus protocol; and a **Smart Contract**, which manages artifact information traceability using a configurable state machine engine.

5.1 BC24 System Overview

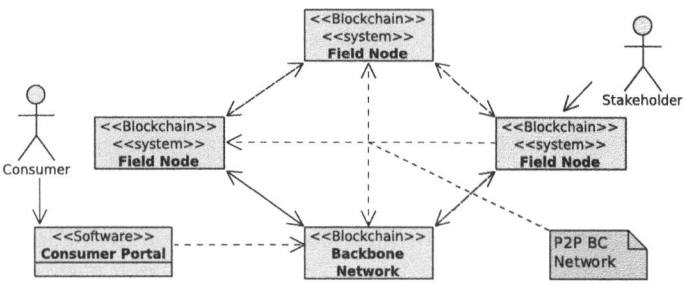

Fig. 1. BC24 Network Block Diagram

Figure 1 presents a SysML Block diagram of the system architecture. The **Backbone Network** is a blockchain network maintained by a consortium of stakeholders, consists of validator nodes that process transactions and ensure the liveness of the consensus algorithm. Each supply chain **Stakeholder** is equipped with a **Field Node**, which runs a blockchain validator and allows stakeholders to interact with the process and its resource traceability features. Each field node is equipped with a unique cryptographic identification that enables secure interaction with the distributed system.

A **Consumer Portal** application is available for participants who only require data visualization, such as consumers or auditors. It is integrated with the blockchain network via an interface and retrieves and displays the corresponding artifact information.

Field nodes contain **wallet software** to securely access private keys used to sign blockchain transactions and interact with the traceability smart contracts. It offers a **GUI application** where stakeholders can register new resources or process their owned resources.

When a resource is processed, specific sensor data may be added depending on the process. In this case, the field node can be considered an Oracle, injecting external data into the submitted blockchain transaction, for example, GPS coordinates for transporters. A **physical token** is required to prove ownership of the corresponding physical product. When resources are processed into new products, the field node generates the relevant blockchain transaction and allows for the creation of new physical tokens.

5.2 BC24 Tracing Contract and State Machine

To ensure secure and non-repudiable storage of traceability, the smart contract stores all the data collected from the field node and provides additional key operations: resource creation, processing, and transfer. It uses the ERC-1155 standard for token management and runs on the Ethereum blockchain. These tokens can be either non-fungible (such as cattle), or fungible, well-suited to represent non-unitary resources (such as beef cuts). We extended ERC-1155 to support metadata management, traceability for fungible resources and access control, where each stakeholder in our system assumes a specific role, granting access to certain processes.

At contract construction, a configurable state machine is initialized. Then, the contract can be called via the **safeTransferFrom** function, transitioning the state machine to the **Transferring** state, or via the **mintResource** function, transitioning to the **Clearance** state. Both states have preconditions. For the transferring state, the **hasAvailableResources** ensures the caller of the **safeTransferFrom** function possess sufficient tokens to transfer an asset to a new stakeholder. For the clearance state, both **Environmental Clearance** and **Domain Clearance** must be satisfied. These are validated with guard conditions based on sensor data, passed as metadata. For example, verifying the GPS coordinates reported by the system match the registered slaughterhouse location, if the result does not match, the environmental clearance will fail, causing an error and aborting the transaction. Similarly, for domain clearance, if the expected requirements are missing, the system will raise an error.

Once the clearance state is validated, the system transitions to the **Resource Creation** state with two possible scenarios: (1) if the resources require no existing input (such as cattle), their creation (minting for blockchain tokens) occurs ex nihilo. The stakeholder allocates a new token with new metadata; (2) if the certified input resources are needed, creation follows a certified process defined by the smart contract's state machine. The system first enters the **Burning** substate, where the required resource tokens are burned after satisfying the **hasAvailableResources** precondition. Then, it transitions to the **Minting** state, creating new tokens based on the quantity of input resources and state machine configuration, and assigning ownership to the function caller. During this step, a reference to the burned resources is added to the new token's metadata to ensure downstream traceability. Unused resources remain available to the stakeholder, as their corresponding physical tokens stay active. When a token is minted, the owner initializes and assigns the corresponding virtual resource token to a physical token. When a token is burnt, the associated physical token becomes unusable. If no errors occur, the state machine returns to the **Contract Ready** state and can receive new orders.

6   Validation

The Trace SAS system is used to verify requirements coverage. First, a breeder uses their field node to register a new animal, entering information and submitting a form through the GUI. A transaction is signed using the built-in wallet on the Pi. Once completed, the animal's ownership and its metadata are stored on both the Backbone Hyperledger Besu network and on the local Besu node

(**R1**, **R2**). The breeder receives confirmation and is prompted to initialize an NFC tag (**R6**).

A month later, the breeder scans the NFC tag to update the animal's treatment (**R5**), with the metadata updated on-chain via a new transaction only they can perform. A few months later, the animal is sold to a slaughterhouse along with its NFC tag. The operator scans the tag, transferring ownership, and after slaughtering the animal, taps the "slaughter" button on its page. The application requests a new NFC tag for the carcass. The operator scans the newly initialized tag, accessing the carcass page with all the animal's information, including vaccination history (**R3**). After processing the carcass, the operation scans the NFC tag, clicks on the "cut" button and enters the cut details. An error occurs if they mistakenly enter five legs instead of four, causing the Trace SAS smart contract to fail domain clearance (**R4**). The operator corrects the entry and resubmits, generating NFC tags for the produced cuts. Later, a butcher scans the NFC tag attached to the cuts to verify the animal's origin for the "Viande Française" label (**R3**). Finally, the butcher prepares roast beef sandwiches, each with 100g of beef and other ingredients (**R7**, **R8**), accompanied with its own NFC tag that the customers can scan to verify the meat's origin.

The previous scenario demonstrates that every requirement is met by the Trace SAS implementation.

7 Discussion and Threat to Validity

This paper focuses on the goals outlined in Sect. 4, but is limited to the requirements we could identify. Beyond that, many issues remain future work. We did not address blockchain architecture security, instead focusing on system and smart contract design. Our solution is vulnerable to common blockchain attacks, and protective measures should be considered for deployment. Collusion between actors should also be taken into account. While a "deceptive" asset could replace a "good" one in the physical world, despite being recorded on the blockchain, it becomes less economically attractive due to the token burning, which prevents the use of the "good" asset within the system. Instead, it would have to be sold on the black market at a discounted price. Spoofing or tampering with physical sensors (e.g., GPS, temperature) is another attack vector. Physical safeguards, such as blocking the system if misuse is detected, could be implemented to prevent human interference. NFC technology, including Mifare tokens, is vulnerable [4], however, newer, more expensive models could have been incorporated into the implementation.

8 Conclusion

This paper presented BC24, a blockchain-based model that integrates fungible asset tracking and secure transformation process traceability, applied to the agro-food supply chain. Our solution leverages a consortium blockchain and

RFID technology to ensure continuous traceability from raw materials to finished products. By extending the ERC-1155 token standard, BC24 effectively manages both fungible and non-fungible assets, providing a flexible framework adaptable to various supply chain scenarios.

Acknowledgments. Special thanks to Université Paris 1 Panthéon-Sorbonne MIAGE Team: Etienne Baumgartner, Mehdi Chebbah, Chadi Grolleau-Raoux, Katia Hammache, Alix Lin, Hugo Marques, Marieme Sow, Quentin Tambone, Paul-Cesar Toux and Florent Zheng for their contribution to this project.

References

1. Agarwal, U., et al.: Blockchain technology for secure supply chain management: a comprehensive review. IEEE Access **10**, 85493–85517 (2022)
2. Dutta, P., Choi, T.M., Somani, S., Butala, R.: Blockchain technology in supply chain operations: applications, challenges and research opportunities. Transport. Res. Part E: Logist. Transport. Rev. **142**, 102067 (2020)
3. Fanizza, F., Omizzolo, M.: Caporalato: an authentic agromafia. Mimesis (2019)
4. Hilt, M., Shao, D., Yang, B.: Rfid security, verification, and blockchain: vulnerabilities within the supply chain for food security. In: Proceedings of the 19th Annual SIG Conference on Information Technology Education, SIGITE '18, pp. 145–145. ACM (2018)
5. Kambilo, E.K., Rychkova, I., Herbaut, N., Souveyet, C.: Addressing trust issues in supply-chain management systems through blockchain software patterns, pp. 275–290. Springer, Cham (2023). https://doi.org/10.1007/978-3-031-33080-3_17
6. Kuhn, M., Funk, F., Franke, J.: Blockchain architecture for automotive traceability. Procedia CIRP **97**, 390–395 (2021)
7. Su, S., Wang, K., Kim, H.S.: Smartsupply: smart contract based validation for supply chain blockchain. In: 2018 IEEE International Conference on Internet of Things (iThings) and IEEE Green Computing and Communications (GreenCom) and IEEE Cyber, Physical and Social Computing (CPSCom) and IEEE Smart Data (SmartData), pp. 988–993. IEEE (2018)
8. Tian, F.: An agri-food supply chain traceability system for china based on rfid and blockchain technology. In: 2016 13th International Conference on Service Systems and Service Management (ICSSSM), p. 1–6. IEEE (2016)
9. Upputuri, B., Tejaswini, R., Vindhya, E., Moahana Roopa, Y.: Blockchain-enabled qr verification system for authenticating gi-tagged products in e-commerce. In: 2024 International Conference on IoT Based Control Networks and Intelligent Systems (ICICNIS), pp. 306–311. IEEE (2024)
10. Vern, P., Panghal, A., Mor, R.S., Kamble, S.S.: Blockchain technology in the agri-food supply chain: a systematic literature review of opportunities and challenges. Manag. Rev. Q. **75**(1), 643–675 (2024)
11. Wieringa, R.: Design Science Methodology for Information Systems and Software Engineering. Springer, Heidelberg (2014)

Suspicious Activity Detection Using Blockchain Process Mining

Felipe Alejandro Manzor Manzor[1]([envelope]) [iD], Adam Burke[2]([envelope]) [iD],
Nagarajan Venkatachalam[2] [iD], and Andrzej Janusz[2] [iD]

[1] Frangipani Labs, Brisbane, Australia
fmanzor@fen.uchile.cl
[2] School of Information Systems, Queensland University of Technology,
Brisbane, Australia
{at.burke,venkat.venkatachalam,andrzej.janusz}@qut.edu.au

Abstract. This study investigates the use of process mining in conjunction with blockchain data analysis to enhance transparency and detect market anomalies in decentralised applications. Using CryptoKitties as a case study, a game built around Non-Fungible Tokens (NFTs), we analyse transaction data to identify hidden patterns and irregularities indicative of unethical practices, including black-market activity and price manipulation. This highlights gaps in blockchain governance models and how audit supported by process and data analytics can help address them.

Keywords: blockchain · audit · process mining

1 Introduction

In 2008, the entire global financial system experienced enormous upheaval as it became clear that multiple major financial institutions did not have good information on the worth of their own assets and liabilities. Banks failed and lives were upended as this systemic lack of transparency in instruments such as collateral debt obligations suddenly unwound. The radical transparency of blockchain technologies [1] has been promoted as both a technical and institutional solution to these problems [2]. On the other hand, the collapse of the FTX cryptocurrency exchange in 2022, itself causing billions of dollars in lost investments, serves as a stark illustration of ongoing transparency challenges, even when blockchain technology underpins a system.

Blockchains are decentralised digital ledgers which record data (typically transactions) in cryptographically signed immutable blocks linked in a chain [1]. The technology is designed to allow trust in anonymous counterparties without intermediaries, often glossed with the term "trustless". Though cryptocurrencies such as Bitcoin are the most well-known distributed ledgers, more complex and domain-specific decentralised applications (DApps) exist. For instance, vChain [3] is a supply chain-focused blockchain platform that aims to enhance traceability, and efficiency across the stages of production and distribution, minimizing fraud, counterfeiting, and inefficiencies.

J. Grabis and Y. Wautelet (Eds.): CAiSE 2025 Workshops, LNBIP 556, pp. 129–141, 2025.
https://doi.org/10.1007/978-3-031-94931-9_11

Process mining [4] analyses event logs from information systems to discover and optimise business processes. By using real data to compute workflows, it allows the comparison of actual processes with expected models. Distinguishing typical and exceptional behaviour makes process mining a powerful tool for financial audit [5].

This paper is a practical investigation on both the potential for abuse in blockchain-based financial trading systems, and the inbuilt transparency required to expose it. It investigates *how blockchain-based process mining can discover patterns of suspicious trading activity in a blockchain-based massively multiplayer trading game.* This novel use of process mining tools in

Fig. 1. CryptoKitty "LilBub", ID: 1129880.

this setting employs them as an auditor or regulator might, not as final proof of disruptive or illegal market activity, but as one form of evidence for this behaviour by a market participant, building a case that could lead to sanction or regulatory penalties. Others have applied process mining to blockchain data [6,7], but this public analysis of suspicious trading is not usually possible for institutional financial markets, such as the New York Stock Exchange, because a full set of counterparty and individual asset identifiers are available only to regulators, if at all.

The data for this investigation comes from the game CryptoKitties [8]. At the height of its speculative bubble in 2017, CryptoKitties involved significant sums, with virtual cats being sold for over USD$100,000 each [8]. Other online games such as *Fortnite* have annual revenues measured in billions[1].

In the remainder of this paper, we review background material in Sect. 2 and survey related work on blockchains and process mining in Sect. 3. Section 4 discusses the dataset and the use of process mining and data science tools. In Sect. 5 we highlight suspicious transactions found with these techniques. Section 6 concludes.

2   Background

CryptoKitties. CryptoKitties is a non-fungible token (NFT) game first published on the Ethereum blockchain in November 2017. An NFT is a digital asset representing ownership of unique items, from artwork to virtual pets, each with distinct properties that make it non-interchangeable. In CryptoKitties, players collect, breed, and trade digital cats, each with unique genetic attributes, or "genes", which determine appearance, rarity, and value. Breeding two CryptoKitties creates a new Kitty, whose characteristics derive from the genetic combination of its parents, including potential mutations. Each Kitty belongs to a specific generation, affecting its breeding cooldown—a waiting period that

---

[1] https://www.statista.com/statistics/1101939/fortnite-annual-revenue.

increases with each breeding cycle. Gene repetition is highly unlikely under normal conditions, however, administrators are allowed to introduce new kittens to the market, such as LilBub, shown in Fig. 1. Players can buy and sell CryptoKitties in an in-game marketplace. Off-market trades are also possible. As these transactions are hosted on the Ethereum blockchain, they are publicly visible and secure, yet lack traditional oversight, enabling direct peer-to-peer exchange without regulatory intervention. This open, trustless environment is foundational to the game's appeal and its susceptibility to speculative trading behaviours.

Market Anomalies and Suspicious Behaviour. Cheating in markets is as old as markets themselves, but in the modern era exchanges and regulators have devised various rules for fair and orderly trading. Markets can exhibit various anomalies, such as collusion, where there are secret agreements among groups or individuals to set prices, avoid forms of competition, or trade in unregulated black markets. Black markets are characterized by features such as under-the-table payments and wide differences in price and asset information available to different participants [9]. Financial markets are also locations where money laundering can occur, that is, proceeds from criminal activity are introduced for use in the regular economy. Non-economic transactions, such as trading at prices far above or below the market, can be symptoms of money-laundering and connections to criminal activity.

Process Mining. Process mining [4] is a suite of related analytics techniques for understanding organisational behaviour. Within process mining, *process discovery* is an unsupervised learning problem which produces structured process descriptions, *models*, from collections of sequential event data [4]. Process discovery requires three mandatory identifiers in an event: 1) an *activity*, which identify the task being performed; 2) a *case identifier*, such as an order id in online shopping, to group together one execution of a process; and 3) a *timestamp* which indicates sequence. The collections of events recording the process under consideration are termed *event logs*. An example process model is in Fig. 2.

Process discovery algorithms are often designed to produce concise process models which have both a straightforward visual interpretation as control-flows, and a data structure with precise formal semantics. In this paper we use Inductive Miner algorithms [10] for their efficiency processing large data sets and formal guarantees, but a large family of discovery algorithms exist, and it is an open area of research.

3   Related Work

Related work includes literature on blockchain applications in corporate governance, process mining in auditing, process mining in decentralized applications, and market anomaly detection.

Blockchain platforms were launched with the promise of radical transparency and radical anonymity delivering both improved governance and financial agency.

This has been a matter of broad advocacy and debate; examples include research on how immutability can enhance trust within corporations [11] and improving accountability and transparency in corporate decision making [12]. Research has also looked at how specific organisational work patterns with blockchain can minimise uncertainty and build confidence among stakeholders [13].

Existing research demonstrates the feasibility of extracting standard XES (eXtensible Event Stream) process mining event logs from blockchain data, and the challenges of using these data sources [14,15]. This paper makes use of those tools and public event logs [14]. Process mining in blockchain environments has focused on DApps and demonstrating the feasibility of mapping transaction flows rather than uncovering blockchain-specific patterns. One study [16] developed heuristics for analysing Ethereum transaction logs, revealing high-level structures of DApp usage and transaction complexity.

Process mining techniques have been shown to effectively detect deviations and compliance issues within purchase processes, with an overview and survey in [5]. Similarly, in blockchain-based processes, process mining can identify deviations from expected workflows and flag compliance violations, leveraging the transparent and traceable nature of blockchain transactions. Process mining has also been used to identify patterns of "weasel" behaviour, such as shirking work or taking credit for other's achievements [17,18]. Here we look at patterns of suspicious trading behaviour, including among possibly colluding traders.

Earlier works on blockchain process mining established its viability with Ethereum DApps like Augur [6] and Forsage [7]. The Augur case study showed that extracting on-chain logs and applying process mining can yield a clear view of how the DApp is used, verifying its design and even detecting unintended behaviors in the smart contract's execution. Forsage pyramid scheme provided evidence that process mining offers valuable insights for smart contract verification and user-behavior analysis a detailed forensic study of Forsage leveraged blockchain's transparency to quantify the scheme's multi-million-dollar gains and losses and to dissect its fraudulent mechanics. Other studies [19] have evaluated process mining's broader utility for transparency and general behavior analysis across Ethereum-based decentralized applications. Against this backdrop, this study takes a different approach by focusing on suspicious activity detection and governance issues in an NFT-based game ecosystem. Rather than emphasizing only process conformance or general transparency, it aims on irregular patterns like black-market collusion and price manipulation (pump-and-dump trading sequences) within CryptoKitties, uncovering evidence of coordinated inflated transactions among a small group of participants.

4   Suspicious Behaviour Discovery Techniques

This section we explain the general analysis methodology, the dataset, and the tools and analysis pipeline.

4.1   Methodology

The study used an iterative, exploratory analysis approach well-accepted for process mining projects [20]. It is similar to the PM^2 method [20], which identifies stages of Planning, Extracting Data, Process Identification, Data Processing, Mining & Analysis, Evaluation, and Process Improvement & Support. Process discovery and analysis happens throughout all the stages after data has been extracted. This paper focuses on the Data Processing, Mining & Analysis stages, with elements of Evaluation. Process Improvement & Support was not part of this project, but would fit the investigation and enforcement activities performed by a market regulator after suspicious behaviour was identified by particular market participants.

Early investigation focused on getting models of typical lifecycle behaviour and sanity checking them against the CryptoKitties smart contract and descriptions of its intended operation. This allowed the investigation of possible exceptions and edge cases. As in an audit, once individual cases of interest were identified, they were cross-checked for patterns of suspicious behaviour.

4.2   Cryptokitties Data

Table 1. Properties of the Cryptokitties event log using a `kittyId` case identifier.

(a) Event log properties

Item	Value
Traces (Kitties)	1,997,605
Events	18,059,296
Activities	12
Start date	2017-11-23
End date	2021-04-15
ETH blocks	2,530,464
Unique Genes	1,993,863

(b) Activity Frequencies

Activity	Mean	Stdv.
Cancel Sale Auction	0.072789	0.354156
Cancel Siring Auction	0.043439	0.256977
Complete Sale Auction	0.259249	0.488925
Complete Siring Auction	0.041854	0.326671
Conceive as Matron	0.591824	1.805093
Conceive as Sire	0.591824	1.913482
Give Birth as Matron	0.593955	1.811559
Give Birth as Sire	0.593955	1.920176
Is Born	0.593955	0.510227
Is Transferred	1.843852	1.988901
Put Up for Sale Auction	0.269602	0.619228
Put Up for Siring Auction	0.100379	0.484080
Total	5.596678	7.775904

An existing tool was used to extract Ethereum data and convert to an XES file [14]. Transactions spanned a three year period, covering Ethereum blocks 4,605,167 (origin block) to 12,243,999. In the process mining approach, each kitty (uniquely identified by its `kittyId`) is treated as a case. This dataset is approximately 8 GB in size. Properties of this dataset are summarised in Table 1, including log properties in Table 1a, and activity detail in Table 1b. As this includes the start of the platform, and the Kitty lifecycles have no defined termination point, the resulting processes should be representative, even though later events will exist for some cases.

Events include a Kitty identifier (`kittyId`), transaction types as activity names, and a timestamp. For CryptoKitties, there are also attributes for details such as gene identifiers, Kitty sire and matron, wallet counterparties, and sale price information. Case identifier, activity identifier, and sequencing attribute are the minimum required inputs for process mining discovery algorithms.

4.3   Analysis Pipeline

Data science tools employed were Python[2]. They included the pm4py process mining library and the DASH plot library for social network analysis. Manual exploration of specific blocks and Kitties was done with blockchain browser tools. The Ethereum Explorer[3] was used for general information on the Ethereum blockchain. The CryptoKitties website also provides viewers specific to the game, which were used to understand fine detail of candidate suspicious cases. Social network analysis was also used to understand transactions among multiple counterparties.

5   Results and Discussion

In this section we describe how data science analytic tools were used to identify suspicious trading behaviour. Process mining was used to produce models of typical Cryptokitties lifecycles and trading patterns across the entire population, and for selected cohorts such as genetic clones and highly traded assets. Social network analysis helped pinpoint exceptional and suspicious trading and holding patterns for these assets.

5.1   Exploratory Process Mining for Asset Lifecycles

The most informative case notion for this data events in the lifecycle of a single Kitty, as identified by the `kittyId`. By defining the `kittyId` as the case identifier, we capture each Kitty's lifecycle events, from its birth as a matron or sire, through transfers, and auctions, and the parenting of other kitties. In the mechanics of the game, Cryptokitties cannot die, so there are no definitively terminal activities.

Figure 2 is a process model representative of typical Kitty lifecycles. It shows birth (Is Born) as an initial activity, though also that this is not the only way a Kitty can be introduced to the system. Kitties can be transferred either through

---

[2] Scripts are available at https://github.com/FelipeManzor/CKTransparency.
[3] https://eth.tokenview.io.

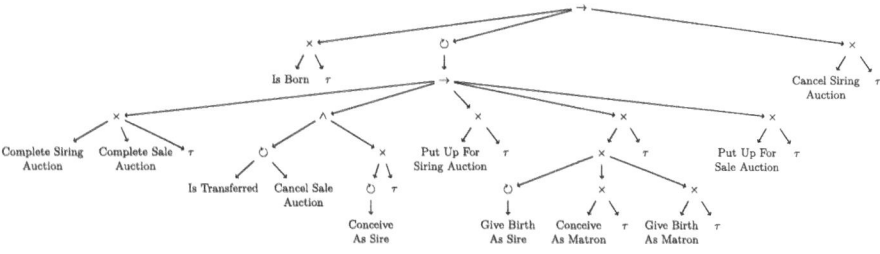

Fig. 2. Process Tree model for Kitties that are genetic clones of "LilBub" (1129880) (see Fig. 1), Kitty lifecycle, 2017–2021. Discovered by the Inductive Miner Infrequent (IMf) discovery algorithm.

a sale auction or a direct transfer. Over the course of a kitty's lifespan, they are unlikely to be sold more than eight times. They can also act as a sire or matron, with the right to breed also being tradable through an auction.

Initial exploratory work included generating a process model for the entire Kitty population. For the process discovery step, we employed the Inductive Miner Infrequent (`IMf`) algorithm provided by the `pm4py` library. This choice was motivated by two main considerations. Firstly, Inductive Miner tends to produce well-structured, block-based process models that are relatively straightforward to interpret compared to other discovery algorithms, and is efficient even on very large event logs. Secondly, the infrequent variant (`IMf`) provides a mechanism to ignore highly infrequent paths that may otherwise clutter the model, especially given the extremely large size of our dataset.

Using the Inductive Miner, the full population model showed repeated short loops and concurrency structures symptomatic of fall-through behaviour, which happens when Inductive Miner cannot find other patterns such as sequences or choice. Interestingly, the full-population model also showed the Is Born activity is not the first recorded event for every Kitty. We also explored a case notion of ownership period of a single Kitty for a particular wallet, but it did not generate further insights.

The analysis then turned to population cohorts guided by hypotheses. Three exploratory analysis hypotheses were generated for further exploration.

AH.1 **High variance activities**. An auditor heurisitic is that suspicious activity is more often found in higher variation parts of a process. Activities with high variation in frequency were then considered as a cohort.

AH.2 **Market rules**. Analytic tools allow empirical tests of whether stated market regulatory rules are followed in practice. For CryptoKitties, these are the rules encoded in the smart contract and the game description.

AH.3 **Price manipulation**. Transactions with artificially inflated prices caused by coordinated activities such as pump-and-dump schemes, and their impact on market integrity.

Table 2. Deviations

Activity	Number of Cases	% Over Total
Is Transferred (>10)	34,734	1.7%
Complete Sale Auction (<2)	20,197	1.0%

As part of exploring hypothesis AH.1, high variation transaction types are listed in Table 2. Given the size of the dataset and the number of cases, we initially chose a threshold of four standard deviations, expecting it to capture only about 0.01% of all observations, as in a Gaussian distribution. However, our findings show that 1.7% of the cases actually exceed this threshold. The *Transferred* activity represents the change of ownership of a kitty, indicated by a new owner address. *Complete Sale Auction* indicates that the kitty was sold through the CryptoKitties Sales Platform, resulting in a change of ownership.

Standard deviations were also informative when producing the many different process models during this project. A key parameter of the Inductive Miner Infrequent algorithm is the *noise threshold*. We set this threshold based on the standard deviations, ensuring that events or paths occurring below a certain frequency were treated as noise and excluded from the main discovered process model. Given that our dataset comprises more than one million kitties, each with multiple transaction events, the process model could become overly complex if every rare event were included. Consequently, using the infrequent variant of Inductive Miner with a tuned noise threshold allows us to derive generalized models of typical kitty lifecycles, while still highlighting significant outliers in separate analyses. This balanced the need for a high-level process overview and the ability to detect unusual or suspicious transactions that may indicate market manipulation or special-edition assets.

5.2 Duplicate Genes

For CryptoKitties, game rules are institutional market rules, the focus for hypothesis AH.2. Though uniqueness is not guaranteed by the platform, as a collectible market, such as for fine art or comic books, the uniqueness of a particular Kitty is part of the value proposition for an owner. The appearance and breeding potential of a Kitty is completely determined by its genetic makeup, and Genetic clones are described by the platform as "responsible for a different trait of a Kitty, and together they combine to make each unique cat [...] there are billions of possible combinations."[4]. Other parts of the documentation emphasise the randomness of breeding and the possibility of mutations.

Each combination of genes is given a unique identifier, `genes`. Using this together with `kittyId` it is straightforward to identify that of the 1,997,605 different kitties in the dataset, there are only 1,993,863 different gene combinations.

---

[4] https://guide.cryptokitties.co/guide/cat-features/cattributes.

This leaves 3,742 kitties with duplicated genes, or 0.18%. This high failure rate - over one in a thousand - is arguably inconsistent with the stated rules.

Kitties with the same genetics may also be duplicated may times over. "Lil-Bub" (ID: 1129880), seen in Fig. 1, has genetic identifier 1528354362908250337. 136 different kitties possess these genes in this dataset. Figure 2 shows their lifecyles as a process model discovered by Inductive Miner. From analysis of other cohorts, this is quite representative of typical Kitty lifecycles. However, 136 Kitties with identical genetics represent an extraordinary dilution of an expensive collectible asset, akin to buying a baseball card advertised as unique which is then reprinted a hundred times by the vendor. These Kitties also participate in 411 transactions, which is 80 times more than the average number of transactions per Kitty, suggesting scenarios such as high information players selling to lower information market participants who do not realise it is a genetic duplicate.

5.3   Market Manipulation

Exploratory hypothesis AH.3 concerns market manipulation. The investigation focused on trading patterns, price, and holding concentration.

Anomalies in CryptoKitties transactions surfaced when analyzing transaction frequency data against established baseline levels, leading to the identification of highly transacted assets. As seen in Table 1b, the mean frequency of the *Is Transferred* activity for each Kitty is 1.84. Kitties traded six times are more than two standard deviations from that mean. Kitties with exceptionally high transaction frequency were identified as anomalies for further investigation. High trading frequencies may simply indicate a popular asset in a deep and liquid market with many participants. However, disparities between market and off-market prices, and transactions at uneconomic prices, often indicate suspicious trading activity.

Among the flagged kitties, one of the most anomalous was the kitty with gene identifier −3019947904495252141 "Dioscuri Balinese" (kitty ID: 995907). This kitty registered an extraordinary 1,684 transfers, positioning it far outside the baseline transaction frequency established within four standard deviations of the average. A deeper review using a blockchain explorer revealed that transactions involving this kitty repeatedly occurred at inflated prices, with examples such as 0.055 ETH and 0.051 ETH. These trades took place outside the official CryptoKitties marketplace, occurring instead in unregulated environments with little to no oversight. Such settings allow for unmonitored and inflated exchanges, which are characteristic of black-market transactions and indicative of artificial price manipulation. This kitty consistently sold (transferred) off-market at prices substantially exceeding the listed value of 0.0419 ETH, often approaching nearly ten times the auction price. Only in-game transaction prices are recorded systematically, with off-market prices are not available from a consolidated source. Two representative transactions and spot prices are shown in Table 3. The relatively high transaction costs of 5–8%, multiplied over more than a thousand transactions, is uneconomic, with much more money spent on transaction costs

Table 3. Examples of uneconomic transactions from 2019 for Kitty "Dioscuri Balinese" (ID: 995907).

Field	Transaction 1	Transaction 2
Block	7217473	8601703
Time (Local)	14-02-2019	23-09-2019
ETH Price	5.28×10^{-2}	5.55×10^{-2}
ETH Transaction Fee	0.27×10^{-2}	0.46×10^{-2}
Fee Ratio	5.19 %	8.29 %

than the underlying value of the asset. Only a single auction (in-game) sale is recorded for this asset.

In addition, only a small number of wallets are involved in trading "Dioscuri Balinese" (ID: 995907). Social network analysis (SNA) reveals this pattern by mapping transaction relationships, where addresses engaged in more than 10 transactions with each other are represented as a cohesive network. These transactions are illustrated in Fig. 3. The long Ethereum wallet identifiers have been replaced with short alphabetic wallet names for clarity. This figure highlights the structure of potential collusion, which is particularly significant in unregulated markets like CryptoKitties, where demand is difficult to track and validate. In this network, nodes represent addresses, and edges represent frequent transactions between them. Key social network metrics, such as *degree centrality* (indicating how connected an address is) and *betweenness centrality* (highlighting addresses that serve as intermediaries in transaction chains), reveal influential addresses within the network that facilitate these trades. High degree centrality among a few nodes suggests a core group repeatedly trading with each other, reinforcing the hypothesis of a coordinated scheme to inflate perceived demand and value.

Many transactions among a small number of participants would suggest an artificial supply scheme. A small group of wallets maintained ownership until the final transactions, a behavior indicative of market manipulation. As many wallets can be anonymously held by a single person, this may even be the actions of a single trader. The frequent, high-value transfers among select wallets signal coordinated market manipulation efforts, where repeated trades at inflated prices create an illusion of demand and scarcity, typical of black-market strategies. For example, these trades can push up the price of this asset with repeated noneconomic sales, before selling it on to another player not in on the scheme.

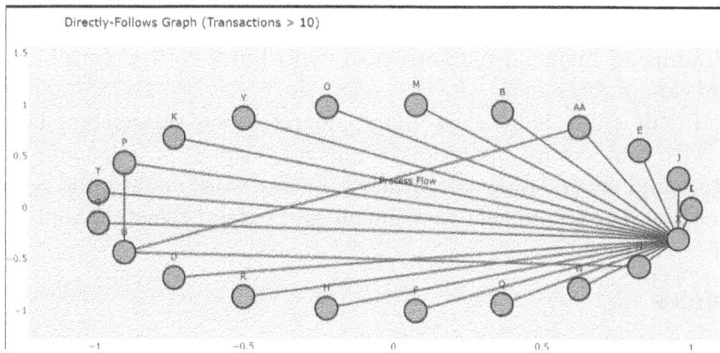

Fig. 3. Wallets with more than ten "Dioscuri Balinese" (ID: 995907) transactions represented as a social network graph.

6   Conclusion

In this research, process mining and social network analysis were used to analyse suspicious behaviour in online trading game CryptoKitties. It identified unusual trading, holding and lifecycle patterns, to uncover suspicious behaviour such as possible pump and dump schemes and off-market co-ordination among close groups of participants. Because financial blockchain data makes available counterparty and asset identifiers available only to regulators in markets based on different technologies, even for organisations with extensive market data feeds, we were able to demonstrate suspicious trading behaviours more precisely than otherwise possible on public data or in the existing literature. This suggests that with the right analytic tools, broader market oversight by a wider range of organisations is possible with blockchain technology, even while a number of suspicious trading behaviours were discovered in practice. The research also illustrates issues in current governance models by revealing violations of stated market rules.

Genetically duplicate CryptoKitties may not themselves represent a blockchain governance crisis, even though millions of dollars worth of assets were involved at the game's peak, and other games now exist. However, similar certification and trading mechanisms would be involved in, for example, an NFT register for real estate. Not maintaining a one-to-one correspondence between physical asset features and the corresponding ledger certificate would have rather more material consequences when there are duplicated claims for the deed to your family home. The mechanism whereby off-market CryptoKitties transactions could happen at inflated prices not readily accessible to market participants is also representative of governance risks.

One limitation of this study is it does not include validation with the direct CryptoKitties developer and player community, which may have provided alternative explanations and highlighted other interesting analysis hypotheses. We would however also argue that analysing blockchain communities from the perspective of established institutional governance expectations, such as those for orderly trading in financial markets, also contributes to a worthwhile ongoing policy and design discussion.

Overall, this study helps show more concrete ways transparent ledgers can combine with time-aware analytics to surface suspicious behaviour in multi-organisation and adversarial environments. Future work might build new process mining tools and concepts that instrument and extend these capabilities.

References

1. Puthal, D., Malik, N., Mohanty, S.P., Kougianos, E., Das, G.: Everything you wanted to know about the blockchain: its promise, components, processes, and problems. IEEE Consum. Electron. Maga. **7**, 6–14 (2018)
2. Sedlmeir, J., Lautenschlager, J., Fridgen, G., Urbach, N.: The transparency challenge of blockchain in organizations. Electron. Mark. **32**(3), 1779–1794 (2022)
3. vChain: About vchain https://www.vchain.io/about. Accessed 2 Feb 2025
4. van der Aalst, W.: Process Mining: Data Science in Action, 2 edn. (2016)
5. Jans, M., Eulerich, M.: Process mining for financial auditing. In: Process Mining Handbook. LNBIP (2022)
6. Hobeck, R., Klinkmüller, C., Bandara, H.M.N.D., Weber, I., van der Aalst, W.M.P.: Process mining on blockchain data: a case study of Augur. In: BPM. LNISA, pp. 306–323 (2021)
7. Kell, T., Yousaf, H., Allen, S., Meiklejohn, S., Juels, A.: Forsage: anatomy of a smart-contract pyramid scheme. In: Financial Cryptography and Data Security, vol. 13951 of LNCS. Springer, Heidelberg (2024). https://doi.org/10.1007/978-3-031-47751-5_14
8. Smith, M.S.: The spectacular collapse of cryptokitties. IEEE Spect. **59**(9), 42–47 (2022)
9. Mackaay, E.: Black markets. In: Law and Economics for Civil Law Systems (2021)
10. Leemans, S., Fahland, D., van der Aalst, W.: Scalable process discovery and conformance checking. Softw. Syst. Model. **17**(2), 599–631 (2018)
11. Panisi, F., Buckley, R., Arner, D.W.: Blockchain and public companies: a revolution in share ownership transparency, proxy-voting and corporate governance? Stanford J. Blockchain Law Policy (2019)
12. Yin, X.: Blockchain technology in corporate governance: advantages and limitations. Acad. J. Bus. Manag. (2023)
13. Müller, M., Ostern, N., Rosemann, M.: Silver bullet for all trust issues? Blockchain-based trust patterns for collaborative business processes. In: Asatiani, A., et al. (eds.) BPM 2020. LNBIP, vol. 393, pp. 3–18. Springer, Cham (2020). https://doi.org/10.1007/978-3-030-58779-6_1
14. Hildebrandt, T., van Dongen, B.F., Röglinger, M., Mendling, J. (eds.): BPM 2019. LNCS, vol. 11675. Springer, Cham (2019). https://doi.org/10.1007/978-3-030-26619-6
15. Moctar-M'Baba, L., Sellami, M., Gaaloul, W., Nanne, M.F.: Blockchain logging for process mining: a systematic review. In: Hawaii International Conference on System Sciences (2022)
16. Müller, M., Ruppel, P.: Process mining for decentralized applications. In: International Conference on Decentralized Applications and Infrastructures (2019)

17. Leyer, M., ter Hofstede, A.H., Syed, R.: Detecting weasels at work: a theory-driven behavioural process mining approach. In: BPM, pp. 337–354 (2023)
18. Bala, S., Jacobowitz, T., Mendling, J.: Spotting the weasel at work: mining inappropriate behavior patterns in event logs. In: International Conference on Enterprise Design, Operations, and Computing, pp. 36–52 (2024)
19. Hobeck, R., Klinkmüller, C., Bandara, H.M.N.D., Weber, I., van der Aalst, W.: On the suitability of process mining for enhancing transparency of blockchain applications. Bus. Inf. Syst. Eng. (2024)
20. van Eck, M.L., Lu, X., Leemans, S., van der Aalst, W.: PM^2: a process mining project methodology. In: Zdravkovic, J., Kirikova, M., Johannesson, P. (eds.) CAiSE 2015. LNCS, vol. 9097, pp. 297–313. Springer, Cham (2015). https://doi.org/10.1007/978-3-319-19069-3_19

Feature Selection in Medical Imaging: A Comprehensive Review

Adrian García Andreu$^{(\boxtimes)}$(iD), Mireia Costa(iD), and Oscar Pastor(iD)

PROS Group, Valencian Research Institute (VRAIN), Universitat Politècnica de València, Camí de Vera, s/n, 46022 València, Spain
{adgaran1,micossan}@vrain.upv.es, opastor@pros.upv.es

Abstract. Modern imaging technologies generate thousands of potential features that can overwhelm computational resources and lead to unreliable models through overfitting. In this context, feature selection methods are essential for identifying the most relevant imaging characteristics while discarding redundant or irrelevant data. This review examines the most adequate methods according to the state-of-the-art. Then, we perform a comparative analysis that evaluates these methods across key dimensions: computational efficiency, ability to capture feature interactions, model dependency, and suitability for high-dimensional or multimodal datasets. Rather than cataloging technical details, we emphasize each approach's fundamental principles and practical trade-offs. Our synthesis provides researchers and clinicians with a practical framework for selecting appropriate feature selection strategies that balance computational efficiency, model performance, and clinical interpretability—ultimately supporting the development of more robust diagnostic tools that can meaningfully improve patient care.

Keywords: Feature Selection Methods · Medical Imaging · Comparative Analysis

1 Introduction

Medical image analysis has become fundamental in modern healthcare [10], assisting clinicians in tasks ranging from disease detection to therapy planning. However, as imaging technologies become more advanced, a single scan can yield hundreds or even thousands of potential features [13]. This "curse of dimensionality" not only overwhelms computational resources but can also endanger the reliability of model predictions [2].

Feature selection, the process of identifying and retaining only the most informative features, is critical in addressing these challenges. By pruning irrelevant or redundant features, feature selection improves computational efficiency and enhances model interpretability and robustness.

Medical imaging, however, presents unique challenges that complicate the direct application of these methods. Images often come from different sources

J. Grabis and Y. Wautelet (Eds.): CAiSE 2025 Workshops, LNBIP 556, pp. 142–154, 2025.
https://doi.org/10.1007/978-3-031-94931-9_12

or conditions, introducing high levels of heterogeneity. Furthermore, the high-dimensional nature of medical imaging data makes models prone to overfitting, potentially compromising diagnostic reliability. Additionally, interpretability is paramount in healthcare settings, where clinicians and regulatory bodies often require clear justifications for automated decisions. With more than a dozen imaging techniques in clinical use, each presenting its own particularities and challenging characteristics, selecting the optimal feature selection approach becomes increasingly complex.

The selection of the most appropriate feature selection method is, therefore, highly dependent on the characteristics of the specific imaging modality and clinical application. Despite extensive research on feature selection methods in general, an in-depth analysis of their applicability in the context of medical imaging—particularly guidance on which method to apply in specific scenarios—remains lacking.

This article addresses this knowledge gap through two primary objectives: (i) conducting a comprehensive state-of-the-art analysis to identify which feature selection methods are currently used in medical imaging contexts and (ii) performing a comparative analysis that evaluates these methods across computational efficiency, ability to capture feature interactions, model dependency, and suitability for high-dimensional or multi-modal datasets.

Rather than exhaustively cataloging technical details, we highlight core principles and practical trade-offs relevant to medical imaging applications. We aim to provide a helpful guide that enables researchers and clinicians to select the most appropriate feature selection strategies for their specific tasks. By emphasizing the balance between performance, efficiency, and interpretability, this work will support the development of more robust diagnostic tools that can meaningfully improve patient care outcomes across various medical imaging contexts.

The remainder of the paper is structured as follows: Sect. 2 presents a state-of-the-art overview of current feature selection categories; Sect. 3 analyzes feature selection strategies concerning different types of medical imaging challenges; Sect. 4 discusses the suitability of these approaches based on the findings in Sect. 3; and Sect. 5 concludes the paper with recommendations and future directions.

2 State-of-the-Art of Feature Selection Methods in Medical Imaging

Feature selection is fundamental to medical imaging analytics, mainly when datasets contain several potentially redundant or non-relevant features. Broadly, feature selection techniques can be organized into filters, wrappers, embedded methods, and metaheuristic approaches, each offering advantages and drawbacks in terms of computational costs, ability to handle non-linear data, interpretability, and scalability.

Filters represent model-agnostic methods: they rely solely on statistical measures such as correlation, p-values, or variance to evaluate individual features without involving any predictive model. In contrast, wrappers and embedded methods are model-based (or model-driven) approaches, meaning they measure a feature subset's quality based on a specific classifier's performance (e.g., SVM, decision tree, or ensemble method). This model-driven selection process can capture complex, non-linear interactions among features but also introduces bias due to the assumptions and limitations of the chosen model. Lastly, metaheuristics represent a flexible group of techniques. They can either operate independently of predictive models (similar to filters) or leverage classifier performance as their selection criterion (behaving like wrappers). This adaptability enables metaheuristics to explore complex feature spaces effectively and introduces additional computational overhead.

This section provides a concise review of these categories of methods, setting the stage for their categorization in the medical imaging context.

Filters

Filter methods use statistical metrics to determine feature relevance or redundancy independently of any predictive model. Their computations usually evaluate how strongly individual features (or small sets) correlate to the target variable. Widely adopted filters include methods such as **CFS** [9], **ANOVA** [12], **Chi/Square** [21], **ReliefF** [6] or **minimum redudancy-maximum relevance (mRMR)** [7]. For instance, ANOVA measures how well a numeric feature separates classes by comparing between-group and withing-group variance, Chi-Square quantifies the independence of a categorical feature and the class label. Techniques like ReliefF sample and compare neighbors from similar or different classes, assigning weights and updating them to highlight underlying patterns. Another technique, mRMR, takes a different approach by simultaneously maximizing feature relevance to the target variable while minimizing redundancy among the selected features.

Filters are computationally efficient and especially suitable for large datasets, making them common in radiomics and other image-based applications. However, they usually miss complex feature interactions, an important aspect to consider.

Wrappers

Wrapper methods measure the utility of a feature subset by iteratively training and testing a predictive model. Standard algorithms such as **Sequential Forward Selection (SFS)**, **Backward Feature Selection (BFS)** and **Recursive Feature Elimination (RFE)** [17] systematically add or remove features until a specific criterion is met. Examples are achieving an accuracy threshold or a certain amount of improvement.

By assessing how each subset actually performs when used by specific models (e.g., SVM or Decision Tree), wrappers can capture feature dependencies that filter-based techniques may overlook. The trade-off spots are why the model's training is repeated over many subsets, which is prohibitively expensive for high-dimensional or when the computational capabilities are limited.

Embeddings

Embedded methods integrate feature selection directly into the training process of predictive models, avoiding separate iterative searches. These techniques tend to rely on parameter regularization or model-intrinsic importance scores (e.g., the Gini coefficient).

Linear models with L1 regularization, also referred to as **LASSO** [20], shrink less relevant coefficients to absolute zero, removing those features from the model. The **ElasticNet** [16] approach expands on this by combining L1 and L2 penalties, preserving some correlated features while still performing selection. Tree-based ensembles such as **Random Forest** [7], determine the feature importance from the frequency or quality of splits on particular features, while methods like gradient boosting increameantally improve residual errors and can similarly track relative importance.

These approaches are usually computationally efficient and occupy a middle ground between filters and wrappers, requiring only a single training process. Their efficacy, however, remains tied to the characteristics of the underlying model algorithm, where a LASSO approach could struggle with non-linearities. At the same time, tree-based ensembles could require additional interpretability measures to meet clinical needs.

Metaheuristics

Metaheuristic techniques take inspiration from biological, evolutionary, or social processes to explore the space of potential feature subsets. **Genetic Algorithms (GAs)**, **Particle Swarm Optimization (PSO)** or **Ant Colony Optimization (ACO)** [3], are all examples in which a population of candidate solutions evolves or adapts based on feedback from a user-defined fitness function that can incorporate predictive performance and other criteria, such as feature interaction.

While these search strategies can be highly effective in discovering underlying relationships or exploring complex search spaces, they can require intensive computation due to repeated model evaluations and often require careful parameter tuning (e.g., population size, mutation, or crossover rates). Moreover, the resulting models may lack the interpretability offered by more straightforward methods.

The flexibility of these approaches allows them to serve as a global filter-like stage (independently pruning irrelevant features according to a heuristic) or as a wrapper-like approach, where a classifier's performance drives each iteration. Such wrapper-like metaheuristics are common in medical imaging since the fitness function can simply be the accuracy of a chosen classification model, guiding the search for an optimal subset until a user-defined threshold is reached.

In summary, filter methods prune irrelevant or redundant features by applying statistical metrics, making them highly scalable but susceptible to missing interactions among variables. Wrappers, by contrast, iteratively train a predictive model to evaluate candidate feature subsets, capturing dependencies but incurring substantial computational costs. Embedded methods balance the strengths of filters and wrappers, integrating feature selection directly into a model's training process to reduce overhead, though they remain tied to the chosen model's assumptions. Finally, metaheuristic approaches offer strong flexibility for global search and can capture intricate data relationships, yet they often require significant computational resources and careful parameter tuning.

In the following section, these methods are categorized according to key factors in medical imaging, such as data dimensionality, imaging modality, feature relationship types, data formats, and clinical interpretability requirements. This categorization serves to clarify when each family of methods is most appropriate in real-world medical imaging scenarios.

3   Characterization of Feature Selection Methods

Feature selection in medical imaging must address the challenges of large (and often multi-modal) datasets, different types of features (e.g., numerical intensities, categorical patient data), and demands for interpretability due to its application in clinical contexts. Building on the methods introduced in the previous section, here we categorize them according to some key considerations: (i) dimensionality (low-dimensional or high-dimensional); (ii) imaging modality (uni-modal or multi-modal); (iii) type of feature relationship (linear or non-linear); iv) data type (either categorical or continuous); and v) degree of interpretability (interpretable or not interpretable). This structured viewpoint clarifies when each technique is most suitable.

Dimensionality (Low-Dimensional vs. High-Dimensional)

In some medical imaging contexts, such as radiomics, datasets often have a large number of features extracted from a limited number of patients, creating overfitting risks and high computational costs. Filter methods, such as Chi-Square, ANOVA and Correlation-based Feature Selection (CFS) are especially popular at initial steps for high-dimensional data because they can prune irrelevant variables quickly. Studies on mammographic images like Abubacker et al. 2014 [1] and heart-disease datasets as the Bashir et al. 2022 work [4], demonstrated that filtering could substantially reduce feature count without a significant drop in terms of classification accuracy. Similarly, mRMR has proven effective in identifying relevant features. For instance, it has been applied in Alzheimer's detection tasks, as shown in the work of HK et al. 2024 [7]. This work highlights the robustness of mRMR in sizeable medical imaging datasets, where it was selected due to its capability to manage an extensive array of features.

Although wrapper methods (e.g., Sequential Forward Selection or RFE) can capture complex feature interactions due to being tied to the model's classification performance, they can become computationally infeasible when the feature pool is exceptionally large, as explained in Tan et al. 2014 [17]. In this work, a Sequential Float Forward Selection approach showed considerably large computation times when selecting features. A more feasible solution is to apply a filter-based dimensionality reduction first step, followed by a second stage on the reduced features set, such as in Vommi et al. 2023 [18], where a first filter step is used to reduce the feature set, and then a wrapper approach is used previously to perform the classification.

Embedded methods like LASSO or random forest can also handle considerably large feature sets when appropriate computing power is available, like in Feng et al. 2020 [5], where embeddings are used to extract radiomic features. Meanwhile, metaheuristic methods often require careful parameter tuning to manage the search space efficiently, which is a significant consideration in high-dimensional scenarios. In practice, combining a computationally more efficient initial step, such as a filter-based method, with a more sophisticated approach can achieve a suitable balance between computational feasibility and model accuracy.

Modality (Uni-modal vs Multi-modal)

Sometimes, the researchers focus on a single modality (e.g., only MRI data). In contrast, others adopt a multi-modal strategy, integrating MRI, CT, PET, or even clinical data like patient demographics or laboratory results. Filter methods remain modality-agnostic since they usually treat each feature independently. A univariate filter (e.g., ANOVA) may still drop irrelevant overall features if multiple modalities are combined into one large feature vector. It could fail to identify synergy between modalities, having critical consequences.

On the other hand, model-based methods, wrappers or embedded ones, can exploit more effectively multi-modal interactions. For instance, Shen et al. 2011 [16] used an ElasticNet-based embedded approach to fuse neuroimaging (MRI) and proteomic biomarkers for diagnosing cognitive impairment and Alzheimer's disease.

Metaheuristics can extend a traditional wrapper framework to incorporate modality-specific weighting by operating on a user-defined fitness function. Rather than treating each modality's features equally, these global search algorithms (e.g., GAs, PSO) can adaptively prioritize different subsets for MRI, CT, or additional imaging sources, seeking the combination that maximizes overall performance across all modalities. For example, in K. et al. 2017 [8], Principal Component Analysis (PCA) and PSO were used to select features from MRI and CT for a posteriori fusing of the obtained feature set. However, multi-modal integration usually expands the feature space further, which may drastically increase computational costs. Similarly to the dimensionality concern, this often makes it necessary to adopt a multi-stage selection pipeline, beginning with a filter method to reduce dimensionality, followed by more computationally intensive methods like an embedding or a wrapper step to refine the selection, making it a more feasible approach.

Feature Relationships (Linear vs. Non-Linear)

Selecting a method that correctly captures the relationship between features is critical. Many radiomic features, such as intensities or shape matrics, might show approximate linear correlations with disease progression, making linear methods like LASSO or some filter methods quite effective. However, relationships usually become non-linear when texture descriptors or different image transformations are present, making linear approaches less effective since they inherently assume the feature relationship. Tree-based embedded methods like random forests or gradient boosting naturally handle non-linearities by recursively partitioning the feature space as in Xie et al. 2019 [19]. This can be determinant, for example, in MRI tumor segmentation, where shape and intensity relationships can show complex, non-linear patterns.

Wrapper strategies can also integrate non-linear classifiers such as SVMs with RBF kernels, but each iteration requires retraining the model, making them potentially costly in high-dimensional contexts. Meanwhile, metaheuristic approaches have enough flexibility to incorporate a non-linear evaluator directly into the fitness function, as shown in the work of Maleki et al. 2021 [11], where the GA heuristic approach is suited for excessively expansive spaces to be comprehensively looked at, illustrating considerably good results when combining a GA approach with a k-NN classifier.

The main consideration is balancing performance gains with runtime overhead due to the computational costs that metaheuristics approaches incur. Investing in a more complex method in data with strongly non-linear signals tends to offer better results. In contrast, mostly linear data can be handled efficiently by more straightforward methods like embedding or filter approaches.

Data Type (Categorical vs. Continuous)

Many imaging pipelines yield numeric features (intensities, geometric descriptors). However, medical datasets often combine categorical elements, such as patient demographics, lesion types, or pathology labels. Chi-Square filters are particularly effective for evaluating which categorical features correlate with a discrete class variable [21], while ANOVA has been successfully applied to numeric imaging features, such as intensities in X-ray or CT for COVID-19 diagnosis at Nasiri et al. 2022 work [12]

When features span multiple data types, tree-based embedded methods can handle both categories without extensive preprocessing. At the same time, metaheuristics are similarly agnostic, provided the fitness function can adapt to different feature encodings with no restrictions. In practice, data preprocessing choices (e.g., one-hot encoding for categorical variables) are often as crucial as the selection algorithm itself. Thus, a pipeline might begin with Chi-Square for purely categorical features, apply ANOVA for numeric ones, and then unify the results or pass them into an embedded or metaheuristic approach for final selection, especially in multi-modal clinical where studies could integrate imaging with tabular data.

Degree of Interpretability (Interpretable vs Not interpretable)

Like all clinical domains, medical imaging represents a high-impact field where diagnostic and treatment decisions require clear justification. Interpretability concerns can influence method selection, especially in regulated contexts.

Filter methods are purely transparent since they rely on statistics such as correlation, p-values, or variance, making it straightforward to explain why certain features are retained or discarded. Linear embedded approaches like LASSO also produce explicit coefficients, enabling clinicians to see which features carry the most weight more easily [5]. For instance, if a particular radiomic texture measure is consistently assigned a high L1-regularized coefficient, its value in diagnostic decisions becomes clearer.

In contrast, ensemble methods (e.g., random forest or gradient boosting) or metaheuristics can enhance performance but make it more difficult to justify each feature's contribution to the final result. For settings where maximizing metrics like sensitivity or specificity is mandatory and regulatory requirements are less strict, these opaque methods approaches may be acceptable. However, suppose there is a need to explain why some specific features could affect the final result. In that case, a simpler filter or linear embedding method might be preferable, even at a mild cost in the final metrics like accuracy.

By examining feature selection through the concerns of dimensionality, imaging modality, feature relationship, data type, and interpretability constraints, researchers gain a more precise roadmap for deciding which approach or approaches are most appropriate for the task at hand. High-dimensional and multi-modal problems may benefit from a rapid filter-based reduction before a second-stage embedding or wrapper fine-tunes the final subset [18]. Conversely, linear embedded methods or straightforward filters may be enough when interpretability is a priority. In some cases, the optimal workflow merges two or more families of methods in sequence or even in parallel, as demonstrated by Atteia et al. 2023 [3], allowing each stage to offset the limitations of the others. The subsequent sections discuss how these factors translate into practical recommendations.

4   Discussion

The previous section demonstrated that no single feature selection approach fits every medical imaging scenario. Although filter methods are computationally fast and well-suited for massive feature sets, their inability to account for complex interactions can be problematic in multi-modal scenarios or disease contexts with subtle feature interdependencies. Wrapper methods (e.g., SFS, RFE) compensate for this shortcoming by iteratively refining subsets based on model performance. Still, their computational cost can become prohibitive in radiomics tasks with thousands of features per image [17].

A practical compromise is a multi-stage approach, where a fast filter is first applied to drop obviously irrelevant or redundant features, then narrow the selection further with a wrapper on the reduced set. This hybrid approach has successfully reduced computational costs while preserving critical features in domains such as gene expression [18] or thermal imaging datasets [14].

Beyond these groups of feature selection techniques, the more generic meta-heuristic approaches (Genetic Algorithms, PSO, ACO) offer high flexibility by tuning a user-defined function to accommodate multi-modal or even mixed-type data [15]. However, while they often uncover complex patterns missed by simpler methods, they also demand considerable computational resources and meticulous parameter adjustments, particularly in high-dimensional scenarios. In practice, a metaheuristic approach can be incorporated as a wrapper-like approach, with the classifier as the core evaluation method. Alternatively, it can serve as a global search strategy to prune features before a more conventional method, which is particularly useful when complex relationships or multi-modality are present in the problem to solve.

Table 1 provides a concise overview of how each method category aligns with the described key factors introduced in the previous section. Users can refer to it as a quick guide to decide whether speed, interpretability, advanced interaction, or multi-modality is the priority. In many real-world projects, a combined pipeline, for instance, filter-based dimensionality reduction followed by an embedded or wrapper-based tuning, optimally balances accuracy and clinical constraints.

Ultimately, selecting the appropriate feature selection strategy depends heavily on practical constraints such as available time, computational resources, and domain expertise rather than purely theoretical considerations. Organizations must balance algorithmic sophistication against implementation feasibility, often making pragmatic compromises to achieve optimal results within their specific operational context.

Table 1. Suitability of Feature Selection Methods by Criterion

Criterion	Filters	Wrappers	Embedded	Metaheuristics
High Dimensionality	**Yes** – Fast and scalable	**Conditional** – Effective only after reducing the feature set	**Yes** – Suitable for low to moderate dimensionalities	**Conditional** – Global search is effective but best applied after filtering to control costs
Multi-Modality	**Conditional** – Treats each feature independently and may overlook cross-modal interactions	**Yes** – Can integrate features from different modalities when the base model supports it	**Yes** – Tree-based methods naturally fuse data from various modalities	**Yes** – Fitness functions can be designed to weight features from different modalities differently
Feature Relationship	**Conditional** – Best for capturing linear correlations; may miss complex interactions	**Yes** – Iterative evaluation can capture non-linear interactions, though with higher cost	**Yes** – Linear methods (e.g., LASSO) work well for near-linear; tree-based methods capture non-linear patterns	**Yes** – Flexible design allows them to uncover complex, non-linear relationships
Data Type	**Yes** – There are specific methods and broader methods to handle both types (e.g., mRMR)	**Conditional** – Depends on the chosen model	**Yes** – Methods like Random Forests handle mixed data; LASSO requires numeric input	**Yes** – Adaptable if data is properly preprocessed
Interpretability	**Yes** – High transparency due to simple, statistical criteria	**Conditional** – The iterative process can obscure individual feature contributions	**Yes** – Linear methods (e.g., LASSO) are very interpretable; ensembles may require additional tools (e.g., SHAP)	**No** – Tends to be less interpretable due to the intensive search space exploration

5   Conclusion

Selecting the most suitable feature selection approach in medical imaging is highly context-dependent. Datasets often exhibit high dimensionality, varied modalities, and even a trade-off between predictive performance and clinical interpretability. As outlined in this work, filter, wrapper, embedded, and meta-heuristic strategies each address different priorities like efficiency, interaction capture, or flexible global search, but no single technique is universally optimal. Instead, pipelines that combine complementary methods often outperform any standalone approach.

Beyond the described methods, ongoing innovations in algorithmic design, including hybrid metaheuristics and advanced interpretability approaches, promise to enhance feature selection performance, scalability, and transparency. A promising future research direction is the deeper integration of complementary approaches, particularly combining deep neural networks' powerful feature extraction capabilities with sophisticated embedded or metaheuristic selection methods. This synergistic approach could yield more robust feature sets that leverage both the representational power of deep learning and the optimization strengths of advanced selection algorithms, potentially addressing complex problems across multiple domains.

As medical imaging data continue to expand in volume and variety, carefully aligning feature selection techniques with clinical requirements will remain critical for developing robust, explainable, and efficient diagnostic models.

Acknowledgement. This work was supported by the Generalitat Valenciana through the CoMoDiD project (CIPROM/2021/023) and a pre-doctoral Grant (ACIF/2021/117), the Spanish State Research Agency through the SREC (PID2021-123824OB-I00) project, and financed with Aid to First Research Projects (PAID-06-24), Vice-rectorate of Research of the Universitat Politècnica de València (UPV).

References

1. Abubacker, N.F., Azman, A., Doraisamy, S., Azmi Murad, M.A., Elmanna, M., Saravanan, R.: Correlation-based feature selection for association rule mining in semantic annotation of mammographic medical images. In: Jaafar, A., et al. (eds.) AIRS 2014. LNCS, vol. 8870, pp. 482–493. Springer, Cham (2014). https://doi.org/10.1007/978-3-319-12844-3_41

2. Altman, N., Krzywinski, M.: The curse(s) of dimensionality. Nat. Methods **15**(6), 399–400 (2018). https://doi.org/10.1038/s41592-018-0019-x. https://www.nature.com/articles/s41592-018-0019-x

3. Atteia, G., Alnashwan, R., Hassan, M.: Hybrid feature-learning-based PSO-PCA feature engineering approach for blood cancer classification. Diagnostics **13**(16), 267 (2023). https://doi.org/10.3390/diagnostics13162672. https://www.mdpi.com/2075-4418/13/16/2672

4. Bashir, S., Khattak, I.U., Khan, A., Khan, F.H., Gani, A., Shiraz, M.: A novel feature selection method for classification of medical data using filters, wrappers, and embedded approaches. Complexity **2022**(1), 8190814 (2022). https://doi.org/10.1155/2022/8190814

5. Feng, Q., Hu, Q., Liu, Y., Yang, T., Yin, Z.: Diagnosis of triple negative breast cancer based on radiomics signatures extracted from preoperative contrast-enhanced chest computed tomography. BMC Cancer **20**(1) (2020). https://doi.org/10.1186/s12885-020-07053-3

6. Heshmati, A., Amjadifard, R., Shanbehzadeh, J.: Relieff-based feature selection for automatic tumor classification of mammogram images. In: 2011 7th Iranian Conference on Machine Vision and Image Processing, pp. 1–5 (2011). https://doi.org/10.1109/IranianMVIP.2011.6121616
7. Hk, R., Deepak Kumar, P., Sharath, Y.: A robust framework for alzheimer's disease detection and staging: incorporating multi-feature integration, MRMR feature selection, and random forest classification. Multimed. Tools Appl. (2024)
8. K, P., Bhat, M., Karki, M.V.: Feature selection based on PCA and PSO for multimodal medical image fusion using DTCWT (2017). https://doi.org/10.48550/ARXIV.1701.08918. https://arxiv.org/abs/1701.08918
9. Li, M., Shang, Z., Yang, Z., Zhang, Y., Wan, H.: Machine learning methods for mri biomarkers analysis of pediatric posterior fossa tumors. Biocybern. Biomed. Eng. **39**(3), 765–774 (2019). https://doi.org/10.1016/j.bbe.2019.07.004
10. Limkin, E., et al.: Promises and challenges for the implementation of computational medical imaging (radiomics) in oncology. Ann. Oncol. **28**(6), 1191–1206 (2017). https://doi.org/10.1093/annonc/mdx034. https://linkinghub.elsevier.com/retrieve/pii/S0923753419324123
11. Maleki, N., Zeinali, Y., Niaki, S.: A k-nn method for lung cancer prognosis with the use of a genetic algorithm for feature selection. Expert Syst. Appl. **164**, 113981 (2021). https://doi.org/10.1016/j.eswa.2020.113981
12. Nasiri, H., Alavi, S.A.: A novel framework based on deep learning and ANOVA feature selection method for diagnosis of COVID-19 cases from chest x-ray images. Comput. Intell. Neurosci. **2022**(1), 4694567 (2022). https://doi.org/10.1155/2022/4694567. https://www.hindawi.com/journals/cin/2022/4694567/
13. Phan, J.H., Quo, C.F., Cheng, C., Wang, M.D.: Multiscale integration of -omic, imaging, and clinical data in biomedical informatics. IEEE Rev. Biomed. Eng. **5**, 74–87 (2012). https://doi.org/10.1109/RBME.2012.2212427. http://ieeexplore.ieee.org/document/6263272/
14. Pramanik, R., Pramanik, P., Sarkar, R.: Breast cancer detection in thermograms using a hybrid of ga and gwo based deep feature selection method. Expert Syst. Appl. **219**, 119643 (2023). https://doi.org/10.1016/j.eswa.2023.119643
15. Rundo, L., Tangherloni, A., Militello, C., Gilardi, M.C., Mauri, G.: Multimodal medical image registration using particle swarm optimization: a review. In: 2016 IEEE Symposium Series on Computational Intelligence (SSCI), pp. 1–8 (2016). https://doi.org/10.1109/SSCI.2016.7850261
16. Shen, L., et al.: Identifying neuroimaging and proteomic biomarkers for MCI and AD via the elastic net. In: Liu, T., Shen, D., Ibanez, L., Tao, X. (eds.) MBIA 2011. LNCS, vol. 7012, pp. 27–34. Springer, Heidelberg (2011). https://doi.org/10.1007/978-3-642-24446-9_4
17. Tan, M., Pu, J., Zheng, B.: A new and fast image feature selection method for developing an optimal mammographic mass detection scheme. Med. Phys. **41**(8), 08190 (2014). https://doi.org/10.1118/1.4890080. https://aapm.onlinelibrary.wiley.com/doi/10.1118/1.4890080
18. Vommi, A.M., Battula, T.K.: A hybrid filter-wrapper feature selection using fuzzy KNN based on bonferroni mean for medical datasets classification: a COVID-19 case study. Exp. Syst. Appl. **218**, 119612 (2023). https://doi.org/10.1016/j.eswa.2023.119612. https://linkinghub.elsevier.com/retrieve/pii/S0957417423001136
19. Xie ,Y., et al.: Use of gradient boosting machine learning to predict patient outcome in acute ischemic stroke on the basis of imaging, demographic, and clinical information. Am. J. Roentgenol. **212**(1), 44–51 (2019). https://doi.org/10.2214/AJR.18.20260. pMID: 30354266

20. Zhao, L., Hu, Q., Wang, W.: Heterogeneous feature selection with multi-modal deep neural networks and sparse group LASSO. IEEE Trans. Multimedia **17**(11), 1936–1948 (2015). https://doi.org/10.1109/TMM.2015.2477058. http://ieeexplore.ieee.org/document/7244241/

21. Çalışkan, A.: Diagnosis of malaria disease by integrating chi-square feature selection algorithm with convolutional neural networks and autoencoder network. Trans. Inst. Meas. Control **45**(5), 975–998 (2023). https://doi.org/10.1177/01423312221147335. https://journals.sagepub.com/doi/10.1177/01423312221147335

Exploring BioNER Frontiers: An In-Depth Evaluation

Manuel Martín$^{(\boxtimes)}$, Mireia Costa , and Oscar Pastor

PROS Group, Valencian Research Institute (VRAIN), Universitat Politècnica de València, Camí de Vera, s/n, 46022 València, Spain
mmarmor@etsinf.upv.es, micossan@vrain.upv.es, opastor@pros.upv.es

Abstract. This paper presents a systematic evaluation of four state-of-the-art BioNER models (BioBERT, PubMedBERT, AIONER, and VANER) across five benchmark datasets covering diseases, genes, proteins, species, and chemical compounds. Although transformer-based architectures have advanced BioNER, direct comparisons remain difficult due to inconsistent annotation guidelines, tokenization schemes, and a lack of standardized benchmarks. To address these issues, we propose a unified pipeline that includes consistent data preprocessing, uniform model fine-tuning, and performance assessment using F1-score. Our results indicate that BioBERT and PubMedBERT often excel, reflecting the benefits of domain-specific pretraining, while AIONER performs competitively through structured sequence modeling and VANER shows variability despite excelling in taxonomic and chemical domains. Beyond model comparisons, we underscore practical considerations—such as ease of implementation, adaptability to novel entities, and resource requirements—and release all code, model configurations, and preprocessed datasets to foster reproducibility and further research.

Keywords: BioNER · Named Entity Recognition · Biomedical Text Mining · Precision Medicine

1 Introduction

Precision medicine represents a breaking change in healthcare, from one-size-fits-all healthcare toward personalized approaches that account for each patient's genetic, environmental, and lifestyle factors. This method has proven indispensable in biomedical research, offering not only enhanced treatment efficacy but also improved resource management and a reduction in unnecessary side effects—specifically, minimizing issues like drug-induced toxicity, hypersensitivity, and off-target adverse effects. According to a recent report [15], global investment in precision medicine is expected to continue rising, propelled by strong interest from the pharmaceutical industry and governmental bodies seeking therapies with demonstrable clinical outcomes. These substantial funding commitments underscore the sector's potential to transform current standards of care and pave the way for evidence-based, individualized medical practice.

© The Author(s), under exclusive license to Springer Nature Switzerland AG 2025
J. Grabis and Y. Wautelet (Eds.): CAiSE 2025 Workshops, LNBIP 556, pp. 155–166, 2025.
https://doi.org/10.1007/978-3-031-94931-9_13

Identifying key entities within scientific literature is crucial for a spectrum of tasks, from elucidating gene-disease associations to facilitating drug repurposing and discovering novel therapeutic targets. Specifically within the context of precision medicine, Biomedical Named Entity Recognition (BioNER) plays a pivotal role by automating the extraction of vital entities such as diseases, genes, chemicals, and species from biomedical texts. This capability is increasingly essential given the exponential growth in research publications, as illustrated in Fig. 1, which underscores a growing reliance on data-driven insights. Consequently, BioNER is not merely a helpful tool but a fundamental component for unlocking the potential of precision medicine by enabling informed clinical and research decision-making through downstream applications such as the effective management of unstructured clinical data and the construction of comprehensive biomedical knowledge graphs.

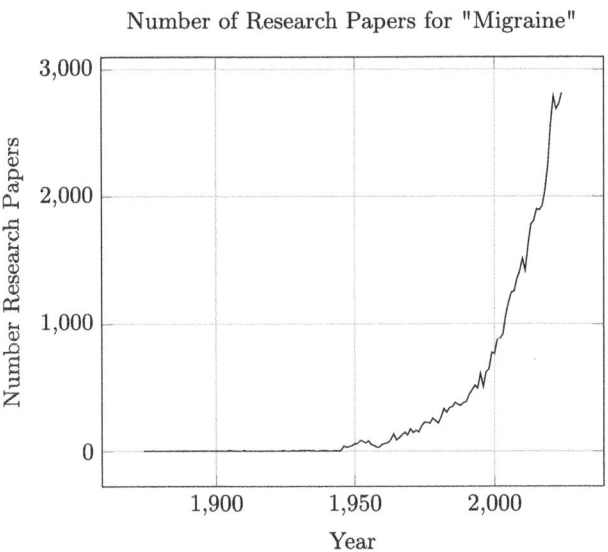

Fig. 1. Research publications on migraine (1900–2020). The graph shows exponential growth in PubMed-indexed papers, with a sharp increase post-2000, reflecting rising scientific interest.

This current generation of transformer-based models has significantly improved BioNER performance through domain-specific pretraining strategies and architectural innovations. Among the most prominent examples are BioBERT [1], which extends BERT's original weights through additional pretraining on PubMed and PMC corpora, and PubMedBERT [5], which trains from scratch exclusively on PubMed abstracts to eliminate potential biases from general-domain data. More recent approaches have introduced additional innovations: AIONER [4] leverages explicit biomedical ontologies through structured sequence modeling, while VANER [7] employs instruction-based fine-tuning for improved knowledge transfer across entity types.

While significant advancements have been made in BioNER approaches, meaningful comparisons between these methods are still constrained by inconsistent annotation guidelines, diverse preprocessing strategies, and the lack of standardized evaluation protocols. This paper tackles these issues through a systematic evaluation of four prominent BioNER models—BioBERT, PubMedBERT, AIONER, and VANER—across five benchmark datasets representing key biomedical entity types: diseases (NCBI Disease Corpus [10]), genes (BC2GM [11]), proteins (JNLPBA [13]), species (Linnaeus [14]), and chemicals (BioNLP [12]). Our unified evaluation pipeline enables fair comparisons via standardized data preprocessing, uniform model fine-tuning, and consistent performance metrics based on F1-scores, while also considering computational requirements, inference speed, and the models' adaptability to novel entities.

The contributions of this work are threefold: (1) To provide a comprehensive performance analysis of state-of-the-art BioNER models across diverse entity types using consistent evaluation methodologies; (2) To identify the specific strengths and limitations of each approach across different biomedical subdomains; and (3) To release all preprocessed datasets, model configurations, and evaluation code to establish a standardized benchmark for the research community, which can be accessed at https://github.com/manumartinm/bioner-benchmarks. This evaluation framework addresses a critical gap in biomedical text mining research and offers clear guidance for selecting appropriate BioNER solutions based on both performance metrics and practical implementation requirements.

The remainder of the paper is organized as follows. Section 2 describes the materials and methods employed. Section 3 presents the results of the systematic model evaluation. Section 4 discusses these findings. Finally, Sect. 5 concludes the paper with future research directions.

2 Materials and Methods

2.1 Materials

Models

The evaluated models fall into three distinct architectural paradigms. The first paradigm includes domain-specific BERT variants—BioBERT [1] and PubMedBERT [5]—which modify the original BERT model to better handle biomedical text. The second paradigm is represented by hybrid neural architectures, for instance, AIONER [4], which merge transformer-based models with additional task-specific components. The third and final paradigm comprises instruction-tuned large language models, like VANER [7], which exploit general-purpose LLMs for biomedical entity recognition through specialized fine-tuning techniques.

We now turn our focus to the domain-specific BERT variants. BioBERT builds upon the original BERT by incorporating extra pretraining on PubMed abstracts and PMC full-text articles, which boosts its ability to process biomedical language. Conversely, PubMedBERT is developed by training solely on PubMed abstracts from the ground up, thereby sidestepping general-domain biases. These differing pretraining methods lead to observable performance differences across BioNER datasets.

Following with the other approaches, we continue with AIONER, which employs a hybrid framework that combines transformer-based contextual embeddings with structured biomedical knowledge from ontologies and curated databases. By integrating relational embeddings with deep learning features, it enhances entity disambiguation and improves recall for specialized biomedical entities.

The final paradigm uses instruction-tuned large language models. The SOTA in this paradigm is VANER, which leverages instruction-tuned large language models like LLaMA and Mistral for biomedical entity recognition. Unlike traditional approaches requiring extensive labeled data, it processes natural language instructions for zero-shot or few-shot recognition. This enables a more flexible approach to BioNER, adapting to new entity types and biomedical subdomains with minimal supervision.

Datasets

For the evaluation, we selected five datasets (see Table 1) based on their suitability for benchmarking biomedical named entity recognition (BioNER) models. The selection was guided by four main criteria: data accessibility, domain-specific coverage, benchmarking relevance, and annotation complexity. These criteria ensured that the datasets provided a diverse and representative evaluation framework.

To ensure **data accessibility**, we prioritized publicly available datasets from established biomedical repositories such as BioCreative, enabling reproducibility and comparability with previous BioNER studies. Regarding **domain-specific coverage**, the datasets encompass a variety of biomedical entities, including diseases, genes, proteins, species, and chemical compounds, allowing us to assess model performance across multiple subdomains.

In terms of **benchmarking relevance**, we selected datasets that have been widely used in prior research, ensuring that the results could be compared against existing state-of-the-art approaches. This choice also guarantees that the datasets align with standardized evaluation protocols in the BioNER field. Finally, to address **annotation complexity**, we included datasets with different annotation structures, ranging from simple entity tagging to multi-class labeling with nested annotations, allowing for a more comprehensive assessment of model capabilities.

Applying these criteria, we selected the **NCBI Disease Corpus**, which provides disease annotations from PubMed abstracts and maintains its original dataset splits. The **BC2GM** dataset, derived from the BioCreative II Gene Mention task, contains gene and protein entity annotations and was partitioned into training, validation, and test sets using an 80-10-10 split. The **Linnaeus** dataset, which focuses on species annotations extracted from PMCOA full-text documents, was included with its original partitions preserved. The **BC5DR** dataset, from the BioCreative V Chemical Disease Relation task, includes annotations for both chemical and disease entities and follows predefined splits. Lastly, the **JNLPBA** dataset, based on the GENIA corpus, contains five biomedical entity types—proteins, DNA, RNA, cell lines, and cell types—consolidated from 48 original subcategories while maintaining its predefined partitioning.

Table 1. Overview of the BioNER datasets used in this study, including entity types, total instances, and dataset splits.

Dataset	Entity Types	Total Instances	Train	Validation	Test
NCBI Disease Corpus	Diseases	7,298	5,433	924	941
BC2GM (BioCreative II)	Genes, Proteins	20,000+	15,000	2,500	2,500
Linnaeus	Species Names	105 documents	55	17	33
BC5DR (BioCreative V CDR)	Chemicals, Diseases	9,385	5,230	2,060	2,095
JNLPBA (GENIA Corpus)	Proteins, DNA, RNA	2,000 abstracts	1,800	100	100

To standardize the evaluation process and ensure consistency across models, all datasets follow the IOB (Inside-Outside-Beginning) annotation format, where "B-ENTITY" marks the beginning of an entity, "I-ENTITY" represents a continuation, and "O" denotes tokens outside any entity. This format, widely used in sequence labeling tasks, enables models to accurately recognize multitoken entity spans and adheres to the standards established in BioCreative tasks, ensuring high-quality annotations for biomedical entity recognition. For datasets without predefined splits, we implemented an 80-10-10 partitioning strategy to maintain comparable training, validation, and test sets across all models, and we applied BERT tokenization uniformly.

2.2   Methods

Following data collection, we implemented a systematic four-phase approach (see Fig. 2): 1) data preprocessing, 2) model training and optimization, 3) model evaluation, and 4) comparative analysis.

The **data preprocessing** phase ensured consistency across our five datasets (NCBI Disease Corpus [10], BC2GM [11], Linnaeus [14], BC5DR [12], and JNLPBA [13]). To address their varying annotation formats, tokenization methods, and tagging schemes, we developed a normalization process that standardized all datasets into a unified format compatible with the Hugging Face datasets library.

Our preprocessing approach consisted of three key components, that intended to ensure the reliability and reproducibility of our benchmarking results. First,

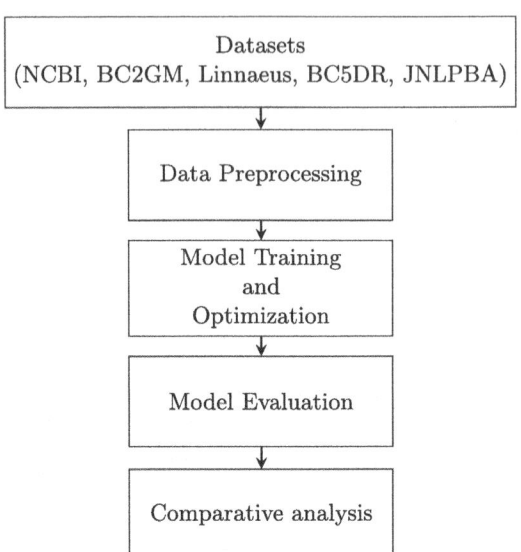

Fig. 2. Pipeline for BioNER model benchmarking (vertical layout).

we performed text normalization by removing extraneous characters, standardizing punctuation, and lowercasing text where applicable to eliminate potential noise. Second, we harmonized all entity annotations into the standard BIO (Beginning, Inside, Outside) tagging format, where the first token of an entity receives a B-ENTITY tag, subsequent entity tokens get I-ENTITY tags, and nonentity tokens are labeled as O. Third, we applied BERT tokenization uniformly across all datasets to ensure consistent token-level processing. For datasets without predefined splits, we implemented an 80-10-10 partition for training, validation, and testing.

The final preprocessed datasets were stored in a format optimized for batch processing and session-based retrieval, allowing for efficient handling of largescale datasets.

The second phase of our methodology focused on **model training and optimization**, where we fine-tuned each biomedical language model on our standardized datasets while addressing model-specific implementation challenges to ensure fair comparison.

BioBERT and PubMedBERT were fine-tuned using Simple Transformers with optimized hyperparameters on NVIDIA A100 GPUs. BioBERT utilized Google Colab with mixed precision (fp16) training, while PubMedBERT featured learning rate decay and weight regularization adjustments. Both required 1.5 h per dataset and demonstrated strong generalization, with PubMedBERT showing particular aptitude for specialized biomedical terminology.

AIONER required modifications to resolve TensorFlow version conflicts, adapting to TensorFlow 2.x with updated layer definitions and Keras API compatibility. Input dimensionality mismatches were corrected by adjusting tokenization and preprocessing pipelines. CRF support was refined through training loop and loss computation modifications, batch processing was optimized to prevent shape mismatches, and architectural adjustments were made to support embedding integration. A modular approach replaced redundant code, improving experimentation capabilities and metric calculation accuracy.

VANER presented challenges due to absent pre-trained weights, requiring author contact to obtain missing models. A Poetry-based dependency management system replaced the missing requirements.txt, resolving conflicts with outdated libraries. Training scripts were refactored to align with current Hugging Face transformers, implementing dynamic path resolution and restructuring the training loop to prevent gradient accumulation issues.

During VANER fine-tuning, a critical tokenization-label alignment issue was identified that had caused near-zero F1-scores. The debugging process was extensive, requiring systematic analysis of the entire entity recognition pipeline. The original implementation failed to maintain correct correspondence between BIO-tagged entity labels and their tokenized input sequences, particularly during subword tokenization. After meticulous tracing of data flow through the model, specialized alignment functions were implemented to ensure tokens and their entity annotations remained properly synchronized. This correction significantly improved performance, transforming the model from non-functional to competitive. Fine-tuning on A100 GPUs achieved results matching the original paper across multiple BioNER datasets. Final models were uploaded to Hugging Face for reproducibility.

The third stage of our approach was **model evaluation**. We selected F1-score as our metric, which is widely adopted in Named Entity Recognition (NER) tasks for its balanced measure of precision (correctly identified entities among predicted ones) and recall (correctly identified entities among all actual entities).

$$F_1 = 2 \times \frac{\text{Precision} \times \text{Recall}}{\text{Precision} + \text{Recall}} \tag{1}$$

where:

$$\text{Precision} = \frac{\text{True Positives}}{\text{True Positives} + \text{False Positives}} \tag{2}$$

$$\text{Recall} = \frac{\text{True Positives}}{\text{True Positives} + \text{False Negatives}} \tag{3}$$

We standardized evaluation across all models using the five selected benchmark datasets (NCBI, BC2GM, Linnaeus, BC5DR, and JNLPBA). Test splits were used exclusively to ensure reported F1-scores reflected true generalization capabilities rather than training data performance.

Automated evaluation scripts were developed for each model-dataset pair, handling token alignment, entity reconstruction, and scoring to maintain methodological consistency. For models requiring tokenization adjustments (such as VANER and AIONER), we implemented custom alignment methods to correctly map model outputs to ground truth labels.

Finally, we conducted a **comparative analysis** to evaluate model performance across datasets using F1-score, precision, and recall metrics. All models were evaluated on identical test splits to ensure fair comparison. The analysis involved collecting and structuring evaluation metrics, normalizing scores to account for dataset variations, and performing error analysis to identify prediction patterns.

For error analysis, we aligned model outputs with ground truth annotations, mapped tokenized outputs to the original text, and categorized discrepancies into predefined error types, with special handling for tokenization mismatches. All comparative analysis procedures were automated with dedicated scripts, which are available alongside evaluation outputs with the original code at https://github.com/manumartinm/bioner-benchmarks.

3 Results

The Results section presents the performance evaluation and comparative analysis of the models studied for biomedical named entity recognition (BioNER). These results are structured to demonstrate how the models performed on various benchmarks and tasks, highlighting their strengths, weaknesses, and overall contribution to advancing the state-of-the-art (Table 2).

Table 2. Performance of BioNER models across various datasets, measured in F1-Score. Best scores for each dataset are highlighted in bold.

Model	NCBI	BC2GM	Linnaeus	BC5DR	JNLPBA
BioBERT	**0.9370**	**0.9082**	0.8670	0.8497	**0.7320**
PubMedBERT	0.8972	0.8803	0.8629	0.7575	0.7011
AIONER	0.8536	0.8954	0.8845	0.9154	0.7132
VANER	0.8781	0.8269	**0.9245**	**0.9400**	0.6919

BioBERT [1] achieved the highest F1-scores on NCBI (0.9370), BC2GM (0.9082), and Linnaeus (0.8670), while also maintaining competitive performance on BC5DR (0.8497) and JNLPBA (0.7320). These results indicate that BioBERT's pretraining on large-scale biomedical corpora provides strong generalization across multiple biomedical domains. PubMedBERT [5], which was trained exclusively on PubMed abstracts, followed closely behind with F1-scores of 0.8972 on NCBI, 0.8803 on BC2GM, 0.8629 on Linnaeus, 0.7575 on BC5DR, and 0.7011 on JNLPBA. The largest gap between BioBERT and PubMedBERT was observed in BC5DR, where BioBERT outperformed by approximately 9 F1-score points.

AIONER [4] obtained high scores on BC5DR (0.9154) and BC2GM (0.8954), indicating strong performance in recognizing chemical and gene/protein entities. However, its F1-scores on NCBI (0.8536), Linnaeus (0.8845), and JNLPBA

(0.7132) were lower, suggesting that its hybrid approach, which integrates structured biomedical knowledge, is more effective in datasets that benefit from external ontological information. VANER [7] achieved the highest scores on Linnaeus (0.9245) and BC5DR (0.9400), showing strong performance in taxonomic and chemical entity recognition. However, its results on NCBI (0.8781), BC2GM (0.8269), and JNLPBA (0.6919) were comparatively lower.

The differences in model performance align with their architectural paradigms. BioBERT and PubMedBERT, as domain-specific BERT variants, demonstrated strong results in disease and gene/protein entity recognition, suggesting that pretraining on biomedical corpora effectively enhances performance in these domains. AIONER, with its hybrid approach that combines contextual embeddings with structured biomedical knowledge, performed well in datasets where external knowledge sources aid entity disambiguation, particularly in chemical and gene/protein recognition tasks. VANER, which employs instruction-tuned large language models, showed high adaptability in taxonomic and chemical entity recognition but exhibited more variation across datasets that require specialized handling of disease and gene/protein mentions.

The characteristics of the datasets also influenced model performance. NCBI, which focuses on disease mentions, showed the highest score with BioBERT, likely due to its pretraining on biomedical literature with strong clinical relevance. BC2GM, a dataset focused on gene/protein entities, also saw its highest performance with BioBERT. Linnaeus, which involves taxonomic entity recognition, had the best results with VANER, suggesting that instruction-tuned models are well suited for structured entity types. BC5DR, which contains both chemical and disease entities, was best handled by VANER, reflecting the model's ability to generalize across distinct biomedical subdomains. JNLPBA, which includes a variety of biomedical entity types, showed generally lower performance across all models, indicating its higher complexity and variability in entity annotation.

All models were evaluated using the same data splits and standard BioNER methodologies to ensure comparability. The reported F1-scores were computed under identical conditions.

4   Discussion

The results of the evaluation highlight several key factors influencing BioNER model performance across different datasets. Differences in dataset characteristics, model architectures, and tokenization strategies impacted the models' ability to generalize across biomedical entity types. Additionally, an error analysis was conducted to identify common challenges in BioNER tasks and to explore areas for improvement in preprocessing and model adaptation.

Influence of Model Architecture

The transformer-based models, **BioBERT** and **PubMedBERT**, demonstrated high performance in datasets with clearly defined biomedical entity boundaries.

These models, pre-trained on large-scale biomedical corpora, leveraged domain-specific embeddings that facilitated entity recognition in structured datasets. However, variations in performance between BioBERT and PubMedBERT suggest that pre-training data composition may play a role in model generalization, particularly in entity-rich environments.

AIONER, incorporating Conditional Random Fields (CRFs) for sequence labeling, achieved competitive F1-scores in datasets with highly structured annotation schemes. CRFs enhanced the model's ability to capture dependencies between adjacent tokens, which was particularly relevant in cases where entities spanned multiple tokens. The integration of pre-trained embeddings from PubMedBERT further contributed to performance stability across datasets.

VANER, which utilized instruction-tuned models, demonstrated high variability in performance across datasets. While achieving the highest scores on Linnaeus and BC5DR, it exhibited lower F1-scores on other datasets. This suggests that instruction-based tuning may provide advantages in recognizing specific entity types but may require dataset-specific adaptation to maintain consistency across diverse biomedical domains.

Error Analysis

The error analysis conducted during this study identified common challenges in BioNER tasks, including:

1. **Nested Entity Recognition:** Many biomedical entities appeared within larger entities, making boundary detection difficult. Transformer-based models, trained primarily on non-overlapping sequences, encountered difficulty distinguishing nested structures, leading to potential misclassifications.
2. **Ambiguous Entity Disambiguation:** Several datasets contained entities with overlapping meanings, increasing the likelihood of misclassification. This issue was more pronounced in datasets where closely related biomedical concepts were annotated differently.
3. **Dataset Alignment Issues:** Variability in annotation guidelines across datasets introduced inconsistencies in entity labeling, affecting training stability. Some datasets included additional entity subtypes not present in other datasets, complicating direct comparisons.
4. **Tokenization Mismatches:** Differences in tokenization strategies resulted in discrepancies between input sequences and entity labels. This was particularly evident in models that employed subword tokenization, where multi-token entities required alignment adjustments to ensure correct BIO-tagging.

Addressing these challenges would require improved preprocessing pipelines, entity alignment methods, and model adaptations capable of handling nested and ambiguous entities more effectively.

Comparison of Accuracy and Implementation Efficiency

From a practical perspective, model selection often involves trade-offs between accuracy and implementation complexity. BioBERT demonstrated the best balance between performance and ease of implementation, achieving high F1-scores across multiple datasets while requiring relatively short fine-tuning times. PubMedBERT exhibited comparable performance but required slightly longer training times.

AIONER introduced additional computational overhead due to its integration of CRFs, which extended training time significantly. Despite this, the model achieved strong results in datasets with structured annotation formats, suggesting that CRFs may provide advantages in certain biomedical NER scenarios.

VANER required the most extensive setup due to the lack of pre-trained models and additional debugging efforts. While it performed well in specific datasets, its implementation required significantly more time, particularly for training and evaluation adjustments. Future optimizations in instruction-based tuning could improve its efficiency and consistency across datasets.

5   Conclusions

This study evaluated multiple state-of-the-art BioNER models across five benchmark datasets, analyzing their performance in recognizing biomedical entities. Historically, biomedical text mining has evolved significantly—from early rule-based and dictionary-driven methods that operated on limited corpora to today's sophisticated machine learning approaches. As biomedical research expanded dramatically since the late 19th century, these rudimentary techniques paved the way for modern transformer-based models. In this study, we assessed transformer architectures (**BioBERT** [1], **PubMedBERT** [5]), hybrid approaches with structured sequence modeling (**AIONER** [4]), and instruction-tuned language models (**VANER** [7]) within a standardized evaluation pipeline using F1-score as the primary metric.

The results demonstrated variations in model performance depending on dataset characteristics, annotation schemes, and architectural differences. Bio BERT achieved the highest scores across most datasets, while PubMedBERT exhibited slightly lower but comparable performance. AIONER demonstrated competitive results, particularly in datasets where structured sequence dependencies played a role. VANER performed best in taxonomic and chemical entity recognition but showed variability across datasets. Error analysis identified challenges such as nested entities, tokenization mismatches, and annotation inconsistencies, emphasizing the need for refined preprocessing pipelines.

These findings underscore the importance of dataset standardization and preprocessing consistency in BioNER tasks, mirroring the historical evolution of biomedical text mining from its rudimentary beginnings to today's transformer-driven innovations. Future work should explore improvements in model architectures, particularly for handling nested and ambiguous entities, as well as further optimization of instruction-tuned models.

Acknowledgments. This work was supported by the Generalitat Valenciana through the CoMoDiD project (CIPROM/2021/023) and a pre-doctoral Grant (ACIF/2021/117), the Spanish State Research Agency through the SREC (PID2021-123824OB-I00) project, and financed with Aid to First Research Projects (PAID-06-24), Vice-rectorate of Research of the Universitat Politècnica de València (UPV).

References

1. Lee, J., et al.: BioBERT: a pre-trained biomedical language representation model for biomedical text mining. https://arxiv.org/pdf/1901.08746
2. Huang, K., Altosaar, J., Ranganath, R.: ClinicalBERT: Modeling Clinical Notes and Predicting Hospital Readmission. https://arxiv.org/pdf/1904.03323
3. Devlin, J., Chang, M.-W., Lee, K., Toutanova, K.: BERT: Pre-training of Deep Bidirectional Transformers for Language Understanding. https://arxiv.org/pdf/1810.04805
4. Zhang, T., et al.: AIONER: Enhancing Biomedical Named Entity Recognition via Adaptive Input-Output Modeling. https://arxiv.org/pdf/2211.16944
5. Gu, Y., et al.: PubMedBERT: Domain-specific language model for biomedical text. https://arxiv.org/pdf/2007.15779
6. Guo, X., Tang, Y., Song, X., Liu, Y., Sun, L., Wang, Y.: Dense Retrieval for Biomedical Literature and Knowledge Extraction. https://arxiv.org/pdf/2108.05542v2
7. Smith, J., Liu, X., Zhou, F., Wang, H., Lin, Z.: VANER: Vision-Augmented Named Entity Recognition for Biomedical Applications. https://arxiv.org/pdf/2404.17835
8. Huang, K., Lu, X., Chen, J., Xu, C.: Clinical XLNet: Modeling Clinical Notes with Permutation Language Modeling. arXiv preprint arXiv:1912.11975 (2019). https://arxiv.org/abs/1912.11975
9. Peng, Y., Yan, S., Lu, Z.: Transfer Learning in Biomedical Natural Language Processing: An Evaluation of BERT and ELMo on Ten Benchmarking Datasets. arXiv preprint arXiv:1906.05474 (2019). https://arxiv.org/pdf/1906.05474
10. National Center for Biotechnology Information: NCBI Disease Corpus. https://github.com/ncbi/datasets
11. Pyysalo, S., et al.: BioCreative II Gene Mention Corpus (BC2GM). https://github.com/spyysalo/bc2gm-corpus
12. National Center for Biotechnology Information: BioNLP Data Resources. https://www.ncbi.nlm.nih.gov/research/bionlp/Data/
13. Hugging Face: JNLPBA Dataset - A benchmark dataset for biomedical named entity recognition, including five entity types: DNA, RNA, protein, cell line, and cell type. https://huggingface.co/datasets/jnlpba/jnlpba
14. Hugging Face: Linnaeus Dataset - A dataset designed for species name recognition in biomedical text, widely used for taxonomic information extraction. https://huggingface.co/datasets/cambridgeltl/linnaeus
15. Precision Medicine Investments and Outcomes Expected. PharmaExec. https://www.pharmexec.com/view/precision-medicine-investments-and-outcomes-expected

3rd Workshop on Modelling and Implementation of Digital Twins for Complex Systems (MIDas4CS)

Third Workshop on the Modelling and Implementation of Digital Twins for Complex Systems (MIDas4CS 2025)

The concept of Digital Twin (DT) has gained significant traction since its introduction within the context of Smart Industry (Industry 4.0). At its core, a Digital Twin is a virtual counterpart of a physical entity—ranging from individual components and complex systems to entire processes or even human beings. The key idea is to establish a bi-directional link between the physical and digital worlds, allowing continuous synchronization of data, state, and behavior. Digital Twins offer numerous benefits, including real-time remote monitoring and control, enhanced efficiency and safety, predictive maintenance and scheduling, scenario and risk analysis, improved collaboration within and across teams, more informed decision support systems, personalized products and services, and clearer documentation and communication. The primary goal of DTs is to support better decision-making for real-world problem-solving. By leveraging digital models to generate actionable insights, decisions can be effectively implemented in the physical world. Although Digital Twins were initially conceived for industrial manufacturing contexts, their adoption has rapidly expanded into diverse domains such as energy management, smart buildings and infrastructure, agriculture, logistics, urban planning, automotive and aerospace, and healthcare. For instance, in healthcare, DTs are being developed to support personalized medicine, patient monitoring, and surgical planning, while in the built environment, they support lifecycle asset management and resilience planning. This workshop series aims to deepen our understanding of the methods used to model and implement DTs across various domains. We welcome contributions from researchers and industry professionals on formal definitions, domain-specific applications, tools for developing and deploying DTs, as well as use case application of DTs.

The third edition of MIDas4CS was organized in conjunction with the 37th International Conference on Advanced Information Systems Engineering (CAiSE 2025). This workshop attracted 9 regular papers and 2 short papers for a total of 11 international submissions. A single-blind peer review process was adopted and each of the paper was reviewed by at least three members of the Programme Committee. From these submissions, 5 submissions were accepted as full papers for presentation at the workshop.

We hope that the reader will find the selection of papers insightful and useful to keep track of the latest advances related to Digital Twins.

Acknowledgments. We thank the authors for their contributions, and the members of the Programme Committee for their invaluable contribution by thoroughly reviewing the submissions. We also wish to thank the organisers of CAiSE 2025 for their support of the organisation of this workshop.

April 2025

Pedro Valderas
Fabrizio Fornari
Luís Ferreira Pires
Marten van Sinderen
João Luiz Rebelo Moreira

Organization

Workshop Chairs

Pedro Valderas	Universitat Politècnica de València, Spain
Fabrizio Fornari	University of Camerino, Italy
Luís Ferreira Pires	University of Twente, The Netherlands
Marten van Sinderen	University of Twente, The Netherlands
João Moreira	University of Twente, The Netherlands

Programme Committee

Abel Armas Cervantes	University of Melbourne, Australia
Barbara Re	University of Camerino, Italy
Estefanía Serral	KU Leuven, Belgium
Victoria Torres Bosch	Universitat Politècnica de València, Spain
Oscar Pastor	Universitat Politècnica de València, Spain
Vinay Kulkarni	TCS Research, India
Philipp Zech	University of Innsbruck, Austria
Ruth Breu	University of Innsbruck, Austria
Souvik Barat	Tata Consultancy Services, India
Taru Itäpelto	University of Twente, The Netherlands

A Meta-model for Integrating Explainable Forecasting with Digital Twins

Tim Kreuzer$^{(\boxtimes)}$ ⓘ, Panagiotis Papapetrou ⓘ, and Jelena Zdravkovic ⓘ

Stockholm University, 16455 Kista, Sweden
{tim.kreuzer,panagiotis,jelenaz}@dsv.su.se

Abstract. Digital twins are virtual replicas of their physical counterparts, providing real-time monitoring and decision-making capabilities. By integrating forecasting-based methods, the potential of digital twins can be augmented significantly, enabling them to execute advanced predictive tasks. However, with digital twins typically involving a human-in-the-loop, the need for explainability becomes crucial for understanding how and why a forecast was made. To effectively integrate explainability methods, forecasting methods, and digital twins, it is essential to define the relations between these components in a structured manner. In this work, we address this issue by providing a meta-model for the integration of explainable forecasting methods with digital twins. We evaluate our meta-model in the context of a smart building digital twin with multiple forecasting and explainability methods. The evaluation demonstrates the inherent trade-off between providing explanations and generating accurate forecasts in this context.

Keywords: Digital Twin · Meta-modeling · Explainability · Forecasting

1 Introduction

Digital twins are virtual replicas of a physical system with the goal of improving the physical system. This can be achieved with, for example, fault diagnosis or adaptive decision-making. As a virtual replica, a Digital Twin (DT) reflects the current status of its physical counterpart in real-time. In addition to that, a feedback loop from the DT to the physical system allows the DT to make a real-time impact on its physical counterpart. Digital twins have originated in the domain of manufacturing, where they have been used for smart manufacturing and shop floor management, and have recently been introduced in multiple other domains such as healthcare, smart cities, or networking.

Digital twins can benefit from integrating artificial intelligence (AI) methods, as they can enable them to predict future outcomes given historical data. These include tasks such as traffic forecasting or path planning, which can be solved by integrating forecasting with DTs [10]. Forecasting-based predictions allow the DT to reduce operating expenses or simulate scenarios with usually high cost or

© The Author(s), under exclusive license to Springer Nature Switzerland AG 2025
J. Grabis and Y. Wautelet (Eds.): CAiSE 2025 Workshops, LNBIP 556, pp. 171–182, 2025.
https://doi.org/10.1007/978-3-031-94931-9_14

ethical implications. As highlighted in a recent review [10], there is little research in the state of the art on forecasting problems within digital twins. In the state of the art, most forecasting algorithms are non-explainable black-box models based on deep learning [14]. To illustrate decision-making to the DT's end-user, it is necessary to combine explainable AI methods with forecasting techniques. *This is the research challenge that we focus on in this study: the integration of forecasting and explainability methods within digital twins.*

Digital twins are applicable in numerous use cases, and their design, functionality, and components vary on a case-by-case basis. Due to this, DTs have been characterized with a high-level symbolic model in early work by Grieves [6], where they are divided into virtual space, physical space, and the data flow between them. Recently, more detailed conceptual models [2,5] and reference architectures [1,26] have been introduced for digital twins, providing a higher level of detail and illustrating the paradigm. Although digital twins have been conceptualized from different angles in the literature, modeling the integration of explainable forecasting with DTs remains an open research problem. Figure 1 shows a symbolic representation of a digital twin of a smart building, where the DT integrates forecasting methods for its internal processing and predictive capabilities. The smart building is equipped with a variety of sensors, streaming data to the DT, which processes them and provides forecasting capabilities among others. The resulting software system is highly complex. A building manager interacting with the DT requires explanations underpinning the forecasts made by the DT to validate them. This demonstrates the importance of integrating explainability with forecasting methods in DTs and highlights the need for a model-based representation.

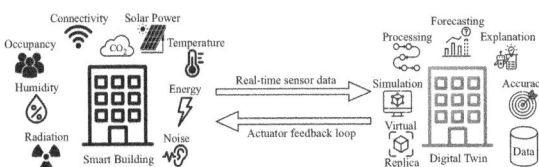

Fig. 1. Digital twin of a smart building integrating explainable forecasting methods.

As previously shown, a digital twin of a smart building is highly complex. Additional challenges, such as data quality and availability, must be faced to implement such a system in a real-world environment. Further, dynamic situations such as heatwaves, or a change of operating hours make the problem more challenging to address. Our proposed meta-model is evaluated in the context of a smart building DT, where we assess how it addresses these challenges while evaluating its applicability. The contributions of this paper are as follows:

1. We introduce a meta-model for the integration of explainable forecasting methods with digital twin. The meta-model captures the relation between explainability methods, forecasting models, and the digital twin.

2. The meta-model is modularized with a component-based approach, where each component fulfills a distinct role within the system.
3. The meta-model captures a set of properties, characterizing the importance of different explainability aspects in DTs.
4. The proposed meta-model is evaluated in the context of a smart building DT with real-world data, where we showcase both explainability and forecasting methods, and their integration with the DT.

2   Background

Digital twins have been successfully implemented in different domains, tackling a variety of problems: Pylianidis et al. [20] have surveyed the literature on digital twins in agriculture, characterizing 28 found use cases where DTs are beneficial in an agricultural setting. In the field of healthcare, Croatti et al. [4] have proposed agent-based digital twins for severe trauma management, serving as a descriptive virtual representation of the patient's medical history. Similar to Pylianidis et al. [20], Opoku et al. [17] have reviewed the literature on digital twins in the construction sector. The authors summarize use cases and present the varying definitions of a digital twin used in the surveyed literature.

Several studies have explored the challenge of forecasting in digital twins. Kharlamova et al. [8] have developed a digital twin to predict the state of charge in electric vehicle batteries, using both GRU and LSTM networks - two prominent recurrent neural network architectures. Likewise, Tu et al. [24] used an LSTM network for traffic flow prediction within a digital twin of a transportation system. Pang et al. [19] examined disease progression in a smart city digital twin, leveraging a temporal convolutional neural network to forecast epidemic trends. These works consistently apply deep learning techniques to generate forecasts within their digital twin. However, none of them employ explainability methods to help end-users understand the underlying reasoning.

The architecture and properties of digital twins have been addressed in multiple studies. Hakiri et al. [7] have listed key characteristics of DTs while also summarizing the state of the art regarding digital twin standardization frameworks. The authors conclude that DTs are typically heterogeneous and use case-specific, and future work should be based on standardized, simplified implementations. Zhang et al. [26] provide a reference architecture for Explainable Human-in-the-loop DTs focusing on the explainability of AI-based predictions and outcomes. Their reference architecture is focused on explainable decision-making, which is crucial for digital twins with a human in the loop, allowing the human to understand the reasoning behind made decisions. In our previous work [9], we have proposed an architectural model for integrating explainability, which is specific to the smart building use case. In contrast, this paper provides a more general meta-model applicable in different domains.

In the context of digital twins, several meta-models have been introduced in the literature. Montini et al. [16] have introduced a meta-model for a human digital twin in a production context. Their proposed model is context-specific and does not include any AI-based component. Tekinerdogan [23] summarizes the relation between systems engineering, digital twin, and modeling with a meta-model. This meta-model is constructed on a high-level basis and does not include forecasting functionality or explainability components, as the DT is represented with a high level of abstraction. Recently, Yang et al. [25] have described a meta-model for shop-floor digital twins, which divides the digital twin across model space, data space, and physical space. None of the related meta-models characterizing digital twins focus on the topic of forecasting-based digital twins or explainability, which highlights the importance of this work.

3 Meta-model

This section introduces our meta-model for integrating forecasting methods and explainability within digital twin systems. The meta-model is designed to be generic for applicability to use cases in different domains by including domain-independent constructs and specifying it at a level of detail that contributes to both guiding its use for DT development and detailed implementations. In Sect. 4, we evaluate our meta-model by deploying it to a real-world use case in the context of a smart building DT. Figure 2 shows the meta-model, highlighting the interactions between the physical system and its digital twin while illustrating the internal data processing for the forecasting task as well as the explainability functionality. Further, a human operator interacts with the DT dashboard.

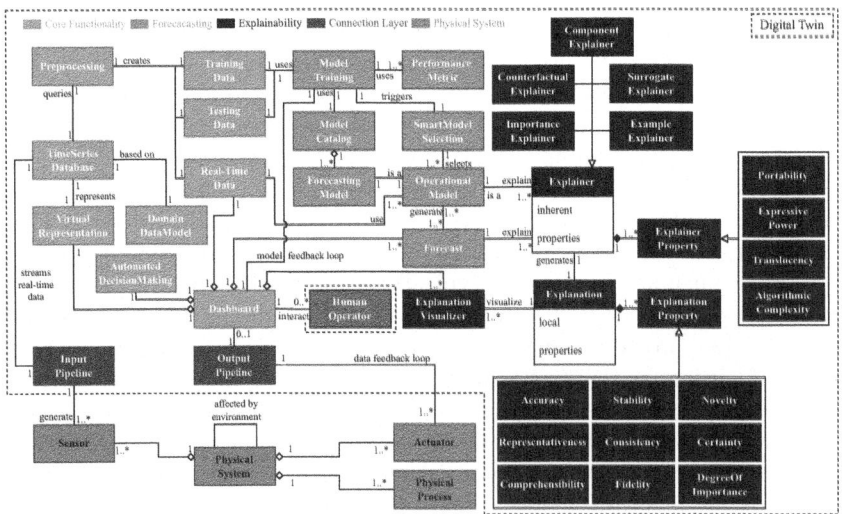

Fig. 2. Proposed meta-model, showing the integration of forecasting and explainability methods in a digital twin. The DT and the physical system are connected with a bidirectional connection layer. Within the DT, forecasting and explainability components are highlighted in green and red, respectively. (Color figure online)

Table 1 describes the elements of the meta-model related to forecasting and explainability. As the core functionality components can be considered state-of-the-art, we describe them in the following paragraphs, but not in the table. In addition to that, Table 2 characterizes the properties of explainers and explanations shown in the meta-model. In our meta-model, the physical system is an important part of the system, as it is both the data source and the target of the feedback loop from the DT. However, as the novelty of this work is focused on the integration of explainable forecasting methods within digital twins, the components and relations of the physical system are not described further.

The DT and the physical system are bidirectionally connected with the connection layer, which contains an *Input Pipeline* that streams sensor data from the physical system to the DT in real time. The virtual-to-physical connection is realized with the *Output Pipeline*, which receives control sequences from the operator via the DT dashboard and forwards them to the system actuators.

Table 1. Forecasting and Explainability elements of the proposed meta-model, as shown in Fig. 2.

Element	Description
Forecasting	Forecasting logic within the DT
Model Training	Model training algorithm based on input data
Performance Metric	Metric for ML model accuracy
Model Catalog	Model architectures used during training
Forecasting Model	Specific model architecture
Smart Model Selection	Optimal model selection based on training results
Operational ML-Model	Trained ML model used in real-time operation
Forecast	Real-time based forecast of the model
Explainability	Explainability logic within the DT
Explainer	Explanation method for the forecasting model
Component Explainer	Explainer based on comprehensible components
Counterfactual Explainer	Counterexample-based explainer
Importance Explainer	Feature-importance-assigning explainer
Surrogate Explainer	Interpretable model approximating the original
Example Explainer	Explainer based on examples
Explainer Property	Property of the explainer algorithm
Explanation	Explanation generated by the explainer
Explanation Property	Property of the explanation itself
Explanation Visualizer	Visualization method used for an explanation

3.1   Core Functionality

Digital twins are based on sensor data, which are in nature temporal. To store and process temporal data, a *Time Series Database* is a key component of a digital twin [1,5,22], which is irrespective of the integration of forecasting and explainability methods. This element facilitates the implementation of forecasting techniques, as they require a substantial amount of data for effective training and accurate predictions [11]. The time series database is based on a domain-specific data model (*Domain Data Model*), representing the concrete data structure used. This contains information such as sampling frequency, measurement units, and possible relations between variables.

The data collected from the sensors are of varied nature due to different manufacturers, sampling rates, and data formats. A *Preprocessing* component is part of the core functionality of the DT to combat this issue. This element is responsible for cleaning and reformatting input data to prepare them for the forecasting models. This includes harmonizing different data formats, imputing missing data, and resampling them to the same frequency. With the preprocessed historic data, a set of *Training Data* and a set of *Testing Data* can be generated for training the forecasting models. *Real-Time Data* streamed from the physical system is also preprocessed and displayed on the DT *Dashboard*. Additionally, a *Virtual Representation* digitally twins the physical system, accessible via the dashboard of the DT. The *Automated Decision Making* component utilizes the data on the dashboard to automate the feedback loop of the DT in two ways: A data feedback loop (Sect. 3.2), and a model feedback loop (Sect. 3.3).

3.2 Forecasting

Forecasting is a self-supervised learning task that does not require labels, due to this, the target variables are known, and no manual data annotations are required. The training and testing data sets are utilized by a *Model Training* element, which implements a training procedure such as gradient descent for machine learning models. Model training is done based on multiple *Performance Metrics*, which describe a forecasting model's predictive power with respect to the ground truth. The training is performed for different model architectures (*Forecasting Model*), which are stored in a *Model Catalog*, where performance metrics are assigned to each model based on the training outcomes.

When model training is finished, a *Smart Model Selection* element decides which models are the most suitable for real-time operation based on the models' measured performance during training. Once in operation, the *Operational Models* receive preprocessed *Real-Time Data* stemming from the sensors and make *Forecasts* using their learned weights. Due to the real-time application of the system, the importance of the latency of model predictions can differ depending on the use case. In the dashboard, both the real-time data and the forecasts are visualized for the *Human Operator* interacting with the DT. Further, the *data feedback loop* connects the DT to the physical system, representing the well-known actuator feedback loop [5].

3.3 Explainability

With the forecast and the operational model, one or more *Explainers* initiate the forecast explanation pipeline. An explainer can either be inherent to the fore-

Table 2. Properties of explainers and explanations in our meta-model.

Property	Description
Portability	The range of models the explainer can be applied to
Expressive Power	The structure of explanations generated by the explainer
Translucency	The extent to which the explainer relies on examining the model's internal structure
Algor. Complexity	The computational demand of generating the explanation
Accuracy	How well the explanation predicts unseen data
Stability	How similar explanations are for similar input instances
Novelty	How well the explanation identifies instances from regions far from the training data distribution
Representativeness	The extent to which the explanation covers multiple instances or the entire model
Consistency	How similar explanations are between models trained on the same task with similar predictions
Certainty	How well the explanation reflects the model's confidence
Comprehensibility	How easily humans can understand the explanation
Fidelity	How closely it approximates the model's predictions
Deg. of importance	How clearly the explanation conveys the data's importance

casting model or applied post hoc as a separate method [13]. The meta-model shows different types of explainers (such as *Counterfactual Explainers* or *Importance Explainers*) which represent distinct explanation approaches. An explainer additionally possesses a set of *Explainer Properties*, which are attributes characterizing the explainer. In the meta-model we list the properties of explanation methods presented in the de facto standard interpretability book of Molnar [15].

Each explainer generates an *Explanation*, which can either be local (related to an individual forecast) or global (explaining the forecasting model as a whole). An individual explanation can be characterized with one or more *Explanation Properties*, which are distinct from explainer properties. We again follow Molnar's [15] definitions for properties of explanations, which align well with the explainer properties. Due to space limitations, we are not describing explainer and explanation properties in further detail, and refer to Molnar's book for an extensive description.

The resulting set of explanations is presented by *Explanation Visualizers*, where each explanation can be used by multiple visualizers. Explanation visualizers can, for example, be temporal importance maps or example-based prototype visualizations. As a result, the visual representations of the explanations are presented for the human operator on the dashboard of the DT. Based on this, the automated decision making component triggers a second feedback loop that we termed *model feedback loop* links to the model training component. This feedback loop dynamically adapts the model training, giving different weights to the input data based on the system's explanations.

4   Evaluation

We evaluate our meta-model for explainable forecasting in digital twins, as seen in Sect. 3, by deploying it to a smart building in the construction domain. This use case has been selected, as the authors are actively engaged in this field, with a real-world use case available for exploration.

4.1   Meta-model

The modeled DT has the goal of reducing energy consumption in a smart building. The physical system provides multiple sensor-based measurements: temperature, humidity, energy consumption, and cooling and heating system data. The sensor data are streamed to InfluxDB, which is used as a *Time Series Database* within the DT. *Preprocessing* includes outlier normalization and scaling to prepare the data for the forecasting algorithms. The 2 years of available historical data are split into 18 months of *Training Data* and 6 months of *Testing Data*. Further, the *Real-Time Data* from the smart building are processed by the DT.

Internally, the digital twin uses stochastic gradient descent as a *Model Training* algorithm, which optimizes for metrics such as the *Performance Metrics* Mean Absolute Error (MAE) and Mean Squared Error (MSE). Since there is a vast number of *Forecasting Model* architectures, the *Model Catalog* only contains three selected architectures: iTransformer [12], a recent transformer-based architecture; GRU [3], a well-known recurrent neural network-based architecture, and N-BEATS [18], a multilayer perceptron architecture, which is inherently interpretable. Table 3 outlines the performance metrics we obtained for the three models in our use case. Notably, iTransformer achieves the lowest error, followed by N-BEATS, with the GRU network having the highest error. With the training performance metrics, iTransformer was selected as it provided the best performance, while N-BEATS was additionally selected, as it offers inherent interpretability. The two models are used as *Operational Models*, making *Forecasts* in real-time.

Table 3. Performance metrics of the forecasting models during model training

Algorithm	MAE	MSE	Interpretable
iTransformer	**0.278**	**0.132**	No
GRU	0.433	0.242	No
N-BEATS	0.322	0.156	Yes

Forecasting and explainability were assessed using two approaches:

iTransformer with TS-MULE: As iTransformer lacks inherent interpretability, the model-agnostic TS-MULE *Explainer* was applied to generate importance-based *Explanations*. These explanations provide insights into the relative influence of input features on forecasts, visualized with color-coded segment importance in Fig. 3. The *Portability* of TS-MULE makes it adaptable to various models, though its *Expressive Power* and *Translucency* are limited due to its reliance on input perturbations.

N-BEATS: This model inherently decomposes forecasts into trend and seasonality components, which are visualized in Fig. 4. Its built-in interpretability eliminates the need for external explainers and adds no *Algorithmic Complexity*. However, it lacks *Portability* and *Translucency* compared to TS-MULE.

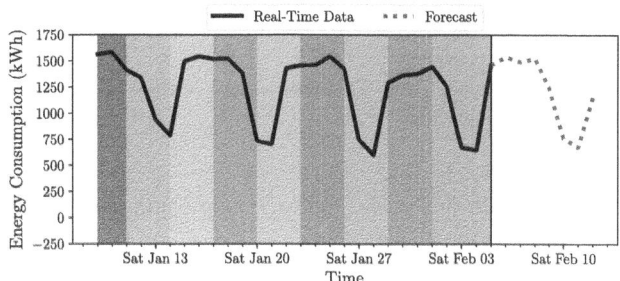

Fig. 3. The Dashboard with the importance-based post-hoc Explanations of iTransformer's Forecast showing feature importance in shades of red for each segment of the Real-Time Data.

The *Dashboard* aggregates *Real-Time Data*, *Forecasts*, and *Explanations*, enabling the building manager (*Human Operator*) to monitor the system. Figures 3 and 4 illustrate this in two exemplary ways. The importance scores in Fig. 3 aid the operator in understanding critical features driving the predictions, where the peaks of the data receive particular importance. Figure 4 highlights the decomposition of energy consumption into trend and seasonality, allowing the operator to recognize systematic patterns. By leveraging the explanations in addition to the forecasts, the operator can identify anomalies or trends and adjust operational strategies accordingly. For example, a snowstorm in winter triggers a sudden outside temperature drop, which requires more heating to keep the building temperature stable. For this, forecasts show how energy consumption evolves over the next day, while explanations highlight that the trend of energy consumption is increasing, which is related to the drop in outside temperature. This allows the operator to more easily comprehend forecasts, and can help them to adjust the air conditioning and heating systems proactively.

In our use case, the dashboard summarizes the current state of the smart building, visualizing historic data, forecasts, and explanations. The building manager, acting as the *Human Operator*, observes the dashboard and can act based on the presented insights: Forecasts and explanations aid the building manager in deciding whether or not to change the building's actuator settings. The *Automated Decision Making*, on the other hand, acts automatically based on the data. For instance, in case of excessive energy usage during a weekend, this component would turn off non-critical lighting and heating actuators. The *data feedback loop* sends control sequences to the building's heating, ventilation,

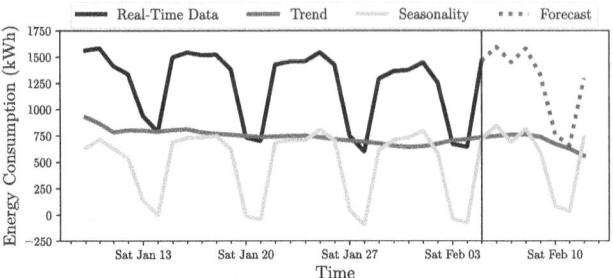

Fig. 4. The dashboard with the Real-Time Data, and N-BEATS' inherent component-based Explanations of its Forecast.

and lighting system, while the *model feedback loop* configures adjustable feature weights for the model training algorithm.

5   Discussion

Overall, when integrating explainable forecasting with digital twins, a balance between explainability and forecasting performance needs to be found. As shown in the performance evaluation in Sect. 4, opaque non-interpretable algorithms often perform better than interpretable algorithms. Generally, algorithms that are more interpretable show lower performance, while better-performing models are not interpretable. This trade-off needs to be taken into account when designing a DT solution utilizing explainable forecasting techniques.

Our meta-model shows the human operator in the center of the application, where they interact with the dashboard, monitoring the status of the system, current forecasts, and explanations. Explainable digital twins are naturally human-centered, as the integration of explainability is most relevant in a human-in-the-loop system [26]. Although the decision-making within our meta-model is fully automatic, involving a human operator is essential, as they can monitor and assess the processes within the DT.

We evaluated our meta-model in the domain of smart buildings, however, the meta-model itself is not domain-specific and can be applied in different scenarios. In the medical context of a human digital twin, patient health values can be forecast, and explanations are key for doctors to make informed decisions in this field [21]. In the manufacturing domain, with a DT of a production line, the production line manager represents the human operator. Forecasts of production efficiency and their explanations would help the operator understand why a change in configuration is beneficial.

In this work, we consider two feedback loops: the data feedback loop between the digital twin and the physical system as well as the DT-internal model feedback loop. The data feedback loop is automated based on the forecasts of the operational model. This emphasizes how forecasting can benefit a digital twin in optimizing its physical counterpart. Explainability indirectly benefits the DT for the same purpose. The model feedback loop improves model training based on the explanations made, which can be factors such as feature importance.

The evaluation of this study was restricted to energy consumption data from the smart building. The smart building we worked with measures multiple other variables, such as temperatures, solar irradiation, or water flow, which were not included in this study. When applying explanation techniques to complex data involving multiple variables, visualization techniques need to adapt accordingly. Using fewer or more sensor variables does not affect our meta-model, nevertheless, it does influence how an explanation visualizer presents explanations to the human operator, as explanations become more complex with more data.

6   Conclusion

In this study, we have introduced and evaluated a meta-model for the integration of explainable forecasting with digital twins. The proposed meta-model describes the interaction of the DT with the physical system while providing a more detailed focus on the integration of forecasting and explainability with the core functionality of the digital twin. We have evaluated our meta-model by deploying it to a use case in the context of a smart building.

This meta-model serves as foundational work for digital twins utilizing explainable forecasting methods. Overall, the contribution is aimed at both practitioners and researchers in the field who can design their digital twins according to our meta-model. We believe that future research should systematically characterize other aspects of AI integration with digital twins using specific meta-models. This would contribute to a shared understanding of digital twins' capabilities, dependencies, and requirements when coupled with AI functionality.

References

1. Aheleroff, S., Xu, X., Zhong, R.Y., Lu, Y.: Digital twin as a service (DTaaS) in industry 4.0: an architecture reference model. Adv. Eng. Inform. **47**, 101225 (2021)
2. Al-Ali, A.R., Gupta, R., Zaman Batool, T., Landolsi, T., Aloul, F., Al Nabulsi, A.: Digital twin conceptual model within the context of internet of things. Future Internet **12**(10), 163 (2020)
3. Bahdanau, D.: Neural machine translation by jointly learning to align and translate. arXiv preprint arXiv:1409.0473 (2014)
4. Croatti, A., Gabellini, M., Montagna, S., Ricci, A.: On the integration of agents and digital twins in healthcare. J. Med. Syst. **44**(9), 161 (2020)
5. De Benedictis, A., Flammini, F., Mazzocca, N., Somma, A., Vitale, F.: Digital twins for anomaly detection in the industrial internet of things: conceptual architecture and proof-of-concept. IEEE Trans. Ind. Inform. (2023)
6. Grieves, M.: Digital twin: manufacturing excellence through virtual factory replication. White Paper **1**(2014), 1–7 (2014)
7. Hakiri, A., Gokhale, A., Yahia, S.B., Mellouli, N.: A comprehensive survey on digital twin for future networks and emerging internet of things industry. Comput. Netw. 110350 (2024)

8. Kharlamova, N., Træholt, C., Hashemi, S.: A digital twin of battery energy storage systems providing frequency regulation. In: 2022 IEEE International Systems Conference (SysCon), pp. 1–7. IEEE (2022)

9. Kreuzer, T., Papapetrou, P., Zdravkovic, J.: AI explainability methods in digital twins: a model and a use case. In: International Conference on Enterprise Design, Operations, and Computing, pp. 3–20. Springer (2024)

10. Kreuzer, T., Papapetrou, P., Zdravkovic, J.: Artificial intelligence in digital twins-a systematic literature review. Data Knowl. Eng. 102304 (2024)

11. LeCun, Y., Bengio, Y., Hinton, G.: Deep learning. Nature **521**(7553), 436–444 (2015)

12. Liu, Y., et al.: itransformer: inverted transformers are effective for time series forecasting. arXiv preprint arXiv:2310.06625 (2023)

13. Loyola-Gonzalez, O.: Black-box vs. white-box: understanding their advantages and weaknesses from a practical point of view. IEEE Access **7**, 154096–154113 (2019)

14. Makridakis, S., Spiliotis, E., Assimakopoulos, V.: The m4 competition: 100,000 time series and 61 forecasting methods. Int. J. Forecast. **36**(1), 54–74 (2020)

15. Molnar, C.: Interpretable machine learning. Lulu. com (2020)

16. Montini, E., Bettoni, A., Ciavotta, M., Carpanzano, E., Pedrazzoli, P.: A meta-model for modular composition of tailored human digital twins in production. Procedia CIRP **104**, 689–695 (2021)

17. Opoku, D., Perera, S., Osei-Kyei, R., Rashidi, M.: Digital twin application in the construction industry: a literature review. J. Build. Eng. **40**, 102726 (2021)

18. Oreshkin, B.N., Carpov, D., Chapados, N., Bengio, Y.: N-beats: neural basis expansion analysis for interpretable time series forecasting. arXiv preprint arXiv:1905.10437 (2019)

19. Pang, J., Huang, Y., Xie, Z., Li, J., Cai, Z.: Collaborative city digital twin for the covid-19 pandemic: a federated learning solution. Tsinghua Sci. Technol. **26**(5), 759–771 (2021)

20. Pylianidis, C., Osinga, S., Athanasiadis, I.N.: Introducing digital twins to agriculture. Comput. Electron. Agric. **184**, 105942 (2021)

21. Rasheed, K., Qayyum, A., Ghaly, M., Al-Fuqaha, A., Razi, A., Qadir, J.: Explainable, trustworthy, and ethical machine learning for healthcare: a survey. Comput. Biol. Med. **149**, 106043 (2022)

22. Tao, F., Zhang, M., Liu, Y., Nee, A.Y.: Digital twin driven prognostics and health management for complex equipment. CIRP Ann. **67**(1), 169–172 (2018)

23. Tekinerdogan, B.: On the notion of digital twins: a modeling perspective. Systems **11**(1), 15 (2022)

24. Tu, Z., Qiao, L., Nowak, R., Lv, H., Lv, Z.: Digital twins-based automated pilot for energy-efficiency assessment of intelligent transportation infrastructure. IEEE Trans. Intell. Transp. Syst. **23**(11), 22320–22330 (2022)

25. Yang, X., Liu, X., Zhang, H., Fu, L., Yu, Y.: Meta-model-based shop-floor digital twin architecture, modeling and application. Robot. Comput.-Integr. Manufact. **84**, 102595 (2023)

26. Zhang, N., Bahsoon, R., Tziritas, N., Theodoropoulos, G.: Explainable human-in-the-loop dynamic data-driven digital twins. In: International Conference on Dynamic Data Driven Applications Systems, pp. 233–243. Springer (2022)

Towards a Digital Twin of a Decanter Centrifuge for Wastewater Management

Massimo Callisto De Donato[1]($\boxtimes$) (iD), Flavio Corradini[1] (iD), Niccolò Francioni[1] (iD), Francesco Giovannini[2] (iD), Barbara Re[1] (iD), and Andrea Scacchia[2]

[1] School of Science and Technology, Computer Science Department, University of Camerino, Via Madonna delle Carceri 7, 62032 Camerino, Italy
{massimo.callisto,flavio.corradini,niccolo.francioni, barbara.re}@unicam.it
[2] EuroEngineering, Viale dei Mutilati e Invalidi del Lavoro 103, 63100 Campolungo-Villa Sant'Antonio, Italy
{f.giovannini,a.scacchia}@eeng.it

Abstract. Over the past few years, with the advent of Industry 4.0, it is noticeable how the Digital Twin concept fits well to fulfill the required needs of increasing efficiency, productivity, and automation. Optimization in Industry 4.0 is important to reduce costs, energy waste and increases productivity, thereby enabling more sustainable processes and environmental benefits. The introduction of Artificial Intelligence in Digital Twins helps create data-driven modeling approaches to monitor, simulate, predict, and optimize visualized entities and contribute to their continuous improvement.

This paper reports an approach for the design of a Digital Twin and Artificial Intelligence used to optimize a decanter centrifuge. The case study uses centrifugal machinery as a reference and outlines a data-driven approach to model the system and determine the optimal working parameters.

Keywords: Digital Twins · Artificial Intelligence · Cyber Physical System · Industry 4.0

1 Introduction and Motivation

The industry has undergone a significant transformation driven by the advent of **Industry 4.0**, which marks a new era characterized by the integration of digital technologies with traditional industrial processes. By leveraging advanced technologies such as Artificial Intelligence (AI), automation, and data analytics, industries can streamline operations, improve resource utilization, minimize downtime, and achieve a higher levels of operational efficiency, productivity and automation [22]. In this scenario, optimization plays a crucial role in Industry 4.0, as it helps to achieve significant cost savings, but also promotes sustainability by reducing environmental impact. Implementing smart optimization strategies helps industries transition to greener practices, reduce carbon emissions, and achieve long-term economic and environmental benefits [18].

J. Grabis and Y. Wautelet (Eds.): CAiSE 2025 Workshops, LNBIP 556, pp. 183–194, 2025.
https://doi.org/10.1007/978-3-031-94931-9_15

Several key technological advances can be recognized as the foundation of Industry 4.0 and contribute to the optimization of industrial processes, such as Cyber-Physical Systems (CPS), Internet of Things (IoT), Big Data Analytics, Cloud Computing and AI [23]. These technologies enable advanced functionalities for real-time data collection, analysis and decision making. Among them, CPS has been identified as the technological backbone for Industry 4.0 [33]. CPSs are industrial automation systems that integrate innovative functionalities through networking to enable connection of the operations of the physical reality with computing and communication infrastructures. CPS are able to fulfill the agile and dynamic requirements of production, and to improve the effectiveness and efficiency of the entire industry, by providing a seamless connectivity and continuous monitoring of equipment and machinery [22]. AI is also recognized as a pivotal technology in Industry 4.0 as it enables software, systems, machines and devices to perceive, sense, develop, understand and learn from their experiences or to augment human activities [1]. AI can be used to perform several tasks such as predictive maintenance of machinery, preventing breakdowns or detecting defects in products [17].

Digital Twin (DT) is an emerging technology that allows a virtual representation of a physical asset and processes, enabling simulations, real-time prediction, optimization, monitoring, controlling, and improved decision making [27]. Thanks to these features, DT contributes to numerous applications in various fields such as smart cities, manufacturing, healthcare [5,7,13,34]. In Industry 4.0, DT technology has become increasingly important in the industrial revolution due to its applicability and benefits in process optimization [12,21]. The integration of big data and AI further enhances its potential and plays a key role in the development of DT-based systems [28].

CPSs and DTs fit naturally into the Industry 4.0 landscape, as one is a resource for the other. CPSs securely collect data from physical processes and perform regulatory control operations at the edge for DTs [25]. Both technologies involve a cyber-physical interaction to improve the management and operation of the physical world. However, DTs focus more on virtual models while CPSs focus on collaboration of *Computing*, *Communication*, and *Control*, known as the 3C [31]. Therefore, models and data are the core elements in a DT, to help interpret and predict the behavior of the physical world based on various data, while sensors and actuators can be considered as the core elements in CPS.

AI is also crucial for DT technology, as it enables real-time data analysis, predictive modeling, and autonomous decision-making. An AI-powered DT continuously learns from sensor data, improving the accuracy of simulations and optimizing industrial processes. This integration enhances predictive maintenance, reduces downtime and enables adaptive manufacturing [3]. Furthermore, AI-driven analytics allow for early fault detection and system efficiency improvements, making Digital Twins essential for Industry 4.0 advancements [32].

In this paper, we report on our experience in developing a DT solution for the optimization of a CPS used in sludge dewatering in the wastewater treatment process. The CPS consists of an industrial centrifuge, also called decanter. The

DT solution aims to support the development of a DT of the physical decanter to enable simulation, prediction, and optimization functionalities based on the virtual counterpart. The 3D representation of the physical asset, combined with real-world sensor data, allows operators to monitor the decanter in realtime. The results of the optimization can be used to drive optimization strategies for the physical decanter based on the operational conditions of the plant. This contributes to the reduction of the energy consumption, minimizing wear and maintenance costs, and contributes to improving the quality of the wastewater treatment process. We describe the implementation of the DT solution that relies on the adoption of an open source DT platform to implement the DT of the decanter. We also discuss the optimization module of the DT platform and the challenges we face in its implementation.

The remainder of this paper is organized as follows: Sect. 2 presents the context and our use case scenario. Section 3 describes the design of the DT solution. Section 4 reports on the implementation of the DT solution. Section 5 reports on the current limitations of the DT solution; Sect. 6 reviews the relevant literature on the use of DT for industrial process optimization; Finally, Sect. 7 concludes the paper with suggestions for future research.

2   Context and Reference Scenario

In this section we describe the use case scenario of the wastewater treatment process where the decanter is used for sludge dewatering.

2.1   Wastewater Treatment Plant

Wastewater treatment is the process of removing contaminants from urban or industrial wastewater to return it to the water cycle. The process consists of a succession of different steps as shown in Fig. 1, during which unwanted substances are removed from the wastewater and concentrated in the form of sludge, resulting in a final effluent that can be discharged into a land, lake, river, or sea without causing harm. The purification cycle consists of a combination of several chemical, physical, and biological processes.

While all the various process steps follow one another to purify the water before discharge, the decanter is placed in the sludge treatment stage where all the unwanted substances are concentrated in the form of sludge. Afterwards, the decanter is used to perform a sludge dewatering process before disposal. The importance of the sludge dewatering process relates, for instance, to the transportation costs involved in the disposal of sludge, which must be loaded and transported to landfills. It follows that the removal of water by dewatering lightens the load for its subsequent disposal.

2.2   Decanter

The **decanter**, as shown in Fig. 2, consists of a solid cylindrical **bowl** rotating at a high speed, with an **auger** inside that rotates at a slightly different speed.

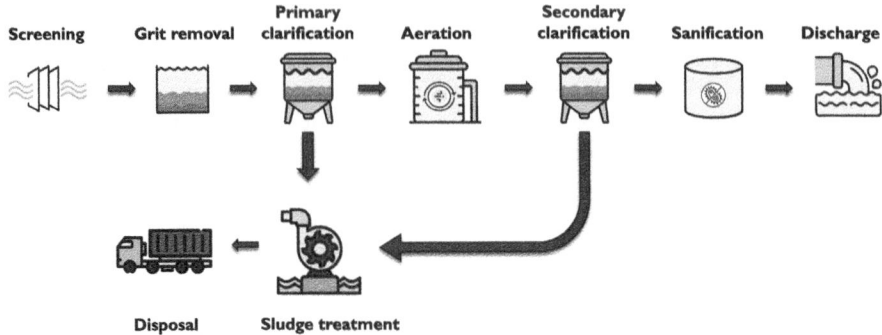

Fig. 1. Example diagram of a wastewater plant

Separation between liquids and suspended solids is achieved by centrifugal force. The differential speed between the bowl and auger provides a conveying motion to collect and remove solids that accumulate on the bowl wall. The clarified liquid then flows down the bowl to exit at one end, while the other end of the bowl is angled inward toward the center, thus providing a beach onto which the solids are conveyed to be discharged from the bowl at the top of the beach [29]. In addition to the rotation of the internal auger, sludge dewatering also occurs with the addition of **polyelectrolyte**, which is a polymer that thickens the solid parts of sludge to facilitate its separation from water.

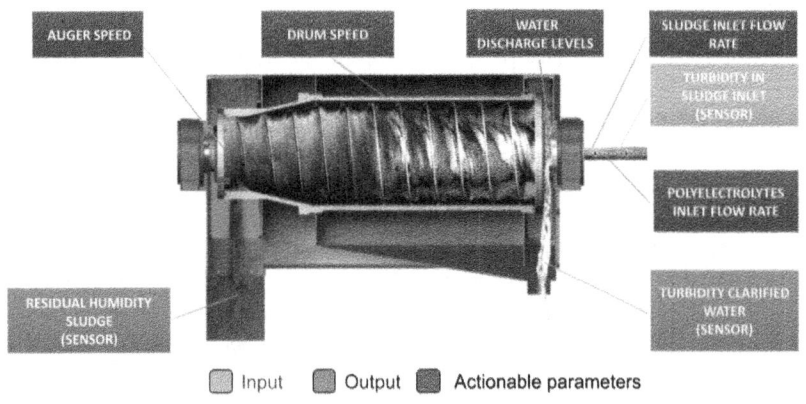

Fig. 2. Decanter sensors diagram

In the decanter, the sludge dewatering can be controlled by changing several parameters such as the rotation speed and the amount of polyelectrolyte. The objective is to find the optimal combination of these parameters that minimize the residual moisture in the sludge, and maximize the purification of the effluent water. Furthermore, since the polyelectrolyte is rather expensive, the optimal solution is to minimize at the same time the amount of this element.

Although the decanter is equipped with several sensors (e.g. bowl and auger speed, sludge moisture, polyelectrolyte dilution), the treatment process strongly depends on the experience of the operators. In particular, the operator decides the parameters of the decanter based on the type of sludge to be treated, and these remain unchanged regardless of the operating conditions. In this scenario, DT and AI can be used to create a virtual replica of the decanter, where sensor data can be used to enable simulation and optimization in the virtual world. The results can be provided to the operator to suggest the optimal configuration of the decanter over time. Furthermore, the optimization can be used to automatically adjust the parameters of the physical decanter.

3   Digital Twin Solution

In this section, we describe the design of the DT solution that we have defined to support the operators in the optimization of the decanter in the wastewater treatment process. The components of the solutions are shown in Fig. 3 and described in the following.

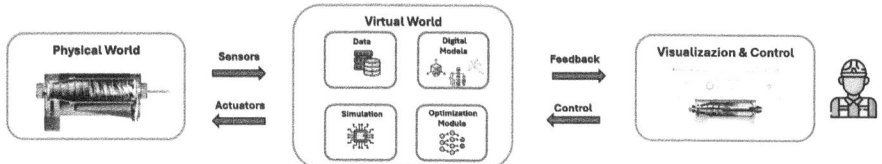

Fig. 3. Digital Twin Design of the case study.

Physical World. This component represents the real world of the treatment plant. At this level we consider the decanter itself, which is the physical counterpart of the DT. The decanter is equipped with sensors to monitor the process and its status, and enabled with a connection to communicate the sensed measurement to the digital counterpart. Actuators are also installed to control the parameters of the decanter based on the feedback from the virtual world.

Virtual World. This component represents the digital space that aggregates digital models and data collected from the physical world. The digital models allow to represent a specific aspect of the physical entity (e.g. 2D/3D representation, behavior model, etc.). Data from the physical world is integrated and used together with the digital models to replicate the state of the physical counterpart. At this level, AI models can be used to implement data-driven models of the DT of the decanter. This combination enables the DT capabilities of real time monitoring, simulation, prediction and optimization.

Visualization and Control. This is the component that enables interaction with the operator. At this level, graphical dashboards and reports can be used to monitor the status of the decanter, analyze the results of the simulated scenario based on the current data, and provide the possible configurations on the decanter to optimize the sludge dewatering process. Depending on the level of automation, the operator can allow the DT to automatically update the decanter parameters based on the optimization results.

4   Digital Twin Implementation

In this section we report on the implementation of the DT solution based on the components described in the previous section.

In the Physical World, the decanter is equipped with several sensors to monitor the sludge dewatering process, such as the residual moisture content of the sludge, measurement of the turbidity of the sludge inlet and the turbidity of the clarified water, bowl and auger speed. The decanter is connected to a Programmable Logic Controller (PLC) to collect the sensor data and control some of the parameters such as bowl speed, the screw speed, and the polyelectrolyte dilution. The PLC is also able to connect to the external systems using standard communication protocols such as HTTPS, MQTT and CoAP.

In the Virtual World, while different DT platform exists [7], we used the open source solution DThingsBoard[1] [8], which provides to us advanced functionalities on top of the IoT platform ThingsBoard[2] DThingsBoard enables the 3D monitoring and visualization of DT models and simulation mechanism to validate the behavior of devices in the design of IoT solutions. Other features based on ThingsBoard are available such as the real-time processing, an embedded rule engine, an alarm systems to report on anomalies on the data. DThingsBoard also supports a set RESTful APIs for the integration with other external systems. In Fig. 4 we described the connection of the physical decanter with DThingsBoard modeled as single device. The collected sensor data can be used to enable the processing functionalities and the creation of customized dashboards.

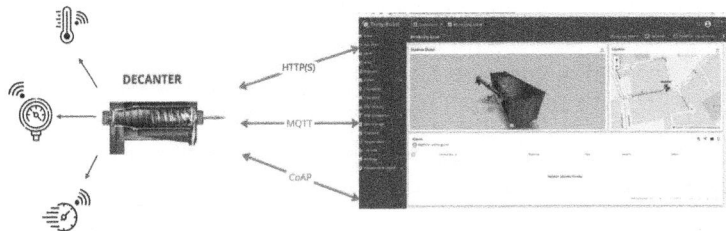

Fig. 4. System overview.

---

[1] DThingsBoard: https://pros.unicam.it/dtplatform.
[2] ThingsBoard: https://thingsboard.io/.

For the Visualization & Control component we implemented a series of graphical dashboards in DThingsBoard. A dashboard consists of the compositions of smaller UI modules called widgets used to easily integrate end-users functionalities such as 2D/3D visualizations, real-time data monitoring, remote device control and alarm management. In Fig. 5 we provided an example of dashboard containing a widget for the 3D visualization of the decanter as well as widgets used to monitor the status of the decanter, including information on sensor data.

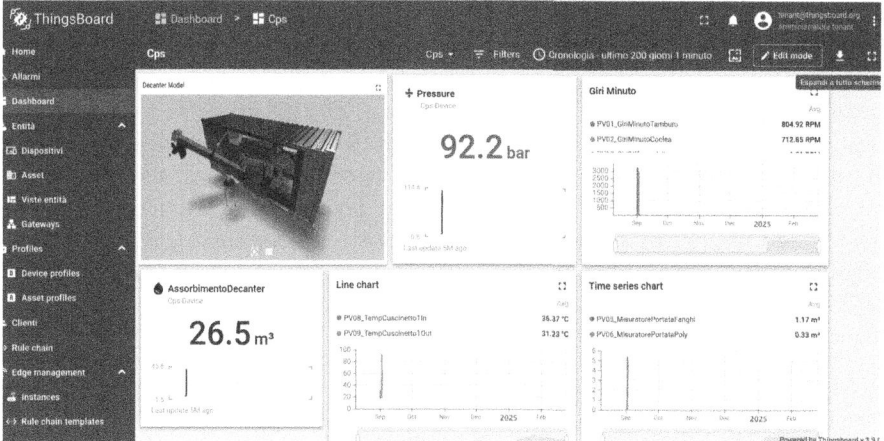

Fig. 5. ThingsBoard dashboard example.

DThingsBoard also allows the definition of dedicated widgets to collect user inputs, which are translated into commands sent to the devices in the real world using the supported communication protocols. We planned to use this feature to allow the operator to modify the decanter parameters based on the optimal configuration of the decanter obtained from the AI models executed in the optimization module under development.

5   Discussion

We describe the implementation of the DT solution where the DThingsBoard platform is used to collect and integrate the sensor data from the physical decanter. This is a fundamental step we have achieved as it allows us to start implementing the DT of the decanter in the virtual world.

The next phase in the implementation of the DT solution is the actual development of an optimization module to be integrated into the DThingsBoard as an additional component. In particular, three possible approaches can be used to this end [27]: **physics-based modeling** is an approach to understanding the behavior of a system by applying the fundamental laws of physics, such as mechanics, thermodynamics and electromagnetism; **data-driven modeling** is an approach that relies on analyzing and learning patterns from data to build models of systems; **hybrid modeling** combines physics-based and data-driven approaches to leverage the strengths of both.

We are evaluating the use of data-driven surrogate-based modeling [4]. This approach allows us to simulate the behavior of a complex system overcoming the lack of knowledge and uncertainties about the behavior to model and limiting the computational requirements needed to run a more detailed mathematical model. Common techniques for building surrogate models include Machine Learning (ML) algorithms such as polynomial response surfaces, kriging, radial basis functions, and artificial neural networks (ANNs) [6].

In Fig. 6 we describe a possible implementation of the surrogate model used for the optimization of the decanter inspired by [15]. The process consists of the following steps. First, a design of experiment is developed to obtain a representative data set of the possible configurations of the CPS. Tests will then be carried out on the decanter to collect the sensor data. The surrogate model will then be created and used as an objective function in an optimization algorithm such as a derivative-free algorithm [30] in order to find the optimal configuration for the CPS. This approach is particularly suitable for black-box optimization or, more generally, when derivative information is not available.

Design of Experiment   **Data Collection**   **Surrogate modeling**   **Optimization**

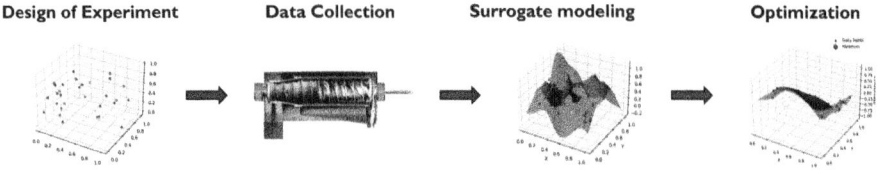

Fig. 6. Surrogate based modeling optimization steps.

Currently, one of the main limitations in implementing a surrogate model for the decanter is the lack of a complete data set. One of the limitations is related to the sensor data from the decanter. We encounter problems related to the electromechanical sensors required to make proper measurements of the dehydration of the sludge, which is one of the parameters to be optimized in the dewatering process. For instance, dried sludge buildup affected the humidity sensor, causing inaccurate readings that corrupted the dataset and prevented the development of an accurate ML algorithm. We also found that historical data set of the sensor data has not been systematically collected and is not sufficiently representative to fully reflect the possible configurations of the decanter. To address this, we are investigating possible experimental design techniques such as the ones described in [2]. In addition, when we designed the experiments, we have to take into account that the tests can only be carried out for a limited period of time in order to avoid production quality defects, since the decanter will be operating in a real wastewater treatment plant subject to the customer's requirements. To mitigate this problem, we are also investigating data augmentation approaches to obtain a larger data set from the one collected, for example, through the use of generative models for the generation of synthetic data [11].

6   Related Work

Several research work focus on the DT for optimization of industrial processes. We report in the following a non-exhaustive list of related work that focus on implementing DTs solutions that rely non data-driven approaches.

In [20] a DT framework is presented for the real-time model predictive control of process parameters of the laser directed-energy deposition (DED) technique, utilizing Long Short-Term Memory (LSTM)-based machine learning as surrogate model and Bayesian optimization to determine the optimal laser power profile.

In [26] a framework is presented for constructing a DT to realize production control optimization in the petrochemical industry. This study introduces guidelines on the use of industrial big data and provides a methodological view on building DT using ML to support process manufacturing industries in optimizing production and improving economic benefits.

In [16] a data-driven DT architecture is proposed for optimized control in process industries. Their DT system reduces severe fluctuations and ensures safe control for industrial processes, employing an adaptive subspace identification method (SIM) to handle multiple faults and provide accurate and timely diagnostic and control information by designing optimized control configurations.

In [34] the authors designed a DT system for iron reverse flotation, with the aim of improving production efficiency by stabilizing product quality and avoiding reagent waste. The system uses a transformer algorithm to monitor product quality based on the process froth image and adjust the reagent system accordingly using an extreme learning machine (ELM) algorithm.

About related works that discuss the optimization of a decanter machinery, we did not found examples based on data-driven approaches as we discussed in our work. Most of them relies in general on numerical simulations and physics-based computational models (e.g. see [14, 19, 24]).

The related works previously reported rely on approaches that are not directly related to the optimization of CPS as in our DT solution. Moreover, differently from them we proposed the adoption of a standard open source DT platform called DThingsBoard. While other DT platforms exist [9], DThingsBoard enable the execution of the DT models into an integrated environment supporting the end users with advanced functionalities that allow 3D monitoring and visualization of DT models. Therefore, our work aims to provide a specific application on this topic supported by an open source technological solution based on DThingsBoard.

7   Conclusion and Future Work

In this paper, we have described our experience in defining a DT solution for modeling a CPS of an industrial machine called a decanter, used for sludge dewatering in the wastewater treatment process.

By leveraging DT technology and AI, the solution aims to support the creation of a virtual representation of the physical decanter through DT models, enabling real-time monitoring based on sensor data collected from the physical decanter, performing simulations, predictions, and optimizations of its parameters based on the operating conditions of the plant. These capabilities provide the operator with real-time monitoring and the ability to evaluate optimization scenarios defined by the DT models.

We described the implementation of the DT solution based on the open-source DT platform called DThingsBoard, which enables the collection of sensor data from the decanter, 3D monitoring and visualization features of DT models and real-time processing. DThingsBoard also provides s graphical dashboard for the operator to interact with the DT of the decanter. As future work, we want to investigate the adoption of model-driven techniques [10] to integrate in DThingsBoard in order to represent the overall wastewater treatment process providing more control on the creation of DT models.

We presented the ongoing implementation of the optimization module to adjust the parameters of the decanter according to the operating conditions of the plant. For the implementation we rely on a data-driven surrogate-based modeling approach where ML algorithms learn patterns from data to make simulation and perdiction of the DT. By combining surrogate models with an optimization algorithm, we aim to define the optimal configuration of the decanter and provide feedback to the operator. We also discussed the challenges we face in implementing the surrogate models due to the limited availability of a representative dataset of sensor data which makes it difficult to apply these types of techniques. To address these issues, we are investigating techniques for designing experiments to collect a meaningful dataset from the physical decanter [2]. We are also investigating the application of data augmentation techniques to create larger data sets from the one collected through the experiments [11].

Acknowledgments. This work has been funded by the European Union - NextGenerationEU, Mission 4, Component 2, under the Italian Ministry of University and Research (MUR) National Innovation Ecosystem grant ECS00000041 - VITALITY - CUPJ13C22000430001, and Mission 4 Component 1 CUP J11J24001890006.

Disclosure of Interests. This research is funded by Euro Engineering Srl. The authors declare that there is no conflict of interest regarding the publication of this paper.

References

1. Ahmed, I., Jeon, G., Piccialli, F.: From artificial intelligence to explainable artificial intelligence in industry 4.0: a survey on what, how, and where. IEEE Trans. Ind. Inform. **18**(8), 5031–5042 (2022). https://doi.org/10.1109/TII.2022.3146552
2. Alam, F.M., McNaught, K.R., Ringrose, T.J.: A comparison of experimental designs in the development of a neural network simulation metamodel. Simul. Model. Pract. Theory **12**(7–8), 559–578 (2004)
3. Arinez, J.F., Chang, Q., Gao, R.X., Xu, C., Zhang, J.: Artificial intelligence in advanced manufacturing: current status and future outlook. J. Manuf. Sci. Eng. **142**(11), 110804 (2020)
4. Barkanyi, A., Chovan, T., Nemeth, S., Abonyi, J.: Modelling for digital twins-potential role of surrogate models. Processes **9**(3), 476 (2021)
5. Barricelli, B.R., Casiraghi, E., Fogli, D.: A survey on digital twin: definitions, characteristics, applications, and design implications. IEEE Access **7**, 167653–167671 (2019)
6. Bhosekar, A., Ierapetritou, M.: Advances in surrogate based modeling, feasibility analysis, and optimization: a review. Comput. Chem. Eng. **108**, 250–267 (2018)
7. Callisto De Donato, M., Corradini, F., Fornari, F., Re, B., Romagnoli, M.: Design and development of a digital twin prototype for the SAFE project. In: International Conference on Enterprise Design, Operations, and Computing, pp. 107–122. Springer (2023)
8. Callisto De Donato, M., Corradini, F., Fornari, F., Re, B., Romagnoli, M.: Enabling 3D simulation in thingsboard: a first step towards a digital twin platform. In: International Conference on Enterprise Design, Operations, and Computing, pp. 325–330. Springer (2023)
9. Corradini, F., Fedeli, A., Fornari, F., Polini, A., Re, B.: DTMN a modelling notation for digital twins. In: Enterprise Design, Operations, and Computing. EDOC 2022 Workshops, Bozen-Bolzano, Italy, 4–7 October 2022. Lecture Notes in Business Information Processing, vol. 466, pp. 63–78. Springer (2022)
10. Corradini, F., Fedeli, A., Fornari, F., Polini, A., Re, B.: FloWare: a model-driven approach fostering reuse and customisation in IoT applications modelling and development. Softw. Syst. Model. 1–28 (2022)
11. Figueira, A., Vaz, B.: Survey on synthetic data generation, evaluation methods and GANs. Mathematics **10**(15), 2733 (2022)
12. Fornari, F., et al.: Digital twins of business processes: a research manifesto. Internet Things 101477 (2024)
13. Fuller, A., Fan, Z., Day, C., Barlow, C.: Digital twin: enabling technologies, challenges and open research. IEEE Access **8**, 108952–108971 (2020)
14. Gleiss, M., Nirschl, H.: Modeling separation processes in decanter centrifuges by considering the sediment build-up. Chem. Eng. Technol. **38**(10), 1873–1882 (2015)
15. Golzari, A., Sefat, M.H., Jamshidi, S.: Development of an adaptive surrogate model for production optimization. J. Petrol. Sci. Eng. **133**, 677–688 (2015)
16. He, R., Chen, G., Dong, C., Sun, S., Shen, X.: Data-driven digital twin technology for optimized control in process systems. ISA Trans. **95**, 221–234 (2019)
17. Javaid, M., Haleem, A., Singh, R.P., Suman, R.: Artificial intelligence applications for industry 4.0: a literature-based study. J. Ind. Integr. Manag. **07**(01), 83–111 (2022). https://doi.org/10.1142/S2424862221300040
18. Javaid, M., Haleem, A., Singh, R.P., Suman, R., Gonzalez, E.S.: Understanding the adoption of industry 4.0 technologies in improving environmental sustainability. Sustain. Oper. Comput. **3**, 203–217 (2022)

19. Kang, X., Cai, L., Li, Y., Gao, X., Bai, G.: Investigation on the separation performance and multiparameter optimization of decanter centrifuges. Processes **10**(7), 1284 (2022)
20. Karkaria, V., et al.: Towards a digital twin framework in additive manufacturing: machine learning and Bayesian optimization for time series process optimization. J. Manuf. Syst. **75**, 322–332 (2024)
21. Lee, D., et al.: Digital twin-based analysis and optimization for design and planning of production lines. Machines **10**(12), 1147 (2022)
22. Lu, Y.: Industry 4.0: a survey on technologies, applications and open research issues. J. Ind. Inf. Integr. **6**, 1–10 (2017)
23. Martinelli, A., Mina, A., Moggi, M.: The enabling technologies of industry 4.0: examining the seeds of the fourth industrial revolution. Ind. Corp. Change **30**(1), 161–188 (2021)
24. Menesklou, P., Nirschl, H., Gleiss, M.: Dewatering of finely dispersed calcium carbonate-water slurries in decanter centrifuges: about modelling of a dynamic simulation tool. Sep. Purif. Technol. **251**, 117287 (2020)
25. Mihai, S., et al.: Digital twins: a survey on enabling technologies, challenges, trends and future prospects. IEEE Commun. Surv. Tutor. **24**(4), 2255–2291 (2022)
26. Min, Q., Lu, Y., Liu, Z., Su, C., Wang, B.: Machine learning based digital twin framework for production optimization in petrochemical industry. Int. J. Inf. Manage. **49**, 502–519 (2019)
27. Rasheed, A., San, O., Kvamsdal, T.: Digital twin: values, challenges and enablers from a modeling perspective. IEEE Access **8**, 21980–22012 (2020)
28. Rathore, M.M., Shah, S.A., Shukla, D., Bentafat, E., Bakiras, S.: The role of AI, machine learning, and big data in digital twinning: a systematic literature review, challenges, and opportunities. IEEE Access **9**, 32030–32052 (2021)
29. Records, A., Sutherland, K.: Decanter centrifuge handbook. Elsevier (2001)
30. Rios, L.M., Sahinidis, N.V.: Derivative-free optimization: a review of algorithms and comparison of software implementations. J. Global Optim. **56**(3), 1247–1293 (2012). https://doi.org/10.1007/s10898-012-9951-y
31. Tao, F., Qi, Q., Wang, L., Nee, A.: Digital twins and cyber–physical systems toward smart manufacturing and industry 4.0: correlation and comparison. Engineering **5**(4), 653–661 (2019)
32. Tao, F., Zhang, H., Liu, A., Nee, A.Y.: Digital twin in industry: state-of-the-art. IEEE Trans. Industr. Inf. **15**(4), 2405–2415 (2018)
33. Xu, L.D., Xu, E.L., Li, L.: Industry 4.0: state of the art and future trends. Int. J. Prod. Res. **56**(8), 2941–2962 (2018)
34. Zhang, D., Gao, X.: A digital twin dosing system for iron reverse flotation. J. Manuf. Syst. **63**, 238–249 (2022)

Digital Twins in Systems-of-Systems on the Internet-of-Vehicles: The Case of Overtaking Maneuver

Flavio Oquendo[✉] [iD]

IRISA – UMR CNRS 6074, Univ. Bretagne Sud, Vannes, France
flavio.oquendo@irisa.fr

Abstract. A software-intensive system-of-systems (SoS) is architecturally designed to exhibit emergent behavior from the interactions between independent constituent systems. With the upcoming generation of connected and automated vehicles, cooperative driving is becoming a major operational domain for safety critical SoS. Overtaking is one of the toughest driving maneuvers for either manual or automated execution, responsible for most of the traffic crashes, e.g., in recent years, almost a third of all people killed on country roads in France died in accidents involving overtaking. This paper investigates a novel approach based on digital twins, where cooperative overtaking is designed to be the emergent behavior outcome of connected and automated vehicles empowered by digital twins, constituting together an SoS. In this approach, each connected and automated vehicle has its own digital twin for cooperative driving, deployed in the cloud, to which it is connected through vehicle-to-network communication. These digital twins, each one influencing the behavior of the corresponding connected and automated vehicle, have their interactions mediated (by design) to raise an emergent behavior resulting in a safe execution of the overtaking maneuver. This novel approach is supported by a model-based engineering workflow and a software toolset for SoS on the Internet-of-Vehicles (IoV).

Keywords: Digital Twins (DTw) · Systems of Systems (SoS) · Connected and Automated Vehicles (CAV) · Internet of Vehicles (IoV) · Overtaking Maneuver

1 Introduction

The pervasiveness of the networks increasingly has made possible to interconnect systems that were independently developed, operated, and managed, yielding a new kind of complex system, i.e., a system that is itself composed of systems, the so-called system-of-systems (SoS) [1, 6]. They are evolutionary developed from systems to achieve missions not possible by a system alone. This is the case of SoSs found in areas as diverse as aeronautics, automotive, manufacturing, healthcare, and transportation [5].

Complexity is indeed intrinsically associated to SoSs by its very nature that implies emergent behaviors [12]. In SoSs, missions are achieved through emergent behaviors drawn from the interaction between constituent systems [10].

J. Grabis and Y. Wautelet (Eds.): CAiSE 2025 Workshops, LNBIP 556, pp. 195–206, 2025.
https://doi.org/10.1007/978-3-031-94931-9_16

Nowadays, the Internet-of-Things (IoT) enables the engineering of SoSs, which are opportunistically formed for achieving specified missions in specific operational environments. In particular, in the subset of IoT known as the Internet-of-Vehicles (IoV), progressively made possible by the advent of the Cellular Vehicle-to-Everything (C-V2X) technology [3], where "things" are connected and automated vehicles (CAV) [22], the challenge is to coordinate those vehicles for performing together traffic-related maneuvers, such as vehicle overtaking, junction crossing, and platooning.

In fact, one of the toughest driving maneuvers for either manual or automated execution is vehicle overtaking, in particular in the case of two-way single roads [8]. Overtaking is responsible for most of the traffic crashes today, e.g., almost a third of all people killed on country roads in France died in accidents involving overtaking in recent years.

The key challenge in coordinating overtaking maneuvers is to solve the problem of how to handle the interactions between a vehicle and its surrounding vehicles in a way that allows a vehicle to safely perform overtaking [16, 17].

More specifically, on the IoV, for the case of connected and automated vehicles operating cooperative maneuvers [21], the consequent research question is: how an automated driving system of a connected vehicle shall interact with its nearby vehicles to safely perform overtaking, knowing that each of its surrounding vehicles is managerially and operationally independent?

To address this research question, we have developed a novel model-based approach for supporting the formation and operation of SoSs to execute cooperative driving maneuvers by empowering connected and automated vehicles with digital twins.

This novel engineering approach brings contributions beyond the state-of-the-art to the formal description of SoSs exposing emergent behaviors relying on mediated interactions between the digital twins of the concerned connected and automated vehicles. The solution presented for the case of a cooperative overtaking maneuver demonstrates its relevant application on the IoV.

The remainder of this paper is organized as follows. Section 2 presents a typical case of overtaking maneuver. Section 3 introduces the concepts underlying our model-based approach, supported by digital twins, for coordinating cooperative overtaking maneuvers. Section 4 describes the engineering workflow supporting this novel model-based approach for digital twin-enabled SoSs. Section 5 exposes an excerpt of the digital twin-enabled SoS solution applied for the cooperative vehicle overtaking maneuver. In Sect. 6, we outline the implemented software toolset for architecting SoS with digital twins supporting the presented model-based approach for IoV. In Sect. 7, we position our proposed model-based approach, integrating digital twins and SoSs, to support cooperative driving with respect to related work. Section 8 concludes the paper.

2 The Case of the Overtaking Maneuver Enabled by C-V2X

Recently, with the advent of the standardized network technology named Cellular Vehicle-to-Everything (C-V2X), which provides one unified solution for V2V (vehicle-to-vehicle), V2I (vehicle-to-infrastructure), V2P (vehicle-to-pedestrian) and, importantly, V2N (vehicle-to-network), by leveraging the existing 5G cellular network infrastructure, it is now feasible to use V2N to provide cloud computing for coordinating safety-critical real-time cooperative maneuvers.

In this technological context, we have studied the situation where every connected and automated vehicle possesses the technical capacity to have its own digital twin, which is deployed in the cloud to support cooperative driving via V2N.

Our emphasis is on how the paradigm of digital twins can enhance the IoV, via V2N, to support cooperative driving of connected and automated vehicles, focusing on the intricate case of overtaking vehicles on two-way country roads.

Fig. 1. Vehicles in a typical overtaking maneuver in a two-way road

Let us recall a typical overtaking scenario on a two-way country road, as depicted in Fig. 1. This overtaking maneuver is the one of a vehicle (the overtaking *ego vehicle*, #2 in the figure) going to pass a slower moving vehicle (the overtaken *target vehicle*, #1 in the figure), travelling in the same lane and direction, on a road. The lane used for the overtaking is an adjacent lane (the one that is further from the road shoulder). For executing the overtaking, the ego vehicle will change lane from the right to the left then drive on the left lane until it pass the target vehicle and later change lane again from the left to the right to come back to the right lane just in front of the target vehicle, while another vehicle may be approaching in the opposite direction during the overtaking maneuver (the *oncoming vehicle*, #4 in the figure). Also, the ego vehicle may be followed by another vehicle just behind of it (the *following vehicle*, #3 in the figure).

Note that in this typical overtaking scenario in a two-way road, the overtaking maneuver consists of one "lane change" from the right lane to the left lane (from position 1 to 2), one "lane keep" on the left lane (from position 2 to 3), and a "lane change" back to the right lane (from position 3 to 4) after passing the target vehicle and finally maintaining a safe headway (position 5), as also depicted in Fig. 1. Note too that between these two lane changes, the ego vehicle needs to move faster than the target vehicle for passing it (the former on the left lane, the latter on the right lane).

To guarantee a safe overtaking maneuver, the ego vehicle must be able to guarantee, when initiating the overtaking maneuver, a safe distance between the ego vehicle and the target vehicle to be overtaken as well as it must take care that the following vehicle is not itself initiating an overtaking maneuver. Under these conditions, it must wait for an appropriate situation to initiate the initial lane change maneuver, taking into account the varying width of the road, and then it must achieve a situation where there is an appropriate gap in front of the target vehicle to safely execute the final lane change to be able to safely return to the right lane before maintaining a safe headway.

3 Cooperative Overtaking Maneuver Enabled by Digital Twins

Having presented a typical vehicle overtaking maneuver, let us now address the cooperative overtaking maneuver supported by C-V2X on the IoV.

There are different strategies for coordinating the overtaking maneuver between connected and automated vehicles equipped with C-V2X. We will focus on the so-called decentralized maneuver coordination [7], which, for cooperative overtaking, is the one resulting of the choreography of the different connected and automated vehicles involved in the overtaking maneuver, in our case, the ego vehicle, the target vehicle, the following vehicle, and the oncoming vehicle.

Fig. 2. Every SoS constituent system is a connected vehicle together with its own digital twin

Under this assumption, in our approach for digital twin-enabled SoS, where digital twins are deployed in the cloud, accessed via V2N, as depicted in Fig. 2, as well as where each vehicle is bidirectionally connected to its digital twin responsible for coordinating maneuvers, also shown in Fig. 2, cooperative driving is performed by connected and automated vehicles that are inherently operationally and managerially independent and have been augmented with corresponding digital twins for coordinating maneuvers.

Our approach actually adopts an SoS perspective, where all the involved vehicles in the driving maneuver opportunistically form together a system of systems during the period of the maneuver.

That SoS for cooperative driving, formed during maneuver execution, is architecturally designed to produce the emergent behavior realizing the cooperative maneuver, which is indeed raised from the mediated interactions between the digital twins representing their target entities, i.e., the corresponding connected and automated vehicles.

Note that every digital twin is related to a connected and automated vehicle, i.e., its physical twin, involved in a specific maneuver, discovered opportunistically at operational time. It is the system of digital system twins that coordinate the maneuvers.

Note also that every digital twin, in this system of digital system twins, has a bidirectional communication with its physical counterpart, i.e., the related connected and automated vehicle. Everyone, thereby, represents the linked physical connected and automated vehicle in the cloud as well is able to command and control its linked physical automated vehicle involved in the specific cooperative maneuver.

More specifically, from the complex system perspective, as systems-of-systems are complex systems, they intrinsically create emergent behavior [12].

Let us now recall what is exactly an emergent behavior and how an emergent behavior can be described.

An emergent behavior is defined as a global behavior that arises out of the interactions between parts of a whole and which cannot be predicted or extrapolated from the behavior of the individual parts. An emergent behavior is a macro-scale behavior, i.e., a behavior of the whole, instead of a behavior of the parts.

In the SoS design framework we have developed along the years, emergent behaviors are architected grounded on the principle of supervenience [15]. Supervenience is the trans-ordinal relation that is applied to describe emergence where the macro-scale property is determined by its micro-scale properties, i.e., the emergent macro-scale properties supervene on the micro-scale properties.

Therefore, based on the supervenience principle, emergent behavior (observed at macro-scale) is determined by micro-scale behaviors subject to upward causation.

Thereby, to architecturally describe an emergent behavior of an SoS, we define micro-scale behaviors that, by upward causation, will form the required macro-scale emergent behavior. Consequently, by applying supervenience, we can define how connected and automated vehicles empowered with digital twins will interact to create an emergent behavior that safely executes a cooperative overtaking maneuver [15].

4 Model-Based Approach for Digital Twin-Enabled SoS on IoV

Let us now present our approach for designing and developing digital twin-enabled SoSs on the IoV and the solution to the case under study in this paper, i.e., the cooperative overtaking maneuver. As mentioned, we focus on decentralized maneuver coordination, in our case enabled by digital twins. In our case, thereby, the decentralized maneuver coordination relies solely on the communication between the digital twins of the involved connected and automated vehicles to support coordinated maneuvers.

The assumption underlying our approach for designing digital twin-enabled SoSs on the IoV is that every digital twin provides a virtual replica of its physical counterpart which is virtually indistinguishable from its physical twin, in the sense that it dynamically replicates the behavior and properties of the physical twin as well as enriches that replica with additional information about the physical counterpart, from a specific viewpoint (in our case, limited to the variables that are relevant for cooperative driving). It is in fact a dynamic digital representation (dynamic in the sense that the physical system and its digital twin are connected from a behavioral viewpoint). It enables thereby to represent the relevant characteristics needed to design and implement specialized digital system twins supporting cooperative driving maneuvers.

The architecture-centric model-based engineering approach we have developed is carried out in three phases as depicted in Fig. 3.

The first phase focuses on the modeling of an SoS architecture for supporting the cooperative driving maneuver addressed in the primary requirements specification. During this phase, the SoS architect conceives a model of the SoS architecture that meets the requirements specification for the cooperative maneuver in question. That model also includes the specifications of the constituent systems and their mediators as well as their coalitions, as defined in [15], to enable emergent behaviors that can realize the required cooperative driving maneuver.

In fact, in our approach for describing SoS architectures [15], SoS models are specified in terms of constituent systems and mediators that mediate their interactions.

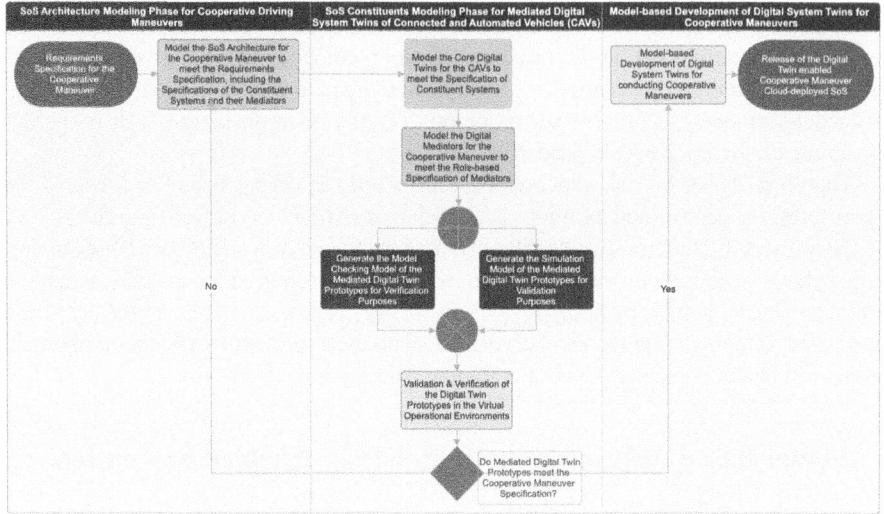

Fig. 3. The model-based approach for SoSs enabled by digital twins on the IoV

The second phase focuses on the refinement of the SoS architecture model specified in the first phase by conceiving models of the specified SoS constituents and corresponding digital system twins of the identified connected and automated vehicles. The outcome of this second phase is the validated and verified models of the digital twin prototypes. These dynamic digital representations aim to act on the one hand as the virtual twins of the identified connected and automated vehicles and on the other hand as mediators of these vehicles during the execution of the cooperative driving maneuver. Note that those physical vehicles may play different virtual roles in different cooperative maneuvers.

The third phase focuses on the implementation of the refined SoS architecture model defined in the second phase by carrying out the model-based development of the mediated digital system twins for the cooperative maneuver resulting in the release the digital twin enabled cooperative maneuver as a cloud application, ready to be deployed on a public traffic cloud.

Let us now zoom into the second phase, which is responsible for conceiving the models of the digital twin prototypes as well as guaranteeing their validation and verification in virtual operational environments.

To achieve that outcome, the initial activity in this phase is to model, if those core twins do not exist, the core digital twins for the connected and automated vehicles involved in the specified cooperative maneuver. Each of these core digital twins concentrates on the behavior and properties of each vehicle in itself and the bidirectional connection between this digital twin and its physical twin as well as on mirroring the physical properties from the physical twin into the digital twin, enhanced with associated informational properties. Those core digital twins, once created and deployed on the cloud, will be reused as they are for all cooperative maneuvers. They are thereby independent of the cooperative maneuvers to be executed.

The next activity is to make those digital twins "learn" how they must behave when they are executing, together with others, cooperative maneuvers according to the different roles that they may play during the maneuvers. In this activity, models for digital mediators are conceived, where each digital mediator specifies how the associated core digital twin must behave to successfully accomplish the cooperative maneuver.

Note that each physical connected and automated vehicle has a digital twin constituted by a core vehicle model that replicates the physical vehicle and possibly several maneuver-based digital mediators, where each of these digital mediators specifies the role of that vehicle in the modelled choreography of a specific cooperative maneuver. Thereby, each digital system twin encompasses its core model that mirrors the physical vehicle as well as several related mediator models, modeling its roles in the choreographies to be executed to realize specific cooperative driving maneuvers.

Once those digital system twins are modelled, from which digital twin prototypes are derived, two concurrent activities are launched: one is in charge of generating the model checking model of the mediated digital twin prototypes for verification purposes and the other activity is in charge of generating the simulation model of the mediated digital twin prototypes for validation purposes.

With those two models generated, the last activity in this phase is to apply the different procedures to validate and verify the modelled digital twin prototypes in the virtual operational environments.

5   Application to Overtaking Maneuver with Digital Twins

Let us now explain the characteristics of the solution we have developed for the cooperative vehicle overtaking maneuver presented so far by applying our model-based approach empowered with digital twins.

The digital twin-enabled SoS framework, we have recently developed, includes an Architecture Description Language (ADL) for Systems-of-Systems (SoS) on the Internet-of-Vehicles (IoV) with Digital Twins (DTw), named *SosADL for IoV with DTw*, which is an extension of *SosADL for IoV* [15], specially defined to support the description of SoS architectures formed by connected and automated vehicles.

SosADL for IoV with DTw focuses on emergent behaviors to choreograph cooperative driving maneuvers by modeling the upward causation between micro-scale behaviors and the intended macro-scale behaviors by supervenience through and at the level of digital twins.

Using *SysADL for IoV with DTw*, one can define an SoS architecture to support the cooperative overtaking on a two-way road, enabling a vehicle, i.e., the ego vehicle, to overtake the vehicle that is ahead of it, i.e., the target vehicle, through self-organization (as we formulated in [13]), while possibly having another vehicle behind of it, i.e., the following vehicle, as well as yet another vehicle approaching from the opposite direction, i.e., the oncoming vehicle.

Recall that, during the vehicle overtaking maneuver, the ego vehicle is in charge of initiating and performing the overtaking maneuver as well as it is responsible for assessing the traffic situation and executing the maneuver safely and efficiently. The target vehicle, i.e., the vehicle ahead of the ego vehicle that will be overtaken, usually traveling at a slower velocity, is expected to maintain its speed and keep its lane during the maneuver unless it signals otherwise, e.g., for turning. The following vehicle is expected to avoid interfering with or attempting to overtake too. Finally, the oncoming vehicle, which approaches from the opposite direction on a two-way road, is expected to maintain or, if needed, to reduce its velocity to ensure that there is enough clearance for the ego vehicle to complete the overtaking safely. All must follow traffic rules.

In our approach, for describing SoS architectures with digital twins for cooperative driving, instead of hard coding the logics of vehicle maneuvers inside and embedded in each vehicle (the so-called, endogenous approach), we define digital mediators that are dynamically created for choreographing specific maneuvers [4], without any modification or additional addon in the involved vehicles, those being completely coded outside of the involved vehicles (the so-called, exogenous approach [15]). Therefore, in our approach for cooperative driving based on digital twins, every connected and automated vehicle involved in an overtaking SoS, equipped with C-V2X and having its corresponding digital twin running in the cloud, is able to initiate or to participate in an overtaking maneuver without any additional addon, as the logics of the maneuver to be performed is inside the digital SoS mediators, also running in the cloud and dynamically linked to the core digital twins of the vehicles involved in the specific maneuver.

Note also that the endogenous approach, in which the maneuver logics is coded and embedded into every vehicle, that is the approach adopted in almost all publications proposing solutions to support overtaking maneuvers, is generally not able to comply with contextual operational conditions, e.g., if there is a vehicle driving from France to Austria via Germany, those endogenous solutions are not able to comply with the regulations of the different countries, as they provide a solution of type "one fits all", while different countries, even in Europe, apply different overtaking traffic rules, e.g., some European countries are bounded by the Vienna Convention on Road Traffic, article 11, while others not. They also have different legislations constraining overtaking and even in a country such as Canada, the legislation varies by province.

Our exogeneous approach applied for supporting cooperative driving based on digital twins of connected and automated vehicles, equipped with C-V2X technology, solves entirely those context related problems, as each digital mediator is created taking into account the local context of the cooperative maneuver, including local traffic rules and legislation, as well as encompass the role-based choreography fragments to be executed to safely perform the suitable dynamic driving tasks in different context-sensitive operational environments.

In addition to the advantages of the exogenous approach enabled by the developed digital twins, our approach based on a formal, mathematically defined [11], ADL enables, through model-to-model transformations, to generate model checking models to verify the correctness of the choreography that executes the intended cooperative maneuver as well as to generate simulation models to validate the intended cooperative maneuver by the vehicular SoS.

Indeed, as cooperative maneuvers are performed by systems of safety-critical real-time systems, expressed as choreographies of related connected and automated vehicles, a central concern is to be able to check their correctness, what is supported in our digital twin enabled approach via the model verification of the digital twin prototypes, which, once being guaranteed correct, will be engineered to be able to be deployed.

Let us now focus on the formal models which guarantee full correctness of the choreography model of cooperative maneuvers executed by connected and automated vehicles under the responsibility of their digital system twins deployed in the cloud.

Let us then express the model to the case of the presented cooperative overtaking, where an ego vehicle is in the right lane, a following vehicle is behind of it and a target vehicle in front of it as well as an oncoming vehicle is approaching coming on the left lane in the opposite direction. Supposing that the target vehicle is driving in a slower speed than the ego vehicle, the ego vehicle can prepare itself to initiate the overtaking maneuver by triggering the dynamic creation of the digital twin-enabled SoS, using the constraint solving mechanisms and method described in [4], and then start the mediated communications between the digital system twins connected to the involved vehicles.

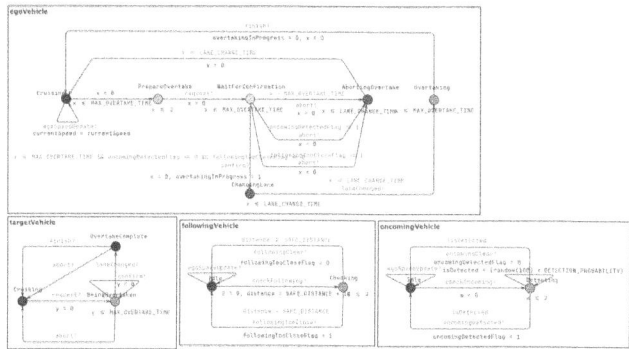

Fig. 4. The model checking model to support verification of the cooperative maneuver

For that overtaking case, the generated model checking model, depicted in a bird's-eye view in Fig. 4 (excerpt), defines the different roles of the vehicles involved in an overtaking maneuver in terms of a network of timed automata, whose correctness is specified via a set of safety and liveness properties expressed in a branching-time timed temporal logic. This formal model specifies the communication and coordination required to achieve the necessary cooperation between the different vehicles involved in the overtaking maneuver driven by the corresponding digital twins acting as mediators of those vehicles during the operational execution of the overtaking maneuver.

6   Software Toolset for Architecting SoS with Digital Twins

We have developed a software toolset, named *SosADL Studio*, for supporting the architecture-centric formal development of SoSs using SosADL, which provides guarantees of correctness of the elaborated SoS architectures [14].

In *SosADL Studio*, by applying model-to-model transformations, SoS architecture descriptions are transformed and converted to input languages of analysis tools, including in particular UPPAAL (uppaal.org/) for exhaustive model checking (case shown in Fig. 4), PLASMA (project.inria.fr/plasma-lab/) for statistical model checking, DEVS (ms4systems.com/) for model simulations in general, and VEINS (veins.car2x.org/) for specifically running vehicular simulations.

Of particular interest for validating SoS emergent behavior based on the digital twin prototypes specified using *SosADL for IoV with DTw*, is the automated generation of concrete SoS architectures, by automated transformations from SosADL to the Kodkod constraint solver (emina.github.io/kodkod), enabling to observe and tune the described emergent behavior of an SoS, created by the solver and run by simulations.

For supporting verification of SoS architectures, both exhaustive model checking and statistical model checking are supported in *SosADL Studio*. The former is based on model-to-model transformations to networks of timed automata extended with data, supported by UPPAAL, with correctness properties specified in TCTL, and the latter is based on PLASMA, with statistical correctness properties specified in DynBLTL.

The extended toolchain for IoV with digital twins, *SosADL Studio for IoV with DTw*, provides the ability to support validation and verification of digital twin-enabled SoS architectures on the IoV, with model-in-the-loop techniques, relying on the approach presented in this paper. Its validation has been carried out in a real pilot project in collaboration with a multinational company.

7 Related Work

The integration of digital twins and systems-of-systems has very recently been identified as the next expected step in the evolution of the digital twin paradigm [20] as well as a major open challenge [2, 9]. In this context, let us address related work.

We focus on the intended area of application of our research on digital twins, i.e., cooperative driving in general and cooperative overtaking in particular.

Almost all the publications in this area report about solutions that vary according to the levels of driving automation [17], which are defined by the Society of Automotive Engineers (SAE) in [22] as: 0 - No driving automation, 1 - Driver assistance, 2 - Partial driving automation, 3 - Conditional driving automation, 4 - High driving automation, and 5 - Full driving automation. From this aspect, most of the papers propose solutions of control engineering to assist the driver or to partially automate critical phases of the overtaking maneuver, based on the capabilities of the automated driving systems, from levels 1 to 3, relying on onboard devices, especially RaDAR, LiDAR or cameras [17].

In the last years, these solutions were enhanced with communication capabilities of more modern vehicles, of levels 3, 4 and even 5, in particular based on V2V communication, relying mainly on Vehicular Ad-Hoc Network (VANet), recently including V2I communication, mainly to interact with roadside units, and more recently also including V2N communication. Notably, with the advent of C-V2X, a few publications have identified the need to develop digital twins for connected and automated vehicles [19].

Cooperative driving is yet a very young field where digital twins have started to be investigated, and yet several issues remain open [18]. Mostly, the focus has been on the ego vehicle as an isolated system where the other vehicles are possible obstacles that make its maneuvers difficult [3].

In the research presented in this paper, we took a different approach by replacing that assumption of a system alone in its context, leading mainly to solutions based on orchestrations conducted by the ego vehicle, to a novel one centered on the concept of system-of-systems, where the ego vehicle as well as the other nearby vehicles interact to perform a choreography that is guaranteed safe for all, while being the emergent behavior raised through supervenience. To guarantee that this choreography coordinating the mediated vehicles is safe, those digital system twins are rigorously developed, starting from the requirements specification of the intended cooperative maneuver, then by architecting the SoS that supports that specific cooperative maneuver, and subsequently by refining the modeled SoS architecture and developing digital twin prototypes that are validated by simulation and verified by model checking.

Therefore, the novel model-based approach, proposed in this paper, for supporting cooperative driving as systems of mediated digital system twins which are bidirectionally linked and synchronized with connected and automated vehicles, brings a major contribution beyond the state of the art related to digital twins: it leverages the concept and the application potential of digital twins, from being a virtual twin of a single vehicle to become the enabling virtual twin for creating emergent behaviors through its mediator role in systems-of-systems, demonstrated here in the area of cooperative driving and in particular of cooperative overtaking maneuvers. These systems of digital system twins are able to deal with different cooperative driving maneuvers in different operational contexts, what is not the case neither of the onboard solutions proposed in the literature nor of orchestrated ones that often dependent on the road infrastructure.

8 Conclusion

In this paper, we have investigated the research question of how an automated driving system of a connected vehicle shall interact with its nearby vehicles to safely perform overtaking, knowing that each of its surrounding vehicles is also a connected and automated vehicle, and that all are managerially and operationally independent.

To answer that research question, we conceived a novel model-based approach based on the integration of digital twins in systems-of-systems, for supporting cooperative driving, where cooperative driving is the outcome of the emergent behavior of involved connected and automated vehicles extended with mediated digital system twins, deployed in the cloud, enabled via C-V2X with V2N access.

Especially, in this paper, we focused on presenting the fundaments of this novel digital twin-enabled model-based approach and its application to support cooperative overtaking, a challenging safety critical maneuver, relying on mediated digital twins in SoS.

Importantly, we approached those opportunistic SoSs on the IoV as dynamic systems of maneuver-specific digital system twins behaving as mediators that coordinate the dynamic driving tasks of the different vehicles involved in the cooperative overtaking maneuver, bringing a novel approach and usage for digital twins.

That approach whose essential points in terms of concept and method were presented has been applied in a real pilot project in collaboration with a multinational company.

References

1. Cavalcante, E., Batista, T., Oquendo, F.: Looking back and forward: a retrospective and future directions on software engineering for systems-of-systems. J. Softw. Evol. Process (2024)
2. Cavalcante, E., Batista, T., Oquendo, F.: Exploring synergies and challenges of system-of-systems and digital twins. In: 4th International Workshop on Architecting and Engineering Digital Twins (AEDT), IEEE ICSA 2025 Companion Proceedings (2025)
3. Deng, R., et al.: Cooperative collision avoidance for overtaking maneuvers in cellular V2X-based autonomous driving. IEEE Trans. Veh. Technol. (2019)
4. Guessi, M., Oquendo, F., Nakagawa, E.: Ark: a constraint-based method for architectural synthesis of smart systems. J. Softw. Syst. Model. (2020)
5. INCOSE: Systems Engineering Vision 2035 (2021). www.incose.org/sevision
6. Maier, M.: Architecting principles for systems-of-systems. J. Syst. Eng. (1998)
7. Maksimovski, D., et al.: A survey on decentralized cooperative maneuver coordination for connected and automated vehicles. In: International Conference on Vehicle Technology and Intelligent Transport Systems – VEHITS. Springer (2021)
8. NHTSA: Analysis of Lane-Change Crashes and Near-Crashes (2009). www.nhtsa.gov
9. Olsson, T., Axelsson, J.: Systems-of-systems and digital twins: a survey and analysis of the current knowledge. In: IEEE International Conference on System-of-Systems Engineering – SoSE (2023)
10. Oquendo, F.: Software architecture challenges and emerging research in software-intensive systems-of-systems. In: European Conference on Software Architecture – ECSA. Springer (2016)
11. Oquendo, F.: The π-calculus for SoS: a novel π-calculus for the formal modeling of software-intensive systems-of-systems. In: Communicating Process Architectures – CPA (2016)
12. Oquendo, F.: On the emergent behavior oxymoron of system-of-systems architecture description. In: IEEE International Conference on System of Systems Engineering – SoSE (2018)
13. Oquendo, F.: Formally describing self-organizing architectures for systems-of-systems on the internet-of-things. In: European Conference on Software Architecture – ECSA. Springer (2018)
14. Oquendo, F., et al.: A formal approach for architecting software-intensive systems-of-systems with guarantees. In: IEEE International Conference on System of Systems Engineering – SoSE (2018)
15. Oquendo, F.: Architecting exogenous software-intensive systems-of-systems on the internet-of-vehicles with SosADL. J. Syst. Eng. (2019)
16. Oquendo, F.: Fuzzy mediating control systems for automating vehicle driving maneuvers: the overtaking case. In: IEEE International Conference of Region 10 – TENCON (2023)
17. Ortega, J., et al.: Systematic review of overtaking maneuvers with autonomous vehicles. J. Transp. Eng. (2024)
18. Pikner, H., et al.: Autonomous driving validation and verification using digital twins. In: International Conference on Vehicle Technology and Intelligent Transport Systems – VEHITS. Springer (2024)
19. Qian, C., et al.: Digital twin based internet of vehicles. In: International Conference on Computer Communications and Networks – ICCCN. IEEE (2024)
20. Ricci, A., et al.: Web of digital twins. ACM Trans. Internet Technol. (2022)
21. SAE: Taxonomy and Definitions for Terms Related to Cooperative Driving Automation for On-Road Motor Vehicles (2021). www.sae.org
22. SAE: Taxonomy and Definitions for Terms Related to Driving Automation Systems for On-Road Motor Vehicles (2021). www.sae.org

Development and Evaluation of Support Tools for Modeling Digital Twin Concepts and Architectures

Gerald Kremer(✉) ⓘ, Svenja Nicole Schulteⓘ, and Rainer Starkⓘ

Technische Universität Berlin, Berlin, Germany
kremer@tu-berlin.de

Abstract. Translating scientific knowledge into practical strategies for Digital Twin development remains a significant challenge. This is particularly important when the concept of Digital Twins is transferred to domains that are not yet familiar with the concept (such as the health sector). This paper presents two tools designed to bridge this gap. First, a Lean Digital Twin Canvas supports the conceptualization and early planning of Digital Twin solutions, helping teams define objectives, scope, and key components of the Digital Twin. Second, a Morphological Box provides a structured approach to determining the fundamental system architecture, ensuring more coherent and adaptable technical foundations. Both methods were evaluated through a questionnaire addressed to students and expert practitioners, who assessed their perceived usefulness. The findings suggest that these practical tools, inspired by established scientific frameworks, are perceived as useful especially for novices in Digital Twin development. The results also indicate that users find development support tools more useful in early development phases (concept design) than in late phases (prototype design).

Keywords: digital twin · design support tool · concept design · system architecture

1 Introduction

Digital Twins have become increasingly important across industries, offering real-time monitoring, enhanced system analysis, and predictive capabilities. Yet, developing Digital Twins remains a complex task, requiring skills that organizations, especially those in domains which are unfamiliar with Digital Twins, may not fully possess.

To address this challenge, practical support tools are needed to guide teams through conceptualization, system architecture design, and implementation. In response, this paper presents two such tools: (1) a *Lean Digital Twin Canvas* that helps users define objectives and scope early in the project, and (2) a *Morphological Box* that provides structured guidance for system development. Both tools were assessed through a questionnaire-based evaluation involving students and expert practitioners.

The primary aim of this work is to determine whether these tools effectively support Digital Twin development across different experience levels and project stages, representing a translation of theoretical knowledge into concrete, practical tools.

J. Grabis and Y. Wautelet (Eds.): CAiSE 2025 Workshops, LNBIP 556, pp. 207–218, 2025.
https://doi.org/10.1007/978-3-031-94931-9_17

1.1 Motivation and Research Objective

Many studies have examined how Digital Twins can be conceptualized, defined, and classified (Kritzinger et al., 2018; Stark et al., 2019). Empirical findings and theoretical derivations led to frameworks and taxonomies describing essential features, from data structures to system architectures (Tao et al., 2019). Despite this robust scientific foundation, few tools offer direct, practical guidance for day-to-day product development, which is especially critical when existing insights from the engineering domain should be transferred to other domains. The gap is worsened by the rising complexity of cyber-physical systems and the diverse skill sets required to build them (Zhuang et al., 2018).

Existing studies have proposed generic methodologies or case-specific insights, but systematically validated tools for guiding Digital Twin developers remain scarce (Trauer, 2024). Therefore, the central question of this research paper is: *How can scientifically grounded knowledge about Digital Twins be translated into concrete, accessible tools that assist developers in conceptualizing and implementing Digital Twins?*

Based on this question, three key aspects emerged. First, which target groups, ranging from novice to expert, benefit most from structured support? Second, during which phases of development (e.g., concept ideation, prototype design) do such tools add the greatest value? Third, what level of detail is needed to balance creativity with concrete guidance? Addressing these questions, the present study developed and evaluated two support tools aimed at bridging the gap.

1.2 Approach and Structure of the Paper

The structure of the paper, including the research approach, is illustrated in Fig. 1.

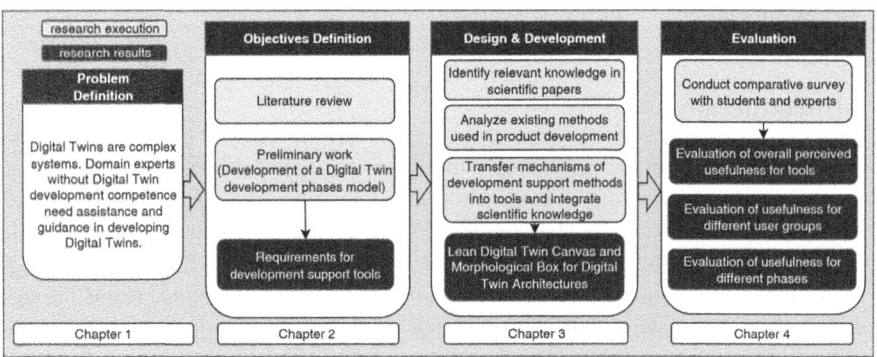

Fig. 1. Structure of the paper and research approach

2 State of Research and Related Works

2.1 Digital Twins and Related Concepts of Academic Research

A Digital Twin is defined as "[…] a digital representation of an active unique product […] or unique product service system […] that comprises its selected characteristics, properties, conditions and behaviors by means of models, information and data within a single or even across multiple life cycle phases" (Stark & Damerau, 2019, p.1). More specifically, a Digital Twin consists of three core components, namely a Digital Master, which consists of models pertaining to the physical system; a Digital Shadow consisting of data pertaining to the physical system; as well as a linkage between the Digital Master and Digital Shadow (Stark & Damerau, 2019).

Several frameworks have been proposed in recent literature to classify Digital Twins. Mendonça et al. (2023) introduce a five-dimensional analytical framework to classify various Digital Twin solutions, analyzing 12 articles to demonstrate its utility. Boyes and Watson (2022) propose a framework focusing on the functional characteristics of Digital Twins, facilitating their characterization and comparison. Stark and Schulte (2021) also illustrate dimensions for describing Digital Twins. These frameworks aim to classify Digital Twins, promoting a better understanding of their capabilities and applications across various domains.

Furthermore, several works describe the architecture of Digital Twins such as the ISO 23247-1:2021 "Automation systems and integration – Digital twin Framework for manufacturing" (International Organization for Standardization, 2021) and the DT Reference Architecture Model (Aheleroff et al., 2021). Both frameworks propose multi-layered architectures, integrating physical and digital entities and utilizing data collection and processing layers. The ISO framework outlines a four-layer structure, distinguishing between the physical unit, communication, modeling, and user application layers. In contrast, the DT Reference Architecture Model adopts a three-layer approach, focusing on the physical, digital, and cyber layers.

Beyond the architectural frameworks, the design of Digital Twins involves several key considerations that significantly influence their functionality and application. Stark et al. (2019) identify six design elements that are essential to the development of Digital Twins. These elements encompass various aspects such as the hardware and software components of the physical system, as well as the models and data associated with the Digital Master and Digital Shadow, respectively. Further, Digital Twins vary in scope and complexity: standalone Digital Twins are typically used in planning phases, descriptive Digital Twins use real-time data for decision support, and predictive Digital Twins rely on forecasts and machine learning (Stadtmann et al., 2023).

There is an increasing amount of literature focusing on the development of Digital Twins. Studies propose a diversity of Digital Twin design and implementation strategies, including structured frameworks and step-by-step methodologies. However, many existing frameworks propose general methodologies that lack detailed guidance for real-world application and thus support for industry practitioners (e.g., Ariansyah et al., 2020; Psarommatis & May, 2023). Other efforts address more specific use cases, which are primarily tailored to particular applications, such as the development of Digital Twins of buildings (Oulefki et al., 2023) and industrial process plants (Martínez et al., 2018) and may not generalize well to other sectors.

A more generalizable and well-known approach is the V-Model (VDI/VDE 2206) (Verein Deutscher Ingenieure, 2021), an established development framework widely used in systems engineering. The framework introduced by Schulte et al. (2025) uses the logic of the V-Model as a sequential process model in a V-shape and applies it to describe and provide support during the phases of the Digital Twin development process. It specifies seven phases, which help structure the workflow from a benefit evaluation to the effective use of the Digital Twin. However, each of these phases could benefit from tools that support users during the individual tasks. The introduction of specific methods, tools, and digital support for each phase of the development process would significantly enhance the usability and applicability of Digital Twins. By integrating these additional resources, industry practitioners would have a more comprehensive, practical framework for Digital Twin development that ensures high-quality outcomes, scalability, and adaptability across various sectors.

2.2 Development Support Tools

Development support tools are structured means that help engineers, designers, and other stakeholders systematically create, refine, and realize new products or systems (Bender & Gericke, 2021). They can serve as assistance tools in development, supporting both direct and indirect development activities (Stark et al., 2021).

Untargeted support fosters creative exploration, relying on methods that stimulate idea generation and challenge conventional thinking (Yilmaz et al., 2015). Classic examples include brainstorming or Osborn's checklist (Trivedi, 2024), which systematically alters or recombines concepts. Such tools often appear in early conceptual phases, when a wide range of solutions is desirable and the goal is to explore unconventional ideas (Ulrich et al., 2020).

In contrast, targeted support refines or evaluates a set of solutions to select an optimal or near-optimal outcome. It often involves more structured decision-making, as seen in house-of-quality diagrams (Akao et al., 1990) or the Pugh Matrix (Guler & Petrisor, 2021). These methods typically appear in later development stages, when teams must converge on a coherent design specification, reconcile trade-offs, and meet defined requirements (Blessing & Chakrabarti, 2009).

Regardless of their focus, support tools share mechanisms for structuring information flow among team members, enabling systematic documentation and communication of requirements, constraints, and ideas (Eppinger & Browning, 2012). In Digital Twin development, these processes remain crucial, as diverse stakeholders must integrate hardware, corresponding models, sensor data, communication protocols, and twinning logic (Negri et al., 2017).

3   Design and Development

3.1   Methods for Digital Twin Development Support

Digital Twin development often unfolds in several phases, beginning with conceptual exploration and advancing toward detailed design and implementation (Negri et al., 2017). In the early conceptual phase, the focus lies on discovering a broad spectrum of options: what functionalities the Digital Twin might include, how it could integrate with existing systems, or which lifecycle stages should be emphasized. During these steps, conceptual knowledge from literature, such as abstract classifications, general best practices, and domain-agnostic frameworks can enhance creativity without imposing excessive constraints. As the Digital Twin project transitions to more advanced stages, developers must refine and converge on specific architectures, components, or data flows (Tao et al., 2019). Here, the priorities shift to validating feasibility, aligning with organizational constraints. This requires decision support tools that draw on either well-established scientific concepts or concrete industry case studies offering proven solution elements (Wynn & Clarkson, 2018). Consequently, the emphasis changes from open-ended exploration to structured selection and optimization.

Accordingly, the overarching objective of this work was to design two complementary tools that map onto these phases. One tool should focus on conceptual support, opening the solution space and integrating high-level theoretical insights, while the other should help structure later phases, where specific solution elements must be identified.

Therefore, existing support methods were first analyzed by expert judgement to assess how well predefined knowledge can be integrated into the methods, and whether the methods support ideating new solutions or refining existing solutions. Table 1 summarizes these methods, indicating their purpose, and to what extent they support the integration of external knowledge, such as research findings or case-study insights.

Table 1. Comparison of analyzed support methods

Method	Purpose	Knowledge Integration	Short Description
Brainstorming	Ideate	Low	Generates many ideas quickly without immediate filtering
6–3–5 Method	Ideate	Low	Structured brainwriting with timed idea rotations
SCAMPER	Ideate	Medium	Modifies existing ideas via systematic prompts (Substitute, Combine, etc.)
TRIZ	Ideate	High	Uses inventive principles to solve technical contradictions
Lean Canvas	Ideate	High	Describes relevant system factors in clusters
Morphological Box	Ideate	High	Combines independent parameters into possible solutions
House of Quality / QFD	Refine	Medium	Aligns product requirements with design specifications
Decision-Matrix	Refine	Medium	Scores concepts on defined criteria to select the best solution

Among the methods, morphological approaches stand out due to their capacity to systematically integrate new knowledge categories. They can help teams generate structured variations across multiple parameters. Similarly, canvases (e.g., adapted from the business model canvas concept) provide a visually intuitive format for capturing high-level insights, which are valuable in early ideation sessions. Hence, we created:

- A canvas-based tool to facilitate discussion and ensure that conceptual knowledge from the dimensions (Stark & Schulte, 2021) is incorporated in the early phases of Digital Twin development (concept design).
- A morphological box to enable more systematic exploration and eventually narrowing of solution elements based on the six design elements (Stark et al., 2019), complemented by specific case-study insights where available, is incorporated in later phases of Digital Twin development (prototype design).

3.2 Developed Artefacts

Two specific artifacts were developed: the first is a canvas-based approach designed for collaborative workshops, inspired by the nine-dimension perspective on Digital Twins (Stark & Schulte, 2021); the second is a morphological box implemented as an HTML application to guide users step-by-step toward a preliminary system architecture. Below, both tools are introduced using an illustrative example of a Digital Twin for a washing machine that autonomously decides when to start the wash cycle based on load measurements and available solar power.

Lean Digital Twin Canvas

The developed Lean Digital Twin Canvas is made public for this research paper and can be found in Kremer et al. (2025a). An illustrative example is shown in Fig. 2. The Lean Digital Twin Canvas is laid out as a poster-sized template that can be filled out by a development team in a group setting. It adopts a "canvas" format, divided into sections corresponding to dimensions of Digital Twins, such as integration breadth, intelligence level, simulation capabilities, and digital model detail (Stark & Schulte, 2021), thereby prompting discussions of key design choices.

The fields in the canvas are divided into:

- Description: In each section, users explain how they envision implementing a particular aspect. For example, under "Integration breadth", a team planning a washing machine Digital Twin might document that it spans the washing machine itself, a built-in scale for load measurement, and a solar panel system for energy generation.
- Analysis: Along the bottom of each canvas field is a visual scale illustrating potential maturity levels for that dimension. Taking "Simulation capabilities" as an illustration, teams can situate their planned Digital Twin between simpler, "stationary" approaches (e.g., a static digital model) and more advanced "co-simulation" methods that integrate multiple dynamic models in real time.
- Obstacles/Open Questions: Each dimension includes a field for obstacles or unknowns. In the washing machine example, possible concerns might include handling unexpected changes in solar panel output due to weather or managing data privacy when uploading usage statistics to a cloud platform.

In a typical usage scenario, the development team gathers around the printed canvas and systematically answers each question. For instance, they could decide that the washing machine's goal is to reduce energy costs, requiring a decision-making intelligence that prioritizes machine runs when solar energy is available. By documenting these points, the canvas not only captures diverse stakeholder input but also reveals interdependencies (e.g., if the team expands the integration breadth to include more household appliances, the intelligence level section may require advanced scheduling algorithms). Once all sections have been completed, the team reviews open questions to refine priorities before moving into a more structured design phase.

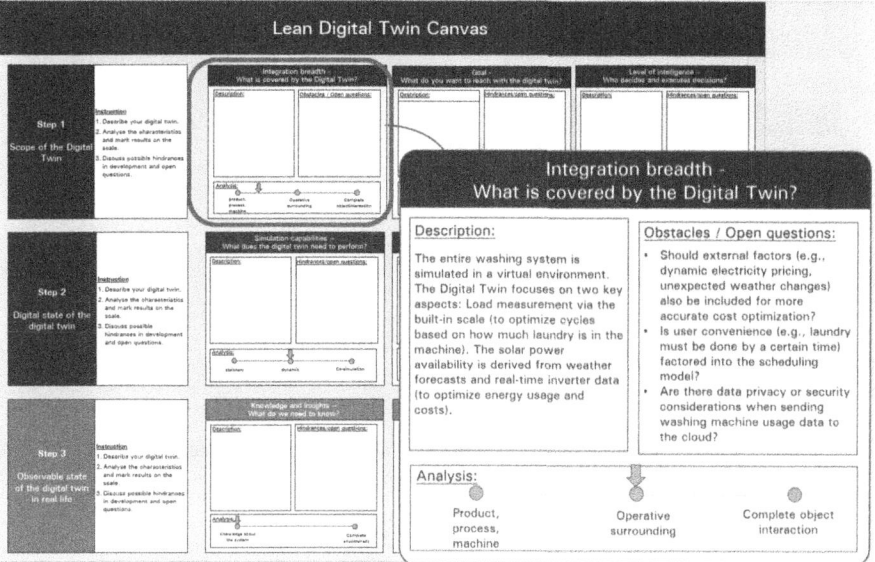

Fig. 2. Lean Digital Twin Canvas with a zoomed-in field that is exemplary filled out

Morphological Box for a Digital Twin System Architecture

The developed Morphological Box is an HTML application and is made public for this paper under Kremer et al. (2025b) and can be found online as a live version under https://gerald734.github.io/. A simplified version, showcasing the input structure is shown in Fig. 3. The Morphological Box guides users through ten structured choices based on the 6 design elements from Stark et al. (2019), which were selected based on experience in projects in Digital Twin development.

In the washing machine scenario, a user first specifies the physical asset (the appliance) and how data is captured (e.g., load measured by scale). Next, they define the electronic control unit (ECU) and the data transfer module (Wi-Fi connection). External data sources (weather forecasts) can then be added, while a data repository (SQL) is chosen to store operational logs. Data preprocessing might include filtering or interpolation in this case, and the Digital Twin's core function is set to optimize start times for each load. The twinning engine (based on a cloud inference server) is chosen. Also, the model type is defined. In the exemplary use case, it is shown that users do not necessarily need to stick to the predefined choices but can also fill in elements of their own choice. In the example, the user might already know that they will want to use a supervised learning model. After completion, the tool automatically generates a schematic depicting the entire architecture, which can be revisited if new requirements arise.

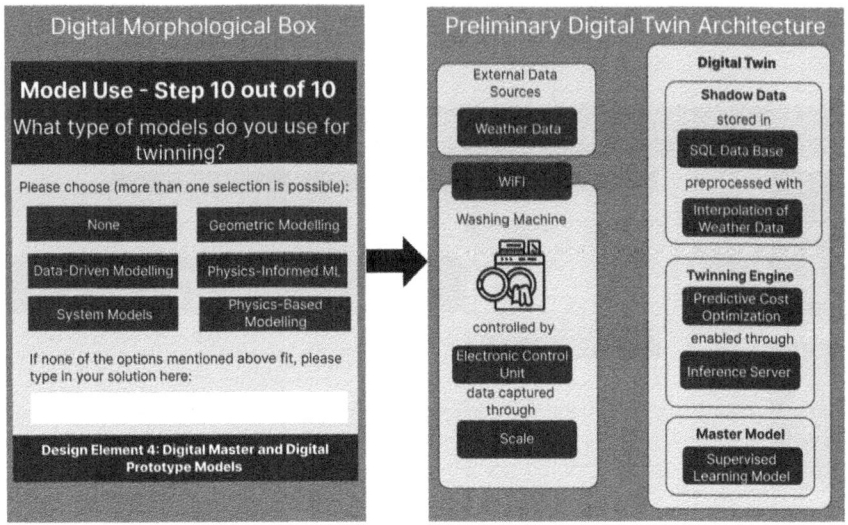

Fig. 3. An exemplary step in the Morphological Box and preliminary architecture

4   Evaluation

4.1   Design of the Evaluation

Two sets of participants were recruited: a cohort of students and a group of experts. The students were enrolled in a project-based course where they developed a cyber-physical product. Although still in training, the students were no absolute beginners, as the practical nature of their course had provided them with experience. The expert group consisted of research associates who had participated in projects involving Digital Twin development, thus combining both theoretical knowledge and practical insights. Prior to testing the tools, each participant was asked to rate their perceived expertise in Digital Twin development. Subsequently, they were introduced to the Lean Digital Twin Canvas and the Morphological Box and completed a questionnaire targeted to measure the perceived usefulness, which employed a seven-point Likert scale ranging from 1 (completely disagree) to 7 (completely agree), based on the questionnaire by Davis (1989). It was aimed to answer our research questions regarding which target group benefits the most from development support tools, during which phase of development they are most valuable, and which level of detail they should provide.

4.2 Results of the Evaluation

A total of 20 participants took part in the survey with 14 students and six experts. Figure 4 shows their average responses on a seven-point scale (1 = completely disagree, 7 = completely agree). The clearest distinction is evident in the participants' perceived experience in Digital Twin development with an average of 3 for students and an average of 5 for experts. Experts see a higher need for support in the development of Digital Twins (6) compared to students (5), with a higher perceived need for support in earlier development phases in both groups. Regarding the perceived impact on faster task completion, the Lean Canvas (LC) is scored on average at approximately 5 by students and approximately 6 by experts, while the Morphological Box (MB) ratings are below those figures for both groups. Similar patterns appear for items on performance, productivity, and effectiveness: in each case, the Lean Canvas and the Morphological Box both receive average ratings in the 4 to 6 range, with experts generally rating them higher than students. For the items "LC improves ease of development" and "MB improves ease of development," students' mean scores are 5.6 and 4.9, respectively, while experts' mean scores are 5.5 and 5.7, respectively. The overall usefulness of the Lean Digital Twin Canvas was rated higher compared to the Morphological Box by both groups. Overall, the experts rated the developed tools slightly higher than students.

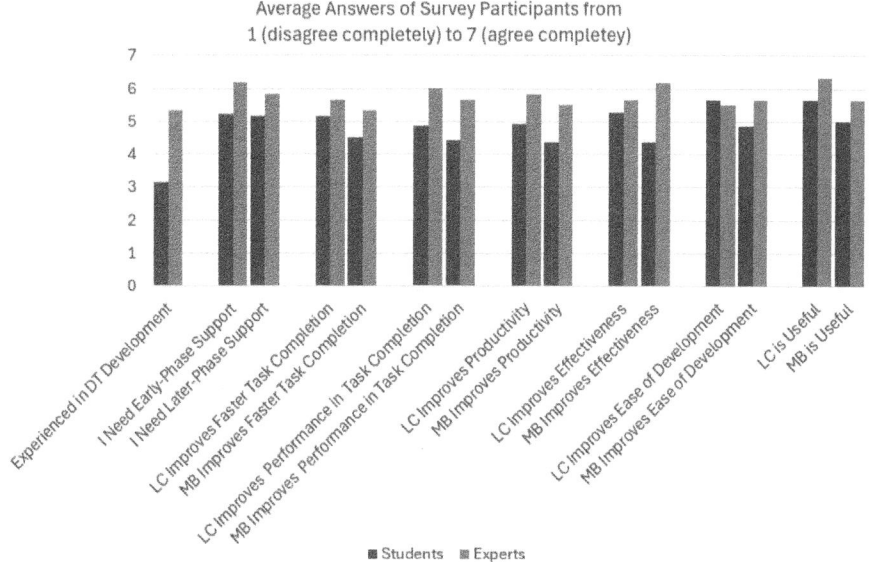

Fig. 4. Survey results regarding the assessment of the developed support tools

4.3 Discussion

The fact that both groups expressed a generally high perceived need for Digital Twin support echoes research findings, which suggest that integrating physical systems with digital elements adds complexity and necessitates methodical guidance (Kritzinger et al., 2018). Expert and novice assessments were very similar. The only recognizable difference in responses could be identified in the level of expertise. While prior studies sometimes highlight differences in tool preferences based on Wynn and Clarkson (2018), our findings suggest that, in practice, both novices and seasoned developers may equally value structured guidance once they begin tackling complex integration and decision-making tasks. Furthermore, the statement provided in literature that untargeted, creativity-focused methods are more useful in early concept-generation phases (Yilmaz et al., 2015) do not align with our results. This suggests that the fundamental need for systematic support in the complex domain of Digital Twins persists throughout. Even though students and experts began with varying degrees of familiarity regarding Digital Twins, both groups found value in having clear support tools for documenting concepts and system architectures. Moreover, the relatively small gap in the perceived utility of analog versus digital formats, or of one method versus another, further underscores the fundamental need for general development support in this domain.

5   Conclusion and Outlook

The findings suggest that structured support tools can help a wide range of users navigate Digital Twin development. The evaluation indicated that both experts and novices find value in the two developed prototype tools. However, the limited number of respondents is a key limitation, and future studies with larger, more diverse samples would offer more detailed insights. Additionally, the participants used the tool for the first time, so that long-term usage effects are not measured. Furthermore, all participants were from the same research institute, potentially limiting variety in the background of participants. Also, the tools were not compared to other development support tools that could potentially be used for Digital Twin development.

Regarding the research questions, the findings show that both inexperienced and experienced developers benefited nearly equally, implying that structured support can be equally useful. The tools also proved useful in early conceptual stages and more advanced design work alike, suggesting that systematic guidance remains important throughout the development process. In terms of tool design, there was no single "best" format; both the more open canvas and the structured morphological approach offered benefits, underscoring the importance of adaptability in translating theoretical knowledge into practical development.

From a practitioner's perspective, these results highlight the benefit of offering multiple, complementary support methods tailored to user preferences and project phases. Even relatively simple tools, when grounded in well-established concepts, can streamline the transition from high-level ideas to structured system architectures. For researchers, the study emphasizes a need for further validations to explore how specific tool features affect team performance and design outcomes in Digital Twin projects. Future research may investigate their adaptability in a broader array use cases. By continuing to refine and evaluate other methods, the field can more effectively bridge the gap between conceptual insights and everyday Digital Twin development practice.

Disclosure of Interests. The authors have no competing interests to declare that are relevant to the content of this article.

References

Aheleroff, S., Xu, X., Zhong, R.Y., Lu, Y.: Digital twin as a service (DTaaS) in industry 4.0: an architecture reference model. Adv. Eng. Inform. **47**, 101225 (2021). https://doi.org/10.1016/j. aei.2020.101225

Akao, Y., Akao, Y., Akao, Y.: Quality Function Deployment: Integrating Customer Requirements into Product Design. Productivity Press (1990)

Ariansyah, D., et al.: Digital twin development: a step by step guideline (SSRN Scholarly Paper 3717726) Soc. Sci. Res. Netw. (2020).https://doi.org/10.2139/ssrn.3717726

Bender, B., Gericke, K.: Pahl/Beitz Konstruktionslehre: Methoden und Anwendung erfolgreicher Produktentwicklung. Springer, Berlin (2021). https://doi.org/10.1007/978-3-662-57303-7

Blessing, L.T.M., Chakrabarti, A.: DRM, A Design Research Methodology. Springer, London (2009).https://doi.org/10.1007/978-1-84882-587-1

Boyes, H., Watson, T.: Digital twins: an analysis framework and open issues. Comput. Ind. **143**, 103763 (2022). https://doi.org/10.1016/j.compind.2022.103763

Davis, F.D.: Perceived usefulness, perceived ease of use, and user acceptance of information technology. MIS Q. **13**(3), 319–340 (1989). https://doi.org/10.2307/249008

Eppinger, S.D., Browning, T.R.: Design Structure Matrix Methods and Applications. MIT Press (2012)

Guler, K., Petrisor, D.M.: A Pugh Matrix based product development model for increased small design team efficiency. Cogent Eng. **8**(1), 1923383 (2021). https://doi.org/10.1080/23311916. 2021.1923383

International Organization for Standardization. Automation systems and integration – Digital twin framework for manufacturing (ISO 23247-1:2021) (2021). https://www.iso.org/standard/ 75066.html

Kremer, G., Schulte, S.N., Stark, R.: Lean Digital Twin Canvas . Technische Universität Berlin (2025a). https://doi.org/10.14279/depositonce-23175

Kremer, G., Schulte, S.N., Stark, R.: Morphological Box for Digital Twin Architectures [Software]. Technische Universität Berlin (2025b). https://doi.org/10.14279/depositonce-23176

Kritzinger, W., Karner, M., Traar, G., Henjes, J., Sihn, W.: Digital twin in manufacturing: a categorical literature review and classification. IFAC-PapersOnLine **51**(11), 1016–1022 (2018). https://doi.org/10.1016/j.ifacol.2018.08.474

Martínez, G.S., Sierla, S., Karhela, T., Vyatkin, V.: Automatic generation of a simulation-based digital twin of an industrial process plant. In: IECON 2018 - 44th Annual Conference of the IEEE Industrial Electronics Society, pp. 3084–3089 (2018). https://doi.org/10.1109/IECON. 2018.8591464

Mendonça, F.M., de Souza, J.F., Soares, A.L.: Making sense of digital twins: an analytical framework. In Camarinha-Matos, L.M., Boucher, X., Ortiz, A. (eds.), Collaborative Networks in Digitalization and Society 5.0, pp. 749–760. Springer, Cham (2023). https://doi.org/10.1007/ 978-3-031-42622-3_53

Negri, E., Fumagalli, L., Macchi, M.: A review of the roles of digital twin in CPS-based production systems. Proc. Manuf. **11**, 939–948 (2017). https://doi.org/10.1016/j.promfg.2017.07.198

Oulefki, A., Amira, A., Kurugollu, F., Alshoweky, M.: Twining buildings: a methodological framework for design and implementation using home assistant technology. In: 2023 International Conference on Electrical, Communication and Computer Engineering (ICECCE), pp.1–6 (2023). https://doi.org/10.1109/ICECCE61019.2023.10442609

Psarommatis, F., May, G.: A literature review and design methodology for digital twins in the era of zero defect manufacturing. Int. J. Prod. Res. **61**(16), 5723–5743 (2023). https://doi.org/10.1080/00207543.2022.2101960

Schulte, S.N., Kremer, G., Stark, R.: Von der Theorie zur Anwendung – Entwicklungsleitfaden für Digitale Zwillinge. Konstruktion, **77**(01–02), 52–57 (2025). https://doi.org/10.37544/0720-5953-2025-01-02

Stadtmann, F., Rasheed, A., Rasmussen, T.: Standalone, descriptive, and predictive digital twin of an onshore wind farm in complex terrain. J. Phys. Conf. Ser. **2626**(1), 012030 (2023). https://doi.org/10.1088/1742-6596/2626/1/012030

Stark, R., Brandenburg, E., Lindow, K.: Characterization and application of assistance systems in digital engineering. CIRP Ann. **70**(1), 131–134 (2021). https://doi.org/10.1016/j.cirp.2021.04.061

Stark, R., Damerau, T.: Digital twin. In: Chatti, S., Tolio, T., (eds.) The International Academy for Production Engineering, CIRP Encyclopedia of Production Engineering, pp. 1–8. Springer, Heidelberg (2019). https://doi.org/10.1007/978-3-642-35950-7_16870-1

Stark, R., Fresemann, C., Lindow, K.: Development and operation of Digital Twins for technical systems and services. CIRP Ann. **68**(1), 129–132 (2019). https://doi.org/10.1016/j.cirp.2019.04.024

Stark, R., Schulte, S.N.: Determination of Digital Twin Maturity Levels Within Value Creation Networks. NAFEMS World Congress (2021)

Tao, F., Zhang, H., Liu, A., Nee, A.Y.C.: Digital twin in industry: state-of-the-art. IEEE Trans. Industr. Inf. **15**(4), 2405–2415 (2019). https://doi.org/10.1109/TII.2018.2873186

Trauer, J.: On the Conception and Implementation of Digital Twins – Supporting Companies in the Development of Digital Twins (2024). https://doi.org/10.13140/RG.2.2.36207.44965

Trivedi, S.: Pedagogical approaches and innovative teaching: simulation activity for new product design using osborn checklist (SCAMPER). In Khaldi, M. (ed.), Advances in Educational Technologies and Instructional Design, pp. 245–261. IGI Global (2024). https://doi.org/10.4018/979-8-3693-1206-3.ch011

Ulrich, K.T., Eppinger, S.D., Yang, M.C.: Product Design and Development, 7th edn. McGraw-Hill, International student edition) (2020)

Verein Deutscher Ingenieure. (2021). Entwicklung mechatronischer und cyber-physischer Systeme (VDI/VDE 2206). https://www.vdi.de/richtlinien/programme-zu-vdi-richtlinien/vdi-2206

Wynn, D.C., Clarkson, P.J.: Process models in design and development. Res. Eng. Design **29**(2), 161–202 (2018). https://doi.org/10.1007/s00163-017-0262-7

Yilmaz, S., Daly, S.R., Seifert, C.M., Gonzalez, R.: How do designers generate new ideas? Design heuristics across two disciplines. Des. Sci. **1**, e4 (2015). https://doi.org/10.1017/dsj.2015.4

Zhuang, C., Liu, J., Xiong, H.: Digital twin-based smart production management and control framework for the complex product assembly shop-floor. Int. J. Adv. Manuf. Technol. **96**(1–4), 1149–1163 (2018). https://doi.org/10.1007/s00170-018-1617-6

Requirements Analysis for a Digital Twin to Increase the Resilience of Multimodal Corridors: A Case Study in the Twente Region

Renata Guizzardi[1]([✉]), Jean Paul Sebastian Piest[1], Arda Akyazi[1], Sekai Ariji[1], Tommy Tao[1], Mohsen Bastani[1], Anne-Ruth Scheijgrond[2], Roland Kromanis[1], Farid Vahdatikhaki[1], Joschka Andreas Hüllmann[1], and Martijn Mes[1]

[1] University of Twente, Drienerlolaan 5, 7522NB Enschede, The Netherlands
r.guizzardi@utwente.nl
[2] Port of Twente, Columbus 17, 7609 RM Almelo, The Netherlands

Abstract. The drought in 2018 and 2022 in The Netherlands caused a reverse modal shift from inland waterways to road transportation within the Twente region in the eastern part of the country. These drought periods resulted in delivery delays, disruption of planning and operational processes, and reduced production capacity, affecting the entire logistics ecosystem in the region, consisting of inland ports and container terminals, logistic and production companies using the ports, and policymakers. As a result, these stakeholders are looking for solutions that increase the resilience of operations in the Twente corridor, helping them prepare, react, recover, and learn from disruptions. To improve the resilience, a digital twin is being developed to monitor the corridor's activities, performance, and infrastructure in real-time, providing alerts and useful information in the face of disruptions. This paper reports the results of the requirements analysis for the development of the digital twin, including the validation and prioritization by involved stakeholders. Although the research focuses on the Twente region, the program of requirements can be reused as a starting point for other multimodal corridors that face similar challenges and disruptions.

Keywords: Multimodal Corridor · Inland Waterways · Resilience · Digital Twin · Requirements

1 Introduction

The logistics industry has always been important to the Dutch economy. Many products from abroad are transported through the main ports in the Netherlands to the inland regions of Europe and other regions of the world, and vice versa [14]. Often, goods are transported in multimodal corridors, that is, through integrated transport networks that combine a primary mode of transport with additional modes, such as inland waterways plus roads and rails [19].

© The Author(s), under exclusive license to Springer Nature Switzerland AG 2025
J. Grabis and Y. Wautelet (Eds.): CAiSE 2025 Workshops, LNBIP 556, pp. 219–230, 2025.
https://doi.org/10.1007/978-3-031-94931-9_18

Climate change has caused significant pressure on multimodal corridors in recent years. It has led to droughts, flooding, infrastructure failures, and downtime, revealing the vulnerability of multimodal corridors and significantly impacting their performance, including negative impacts on direct stakeholders. These disruptions also affected multimodal transport in the Twente region, causing problems in many aspects, as can be seen in the example of the reverse modal shift caused by drought in this region in 2018 and August 2022[1], which resulted in a considerably larger number of trucks on the roads. Vulnerabilities in multimodal corridors have serious consequences and need to be addressed. It is important to note that these problems are not unique to the Twente region; other European multimodal corridors have experienced similar challenges [21].

Port authorities, terminal operators, transport operators, production companies, recycling companies, and policymakers are interested in improving the resilience of the operations of this multimodal corridor. Resilience here means anticipation through preparation, detecting risks and vulnerabilities as early as possible, efficiently recovering from disruptions, and returning to normal operations as fast as possible, analogous to the definition of Park et al. [15], who describe resilience as the capacity to adapt to changing conditions without catastrophic loss of form or function [2].

Digital Twin (DT) technology has emerged as a promising way to increase the resilience of logistics systems, offering real-time visibility of physical supply chains in a digital environment combined with advanced analytics, simulation models, and optimization techniques [13]. When applied to multimodal transport, DT allows stakeholders to collaboratively monitor the operations and performance of the multimodal corridor, simulate various scenarios and interventions, predict disruptions, and optimize performance dynamically. What makes DT especially attractive for solving the problems previously described is that DTs not only help monitoring the real environment to make predictions and support decision making, but also allow real-time interventions in the physical world based on the monitoring results.

In software development in general, and in the development of DTs in particular, requirements specification, validation, and prioritization play an important role. Requirements specification includes capturing the needs of all involved stakeholders, considering their preferences, and resolving possible conflicts regarding these requirements. Requirements validation is used to determine the correct requirements, avoiding inconsistencies, incompleteness, inaccuracies, and other defects, and to check if the requirements can properly guide the design and implementation of the system. It reduces the risks associated with software projects by helping to detect and correct errors that may occur unintentionally [20]. Requirements prioritization is the process of defining the relative importance of the requirements for the stakeholders. It is a key step in making critical decisions that enable the software under consideration to function as expected and increase its economic value. Prioritizing requirements before architectural

---

[1] https://www.rijkswaterstaat.nl/nieuws/archief/2022/09/droogte-en-laagwater-belemmeren-werkzaamheden-twentekanalen.

design and coding will significantly help implement the important software components earlier [1]. These techniques assist in implementing the system based on the desired features of the stakeholders and according to schedule and budget.

Goal-Oriented Requirements Engineering (GORE) is an approach to identify, analyze, and refine stakeholders' goals to derive system requirements [11]. It focuses on understanding the "why" behind the elicited system functionalities, ensuring that the developed system aligns with organizational objectives and stakeholder intentions. Typically, GORE is hierarchically structured by deriving high-level objectives from stakeholders, which are then decomposed into specific sub-goals [11]. Multiple frameworks for goal-oriented requirements engineering exist, e.g., KAOS [16] and i^* [5]. Our work adopts i^*, which allows the representation of actors (i.e., stakeholders), along with their goals and tasks, as well as how these actors depend on each other to fulfill their goals, execute their tasks, or obtain information/resources. Modeling dependencies allows early identification and assessment of potential conflicts or trade-offs between stakeholder goals.

This paper presents the results of a requirements engineering process performed for the DT under development to increase the resilience of multimodal corridors, focusing specifically on the Twente corridor. For that, we interviewed nine stakeholders of the given logistics ecosystem to grasp their needs and wants. Next, we combined the use of a goal-oriented requirements analysis and a requirements table to present the result of the requirements specification phase in detail. Finally, we validated and prioritized these requirements by conducting a survey with the stakeholders interviewed to check if the specified requirements are correct and what their priorities are about the functionalities of the system.

The remainder of this paper is organized as follows. Section 2 discusses the background information and related works on DTs in the logistic sector; Sect. 3 presents the requirements engineering method applied in this work; Sect. 4 focuses on our DT requirements, presenting the developed goal models and the requirements table resulting from requirements specification, validation, and prioritization; and Sect. 5 concludes this paper.

2   Digital Twins in Logistics

A DT is a virtual representation of a physical object/system that allows for simulation, monitoring, and performance optimization using AI and other simulation techniques [10]. A DT is based on a fully automated data flow and bi-directional interaction. In other words, changes in physical objects result in changes in digital objects and vice versa.

DTs in logistics can improve the resilience of multimodal logistics by improving the flexibility and adaptability of complex supply chain networks through multiple means. First, DTs allow real-time monitoring and predictive analytics by integrating diverse data sources such as weather forecasts, IoT sensor data, logistics planning systems, and infrastructure data [4,9]. Visualization and analytics help diagnose operations problems, detect inefficiencies, and anticipate failures [6,17]. Furthermore, mitigation strategies can be developed by simulating disruption scenarios (e.g., low water levels affecting inland shipping) so that stakeholders can make proactive decisions to maintain supply chain continuity [7,18]. Second, conventional logistics rely on static modal planning, likely resulting in infeasible plans once disruptions occur. A DT can form the basis for dynamic adjustment of decision-making based on real-time conditions [8,12]. Predictions and prescriptive analytics allow rapid application of alternative transport plans, such as rerouting cargo or adjusting inventory levels, thereby reducing costs and optimizing resource utilization [3].

Several DT projects have been initiated within the context of multimodal logistics, e.g., the DT Fairway Corridor (DTFC)[2] or the TRANS2[3] projects that focused on the Rhine-Maas corridor. These projects have produced relevant research output and prototypes, providing insights for developing DTs for multimodal corridors. Moreover, Busse et al. [4] focuses on DTs for multimodal supply chains, including waterways. Other research focuses on the design of DTs for logistics more generally, e.g., smart cities [12,18] and supply chains [9]. More conceptual works offer reference models and ontologies for architecting DTs or merely review the literature [6–9]. These related works only present DT requirements at a high-level, and to the best of our knowledge, there are no publications detailing the requirements engineering process used in developing a DT in the logistics sector.

3   Applied Requirements Engineering Method

This research follows four phases: Requirements Elicitation, Goal Modeling, Requirements Specification, and Requirements Validation and Prioritization. The work has been carried out by three requirements analysts (analysts, for short).

For **Requirements Elicitation**, requirements analysts A and B conducted interviews with nine members of the Twente corridor ecosystem. These were semi-structured interviews focusing on the main challenges faced by the companies, and their goals and requirements with respect to the DT. The analysts were also open to hearing any additional recommendations for improving the resilience of multimodal transport operations. The results of these interviews were documented by analyst A.

After the interviews, analyst B proceeded to the **Goal Modeling** phase, based on a synthesis of the information provided by all stakeholders. Our goal models describe the high-level requirements using i^* modeling constructs. Two sets of models have been created: model set (i) representing the current situation (*as-is models*), concerning stakeholders main goals and information needs and how they depend on each other to obtain their required information; and model set (ii) modeling the future situation (*to-be models*) considering the DT under development and how this affects the previous dependencies. These models were

---

[2] https://www.fairwaydanube.eu/.

[3] https://www.deltares.nl/en/expertise/projects/trans2-for-more-future-proof-waterways.

validated with the support of a Requirements Engineering expert and a multimodal transport expert who work closely with the members of Twente corridor ecosystem.

The goal models offer a preliminary understanding of the stakeholders' high-level requirements, but to allow implementation, these requirements are refined during a **Detailed Requirements** phase, conducted by requirements analyst C. This phase started with an inspection of the interview documentation. Since each interview was documented separately, the first result of the inspection was the creation of a requirements table per stakeholder. These requirements tables were then integrated, resulting in a unique initial requirements table for the DT. This process involved sorting out common or similar requirements among the various stakeholders. Each line of the initial requirements table corresponds to a functional or a non-functional requirement for the DT.

Finally, requirements analyst C conducted a survey[4] based on the requirements table and submitted it to the nine interviewed stakeholders for **Validation and Prioritization**. Each survey question corresponds to one requirement from the table, to be rated by the respondents following a 4-point Likert scale, ranging from 1 to 4, regarding the need of the corresponding requirement (following the established requirements prioritization procedure). In this way, stakeholders could express their priority level for each requirement. At the end of the survey, an open question collected new requirements that were not found in the initial requirements table. This phase resulted in a final requirements table with an added column expressing the requirements' priorities (averaged from the responses collected via the survey).

4 Goal Models and Requirements

4.1 Goal Models

The goal models presented in this section represent the high-level requirements of the DT stakeholders. Figure 1 depicts a model of the current situation, showing how the different stakeholders currently depend on each other for information (represented as i^* resource dependencies). For example, the LOGISTIC COMPANIES currently rely on the TRANSPORTERS to have information about *load capacity, type of transport, transportation cost*, and *availability*. The LOGISTIC COMPANIES depend on information from the GOVERNMENT WATER MANAGEMENT DEPARTMENT about the *infrastructure (bridges, water locks), road work/blockages* and *traffic congestion*. The ports of Twente and Zwolle and the Transporters have their own information needs, for which they also depend on other actors.

Looking at the number of mutual dependencies between the actors in the model of Fig. 1, one can understand the reason for some inefficiencies. Each dependency on information requires constant and direct interactions between the actors. For instance, the LOGISTIC COMPANIES needs information from the

---

[4] This survey may be found at https://forms.gle/i8gH5yaS64KK7y82A.

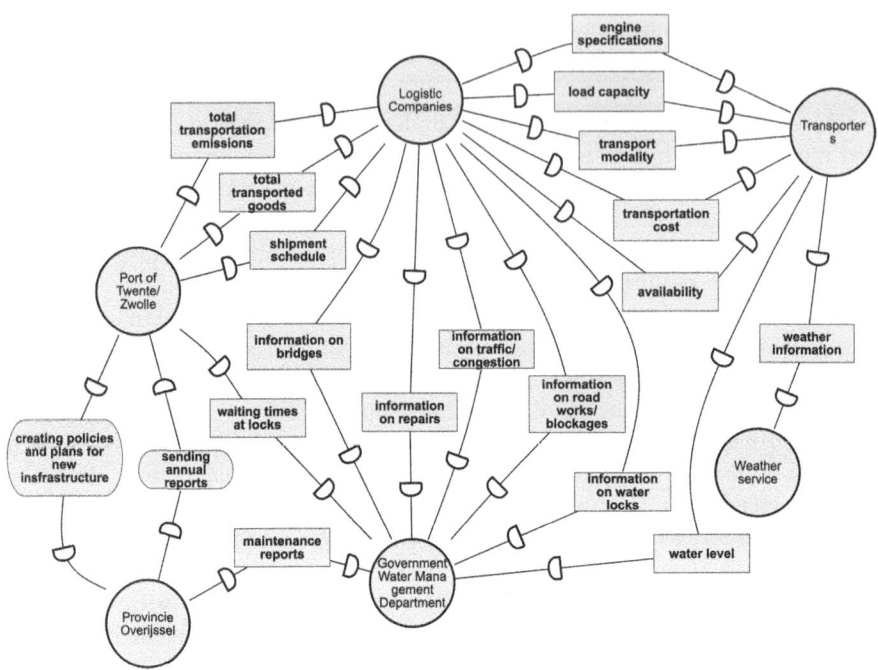

Fig. 1. Goal model depicting how stakeholders currently depend on each other to gather information

GOVERNMENT WATER MANAGEMENT DEPARTMENT to get informed about possible obstructions and congestion on the desired route. To decide which transportation modality to use and which transporter to hire to transport the goods, information from the TRANSPORTERS is needed. The way information is currently gathered and processed often hinders the LOGISTIC COMPANIES's goal of *fast decision-making*. For example, having to *contact transporters directly* and *needing information on infrastructure blockages* end up delaying decisions and making the logistic process less efficient.

All stakeholders have been at the center of the DT requirements engineering process. In general, they expect that the development of the DT will provide the required information more promptly and consistently so that they may take proactive action in case of imminent disruptions, improving their decision-making efficiency and the multimodal corridor's resilience.

The goal model in Fig. 2 depicts how the DT can be included in this setting to make predictions, facilitate real-time monitoring of the multimodal corridor, and provide relevant information to the stakeholders in need. As can be noted, the DT has the main goal of *optimizing logistics and supply chains*. For that, it must accomplish several subgoals, such as *providing the best modality of transport, providing suggestive actions against reverse modal shift, providing overview of historical data, assessing the performance of the canals*, and *simulat-*

ing scenarios. To accomplish these subgoals, the DT must execute the following tasks: *provide an overview of available transporters, predict water levels, predict congestion, actively monitor the canals,* and *monitor operations of the infrastructure.* The model shows new information dependencies, now going from the DT to the TRANSPORTERS and to the GOVERNMENT WATER MANAGEMENT DEPARTMENT. Moreover, it shows how the information needs of the PORTS OF TWENTE/ZWOLLE and the LOGISTIC COMPANIES are fulfilled by the DT in the form of performance reports and historical analysis. Since a Digital Twin works by connecting the digital and real worlds in an automated way, previous inefficiencies related to the multiple dependencies and constant interaction of stakeholders will be alleviated (see again the discussion related to Fig. 1.

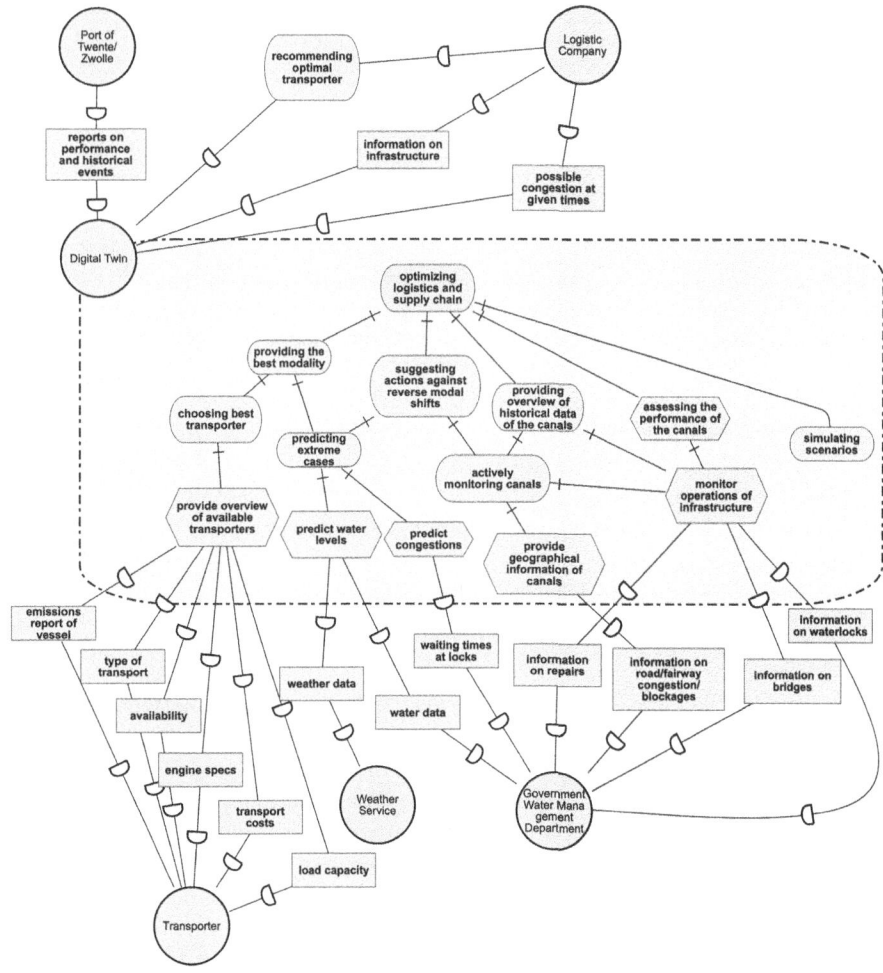

Fig. 2. Future dependencies considering the development of the DT, along with the system's internal view

4.2 Validated and Prioritized Requirements

As mentioned in Sect. 3, requirements were collected through interviews with the involved stakeholders, documented and inspected to enable requirements specification. A survey was conducted to validate and prioritize the specified requirements. Unfortunately, only three of the nine interviewed stakeholders responded to the survey. Thus, the results reported here are preliminary and subject to further validation rounds.

Table 1. "Environmental Information" view of the Final Requirements Table

ID	Requirements	Comment	Priority
	Water information		
1.1.1	System displays real-time water level, depth and flow	IJssel River, Twente Canal, around locks and bridges	4
1.1.2	System alerts users when the water level is lower/higher than a certain level	Such as when the IJssel River water level is lower than possible water pumping water level, it alerts users	4
1.1.3	System calculates and displays predicted water level/depth for next several weeks	Based on past data, weather forecast, etc.	4
1.1.4	System alerts users when predicted water level/depth is lower/higher than a certain level	Such as When the predicted IJssel River water level is lower than possible water pumping water level, it alerts users	4
1.1.5	System allows users to set specific conditions to activate the alarm	Such as: Give an alert when the water level is lower than 8 m	3
1.1.6	System displays water temperature		2
	Weather information		
1.2.1	System displays weather forecast	Including temperature, wind, etc.	2
1.2.2	System alerts users when adverse weather is forecasted/observed		2

Together Table 1 and Table 2 provide a partial view of the Functional Requirements Table. The complete table is not presented here due to page limitations but can be found in the project's repository folder[5]. The tables are organized with the following columns: ID (for the requirement identifier), Requirement (short description of the requirement), Comment (additional comments about the requirement) and Priority (requirement priority level). The priority level score can be interpreted as follows: 4 ("Must have" the requirement); 3 ("Should have" the requirement); 2 ("Could have" the requirement); N ("Will not have" the requirement); and S (Suggested by stakeholder in response to the survey).

---

[5] https://doi.org/10.17605/OSF.IO/QU6XH.

Table 2. Partial "Operational Management" view of the Final Requirements Table

ID	Requirements	Comment	Priority
	Operational plan management		
2.1.1	System alerts users about the possible need to adjust the loading layer, capacity, and transport routes	Such as When the water level rises, the loading layer height needs to be adjusted because it may be caught by the bridge's maximum passing height limit when passing through the bridge. Based on water levels, vessel type, cargo loads, bridge height restrictions, malfunction on the route, etc.	4
2.1.2	System displays information on narrow and difficult waterways, obstructions on waterways, obstructions on transportation routes		4
2.1.3	System allows users to create and save operational plan	Transportation method (ship, truck, rail, and its type), route, scheduling, cargo handling operation plan, etc.	3
2.1.4	System allows users to modify/adjust the operational plan		3
2.1.5	System allows users to view the operational plan		3
2.1.6	System provides real-time estimated time of arrival, cargo status, and estimated time of plan completion	Based on transportation status	3
2.1.7	System calculates and suggests optimal transportation plan to transport destination	Based on distance, water conditions, road conditions, CO_2 emission and other various information on the transportation route	3
2.1.8	System calculates and suggests optimal scheduling and provides information such as optimal sailing speed	Based on vessels, canals, lock passage times, and a variety of other operational factors	3

The requirements table is classified into categories and sub-categories according to the type of information to which it refers. Table 1 contains the first two sub-catogories and Table 2 the third (see lines without ID value). An overview of all sub-categories is presented below:

- Water information: Requirements related to real-time information about water levels and predictions of water level fluctuations.
- Weather information: Requirements related to weather forecasts.
- Operational plan management: Requirements related to the operational plan.
- Ship information: Requirements for real-time ship monitoring and other ship-related information.

– Facilities management: Requirements related to canal facilities.
– Bridge and lock management: Requirements related to the infrastructure, i.e. bridges and locks, including their real-time status (functioning or blocked).
– Cost management: Requirements related to the tracking and optimization of transportation costs.
– Fuel/CO2 emission management: Requirements related to the tracking and optimizing of fuel consumption and CO2 emissions.
– Storage management: Requirements related to storage management.
– Communication channel: Requirements related to communication channels.
– Information hub: Requirements related to information providing platforms.
– Account: Requirements related to accounts within the system.
– Payment: Requirements related to the payment process at the canal facilities.

The five elicited non-functional requirements are the following: a) the system provides only reliable and accurate data; b) the system provides long-term, accurate water level forecasts with over 70% accuracy; c) sensitive information (e.g., vessel location, cargo information, etc.) is protected by a sophisticated security mechanism; d) the UI is understandable and actionable even for users without technical background; and e) the UI displays on smartphones, tablet, laptops and desktops.

The analysis of the survey results shows that 11 out of the 62 functional requirements received the highest priority 4, with high percentages in the *Water information* and *Bridge and lock management* requirement sub-categories. All five non-functional requirements received high priority values, either 4 or 3. We advise that the DT development starts from the functional requirements marked as 4 and progressively adds the functionalities in descending order with respect to the priority level. As for the non-functional requirements, we expect more non-functional requirements to arise during the development phases. Therefore, all should be observed from the start of the development.

The lowest rated requirement was *3.1: System allows users to manage inventory information for their warehouses*, and the only one marked as N in the table. Since the stakeholders did not find this requirement important, it can be removed from the table, and thus, such functionality will not be developed in the DT. Survey respondents proposed the following new requirements: *2.1.14: System provides comparisons based on water level predictions, by ship vs. truck or other transportation modalities* and *5.3.1: System provides 3D visualization simulation tool*. These new requirements have priority level score S.

5   Conclusion

In this paper, we reported on the requirements engineering process to develop a Digital Twin (DT) to improve the resilience of multimodal corridors. We focus on the case of the Twente region in The Netherlands. However, given that this problem is recurring in other European regions (and possibly in other areas of the world), we hope that this research serves as a starting point for developing

DTs to improve resilience in multimodal transport, in general. In this context, the requirements we captured, analyzed, and validated can be reused to guide the development of DTs for other multimodal corridors, focusing on monitoring real-time data, making predictions, and providing timely information and actionable insights to different stakeholders so they can proactively mitigate risks and/or recover from climate-based or other types of disruptions.

We acknowledge the main limitation of the work, i.e., the number of participants in the requirements validation phase, which was a little over 30% of the total number of stakeholders consulted. To correct this, we hope to consult the remaining stakeholders in the near future. Given our experience so far, we expect that the list of requirements will remain more or less stable, but the prioritization level of each requirement may change. A few new requirements may possibly be suggested. Given that the stakeholders are of different types, including logistic companies, ports, policymakers, and production companies, we believe that the involved participants are representative of the DT's future users. Moreover, DT development is cyclic and we hope that in a new development cycle we will be able to involve more stakeholders, leading to a more consistent validation of the requirements.

Many of the elicited requirements regard what kind of processes should be monitored (e.g. changes in water level, transportation delays, etc.) and predicted (e.g. natural disasters and other disruptions). For that, the next development steps involve the implementation of algorithms and quantitative analyses techniques to fulfill such requirements.

This is still an ongoing project. The DT development cycle should proceed with the design, implementation and validation, possibly leading to several cycles before a complete version of the DT is ready for use. We will use the gathered requirements for prototyping, supporting requirements validation by allowing stakeholders to test the developed prototype. Our future research agenda comprises all the remaining DT development cycles.

References

1. Achimugu, P., Selamat, A., Ibrahim, R., Mahrin, M.N.: A systematic literature review of software requirements prioritization research. Inf. Softw. Technol. **56**(6), 568–585 (2014)
2. Bak, O., Shaw, S., Colicchia, C., Kumar, V.: A systematic literature review of supply chain resilience in small-medium enterprises (SMES): a call for further research. IEEE Trans. Eng. Manage. **70**(1), 328–341 (2023)
3. Bakhshi, S., et al.: Digital twin applications for overcoming construction supply chain challenges. Autom. Constr. **167**, 105679 (2024)
4. Busse, A., Gerlach, B., Lengeling, J.C., Poschmann, P., Werner, J., Zarnitz, S.: Towards digital twins of multimodal supply chains. Logistics **5**(2), 25 (2021)
5. Dalpiaz, F., Franch, X., Horkoff, J.: istar 2.0 language guide (2016)
6. Ferko, E., Bucaioni, A., Behnam, M.: Architecting digital twins. IEEE Access **10**, 50335–50350 (2022)
7. Ge, C., Qin, S.: Digital twin intelligent transportation system (DT-ITS)-a systematic review. IET Intel. Transp. Syst. **18**(12), 2325–2358 (2024)

8. Irfan, M.S., Dasgupta, S., Rahman, M.: Towards transportation digital twin systems for traffic safety and mobility: a review. IEEE Internet of Things J. (2024)
9. Koot, M., Mes, M.R., Iacob, M.E.: Building an ontological bridge between supply chain resilience and IoT applications. In: International Conference on Enterprise Design, Operations, and Computing, pp. 79–96. Springer, Cham (2023)
10. Kritzinger, W., Karner, M., Traar, G., Henjes, J., Sihn, W.: Digital twin in manufacturing: a categorical literature review and classification. IFAC-PapersOnLine 51(11), 1016–1022 (2018)
11. van Lamsweerde, A.: Goal-oriented requirements engineering: a guided tour. In: Proceedings Fifth IEEE International Symposium on Requirements Engineering, pp. 249–262. ISRE-01, IEEE Comput. Soc (2002)
12. Liu, Y., et al.: Digital twin-driven approach for smart city logistics: the case of freight parking management. In: Dolgui, A., Bernard, A., Lemoine, D., von Cieminski, G., Romero, D. (eds.) APMS 2021. IAICT, vol. 633, pp. 237–246. Springer, Cham (2021). https://doi.org/10.1007/978-3-030-85910-7_25
13. Liu, Y., Pan, S., Ballot, E.: Unveiling the potential of digital twins in logistics and supply chain management: services, capabilities, and research opportunities. Digital Eng. 3, 100025 (2024)
14. Notteboom, T.E.: Concentration and the formation of multi-port gateway regions in the European container port system: an update. J. Transp. Geogr. 18(4), 567–583 (2010). special Issue on Comparative North American and European gateway logistics
15. Park, J., Seager, T.P., Rao, P., Convertino, M., Linkov, I.: Integrating risk and resilience approaches to catastrophe management in engineering systems. Risk Anal. 33(3), 356–367 (2012)
16. Ponsard, C., Massonet, P., Molderez, J.F., Rifaut, A., Lamsweerde, A.V., Van, H.T.: Early verification and validation of mission critical systems. Formal Methods Syst. Des. 30(3), 233–247 (2006)
17. Roman, E.A., Stere, A.S., Roca, E., Radu, A.V., Codroiu, D., Anamaria, I.: State of the art of digital twins in improving supply chain resilience. Logistics 9(1), 22 (2025)
18. Saroj, A.J., Roy, S., Guin, A., Hunter, M.: Development of a connected corridor real-time data-driven traffic digital twin simulation model. J. Transp. Eng. Part A: Syst. 147(12), 04021096 (2021). https://doi.org/10.1061/JTEPBS.0000589
19. SteadieSeifi, M., Dellaert, N., Nuijten, W., Van Woensel, T., Raoufi, R.: Multimodal freight transportation planning: a literature review. Eur. J. Oper. Res. 233(1), 1–15 (2014)
20. Upadhyay, P.: The role of verification and validation in system development life cycle. IOSR J. Comput. Eng. 5(1), 17–20 (2012)
21. Wojciechowski, P.: Fifth work plan of the European coordinator (2022). https://transport.ec.europa.eu/system/files/2022-10/5th_workplan_ralp.pdf

Joint Process Mining with Unstructured Data workshop (PMUD) and International Workshop on Multimodal Process Mining (MMPM)

1st International Workshop on Process Mining with Unstructured Data (PMUD 2025) and 1st International Workshop on Multimodal Process Mining (MMPM 2025)

The Process Mining with Unstructured Data (PMUD) workshop aims to provide a forum for researchers and practitioners to present and discuss how unstructured data can support process mining tasks.

Traditional process mining techniques take structured data as input. However, many valuable insights can be hidden in unstructured data sources, such as emails, social media interactions, legal documents, images, or sensor data. Most state-of-the-art techniques ignore such data, thus missing valuable insights regarding the process. Furthermore, relying solely on structured data can lead to a rigid analysis framework, as structured data often adheres to predefined formats and categories.

Recently, a growing array of approaches to deal with various kinds of unstructured data has emerged in the literature. Among them, NLP techniques have attracted considerable interest thanks to recent breakthroughs such as Large Language Models. Examples include using NLP techniques to extract process models from textual documents, or using LLM to interact with the user at runtime. Some studies also advocate using unstructured data to extract inter-case patterns, thus supporting process-level and object-centric approaches.

Despite the promising results, dealing with unstructured data remains one of the main challenges when applying process mining.

The Multimodal Process Mining (MMPM) workshop aims to bring together researchers and practitioners to explore the integration of multimodal data in process mining. This workshop focuses on the challenges, methodologies, and applications of incorporating diverse data types such as video, audio, and textual data into process mining techniques to enhance process understanding and analysis.

As a special case of multimodal unstructured data, audiovisual streams present both unparalleled opportunities and distinct challenges for process mining. Videos capture rich contextual cues: visual gestures, manual operations, spatial layouts, and environmental changes that cannot be encoded in traditional event logs. However, extracting meaningful events from continuous footage requires advanced computer-vision pipelines for object detection, action recognition, and temporal segmentation, often complemented by speech-to-text transcripts or sensor metadata.

The first edition of PMUD and MMPM received five submissions as regular papers, which were reviewed by at least three members of the program committee. The review process led to three papers being accepted: two as full papers and one as a short paper.

The paper Leveraging LLMs to discover causal dependencies: a case study on a university program" by Claudia Diamantini, Chiara Gobbi, Alessandro Mele, Domenico

Potena, and Cristina Rossetti investigates process model elicitation within the educational domain, conceptualizing university courses as activities connected by prerequisite relationships. The study introduces a methodology that leverages Large Language Models (LLMs) to automatically infer causal dependencies between courses through the analysis of course syllabi. By employing pairwise prompting combined with step-back and chain-of-thought reasoning techniques, the proposed technique extracts dependency information to construct a Directly-Follows Graph, which is subsequently validated by domain experts. Experimental results demonstrate that LLMs can effectively uncover and explain course dependencies, offering valuable insights for curriculum design and improving student guidance on course sequencing. Additionally, the approach reveals potential issues in existing prerequisite structures, demonstrating its broader applicability to educational planning and adaptive learning environments.

The paper Enabling Process Mining on Multimodal Robotic Data" by Flavio Corradini, Sara Pettinari, Barbara Re, Lorenzo Rossi, and Massimiliano Sampaolo addresses the growing challenge of making sense of the vast, heterogeneous streams of information produced by contemporary robotic systems. By systematically transforming low-level sensor readings, video sequences, and inter-module communication logs into coherent, high-level activity traces, this work pioneers the application of process mining techniques to robotics. In particular, the authors employ Conditional Random Fields to segment and label time-series sensor data and fine-tune a Florence-2 vision model to recognize human-interpretable actions from video feeds. Through these methods, they demonstrate how to bridge the gap between raw multimodal inputs and analysable process representations. Finally, the paper identifies the principal obstacles—such as data alignment, noise reduction, and scalability—and outlines a roadmap of opportunities for extending process-mining-based performance evaluation and anomaly detection in complex robotic deployments.

The paper Exploring Business Process Model Similarity with LLMs: Challenges and Potentials " by Francesca Zampino and Antonella Longo explores the use of Large Language Models (LLMs), a technology that is being increasingly adopted to support various tasks within the BPM community with promising results, to evaluate process model similarity, a well-studied and still challenging problem. While conventional approaches usually analyze structural and semantic aspects separately, LLMs offer the ability to evaluate both dimensions simultaneously, enabling more accurate comparisons. The study compares the results obtained by the proposed approach with those obtained by the winning approaches of a previous contest, which provided a ground-truth. The results demonstrate that LLM-based methods, particularly when enhanced with prompt engineering, outperform traditional techniques in terms of precision, recall, and F-score. These findings point to the exciting potential of LLMs in the realm of business process analysis and present valuable opportunities for further refinement in future research.

We would like to thank all the authors who submitted papers for publication in this book. We are also grateful to the members of the Program Committee for their excellent work in reviewing the submitted and revised papers with expertise and patience.

April 2025

Laura Genga
Alex Mircoli
Roberto Nai
Aleksandar Gavric
Maxim Vidgof

Organization

Workshop Chairs

Laura Genga	Eindhoven University of Technology, The Netherlands
Alex Mircoli	Università Politecnica delle Marche, Italy
Roberto Nai	Università di Torino, Italy
Aleksandar Gavric	TU Wien, Austria
Maxim Vidgof	Vienna University of Economics and Business, Austria

Program Committee

Luciana Barbieri	University of Campinas, Brazil
Boualem Benatallah	Dublin City University, Ireland
Patrizio Bellan	Fondazione Bruno Kessler, Italy
Alessandro Berti	RWTH Aachen University, Germany
Dominik Bork	TU Wien, Austria
David Chapela-Campa	University of Tartu, Estonia
Luigi Di Caro	University of Turin, Italy
Chiara Di Francescomarino	University of Trento, Italy
Davide Di Ruscio	Università degli Studi dell'Aquila, Italy
Claudia Diamantini	Università Politecnica delle Marche, Italy
Istvan David	McMaster University, Canada
Sébastien Gérard	CEA List, France
Ana-Maria Ghiran	Babeş-Bolyai University, Romania
Jānis Grabis	Riga Technical University, Latvia
Gert Janssenswillen	Hasselt University, Belgium
Agnes Koschmider	University of Bayreuth, Germany
Hugo A. Lopez-Acosta	Technical University of Denmark, Denmark
Xixi Lu	Utrecht University, The Netherlands
Niels Martin	Hasselt University, Belgium
Jan Mendling	Humboldt-Universität zu Berlin, Germany
Iulian Ober	University of Toulouse, France
Andreas Oberweis	Karlsruhe Institute of Technology, Germany
Adela del Río Ortega	Universidad de Sevilla, Spain
Cristina-Claudia Osman	Babeş-Bolyai University, Romania
Sara Pettinari	Gran Sasso Science Institute, Italy
Domenico Potena	Università Politecnica delle Marche, Italy
Henderik A. Proper	TU Wien, Austria
Majid Rafiei	SAP SE, Germany

Leveraging LLMs to Discover Causal Dependencies: A Case Study on a University Program

Claudia Diamantini[1] , Chiara Gobbi[1] , Alessandro Mele[1](✉) ,
Domenico Potena[1] , and Cristina Rossetti[1,2]

[1] DII, Università Politecnica delle Marche, via Brecce Bianche, 60131 Ancona, Italy
a.mele@pm.univpm.it
[2] DAUIN, Politecnico di Torino, Corso Duca degli Abruzzi 24, 10129 Turin, Italy

Abstract. Defining a process model is essential for understanding organizational workflows and guiding future activities. While process discovery techniques can derive models from event logs, designing a process model from scratch remains challenging, as it relies on human experts to interpret requirements. This work explores process model elicitation in the educational domain, where courses in a university program are treated as activities with prerequisite relationships. We propose a methodology leveraging Large Language Models to automatically infer causal dependencies among courses by analyzing their syllabi. Using pairwise prompting with step-back and chain-of-thought reasoning, the extracted dependencies are used to build a Directly-Follows Graph, subsequently evaluated by domain experts. Experimental results show that Large Language Models can effectively identify and justify course dependencies, providing valuable insights that can enhance curriculum design and provide students with clearer guidance on course sequencing. The approach also highlights gaps in prerequisite structures, suggesting a broader application in educational planning and dynamic learning environments.

Keywords: Process mining · Large language models · Educational process mining

1 Introduction

Explicitly defining a process model is a crucial activity for understanding how an organization operates and for guiding future activities. A process model can be derived from the information contained in an event log using process discovery techniques, when an event log is available. However, during the process design phase, only the requirements are known, and is challenging to define a process model. In this case, human experts are required to interpret the requirements and formalize them into a process model.

We focus on the design of process models from scratch in the educational domain, considering the study of a set of available courses as activities to be performed in order to acquire the skills provided by a study program (i.e., the process). In this scenario, process model elicitation corresponds to identifying the set

J. Grabis and Y. Wautelet (Eds.): CAiSE 2025 Workshops, LNBIP 556, pp. 237–248, 2025.
https://doi.org/10.1007/978-3-031-94931-9_19

of causal dependencies between available courses, meaning that fully understanding the content of a course requires the skills acquired in another course. In an academic scenario, this set of dependencies is useful, for instance, to verify the manifesto of a degree program, specifically the allocation of courses across semesters and years. Moreover, in contexts where students can attend courses in any order without any content-related prerequisites, causal dependencies provide a useful guideline for students, suggesting the order in which courses should be taken.

The issue becomes even more complex in dynamic online learning systems, where several courses are available and frequent change or addition of courses occur. In these environments, every time a new course is introduced, all instructors would need to reassess and redefine the prerequisite relationships for their courses in light of the new ones. This process is highly challenging as it requires continuous effort to keep the dependency structure up to date, making manual maintenance impractical.

In this work, we investigated upon the use of Large Language Models (LLMs) for automatically discovering dependencies among available courses, based on the topics covered in each course's syllabus. Specifically, we leverage the ability of LLMs to both analyze and establish relationships among course topics. The proposal uses a pairwise prompting supported by a step-back [20] and chain-of-thought [18] approach. The discovered dependencies are used to build a Directly-Follows Graph (DFG). The results are evaluated by domain experts and show that LLMs can both identify, with a good precision, and justify dependencies.

The work is organized as follows. Section 2 provides an overview of related work, Sect. 3 describes the proposed approach through a real-world case study, Sect. 4 discusses the experimental results, and Sect. 5 concludes the paper and delineates future work.

2   Related Work

LLMs are advanced Artificial Intelligence (AI) systems that learn from vast collections of corpora to process and generate text. These models leverage deep learning techniques, with the transformer architecture being the most widely used [17]. This enables LLMs to recognize intricate linguistic patterns and relationships across words and sentences allowing despite the complexities of human language [10,19].

By acquiring broad knowledge across multiple domains, these models enhance language comprehension and open new possibilities for improving the identification of causal dependencies [8,14]. These advances in LLMs have sparked new interest in their application to causal discovery tasks. [11] explores how LLMs can initialize differentiable causal discovery models, improving robustness and scalability. Similarly, [9] analyzes factors influencing LLM performance in causal discovery. Furthermore, [12] investigates autonomous LLM-augmented causal reasoning, showcasing their ability to enhance causal inference tasks. In addition, [1] discusses how LLMs can be leveraged for causal discovery, providing insights into their potential advantages over traditional methods.

Most LLM-based approaches to causal dependencies discovery, predominantly rely on pairwise prompting [2,13,14] where the model is required to produce causal relations like "Does A cause B?" using different prompt formulations. Some other work proposes a triplet-based prompting strategy combined with chain-of-thought reasoning [18] that enhances accuracy and mitigates cyclic dependencies when inferring relationships [16].

Process mining has greatly benefited from LLM integration. [3] shows that some LLMs can effectively perform multiple tasks, such as anomaly detection, process model generation, and process model understanding. The application of LLMs in process mining is also discussed in [5], which provides a detailed analysis of their potential. Additionally, [6] proposes the analysis of business processes models through natural process querying language and [7] develops a LLM specialized in the interpretation, analysis and optimization of business processes.

Despite these advancements, several challenges persist. While LLMs have demonstrated potential in causal discovery and process mining, concerns regarding their interpretability, robustness, and reliability remain critical areas of investigation. [15] introduces a benchmark designed to evaluate LLMs in process mining contexts, addressing existing gaps in performance evaluation, while [4] investigates methods for evaluating LLM outputs in PM tasks, an essential aspect for real-world applicability.

In our approach, we investigate the use of LLMs to extract causal dependencies among courses available in a course set. In details, we use a pairwise prompting supported by a step-back [20] and chain-of-thought [18] approach.

3   Methodology

The proposed methodology aims at extracting causal dependencies among courses available in a university study plan, based on the topics covered in the syllabus of each course.

In order to provide an illustrative example, we focus on a 3-year Bachelor's Degree program in Computer and Automation Engineering from the Università Politecnica delle Marche, Italy[1]. In particular, we focus on courses of the 2023–2024 academic year[2]. Foundational courses, such as *Mathematical Analysis 1* and *2*, *Linear Algebra and Geometry*, *Physics 1* and *2*, *Fundamentals of Computer Science* and *Business Economics* are all concentrated in the first year. Starting from the second year, courses specific to the degree program are introduced, including *Fundamentals of Automation*, *Elements of Electronics*, *Electrotechnics*, *Automation Control* and *Object Programming*. In the second year, students have the opportunity to select two courses from the ones offered by the university, based on their area of interest. Finally, in the third year, there are only two mandatory courses, and all the others are electives, allowing students to choose

---

[1] https://www.univpm.it/Entra/Universita_Politecnica_delle_Marche_Home/L/1.
[2] https://guide.univpm.it/guide.php?fac=ingegneria&lang=lang-eng.

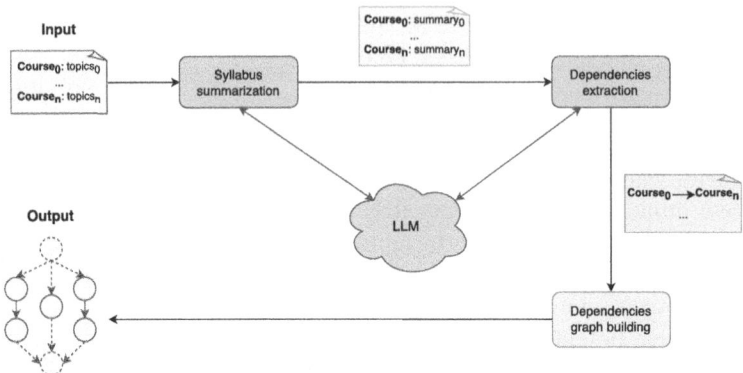

Fig. 1. The proposed methodology.

their specialization path. Examples of specialized courses include: *Web Technologies*, *Databases*, and *Technologies for Automation and Robotics*.

The methodology adopts a step-back [20] and chain-of-thought [18] prompting approaches, which consist of providing the LLM with an initial prompt and then refining the output through additional prompts to obtain the final result. This approach results useful to instruct the LLM to refine its reasoning process incrementally, ensuring a coherent final output. The steps of our methodology are detailed in Fig. 1.

Syllabus Summarization. In this section, we define the steps to obtain the initial prompt provided to the LLM. The course-related information were extracted from the syllabus of courses. The syllabus provides details for each course of the degree program, including the teacher and the topics covered in the course.

The starting prompt consists on providing the LLM with list of courses, each of one is described by the name and the topics covered in the course. To mitigate biases introduced by course naming, we begin by assigning a neutral code to each course in the syllabus, thus redirecting the model's attention to the substantive content of the program. For the sake of simplicity, in the following, we still refer to courses with their names instead of their codes. The task assigned to the LLM is to summarize, for each course, the most important concepts to learn. This step is fundamental, since we provide the LLM with a knowledge base for future queries. Figure 2 shows an excerpt of the prompt to derive summarization.

Dependencies Extraction. In this step, we aim at deriving the set of *causal dependencies* among the courses listed in the degree program. A causal dependency between courses A and B ($A \rightarrow B$) means that in order to attend B, some topics covered in course A are required. This step is further divided in sub steps: we query the LLM (i) to derive the initial set of causal dependencies based on the provided knowledge base, (ii) to obtain the explanations that guided the LLM

This is the list of courses from the syllabus:

Course: C1 {Mathematical analysis 1}
Program: sets, relations and functions. natural, integer, rational and real numbers. complex numbers, trigonometric and exponential representation.

Course: C2 {Mathematical analysis 2}
Program: functions of several variables. curves, line integrals, vector fields, differential forms. multiple integrals with applications. ordinary differential equations. laplace transform on r.

Course: C3 {Business Economics}
Program: economic and financial aspect of management, enterprise in the economic system, corporate legal forms.

. . .

Your task is to summarize their programs highlighting the most important concepts to learn.

Fig. 2. Excerpt of the starting prompt provided to the LLM to derive summarization. The course names are enclosed in curly brackets for simplicity only and have not been included in the prompt

in defining them, and (iii) to determine whether, based on the explanations just provided, it would insert new dependencies or delete discovered ones, obtaining the final set.

The first sub step consist on providing the LLM with the definition of causal dependency. To achieve this, the LLM is provided with the following prompt: *Given two courses A and B, the causal dependency $A \rightarrow B$ means that in order to study B, it is essential to have previously studied A.* Then we assign the following task to the LLM: *Find causal dependencies $A \rightarrow B$, where A and B must be only in this list of given courses.* With this indications, the LLM is provided with a precise definition of causal dependency and is forced to adhere to the specified course names. Luckily, in our case study, the LLM has not discovered dependencies among non-existing courses.

The second sub step involves querying the LLM to obtain the reasons behind the definition of the dependencies. This is a crucial step because it forces the LLM to articulate its reasoning explicitly, rather than simply presenting a set of conclusions. Revealing these justifications allows verification of whether the dependencies align with the actual course content. Figure 3 shows the reasoning provided by the LLM for the dependency *Mathematical analysis 1 → Mathematical analysis 2.*

Mathematical Analysis 1 → Mathematical Analysis 2

Explanation: mathematical analysis 1 covers foundational calculus concepts such as limits, continuity, differentiation, integration, and basic infinite series. Understanding these single-variable calculus principles is essential before advancing to mathematical analysis 2, which deals with functions of several variables, multiple integrals, and advanced topics like differential equations. The multi-variable calculus in mathematical analysis 2 builds directly upon the single-variable calculus learned in mathematical analysis 1.

Fig. 3. An example of causal dependency explanation.

The last sub step consists on querying the LLM to revisit the dependencies in light of its own justifications, reflecting on whether the previous dependencies it articulated are correct and complete. In this step, the LLM detects inconsistencies or realizes that certain dependencies are misaligned with the actual course content and with the explanations it gave in the previous step and then it revises the dependencies accordingly. This ensures that the LLM not only clarifies how it arrived at particular prerequisites but also critically reevaluates its own reasoning, refining and strengthening the set of causal dependencies across the courses.

Dependencies Graph Building. The resulting set of causal dependencies is then used to construct a DFG. Let $\mathcal{G} = (V, E)$ be a graph, where each node $v \in V$ represents a course, and each directed edge $\langle v_i, v_j \rangle \in E, v_i, v_j \in V$ represents the causal dependency $v_i \rightarrow v_j$. In order to obtain a connected graph, we added two artificial nodes, i.e., $START$ and END. For each course for which the LLM has not identified incoming dependencies, we add an artificial edge from the $START$ node and the course. For example, the *Business Economics* course, being from a different disciplinary field, does not require engineering-related skills. For all the courses for which the LLM has not identified outcoming dependencies, we add artificial edges to the END node.

4   Experiments

This section aims to illustrate (i) the experimental setup, (ii) the obtained dependencies, and (iii) the corresponding evaluation phase. The proposed methodology was implemented in Python and using the *gpt-o1-preview* LLM, accessible via OpenAI APIs[3]. Regarding the LLM, the seed shall aim at ensuring experiment reproducibility. For space reason, in this work we show only an excerpt of the dependency graph; the complete material is available at the following repository[4]. The evaluation step is conducted as follows: the graph generated by the

---

[3] https://platform.openai.com/docs/overview.
[4] https://github.com/KDMG/causal_dependencies_degree_courses/tree/main.

LLM ($\mathcal{G}$) is compared with the reference graph ($\mathcal{G}^*$) built by asking course professors to indicate which other courses a student should take before enrolling in their own course. Then, all dependencies discovered by the LLM that are also present in the baseline graph are evaluated by professors.

4.1 Results

The dependency graph derived from LLM ($\mathcal{G}$) contains 40 edges, 19 of which identify causal dependencies not present in $\mathcal{G}^*$. Due to space constraints, Fig. 4 illustrates an excerpt of $\mathcal{G}$. The excerpt highlights (with dashed edges) the artificial links between the *START* node and the courses for which the LLM has no discovered dependencies, i.e., *Linear Algebra and Geometry*, *Mathematical Analysis 1*, *Business Economics*, and *General Physics 1*. Note that the graph $\mathcal{G}$ obtained can be interpreted as a process model that provides students with guidance on how to build the required knowledge before progressing to more advanced topics in the study plan. Specifically, the dependencies in the graph highlight different types of prerequisite relationships: AND-gateways where multiple prerequisites are recommended before taking a course and OR-gateways, which indicate that completing a course enables students to access multiple subsequent courses for which they have acquired the necessary foundations.

Figure 4 also highlights (with blue edge) a *transitive* dependency. A transitive dependency is a dependency that can be derived from others. Given the dependency *Mathematical Analysis 1* → *Mathematical Methods for Automation Engineering*, we observe that can be derived from *Mathematical Analysis 1* → *Mathematical Analysis 2* and *Mathematical Analysis 2* → *Mathematical Methods for Automation Engineering*. Discussions with domain experts revealed that all transitive dependencies were intentionally omitted in the definition of $\mathcal{G}^*$. Consequently, before the evaluation stage, all transitive dependencies were removed from $\mathcal{G}$, resulting in a total of 37 edges, of which 17 dependencies (E') were identified by the LLM and missing in $\mathcal{G}^*$. Table 1 reports some examples of the resulting dependencies and the corresponding explanation provided by the LLM.

Table 1. Example of dependencies discovered by LLM not in $\mathcal{G}^*$.

Dependency: *Mathematical Analysis 1 → Probability and Statistics*
Explanation: Calculus concepts from mathematical analysis 1, such as integration and differentiation, are essential in probability and statistics for working with probability density functions, calculating probabilities, and understanding continuous random variables. The ability to compute limits and work with infinite series is also important for topics like convergence in distributions and the Central Limit Theorem in probability and statistics
Dependency: *Mathematical Analysis 1 → Fundamentals of Electronics*
Explanation: Calculus concepts from mathematical analysis 1 are important in fundamentals of electronics for analyzing circuit behavior over time, especially when dealing with capacitors, inductors, and time-varying signals. Understanding differential equations and integrals is necessary for transient analysis and frequency response in electronics
Dependency: *Mathematical Analysis 2 → Automatic Control*
Explanation: Automatic control requires strong calculus skills from mathematical analysis 2, as control systems analysis and design involve differential equations, Laplace transforms, and continuous-time system modeling. Understanding multi-variable calculus and the mathematical tools for analyzing system dynamics is crucial in automatic control
Dependency: *Linear Algebra and Geometry → Probability and Statistics*
Explanation: The necessity of linear algebra for probability and statistics depends on the depth of topics like multivariate distributions, covariance matrices, and linear regression If probability and statistics covers these advanced topics extensively, linear algebra becomes essential However, for introductory probability and statistics focusing on univariate distributions and basic statistical methods, linear algebra may not be strictly required Therefore, the dependency should be clarified based on the course's emphasis
Dependency: *Linear Algebra and Geometry → Mathematical Methods for Automation Engineering*
Explanation: mathematical methods for automation engineering involves functional analysis and linear operators, which are built upon linear algebra concepts from linear algebra and geometry, including vector spaces and linear transformations The abstract mathematical structures studied in mathematical methods for automation engineering require a deep understanding of linear algebra

4.2   Discussion

After the post-processing step in which the transitive edges were excluded, a total of 20 correct edges were identified by the LLM, compared to the 51 in $\mathcal{G}^*$; 31 dependencies are not recognized by the LLM and 17 are found by the LLM but are not present in $\mathcal{G}^*$. Here, we focus on these latter as they may not be incorrect. In fact, $\mathcal{G}^*$ cannot be considered 100% reliable for several reasons. First, human experts who contributed to its development may have omitted some dependencies for the sake of simplicity or because they considered them less important than others. Moreover, while the LLM used only the content of the syllabus, the expert also relied on its own knowledge and experience. This forces us to consider the dependencies in E' to avoid erroneously labeling them as

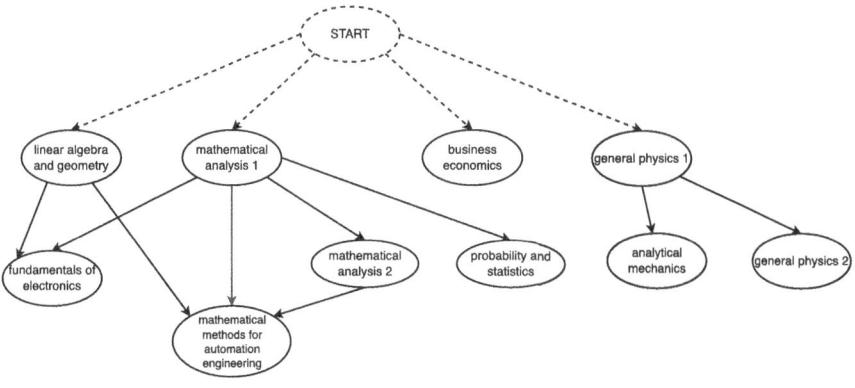

Fig. 4. Excerpt of $\mathcal{G}$.

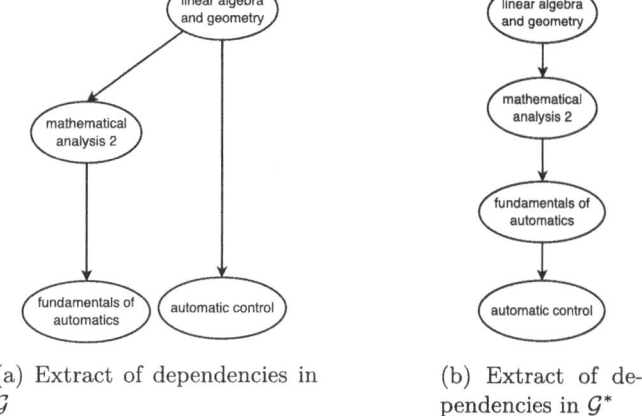

(a) Extract of dependencies in $\mathcal{G}$

(b) Extract of dependencies in $\mathcal{G}^*$

Fig. 5. Example of indirect dependency.

wrong. In fact, some of these dependencies might be correct from the evaluator point of view, and this can be useful to possibly refine and adjust the source graph.

Before the actual evaluation, we identify among E' a subset that we call *indirect dependencies*. These dependencies represent those edges that are not explicitly present in $\mathcal{G}^*$, but can be found in an existing path. For example, assume $\{(A, B), (B, C), (C, D)\} \in E^*$ and $(A, D) \in E'$ a dependency returned by the LLM but not present in $\mathcal{G}^*$. The edge (A, D) cannot be considered wrong, because there is in fact in $\mathcal{G}^*$ a path connecting node A to node D, so this dependence exists but in an indirect way. We identified a total of 9 indirect dependencies in E'. For instance, consider the dependency *Linear Algebra and Geometry* $\rightarrow$ *Automatic Control* (Fig. 5): in $\mathcal{G}^*$ the path *Linear Algebra and Geometry* $\rightarrow$ *Mathematical Analysis 2* $\rightarrow$ *Fundamentals of Automatics* $\rightarrow$ *Automatic Control* exists. It can be stated that, in order to fully comprehend *Automatic Control*, it is essential to have studied *Linear Algebra and Geometry*. As such, the indirect dependency *Linear Algebra and Geometry* → *Automatic Control* can be considered as correct.

These observations cause the total number of dependencies that we consider to be correct to rise from 20 to 29. It now remains to discuss the remaining 8 dependencies that are neither present in $\mathcal{G}^*$ nor indirect. Of these, 4 were assessed by the evaluators as incorrect. The other 4 are discussed in detail below. The dependencies *Numerical Analysis* → *Modeling and Identification of Dynamic Processes* and *Numerical Analysis* → *Fundamentals of Automatics*, which connect *Numerical Analysis* to automation courses, was positively assessed by the evaluators because methods to solve linear and non-linear systems as well as concepts of eigenvalues, derivatives and integrals studied in *Numerical Analysis* may serve as useful mathematical knowledge to better approach the design of dynamic control systems. As concerns the dependency *Object-Oriented Programming* → *Operating Systems*, evaluators believed that the implementation of concurrent programming (present in the course's syllabus) may involve the use of constructs from object-oriented programming. In addition, the practice lectures require knowledge of Java. Thus, this dependency was evaluated as correct, although it may be considered a weak link. Finally, also the dependency *Algebra and Logics* → *Object-Oriented Programming* was labeled as correct, since the notions of logical reasoning and algebraic structured studied in *Algebra and Logics* can be useful, even if not strictly necessary, for a better approach to a programming course. On the basis of this discussion, the total number of correct dependencies in $\mathcal{G}$ are 33.

It is interesting to note that evaluators agreed with the explanations provided by the LLM. For instance, concerning the above-mentioned dependencies involving *Numerical Analysis*, both the LLM and the evaluators stated that the mathematical methods studied in the course helps the understanding, modeling and solving dynamic processes. In addition, the LLM seems capable of assigning an importance weight to dependencies with terms such as "necessary" or "not strictly required". For example, the LLM assessed the course *Algebra and Logics* as useful but not strictly necessary for *Object-oriented programming*, just as the evaluators.

An important consideration concerns the identification of clusters. In fact, in $\mathcal{G}^*$ we can find homogeneous groups of courses belonging to macro-areas, thus accounting for disciplines belonging to the same field of study. Experts identified 4 different clusters $c_1 = $ *Mathematical and physical foundations*, $c_2 = $*Computer science*, $c_3 = $*Automation* and $c_4 = $*other*. Courses {*Mathematical Analysis 1, Mathematical Analysis 2, Linear Algebra and Geometry, General Physics 1, General Physics 2, Numerical Analysis, Algebra and Logics*} belong to c_1; {*Fundamentals of Computer Science, Operating Systems, Computer Architecture and Cloud Computing, Web Technologies, Object-oriented Programming, Databases, Software Engineering, Mobile Programming*} belong to c_2; {*Fundamentals of Automatics, Industrial Automation, Automatic Control, Automation Laboratory,*

Robotics and Automation Technologies, Modeling and Identification of Dynamic Processes, Methods and Techniques for Automation, Computer Aided Control Design} belong to c_3. The LLM correctly finds the 66.66% of dependencies within each cluster, meaning that the majority of edges between courses of c_i are present in $\mathcal{G}$.

5   Conclusion and Further Works

This paper introduces a new approach to extract causal dependencies among courses, demonstrating its application to an Italian university degree program.

The study demonstrated that the DFG obtained using the LLM exhibits high precision but suffers from low recall, as some prerequisite relationships present in the reference graph are not detected by the LLM. This limitation is due to the varying and often insufficient level of detail in the course programs, making it challenging for the LLM to identify dependencies. On the other hand, professors, who have more vast and precise knowledge, proposed additional links. For this reason, providing to the LLM more comprehensive materials, such as more detailed syllabus, could help compensate for these limitations. Notably, the LLM also inferred additional dependencies that were not present in $\mathcal{G}^*$ but were reasonable. This suggests that LLMs can provide valuable insights that complement or refine existing knowledge.

In conclusion, it could be interesting to test the LLM by providing it with more comprehensive information beyond just the official course programs. This is especially relevant in dynamic online learning systems, where course offerings change dynamically. Furthermore, this approach could support future research to understand whether the courses offered within a study program are sufficient to cover all the required prerequisites. In this work, the focus has been on identifying dependencies between the courses while ensuring that the LLM does not generate new course names. However, an extension of this study would be to assess whether the set of courses available in a program adequately covers the fundamental knowledge required for all the courses in the program. This means that the methodology could also play a crucial role in designing an entire educational curriculum for schools and universities other than optimizing the structure of an already existing study program, ensuring that it provides a coherent and comprehensive learning path.

References

1. Ban, T., Chen, L., Lyu, D., Wang, X., Zhu, Q., Chen, H.: Llm-driven causal discovery via harmonized prior. IEEE Trans. Knowl. Data Eng. (2025)
2. Ban, T., Chen, L., Wang, X., Chen, H.: From query tools to causal architects: harnessing large language models for advanced causal discovery from data. arXiv preprint arXiv:2306.16902 (2023)
3. Berti, A., Kourani, H., van der Aalst, W.M.: PM-LLM-benchmark: Evaluating large language models on process mining tasks. arXiv preprint arXiv:2407.13244 (2024)

4. Berti, A., Kourani, H., Häfke, H., Li, C.Y., Schuster, D.: Evaluating large language models in process mining: capabilities, benchmarks, and evaluation strategies. In: International Conference on Business Process Modeling, Development and Support, pp. 13–21. Springer (2024)
5. Berti, A., Qafari, M.S.: Leveraging large language models (LLMS) for process mining (technical report). arXiv preprint arXiv:2307.12701 (2023)
6. Berti, A., Schuster, D., van der Aalst, W.M.: Abstractions, scenarios, and prompt definitions for process mining with LLMS: a case study. In: International Conference on Business Process Management, pp. 427–439. Springer (2023)
7. Buss, A., Kratsch, W., Schmid, S.J., Wang, H.: Processllm: a large language model specialized in the interpretation, analysis, and optimization of business processes. In: International Conference on Business Process Management, pp. 221–232. Springer (2024)
8. Chen, L., Ban, T., Wang, X., Lyu, D., Chen, H.: Mitigating prior errors in causal structure learning: Towards LLM driven prior knowledge. arXiv preprint arXiv:2306.07032 (2023)
9. Feng, T., Qu, L., Tandon, N., Li, Z., Kang, X., Haffari, G.: From pre-training corpora to large language models: What factors influence LLM performance in causal discovery tasks? arXiv preprint arXiv:2407.19638 (2024)
10. Hadi, M.U., et al.: A survey on large language models: applications, challenges, limitations, and practical usage. Authorea Preprints **3** (2023)
11. Kampani, S., Hidary, D., van der Poel, C., Ganahl, M., Miao, B.: LLM-initialized differentiable causal discovery. arXiv preprint arXiv:2410.21141 (2024)
12. Khatibi, E., Abbasian, M., Yang, Z., Azimi, I., Rahmani, A.M.: ALCM: autonomous LLM-augmented causal discovery framework. arXiv preprint arXiv:2405.01744 (2024)
13. Kiciman, E., Ness, R., Sharma, A., Tan, C.: Causal reasoning and large language models: opening a new frontier for causality. Trans. Mach. Learn. Res. (2023)
14. Long, S., Schuster, T., Piché, A.: Can large language models build causal graphs? arXiv preprint arXiv:2303.05279 (2023)
15. Redis, A.C., Sani, M.F., Zarrin, B., Burattin, A.: Processtbench: an LLM plan generation dataset for process mining. arXiv preprint arXiv:2409.09191 (2024)
16. Vashishtha, A., Reddy, A.G., Kumar, A., Bachu, S., Balasubramanian, V.N., Sharma, A.: Causal inference using LLM-guided discovery. arXiv preprint arXiv:2310.15117 (2023)
17. Vaswani, A., et al.: Attention is all you need. In: Advances in Neural Information Processing Systems, vol. 30 (2017)
18. Wei, J., et al.: Chain-of-thought prompting elicits reasoning in large language models. Adv. Neural. Inf. Process. Syst. **35**, 24824–24837 (2022)
19. Zhao, W.X., et al.: A survey of large language models. arXiv preprint arXiv:2303.18223 1(2) (2023)
20. Zheng, H.S., et al.: Take a step back: evoking reasoning via abstraction in large language models. arXiv preprint arXiv:2310.06117 (2023)

Exploring Business Process Model Similarity with LLMs: Challenges and Potentials

Francesca Zampino[1,2(✉)] [iD] and Antonella Longo[1] [iD]

[1] University of Salento, Lecce, Italy
{francesca.zampino,antonella.longo}@unisalento.it
[2] HSPI Spa, Rome, Italy
http://www.unisalento.it

Abstract. Process model similarity is vital for ensuring consistency, comparability, and evolution of business processes. In recent years, Large Language Models (LLMs) have been increasingly adopted to support various tasks within the BPM (Business Process Management) community, showing promising results. However, one area that remains underexplored is the use of LLMs for evaluating the similarity of process models. This task is particularly challenging as it involves capturing both the structural and semantic dimensions of similarity in business process models, while traditional methods typically address only one aspect at a time. Unlike conventional approaches, which analyze structural and semantic aspects separately, LLMs offer the ability to evaluate both dimensions simultaneously, enabling more accurate comparisons.

The results demonstrate that LLM-based methods, particularly when enhanced with prompt engineering, outperform traditional techniques in terms of precision, recall, and F-score. These findings point to the exciting potential of LLMs in the realm of business process analysis and present valuable opportunities for further refinement in future research.

Keywords: Process Model Matching · Large Language Models · Benchmarking AI Performance

1 Introduction

Similarity matching between process models involves identifying correspondences between models that often differ in semantics, structure, and granularity [5,9]. Traditional approaches relying on purely syntactic measures struggle with complex cases, frequently resulting in false positives, and they fail to capture structural dependencies-such as those imposed by gateways-which control process flow [6]. Recent advances in generative AI and Large Language Models (LLMs) promise improvements by integrating semantic understanding and, to some degree, structural analysis. Although methods using ontologies, word embeddings, and models like BERT enhance semantic similarity, they do not fully address the complex structures of process models.

© The Author(s), under exclusive license to Springer Nature Switzerland AG 2025
J. Grabis and Y. Wautelet (Eds.): CAiSE 2025 Workshops, LNBIP 556, pp. 249–256, 2025.
https://doi.org/10.1007/978-3-031-94931-9_20

Our approach overcomes these limitations by combining semantic and structural matching. We investigate several LLMs-tailoring prompt engineering to better capture both the nuanced meanings and the underlying process structure-and benchmark their performance against the PM Matching 2015 contest gold standard [7]. This study provides a structured evaluation of LLM-based methods, highlighting their potential to outperform traditional similarity metrics while mitigating their shortcomings.

The manuscript is organized as follows. Section 2 presents a brief literature review on business process models and LLM integration; Sect. 3 details our evaluation methodology and results using the contest's ground truth; finally, Sect. 4 discusses the findings and outlines the challenges and potentials of LLMs in process similarity analysis.

2   Background

Since 2018, LLMs have significantly impacted the BPM community by automating workflow extraction from unstructured documents and enhancing process discovery. [10,12]. LLMs enhance business process discovery by analyzing textual data such as customer interactions, emails, and reports to identify patterns and optimize workflows. Beyond improving natural language interaction, LLMs are also finding advanced applications in Business Process Modeling where their ability to understand and generate text is crucial.

Evaluating the similarity between process models is essential for ensuring consistency and aligning operations with business goals. However, this is challenging due to differences in structure, terminology, and behavior, as noted by Dijkman et al. [6]. Traditional matching methods often struggle with these complexities, particularly in capturing semantic nuances and structural dependencies.

This paper focuses on the application of Large Language Models (LLMs) for process model similarity assessment. A literature review was conducted using Scopus with the query "business AND process AND large AND language AND models," identifying key LLM-based methods for improving process model matching. Works published since 2018 were filtered for relevance, particularly those by Bernardi et al. [1,2], who demonstrated that LLMs trained on large datasets can recognize recurring process patterns, leading to the BPLLM framework. Similarly, Lagos et al. [8] integrated semantic similarity into process modeling by using ontologies and models like BERT, enhancing the matching of activities across various terminologies. These contributions highlight the growing potential of LLMs to offer a more nuanced, accurate, and efficient comparison of business process models, improving integration, optimization, and redundancy detection.

LLMs Challenges and Potentials. LLMs offer significant promise in process model similarity matching, but their effectiveness is heavily dependent on the design of input prompts. Although LLMs such as BERT and Llama can capture complex semantic and structural dependencies, poorly designed prompts can result in vague or inaccurate output [11]. However, prompt engineering allows for targeted refinement of LLM performance, enabling better handling of the variability and complexity of business processes.

Figure 1 illustrates the challenges and potential of applying prompt engineering to business process models, highlighting the need for clear and structured instructions to improve the accuracy of the match.

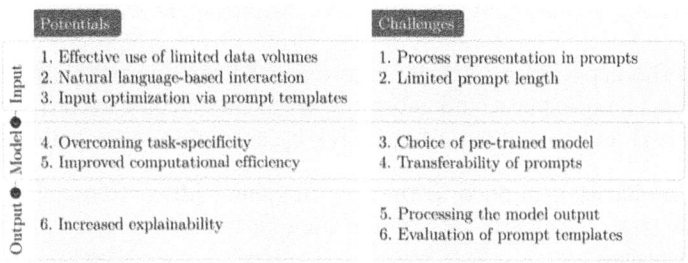

Fig. 1. LLMs Challenges and Potentials [3]

The Process Model Matching Contest. To benchmark LLMs against established methods, we use the Process Model Matching Contest 2015 [7], which focused on process model matching in process mining. Participants applied NLP techniques, such as Word Embeddings (Word2Vec, GloVe, BERT), Cosine Similarity, and Levenshtein Distance, on three datasets: University Admission (9 models of administrative processes for university admissions), Birth Registration (9 models for the birth registration process), and Asset Management (72 models covering various asset management procedures).

The matching techniques were evaluated against a manually created gold standard [7], using the macro-average F-measure.[1]

3   Overview of the LLMs Applied

This work applies multilingual BERT and Llama-based matching systems to assess business process similarity. Unlike traditional methods focusing on the semantic level, our approach captures task names and the entire process structure, including relationships between tasks, events, gateways, and control flows. We will compare these LLM systems with the best-performing approach from the process model matching contest [7].

We selected BERT multilingual for its ability to capture semantic relationships across languages in BPMN datasets and Llama for its effectiveness in

---

[1] University Admission: the two most effective methods identified were RMM/NHCM (0.668) and RMM/NLM (0.636); Birth Registration: the highest scores were achieved by OPBOT (0.54) and pPalm-DS (0.426). Asset Management: the best methods were AML-PM (0.677) and RMM/NHCM (0.661).

domain-specific insights through prompt engineering. By testing both models separately, we aim to identify the most effective tool for process model similarity.[2]

BERT Multilingual Model. The BERT model is used in its pre-trained form (bert-base-multilingual-cased) to generate semantic and structural representations of process models, enabling similarity measurement without prompt engineering.

The methodology [4] begins by converting BPMN models into XML. Key elements, task names, lanes, and gateways, are extracted and converted into text, then tokenized and embedded using BERT by averaging token embeddings.

– Cosine similarity is applied to the resulting embeddings to quantify the similarity between elements, with values ranging from 0 (completely dissimilar) to 1 (identical).

To combine both semantics and structure, the method merges all elements, tasks, lanes, and gateways, into a single textual representation before embedding. This approach allows for the calculation of a global similarity score that considers the relationships among the elements. It explicitly includes roles (lanes) and control flows (gateways) in the comparison.

For models in PNML and EPML formats, a parallel process is undertaken: XML parsing, extraction of elements (such as places and transitions in Petri Nets), conversion of the text, and embedding utilizing BERT.

The model produces:

– **Global Similarity**, cosine similarity between concatenated textual representations.
– **One-to-one Similarities**, similarity scores for individual components (tasks, lanes, gateways, places, transitions).

By integrating semantic content with structural context, this approach supports consistent and comprehensive similarity analysis across BPMN, PNML, and EPML models.

LLAMA Model. In our experiment with LLAMA, we applied the same prompt engineering principles across different process modeling formats, including BPMN (Business Process Model and Notation), Petri Nets, EPML (Event-driven Process Chain Markup Language), and PNML (Petri Net Markup Language).

As shown in the example with BPMN(Figure 2), we designed a structured prompt to compare two process models in XML format, assess their similarity, and identify semantic and structural correspondences. The same methodology was then extended to other modeling languages, ensuring consistency across different notations.

---

[2] https://github.com/Frazampino/ZampinoLongoPMUD.

```
import xml.etree.ElementTree as ET
import ollama

def compare_bpmn_with_ollama(bpmn_file_1, bpmn_file_2):
    with open(bpmn_file_1, 'r') as file1:
        bpmn_1_content = file1.read()

    with open(bpmn_file_2, 'r') as file2:
        bpmn_2_content = file2.read()

    #Example prompt
    prompt = f"""Compare the following two BPMN models in XML format and assess their matching:

BPMN Model 1: {bpmn_1_content}
BPMN Model 2: {bpmn_2_content}

1. Provide a matching score from 0 to 1, where 0 means no match and 1 means perfect match,
along with a brief explanation of the
score.
2. Identify one-to-one mappings between tasks in both models based on their semantic meaning and structure.
Provide the mapping in a list format
(e.g., Task 1 in Model 1 -> Task A in Model 2).
3. If gateways or other elements have significant differences, note them separately.

Respond in a clear and structured format."""

    response = ollama.chat(model="llama3", messages=[{'role': 'user', 'content': prompt}])

    content = response['message']['content']

    return content
```

Fig. 2. Example prompt for BPMN

- Explicit Instructions: we provided clear instructions to the model for identifying correspondences between elements in BPMN, Petri Nets, EPML, and PNML. This included both semantic matching (understanding the meaning of activities, transitions, places, and events) and structural matching (analyzing the relationships between elements).
- Example Prompts[3]: we supplied tailored examples of correct matches, highlighting similarities between activities in BPMN, transitions in Petri Nets, functions in EPML, and elements in PNML. Additionally, we considered relationships between places in Petri Nets, events in BPMN and EPML, and other structurally relevant components.
- Process Layout: we emphasized the structural relationships between elements across all modeling formalisms, ensuring that the model captured both semantic and structural correspondences accurately.
- Iterative refinement: we refined the prompts iteratively to enhance the identification of correspondences, particularly for complex models with significant structural variations.
- Domain-Specific Prompts: we customized prompts for each process modeling notation, ensuring that responses were relevant and aligned with the specific characteristics of BPMN, Petri Nets, EPML, and PNML.

---

[3] https://github.com/Frazampino/ZampinoLongoPMUD.

To measure the similarity between different process models, we used LLAMA and Sentence Transformer to generate vector representations of elements across BPMN, EPML, and PNML. By designing prompts that emphasized semantic matching, structural alignment, and the extraction of correspondences between key elements in each formalism, we enabled a comprehensive comparison of different process modeling languages.

4   Discussion and Results

The study focused on comparing the methods developed during the PM Matching contest [7] with those presented in the paper, employing Large Language Models (LLMs). The LLM-based methods were applied to the same models used during the contest to ensure a fair and consistent evaluation. This allowed for a direct comparison between the two sets of approaches. The evaluation relied on a ground truth, often referred to as a gold standard, which served as a benchmark for assessing performance and, as mentioned earlier in the paper, was defined by the contest. The gold standard serves as a binary reference set of correct task correspondences between two process models. Unlike a numeric similarity score, the gold standard defines whether a pair of tasks from two models should match. To perform this comparison, we first extracted the University Admission, Birth Registration and Asset Management models from the PM Matching Contest and applied the BERT multilingual and LLAMA systems to compare these business process models.

4.1   LLM vs. PM Matching Contest Results: A Comparative Analysis

Building on Sect. 3, we evaluated BERT multilingual and Llama for similarity matching across three process model datasets: University Admission (BPMN), Birth Registration (PNML), and Asset Management (EPML)-and compared their performance with the top results from the PM Matching Contest.

Table 1 show the highest Recall, Precision, and F-score **macro averages** obtained in the contest for each dataset, along with the best averages achieved using BERT and Llama. The macro average is defined in Sect. 2 and is calculated in the same way as the evaluation methodology used in the Process Model Matching Contest 2015.

- **University Admission (BPMN):** Llama achieved the highest precision (0.8571) and F-score (0.821), outperforming BERT and both contest methods. BERT, however, reached a perfect recall (1.000), while Llama followed with 0.7857.
- **Birth Registration (PNML):** Llama obtained the best recall (1.000) and the F score (0.655), while BERT led in precision (0.794). Contest methods scored lower across all metrics.

Table 1. Results across three datasets

Method	Precision	Recall	F-score
Llama	0.857	0.786	**0.821**
BERT	0.467	1.00	0.704
1st Method	0.597	0.61	0.566
2nd Method	0.673	0.466	0.509

(a) University Admission

Method	Precision	Recall	F-score
Llama	0.570	1.00	**0.655**
BERT	0.796	0.474	0.591
1st Method	0.468	0.713	0.565
2nd Method	0.474	0.679	0.540

(b) Birth Registration

Method	Precision	Recall	F-score
Llama	0.770	0.850	**0.807**
BERT	0.590	1.00	0.740
1st Method	0.786	0.595	0.677
2nd Method	0.957	0.505	0.661

(c) Asset Management

- **Asset Management (EPML):** Llama scored highest in precision (0.770) and F-score (0.807), while BERT achieved the top recall (1.000). Both outperformed the contest baselines.

The key difference is that BERT uses its multilingual functions to efficiently process BPMN activity names and other elements of the process structure without prompting. On the other hand, Llama performs even better with prompting, as it can more effectively capture the relationships between tasks, events, gateways, and control flows within the process. This highlights the power of transformer-based models in understanding process structures and their interdependencies, offering a significant advantage over traditional methods.

5   Conclusion

In conclusion, this study investigates the potential and challenges of leveraging Large Language Models (LLMs) for comparing business process models. By evaluating the performance of LLM-based approaches (specifically BERT and Llama) against traditional similarity matching techniques from the Process Model Matching Contest 2015, we highlight both their strengths and limitations.

- Improved Accuracy through Prompt Engineering: Llama, with tailored prompt engineering, demonstrated significant improvements in precision, recall, and F-score, outperforming traditional methods. This showcases the potential of LLMs to adapt to domain-specific needs for more accurate results.
- Benchmarking and Fine-tuning: Further testing across diverse datasets is needed to evaluate the generalizability of these models. Both models require further optimization, especially in business process analysis, through refined tuning parameters and training datasets.

LLMs significantly enhance the analysis of business process model similarity. It is essential to conduct further research to improve recall accuracy and ensure their widespread applicability in real-world situations.

References

1. Bernardi, M.L., et al.: A preliminary study on business process-aware large language models. In: Proceedings of Ital-IA 2024: Thematic Workshops co-located with the 4th CINI National Lab AIIS Conference on Artificial Intelligence, vol. 3762, pp. 441-446. CEUR-WS.org (2024)
2. Bernardi, M.L., et al.: Conversing with business process-aware large language models: the BPLLM framework. J. Intell. Inf. Syst. (2024)
3. Busch, K., et al.: Just tell me: prompt engineering in business process management. In: Enterprise. Business-Process and Information Systems Modeling, Lecture Notes in Business Information Processing, pp. 123–134. Springer, Heidelberg (2023)
4. Devlin, J., et al.: BERT: pre-training of deep bidirectional transformers for language understanding. arXiv:1810.04805 (2018)
5. Dijkman, R., Dumas, M., García-Bañuelos, L.: Graph matching algorithms for business process model similarity search. In: Dayal, U., Eder, J., Koehler, J., Reijers, H.A. (eds.) BPM 2009. LNCS, vol. 5701, pp. 48–63. Springer, Heidelberg (2009). https://doi.org/10.1007/978-3-642-03848-8_5
6. Dijkman, R., Dumas, M., Van Dongen, B., Käärik, R., Mendling, J.: Similarity of business process models: metrics and evaluation. Inf. Syst. **36**(2), 498–516 (2011)
7. Kolb, J., et al.: The process model matching contest 2015. In: Enterprise Modelling and Information Systems Architectures. Lecture Notes in Informatics (LNI), pp. 127–140. Gesellschaft für Informatik, Bonn (2015)
8. Lagos, N., Mos, A., Cortes Cornax, M.: Towards semantically-aided domain specific business process modeling. Data Technol. Appl. (2018)
9. Ali, M., Shahzad, K., Muzaffar, S.I., Malik, M.K.: Deep analysis of process model matching techniques. IEEE Access **8**, 99239–99253 (2020). https://doi.org/10.1109/ACCESS.2020.2997097
10. Naveed, H., et al.: A comprehensive overview of large language models. arXiv preprint arXiv:2307.06435 (2023)
11. Vidgof, M., Bachhofner, S., Mendling, J.: Large language models for business process management: opportunities and challenges. In: Proceedings of BPM 2023, pp. 123-134. Springer, Heidelberg (2023)
12. Zhao, W.X., et al.: A survey of large language models. arXiv preprint arXiv:2303.18223 (2023)

Enabling Process Mining on Multimodal Robotic Data

Flavio Corradini[1] , Sara Pettinari[2(✉)] , Barbara Re[1] , Lorenzo Rossi[1] ,
and Massimiliano Sampaolo[1(✉)]

[1] School of Science and Technology, University of Camerino, Camerino, Italy
{flavio.corradini,barbara.re,lorenzo.rossi,
massimilian.sampaolo}@unicam.it
[2] Gran Sasso Science Institute, L'Aquila, Italy
sara.pettinari@gssi.it

Abstract. Robotic systems are increasingly deployed across diverse domains, performing multiple operations while continuously interacting with the environment and making decisions. This results in large volumes of multimodal data from various sources, including sensor readings, video feeds, and communication data. In this domain, process mining holds the potential for extracting behavioral patterns, identifying anomalies, and evaluating performance metrics in robotic systems. However, its application remains largely unexplored due to the fine-grained, multimodal nature of robotic data. In this work, we investigate how robotic data should be processed to enable process mining applications. We explore activity recognition techniques to transition from robotic fine-grained data to high-level activities, applying Conditional Random Fields to sensor data and fine-tuning the Florence-2 model for video data. Furthermore, we outline key challenges and opportunities in preparing robotic data for process mining, laying the groundwork for future research on process mining-based analysis of robotic systems.

Keywords: Robotic Systems · Process Mining · Multimodal Data · Event Logs · Activity Recognition

1 Introduction

Robots are increasingly deployed in various domains, such as manufacturing, healthcare, and agriculture, where they perform multi-purpose activities [29]. They continuously interact with the environments, making decisions based on data collected from diverse sources. These multimodal data include sensor readings, video feeds, audio signals, communication data, and operational logs, each providing a different perspective on the robot's activities.

The application of process mining in robotic settings presents an opportunity to enhance the understanding and optimization of robots' behavior by enabling a holistic analysis of their operations [8]. Although process mining has demonstrated effectiveness in analyzing business and industrial processes, its

J. Grabis and Y. Wautelet (Eds.): CAiSE 2025 Workshops, LNBIP 556, pp. 257–269, 2025.
https://doi.org/10.1007/978-3-031-94931-9_21

application to robotic systems is largely underexplored. Indeed, the multimodal, fine-grained nature of robotic data introduces significant challenges in abstracting high-level activities, necessary to enable the application of process mining techniques. These complexities have limited the development of process mining methodologies tailored to robotic systems, underscoring the need for novel approaches that can abstract activities from multimodal data while preserving contextual information. To enable process mining in robotic domains, activity recognition techniques must integrate multiple data modalities into an event log. This would support a holistic analysis of robotic behavior by merging insights from various sources, such as sensor data and video recordings.

This paper explores the intersection of robotic systems and process mining techniques, focusing on how robotic data must be processed to enable effective application of process mining. We examine the characteristics of robotic data and the requirements for applying process mining in such environments, highlighting the need for methodologies capable of handling multimodal data. To support this discussion, we experiment with two activity recognition techniques on publicly available robotic datasets that could complement each other in a multimodal context. For sensor data, we utilize Conditional Random Fields (CRFs) [23] to infer activities based on position data, while we fine-tune the Florence-2 [36] model for video recordings. Finally, we highlight the challenges and opportunities in developing multimodal event logs of robotic systems.

The rest of the paper is organized as follows. Section 2 presents the differences between robotic data and IoT data. Section 3 details robotic data. Section 4 presents experiments with activity recognition techniques. Section 5 explores the challenges and opportunities in processing robotic data for process mining. Finally, Sect. 6 concludes the paper.

2   Demystifying Robotic Data from IoT Data

The integration of process mining with robotic systems follows naturally from the established application of process mining in the IoT domain [20]. While both technologies enhance automation and process optimization, robotic systems differ in their ability to operate autonomously and interact with the environment, which directly influences the nature and complexity of the data they generate. Robots use contextual knowledge to interpret their surroundings and can perform different activities to achieve a goal. To enable this, robotic systems integrate multiple sensors and actuators, resulting in inherently complex and multimodal decision-making processes [12]. This section aims to present the core differences between robotic and IoT systems and their impact on the produced data. It first presents an illustrative example, followed by a comparison of system characteristics. Notably, we focus on multipurpose robots, meaning robots capable of moving, manipulating objects, and interacting in various ways.

Illustrative Example. As an illustrative example, we consider a warehouse where orders are processed using both a mobile picking robot and IoT devices.

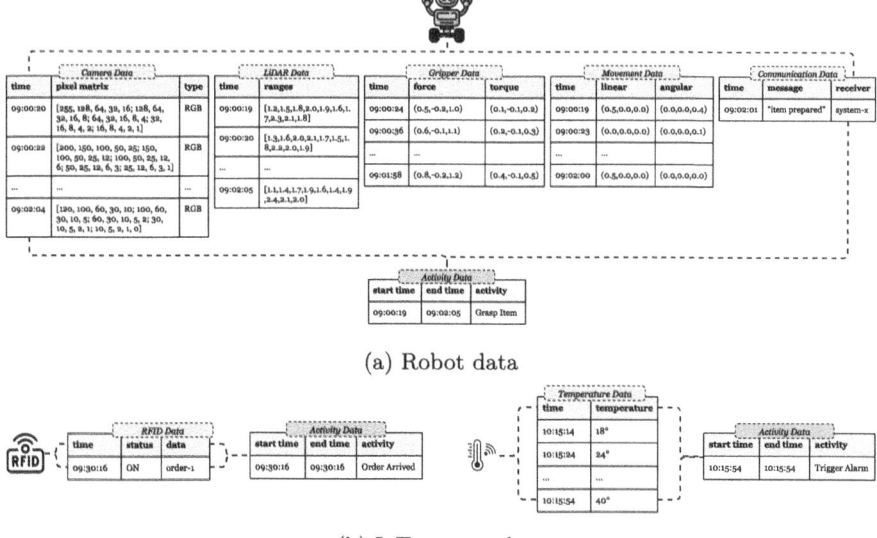

(a) Robot data

(b) IoT sensors data

Fig. 1. Data comparison

When an order is placed, a mobile robot retrieves the item from the warehouse using cameras and LiDAR to detect shelves and obstacles. It adjusts its grip pressure with force-sensitive grippers to handle fragile items. If the item is unavailable or misplaced, the robot dynamically modifies its trajectory, attempting to retrieve the item from an alternative location or triggering human intervention. Throughout its operations, the robot continuously generates multimodal data, including camera images, LiDAR point clouds, position information, gripper force feedback, wheel motion data, and human interaction events. For example, during the *grasp item* activity, the robot utilizes a gripper actuator, wheels, camera, and LiDAR sensors while making control decisions. Differently, during *navigation*, it primarily relies on wheel actuation, LiDAR, camera, and position sensors. Each high-level activity is thus associated with a distinct set of multimodal data sources, as exemplified in Fig. 1a. Once an order is assembled, an RFID sensor scans the order to update the inventory database, and environmental sensors monitor temperature and humidity. If an anomaly, like excessive temperature, happens, an alert is generated from the central system. The IoT devices generate continuous data streams, including RFID signals, and temperature and humidity readings. These streams can indicate specific events within the warehouse, such as *order arrived* upon RFID activation or *trigger alarm* based on extremely high temperatures, as shown in Fig. 1b. Therefore, the IoT data can provide insights into the warehouse or order status, while the robot data can also be used to abstract the autonomous activities it performs.

Characteristics. To compare the characteristics of robotic and IoT systems we leverage the classification from the *Robotics Multi-Annual Roadmap* [33], which identifies robotic capabilities that reflect system performance characteristics independent of specific configurations or application domains. In this context, we focus only on those characteristics directly related to system behavior. Based on this comparison, we examine how these characteristics influence the data produced by robotic and IoT systems.

Decisional Autonomy refers to the ability of a system to act autonomously. Robots can operate autonomously or semi-autonomously, performing a sequence of activities to achieve a goal by making real-time decisions based on sensor readings. Additionally, robots may use AI to make decisions in unpredictable environments. A robot with decisional autonomy captures sensor readings, actuator feedback, and decision logs. The data reflects complex decision-making paths (e.g., if an obstacle is detected, the robot may choose to reroute or change activity). In contrast, IoT systems primarily function as monitoring and control mechanisms. They collect sensor data (e.g., temperature, pressure, motion) and transmit it for analysis or trigger simple, predefined automated actions (e.g., activating irrigation). Therefore, an IoT system typically can generate data mainly related to sensor readings or triggered actuators, which can at most recall a predefined decision (e.g., when the humidity is below a threshold, the irrigator is activated).

Interaction is the ability of a system to interact physically, cognitively, and socially with humans, or other systems. Robots can actively interact with other robots, systems, or humans. As a result, they can generate data related to dynamic interactions with humans, which may occur for social purposes (e.g., conversation data) or within a human-robot collaborative task, such as jointly working on the same workpiece (e.g., sensor readings, actuator feedback, communication data). Additionally, robots can produce data through interactions with other robots or systems (e.g., shared messages exchanged during coordinated operations). In contrast, interaction in IoT systems is mostly passive and limited to data collection and notification. These systems cannot physically interact with their environment or other systems. However, they can send notifications to human operators or other systems (e.g., alerts for a failure).

Adaptability denotes the ability of the system to adapt to different scenarios, environments, and conditions. Robotic systems can exhibit high adaptability due to their operation in dynamic, unpredictable environments [13] where objects, obstacles, and human interactions are constantly changing. This requires real-time perception and decision-making to manage these variations (e.g., adjusting grip force based on object weight), allowing robots to adapt their activities based on new information. As a result, robots generate sensor data, activity switching, and actuator changes during adaptation. Differently, IoT systems deal with lower variability, as most IoT sensors are designed for structured, repetitive data collection. Therefore, their workflow variability is typically low because IoT is reactive rather than adaptive. However, adaptation can happen based on preprogrammed rules or external inputs (e.g., a smart thermostat adjusting the temperature threshold based on learned user behavior).

Summing up, the key distinction is that robots can perform multipurpose activities, leveraging multimodal data, such as sensor readings, communication data, and actuator feedback, while actively changing the environment. In contrast, IoT systems are primarily designed to perform predefined actions, in an environment that may change only due to external factors. This difference significantly impacts the data they produce and the challenges associated with abstracting high-level activities from fine-grained data. Specifically, for the robotic domain, it is necessary to preprocess all the multimodal data robots generate to extract the performed activities and the associated decision-making processes.

3   On Robotic Data

A robotic mission consists of high-level tasks performed to achieve a final objective while operating in dynamic environments that may include people, objects, and robots [29]. To accomplish a mission, robots rely on multiple sensors and actuators to perceive and interact with their surroundings, resulting in the generation of multimodal data.

Several publicly available datasets provide multimodal recordings of robotic activities [7]. For grasping and manipulation activities, the dataset presented in [19] is video-based and captures a robotic arm performing grasping and stacking activities. In contrast, the dataset from [37] consists of tactile sensor recordings focused on detecting grasping stability and slip events during object lifting, providing valuable insights into force-based manipulation. For spatial movement and navigation, [15] is a widely used benchmark, providing high-resolution visual and LiDAR scans of structured urban environments. Considering unstructured environments, [5] provides motion tracking data, including GPS, IMU, and video recordings, for ground robot navigation in forested areas, while [6] captures multimodal data from a quadrotor, like IMU, rotor tachometers, and images.

However, most robotic datasets focus on fine-grained data [7], lacking information about the high-level activities they represent. Only a few datasets provide both fine-grained data and high-level activity annotations. For instance, the TALE dataset [8], specifically designed for process mining applications, collects data from a multi-robot agricultural scenario, where drones and tractors collaborate. Whereas, the ATLAS Dione dataset [31], designed for activity recognition, provides video recordings of a surgeon robot.

4   Processing Robotic Data

Processing robotic data involves extracting performed activities from data generated by multiple sources. In this section, we explore the application of two activity recognition techniques to different robotic datasets, assessing their suitability for preparing fine-grained data for process mining. Specifically, we apply CRFs for sensor-based activity recognition and fine-tune the Florence-2 vision foundation model for video-based activity recognition. Notably, the scripts for replicating the experiments are available online[1].

4.1   CRFs to Process Position Data

CRFs [23] are probabilistic graphical models commonly used in fields like natural language processing and sequence labeling. They are discriminative models that condition probabilities on observation sequences. Unlike generative models, which compute probabilities for every possible observation sequence, CRFs focus on specifying the probability of label sequences given the observations, denoted as $P(Y|X)$, rather than joint probabilities $P(X,Y)$. These models have been applied in various contexts, including activity recognition from sensor data [35] and the abstraction of activities to simplify process models [34].

In our experiment, we applied CRFs to position data from the TALE dataset. Specifically, we utilized the dataset high-level annotations for both model training and final validation. We focused only on data recorded by the flying robot. The dataset consists of 36 distinct executions of the simulation, each generating multiple data streams, including physical data, such as robot position and battery, communication events, and high-level activity annotations. Among the high-level activities annotated in the dataset, we selected only those directly related to the spatial movement of the robot, specifically *takeoff*, *explore*, and the *idle* state, representing periods when the robot was stationary. Firstly, we aligned the position data with the high-level activity annotations by matching their timestamps. After that, we concatenated data from all simulation executions, creating a final training dataset of over 100,000 records. A crucial step during training was feature selection, as it significantly impacted the results, which were evaluated using traditional metrics, i.e., *precision*, *recall*, and *f1-score*. Through an iterative refinement process, we identified the optimal features for training the model, i.e., the deltas of the flying robot's coordinates (dx, dy, and dz), representing the change in position between consecutive rows, and the activity label from the previous row.

As shown in Table 1a, the model demonstrated excellent performance in abstracting activities from position data, particularly for the *explore* and *idle* activities. However, the *takeoff* activity exhibited inconsistencies. By analyzing the results, we noticed that the robot's position data lacks a direct relationship with the *takeoff* activity, despite the semantic connection. Indeed, the *takeoff* activity is logged by the flying robot when it records the intent of taking off, rather than after a significant position change. This underscores how context data can be leveraged to correct and align high-level activities, providing a more accurate representation of system behavior.

---

[1] https://bitbucket.org/proslabteam/robot_activity_recognition.

Table 1. Performance in processing robotic data

Activity	Precision	Recall	F1-Score
EXPLORE	0.97	0.97	0.97
IDLE	1	0.99	1
TAKEOFF	0	0	0

(a) CRF results

Epochs	Training Loss	**Validation Loss**
50	0.891	0.512

(b) Fine-tuned Florence-2 results

4.2   Fine-Tuning of Florence-2 for Video Data

Florence-2 [36] is an advanced vision foundation model pre-trained on the *FLD-5B* dataset, which includes a total of 5.4 billion annotations across 126 million images. It was designed to take text prompts as task instructions and generate desirable results in text forms, whether it be captioning, object detection, grounding, or segmentation. This model was selected for its unprecedented *zero-shot* and *fine-tuning* capabilities [36]. This zero-shot capability offers a promising opportunity to leverage the knowledge acquired during the model pre-training, without requiring the development of a specific model for each use case.

In the experiment with Florence-2 and the ATLAS Dione dataset, the zero-shot approach yielded suboptimal results, underscoring the need for fine-tuning to adapt the model to these specific activities. For fine-tuning, we used 84 videos for training and 15 videos for validation, extracting 5 frames per second and training the model over 50 epochs. Each epoch of fine-tuning took approximately 1 h and 30 min, resulting in a total training time of nearly three and a half days. Although we used a limited number of epochs, this process significantly enhanced recognition results, enabling the fine-tuned model to accurately identify activities in the videos and generate a file with both the activities and their timestamps. Despite these improvements, the model still exhibited confusion in discriminating certain very similar activities, such as *suture tie* and *suture pull through*. Table 1b displays the training and validation loss after the fine-tuning using the Cross-Entropy loss function. The results are satisfactory, the gap between the two measures indicates that the model generalizes well on the validation set and could likely benefit from more extensive training by increasing the number of epochs.

5   Challenges and Opportunities

Leveraging our expertise in the robotic domain and process mining, existing state-of-the-art, and conducted experiments, we identify the following challenges and opportunities: (*CH1*) the processing of multimodal robotic data, (*CH2*) the necessity for robotic data that explicitly captures and explains robot activities, (*CH3*) the segmentation of data to link them to specific process executions, and (*CH4*) the transformation of robotic data into event logs that provides a holistic view of system operation, by integrating high-level and multimodal data.

Processing Multimodal Robotic Data. In the literature, several process mining-related approaches aim to abstract high-level activities from fine-grained data. Pattern-based techniques aim to map fine-grained data to correspond-ing high-level activities in a supervised manner [11,27,32]. However, in robotic systems, multiple sensors generate multimodal data, which requires substan-tial effort to accurately link it to high-level activities. Whereas, context-based approaches focus on using fine-grained IoT sensor data to detect human rou-tines [10,21,24]. These approaches could be adapted to automatically extract the activities performed by robots, leveraging the knowledge of their context. Notably, comprehensive surveys on the application of both supervised and unsu-pervised abstraction techniques have been presented in [18,38]. For video data processing, process mining approaches are still in early stages [25]. While some unsupervised methods have been proposed to derive process models from video recordings [22,28], they still require significant effort in incorporating domain knowledge. To address this challenge, [14] leverages an LLM to extract knowl-edge from videos and identify relevant evidence from individual frames. In our experiments, we evaluated CRFs and Florence-2 on position and video data, respectively. While both performed well on their modalities, there is still a lack of approaches for abstracting activities from multimodal data, like robotic ones.

CH1. Processing Multimodal Robotic Data

Challenge. Developing novel techniques or adapting existing ones to process robotic data is needed to infer high-level activities from multimodal data with-out relying on supervised learning or extensive domain knowledge.
Opportunities. Adopting techniques that can infer high-level activities from multimodal data, only leveraging descriptions of the robot's context and capa-bilities, could significantly enhance the applicability of process mining. This approach would enable the processing of robotic datasets lacking annotations, making them suitable for process mining-based analysis.

Annotating Robots Activities. Robots are getting increasingly multi-purpose and capable of autonomously identifying which activities to perform [29]. There-fore, robotic developers and vendors should design robots to generate data about the activities they are executing, enabling the creation of comprehensive datasets containing multimodal and high-level data. Currently, most robotic datasets that capture high-level activities rely on manual annotation [7]. While this approach is suitable for static behaviors, it becomes impractical for autonomous robots that dynamically adapt using AI. This dynamicity highlights a critical gap in cur-rent robotic behavior analysis, which mainly depends on human observation [3]. Autonomous robots operate in ways that are not always transparent to end-users, further complicating efforts to understand or verify the performed activi-ties [9,30]. To address these challenges, the robotics community should provide methods to automatically extract and interpret high-level activities from robots' execution data. Leveraging multimodal data, AI models, and robots' knowledge, developers can train models to provide accurate event data for end-users, enhanc-ing transparency and advancing robotic activity analysis research.

```
┌─────────────────────CH2. Annotating Robots Activities──────────────────────┐
```

Challenge. Obtaining high-level activities from robot executions requires support from the robotics community to enable the automatic generation of high-level data in conjunction with multimodal information.

Opportunities. Empowering robots to autonomously record and interpret their activities offers significant opportunities for advancing robotic behavior analysis. This enables the application of process mining techniques to analyze not only how and why robots behave in specific ways but also their impact on the overall system. This capability would create a synergy between robotics and process mining, driving the advancement of both fields and their real-world applications.

Segmenting Robotic Data. The unstructured nature of robotic data necessitates trace segmentation to prepare it for process mining techniques. In the process mining domain, segmentation is a well-known challenge [4,17], as it involves associating data with specific process executions to define a case identifier. Without a well-defined trace structure, traditional techniques struggle to organize event data for meaningful analysis. In robotic systems, a case could be defined by a specific robot identifier or encompass predefined periods, such as an entire workday. The segmentation of logs into cases should be determined by the analyst based on the objectives of the analysis. However, due to the involvement of multimodal data, multiple interacting objects and entities, and various tasks, defining a single-case concept becomes ambiguous. This challenge can be addressed by identifying different perspectives for segmenting the data and applying object-centric process mining techniques, which enable the simultaneous tracking of multiple objects and perspectives [1].

```
┌───────────────────────CH3. Segmenting Robotic Data─────────────────────────┐
```

Challenge. Segmenting robotic data is required to associate it with a case identifier, which is necessary for applying traditional process mining techniques, or to identify multiple perspectives, for object-centric process mining techniques.

Opportunities. Developing standardized formats and frameworks for robotic event data could facilitate the segmentation and integration with process mining techniques. Additionally, by tracking multiple objects and perspectives, object-centric approaches could provide a holistic view of robotic systems behavior.

Representing Robotic Event Logs. Extracted high-level and multimodal data from the robotic system must be aligned with the formats required for process mining techniques. Several studies have explored methods to represent data from IoT and robotic systems. For instance, [26] extends the XES standard to log IoT device values during an event's lifecycle, while [8] uses the XES *inprogress* state to incorporate fine-grained robotic data. From an object-centric perspective, [16] proposes DOCEL, an OCEL extension, to capture evolving dynamic object attributes. Alternatively, [2] separates events from continuous data streams and correlates them using timestamps and shared objects. Indeed, to fully leverage the rich perception capabilities of robots in understanding their surrounding context, it is necessary to align and represent data from diverse sources, such as sensor readings and communication, with the high-level activities performed by robots, enabling the creation of event logs that provide a holistic view of robot behavior.

CH4. Representing Robotic Event Logs

Challenge. Establishing standard methods to represent the interleaving of high-level and multimodal data is necessary for accurately storing the execution information of a robotic system and linking the performed activities to the robot's contextual dynamics.

Opportunities. Standardized robotic event logs would facilitate the development of new process mining techniques or the enhancement of existing ones to effectively incorporate robots' dynamics. These logs would enable tracking of all data collected during an activity's execution, providing insights into the robot's environment and state throughout its operations.

---

6   Conclusions

This paper investigates the intersection of robotic systems and process mining techniques, focusing on how these systems generate data and how it should be processed to be suitable for applying process mining techniques. To this end, we experimented with techniques for processing multimodal robotic data to abstract high-level activities from two robotic datasets. We also discussed the challenges and opportunities in preparing robotic data for process mining, aiming to guide the development of methodologies that support its application. This exploration aims to bridge the gap between the process mining and robotics communities by laying the foundation for future research, including methodologies to facilitate event log extraction and enhance process mining in increasingly robotized environments. Therefore, working with robotic data that includes both high-level and multimodal data would facilitate the development or extension of techniques to analyze robot behavior and context information, such as spatial positioning or battery levels. Moreover, analyzing multimodal data in real-time would allow the capture and examination of robots' decision-making processes as they occur, enabling robots to adapt and optimize activities based on immediate insights.

Acknowledgments. This work has been partially funded by (a) the PRIN project 2022JKA4SL - HALO: etHical-aware AdjustabLe autOnomous systems, and (b) the European Union - NextGenerationEU under the Italian Ministry of University and Research National Innovation Ecosystem grant ECS00000041 - VITALITY - CUP J13C22000430001.

References

1. Aalst, W.: Object-centric process mining: dealing with divergence and convergence in event data. In: Ölveczky, P.C., Salaün, G. (eds.) SEFM 2019. LNCS, vol. 11724, pp. 3–25. Springer, Cham (2019). https://doi.org/10.1007/978-3-030-30446-1_1

2. van der Aalst, W.: Experiences from the internet-of-production: using "data-models-in-the-middle" to fight complexity and facilitate reuse. In: Business Process Management. LNBIP, vol. 492, pp. 87–91. Springer, Heidelberg (2023). https://doi.org/10.1007/978-3-031-50974-2_7

3. Afzal, A., Le Goues, C., Hilton, M., Timperley, C.S.: A study on challenges of testing robotic systems. In: Software Testing, Validation and Verification, pp. 96–107. IEEE (2020)

4. Agostinelli, S., Marrella, A., Mecella, M.: Exploring the challenge of automated segmentation in robotic process automation. In: Cherfi, S., Perini, A., Nurcan, S. (eds.) RCIS 2021. LNBIP, vol. 415, pp. 38–54. Springer, Cham (2021). https://doi.org/10.1007/978-3-030-75018-3_3

5. Ali, I.: Finnforest dataset: a forest landscape for visual slam. Robot. Auton. Syst. **132**, 103610 (2020)

6. Antonini, A., et al.: The blackbird uav dataset. Int. J. Rob. Res. **39**, 1346–1364 (2020)

7. Corradini, F., Pettinari, S., Re, B., Rossi, L., Sampaolo, M.: Robotic datasets for process mining. In: Intelligent Information Systems - CAiSE Forum. LNBIP, vol. To Appear. Springer, Heidelberg (2025)

8. Corradini, F., Pettinari, S., Re, B., Rossi, L., Tiezzi, F.: A methodology for the analysis of robotic systems via process mining. In: Enterprise Design, Operations, and Computing. LNCS, vol. 14367, pp. 117–133. Springer, Heidelberg (2023). https://doi.org/10.1007/978-3-031-46587-1_7

9. Das, D., Banerjee, S., Chernova, S.: Explainable AI for robot failures: generating explanations that improve user assistance in fault recovery. In: Human-Robot Interaction, pp. 351–360. ACM (2021)

10. Di Federico, G., Burattin, A.: Cvamos-event abstraction using contextual information. Future Internet **15**(3), 113 (2023)

11. van Eck, M.L., Sidorova, N., van der Aalst, W.: Enabling process mining on sensor data from smart products. In: International Conference on Research Challenges in Information Science, pp. 1–12. IEEE (2016)

12. Farooq, A., Iqbal, K.: Towards transparent ethical AI: a roadmap for trustworthy robotic systems. In: International Conference on Intelligent Robots and Systems Workshops (2024)

13. García, S., Strüber, D., Brugali, D., Fava, A.D., Pelliccione, P., Berger, T.: Software variability in service robotics. Empir. Softw. Eng. **28**(1), 24 (2023)

14. Gavric, A., Bork, D., Proper, H.A.: Multimodal process mining. In: International Conference on Business Informatics, pp. 99–108. IEEE (2024)

15. Geiger, A., Lenz, P., Stiller, C., Urtasun, R.: Vision meets robotics: the kitti dataset. Int. J. Rob. Res. **32**, 1231–1237 (2013)

16. Goossens, A., De Smedt, J., Vanthienen, J., van der Aalst, W.: Enhancing data-awareness of object-centric event logs. In: Process Mining Workshops. LNBIP, vol. 468, pp. 18–30. Springer, Heidelberg (2022). https://doi.org/10.1007/978-3-031-27815-0_2

17. Günther, C.W., Rozinat, A., van der Aalst, W.: Activity mining by global trace segmentation. In: Rinderle-Ma, S., Sadiq, S., Leymann, F. (eds.) BPM 2009. LNBIP,

vol. 43, pp. 128–139. Springer, Heidelberg (2010). https://doi.org/10.1007/978-3-642-12186-9_13

18. Houdt, G.V., de Leoni, M., Martin, N., Depaire, B.: An empirical evaluation of unsupervised event log abstraction techniques in process mining. Inf. Syst. **121**, 102320 (2024)

19. Hundt, A., et al.: The costar block stacking dataset: learning with workspace constraints. In: Intelligent Robots and Systems (2019)

20. Janiesch, C., et al.: The internet of things meets business process management: a manifesto. IEEE Syst. Man Cybern. Maga. **6**(4), 34–44 (2020)

21. Janssen, D., Mannhardt, F., Koschmider, A., van Zelst, S.J.: Process model discovery from sensor event data. In: Leemans, S., Leopold, H. (eds.) ICPM 2020. LNBIP, vol. 406, pp. 69–81. Springer, Cham (2021). https://doi.org/10.1007/978-3-030-72693-5_6

22. Knoch, S., Ponpathirkoottam, S., Schwartz, T.: Video-to-model: unsupervised trace extraction from videos for process discovery and conformance checking in manual assembly. In: Fahland, D., Ghidini, C., Becker, J., Dumas, M. (eds.) BPM 2020. LNCS, vol. 12168, pp. 291–308. Springer, Cham (2020). https://doi.org/10.1007/978-3-030-58666-9_17

23. Lafferty, J.D., McCallum, A., Pereira, F.C.N.: Conditional random fields: probabilistic models for segmenting and labeling sequence data. In: International Conference on Machine Learning, pp. 282–289. Morgan Kaufmann (2001)

24. de Leoni, M., Pellattiero, L.: The benefits of sensor-measurement aggregation in discovering iot process models: a smart-house case study. In: Marrella, A., Weber, B. (eds.) BPM 2021. LNBIP, vol. 436, pp. 403–415. Springer, Cham (2022). https://doi.org/10.1007/978-3-030-94343-1_31

25. Lepsien, A., Koschmider, A., Kratsch, W.: Analytics pipeline for process mining on video data. In: BPM Forum. LNBIP, vol. 490, pp. 196–213. Springer, Heidelberg (2023). https://doi.org/10.1007/978-3-031-41623-1_12

26. Mangler, J., Grüger, J., et al.: Datastream xes extension: embedding iot sensor data into extensible event stream logs. Future Internet **15**(3), 109 (2023)

27. Mannhardt, F., de Leoni, M., Reijers, H.A., van der Aalst, W., Toussaint, P.J.: From low-level events to activities - a pattern-based approach. In: La Rosa, M., Loos, P., Pastor, O. (eds.) BPM 2016. LNCS, vol. 9850, pp. 125–141. Springer, Cham (2016). https://doi.org/10.1007/978-3-319-45348-4_8

28. Melfsen, A., Lepsien, A., Bosselmann, J., Koschmider, A., Hartung, E.: Describing behavior sequences of fattening pigs using process mining on video data and automated pig behavior recognition. Agriculture **13**(8), 1639 (2023)

29. Menghi, C., Tsigkanos, C., Pelliccione, P., Ghezzi, C., Berger, T.: Specification patterns for robotic missions. IEEE Trans. Softw. Eng. **47**(10), 2208–2224 (2021)

30. Sakai, T., Nagai, T.: Explainable autonomous robots: a survey and perspective. Adv. Robot. **36**(5–6), 219–238 (2022)

31. Sarikaya, D., Corso, J.J., Guru, K.A.: Detection and localization of robotic tools in robot-assisted surgery videos using deep neural networks for region proposal and detection. IEEE Trans. Med. Imaging **36**(7), 1542–1549 (2017)

32. Seiger, R., Franceschetti, M., Weber, B.: An interactive method for detection of process activity executions from iot data. Future Internet **15**(2), 77 (2023)

33. SPARC: Robotics 2020 - multi-annual roadmap (2017)

34. Tax, N., Sidorova, N., Haakma, R., van der Aalst, W.: Event abstraction for process mining using supervised learning techniques. In: Bi, Y., Kapoor, S., Bhatia, R. (eds.) IntelliSys 2016. LNNS, vol. 15, pp. 251–269. Springer, Cham (2018). https://doi.org/10.1007/978-3-319-56994-9_18

35. Vail, D.L., Veloso, M.M., Lafferty, J.D.: Conditional random fields for activity recognition. In: International Joint Conference on Autonomous Agents and Multi-agent Systems, pp. 1–8. IFAAMAS (2007)
36. Xiao, B., et al.: Florence-2: advancing a unified representation for a variety of vision tasks. In: Conference on Computer Vision and Pattern Recognition, pp. 4818–4829. IEEE (2024)
37. Yan, G., Schmitz, A., Funabashi, S., Somlor, S., Tomo, T.P., Sugano, S.: A robotic grasping state perception framework with multi-phase tactile information and ensemble learning. IEEE Rob. Autom. Lett. **7**, 6822–6829 (2022)
38. van Zelst, S.J., Mannhardt, F., de Leoni, M., Koschmider, A.: Event abstraction in process mining: literature review and taxonomy. Granular Comput. **6**, 719–736 (2021)

Joint Workshop on Large Language Models in Service-Oriented Architectures Design: Innovations and Applications (LLM-SOA) and Generation of Synthetic Datasets for Information Systems (GENSYN)

Workshop on Large Language Models for Service-Oriented Architectures and Systems Design and Workshop on Generation of Synthetic Datasets for Information Systems (LLM-SOA and GenSyn)

Large Language Models (LLMs) and synthetic data generation techniques have emerged as key enablers of innovation in modern Information Systems, addressing distinct but complementary challenges in their design, implementation, and evolution. On the one hand, the rise of LLMs has opened new opportunities in the design and engineering of Information Systems, especially within service-oriented ecosystems, by enabling advanced capabilities such as (semi-)automated service discovery and composition. On the other hand, synthetic data generation techniques address growing concerns around data privacy, scarcity, and accessibility, thus providing scalable alternatives for benchmarking, training, and validating AI and data-driven systems.

This year, the first edition of the "Workshop on Large Language Models for Service-Oriented Architectures and Systems Design (LLM-SOA)" and the first edition of the "Workshop on Generation of Synthetic Datasets for Information Systems (GenSyn)" were jointly held, co-located with the 37th International Conference on Advanced Information Systems Engineering (CAiSE 2025), which took place in Vienna, Austria. The LLM-SOA workshop provided a dedicated forum for investigating how LLMs can be employed to improve the design of service-oriented architectural solutions as well as their use in tasks such as service discovery and composition. Meanwhile, the GenSyn workshop focused on the generation of synthetic datasets, covering both classical and generative AI methods that support diverse Information System Engineering (ISE) application domains, i.e., IoT, digital twins development, and business process modeling. More information on the LLM-SOA workshop is available at https://dbwis.gitlab.io/llm-soa/, whilst for the GenSyn workshop it is available at https://gensyn-ws.github.io/.

The LLM-SOA workshop received eight submissions. For each paper, at least two single-blind reviews were collected. The GenSyn workshop received two submissions. For each paper, three single-blind reviews were collected. Considering the reviews and the maximum acceptance rate of Springer (which is set around 50%), three papers were accepted as full papers for presentation at the LLM-SOA workshop along with three papers accepted as short papers. As for the GenSyn workshop, one full paper was accepted for presentation.

The papers presented at the LLM-SOA workshop covered different research areas: the paper by Smardas et al. discussed a RESTful API system aimed at managing OpenAPI specifications of RESTful services for the automatic derivation of the maturity level of RESTful services, using LLMs. Falconi et al. presented a study on improving content-based data product retrieval in federated environments (specifically, in Data Mesh architectures) using LLMs and sampling techniques, shifting from a metadata-based discovery to a content-based discovery approach; Martire et al. explored the use of LLMs and RAG (Retrieval-Augmented Generation) in a service-oriented ecosystem for football talent scouting; Tamburri et al. identified a need to create better understanding of the combination of DevOps and LLMs (referred to as LLMOps by the authors) in the logistics industry, examining its maturity in the scope of an industrial case study; Pellegrini et al. investigated a modular automated newsroom leveraging LLMs to streamline news processing and enhance editorial workflows, through a Service-Oriented Architecture; Khaliq et al. provided a literature review on the use of LLMs in Legal Natural Language Processing (NLP). Regarding the GenSyn workshop, the paper from Ghinani et al. explored a two-phase training strategy combining pretraining with synthetic data and fine-tuning using Active Learning (AL) with uncertainty sampling, showing that combining synthetic data with AL significantly reduces real data requirements while achieving superior precision, especially when real data is limited.

Beyond paper presentations, the workshop programs were enriched by two insightful keynote sessions. In particular, the LLM-SOA workshop featured a keynote presented by Emanuel Sallinger (TU Wien) entitled "LLMs for Explanations in Knowledge Graphs: Explaining Enterprise Knowledge Graphs with Large Language Models and Ontological Reasoning", while the GenSyn workshop featured a keynote presented by Paul Tiwald from MostlyAI entitled "Data Without Barriers: Synthetic Data as a Catalyst for Responsible Innovation".

We sincerely thank all the authors who presented at both the LLM-SOA and GenSyn workshops. Their valuable contributions and active engagement were essential to making these workshops impactful. Special thanks go to our keynote speakers and to the Program Committee members of both the LLM-SOA and GenSyn workshops for their high-quality reviews, which greatly contributed to the success of the workshops. Lastly, we would also like to thank the workshop chairs of CAiSE 2025, Jānis Grabis and Yves Wautelet, for their continued support.

April 2025

Massimiliano Garda
Ada Bagozi
Ala Arman
Claudio Di Sipio
Arianna Fedeli
Riccardo Rubei
Eduard Kamburjan

LLM-SOA and GenSyn Organization

LLM-SOA Workshop Co-organizers and Program Committee Co-chairs

Massimiliano Garda	University of Brescia, Italy
Ada Bagozi	University of Brescia, Italy
Ala Arman	University of Rome "La Sapienza", Italy

LLM-SOA Workshop Advisory Board

Massimo Mecella	University of Rome "La Sapienza" Italy
Monique Snoeck	KU Leuven, Belgium
Barbara Pernici	Politecnico di Milano, Italy
Devis Bianchini	University of Brescia, Italy

LLM-SOA Workshop Program Committee

Amirali Amiri	TU Wien, Austria
Anisa Rula	University of Brescia, Italy
Basem Suleiman	University of New South Wales, Australia
Catarina Ferreira da Silva	University Institute of Lisbon, Portugal
Damian Andrew Tamburri	University of Sannio, Italy
Flavia Monti	University of Rome "La Sapienza", Italy
Francesco Leotta	University of Rome "La Sapienza", Italy
Giovanni Quattrocchi	Politecnico di Milano, Italy
Maurizio Atzori	University of Cagliari, Italy
Michele Melchiori	University of Brescia, Italy
Mingyi Liu	Harbin Institute of Technology, China
Mohamed Ragab	Southampton University, UK
Nafaa Jabeur	German University of Technology in Oman, Oman
Stephan Reiff-Marganiec	University of Derby, UK

GenSyn Workshop Co-organizers and Program Committee Co-chairs

Claudio Di Sipio	University of L'Aquila, Italy
Arianna Fedeli	Gran Sasso Science Institute, Italy
Riccardo Rubei	University of L'Aquila, Italy
Eduard Kamburjan	University of Copenhagen, Denmark

GenSyn Workshop Program Committee

Chenyu Wang	Singapore Management University, Singapore
Christophe Debruyne	University of Liège, Belgium
David Manrique Negrin	Eindhoven University of Technology, The Netherlands
Guang Yang	Singapore Management University, Singapore
Hong Jin Kang	Singapore Management University, Singapore
José Antonio Hernández López	Linköping University, Sweden
Martin Weyssow	Singapore Management University, Singapore
Shaukat Ali	Simula Lab, Norway
Stefan Klikovits	Johannes Kepler Universität Linz, Austria
Vittoriano Muttillo	University of Teramo, Italy
Xin Zhou	Singapore Management University, Singapore

LLM-Enhanced Derivation of the Maturity Level of RESTful Services

Antonios Smardas and Kyriakos Kritikos(✉) ⓘ

Department of Information and Communication Systems Engineering, School of Engineering,
University of the Aegean, Mytilene, Greece
icsdd22002@icsd.aegean.gr, kkritikos@aegean.gr

Abstract. This paper presents a RESTful API responsible for the management of the OpenAPI specification of RESTful services. This API is capable of publishing and matching RESTful services based on their OpenAPI specifications as well as generating these specifications from their source code and deriving their maturity level, where the latter two capabilities are backed up by the use of LLMs. Apart from presenting this API, the paper focuses on experimentally evaluating its maturity level derivation capability when different state-of-the-art LLMs are utilized to support it. The experiment results seem promising and pave particular directions for further improving this capability.

Keywords: SOA · LLM · OpenAPI · maturity level · RESTful services

1 Introduction

Service-Oriented Architecture (SOA) is a key architecture for developing web-based applications that comprise one or more web services. This architecture promotes the re-use of existing functionality while it is vendor-neutral and relies on open standards. The core of this functionality is web services, i.e., software that can be remotely invoked and implements a well-defined business capability. Two main implementations of web services exist, SOAP and RESTful services.

RESTful services seem to represent nowadays the greatest percentage of services with respect to the two aforementioned implementations. Such services conform to the REST architectural style while they rely on open protocols and standards, including HTTP and XML. Their wide adoption is mainly due to the fact that they are lightweight and easy to implement by utilizing well-known programming languages and frameworks.

While the vision of SOA centers around re-usability, every attempt to support this at the global level has failed. Apart from the UDDI standard that became obsolete and deprecated, although relying mainly on SOAP services, other efforts like ProgrammableWeb, mainly focusing on RESTful services, were shut down. While new proposals come into play, like RapidAPI[1], they present limited, structural ways to discover the services one actually needs while they are proprietary, requiring an organisation to pay money for their use.

---

[1] https://rapidapi.com/.

J. Grabis and Y. Wautelet (Eds.): CAiSE 2025 Workshops, LNBIP 556, pp. 277–288, 2025.
https://doi.org/10.1007/978-3-031-94931-9_22

To this end, the goal of our work is to develop and offer an open RESTful API that everyone can utilize to both publish new RESTful services as well as discover existing ones that can implement part of an application's functionality. This API intends to rely on Information Retrieval (IR), Semantic Web (SW) and Generative Artificial Intelligence (AI) technologies in order to fulfil its main goal. Further, apart from semantically publishing and matching RESTful services, the API aims at offering additional capabilities, like the generation of the OpenAPI[2] specification of a RESTful service based on its source code and the derivation of its maturity level. Such capabilities mainly rely on Generative AI technologies and especially LLMs to be implemented. LLMs have already shown promising results in many tasks related to the development of (web) applications and the management of business processes (BPs) [1, 2], like the production of UML design models and BP specifications from textual descriptions. To this end, they seem to be a suitable choice also for realizing the two aforementioned capabilities.

We believe that these two capabilities represent interesting, suitable and added-value extensions to a service registry, i.e., the role intended to be played by our API either at the global level or the local level of an organization that intends to re-use its own services. The capability to generate an OpenAPI specification from a RESTful service's source code plays a two-fold purpose: (a) it can enable to produce such a specification automatically, especially when the respective tooling or libraries are absent for a certain programming language and (b) it can produce a more qualitative OpenAPI specification including all appropriate elements that enable the user to select and invoke a required RESTful service. In particular, apart from fully incorporating necessary OpenAPI elements, like response and error schemas, it can enable to automatically add textual descriptions of paths/methods, input parameters, and outputs as well as of the whole API. This can be quite beneficial for service discovery purposes, especially in cases where respective annotations are missing from a RESTful service's source code (e.g., due to tight delivery schedules that the programmers or DevOps need to conform to).

The capability to derive the maturity level of a RESTful service and especially its OpenAPI specification also plays a two-fold purpose: (a) the maturity level witnesses how well the REST architectural style is realized and how easy it is to integrate and invoke a RESTful service and (b) the maturity level can be used for service matching purposes, constituting another service feature for which respective user requirements can be posed.

The main focus of this paper is on presenting our open RESTful API for the management of RESTful services and supplying some initial experimental results, concentrating mainly on the maturity level generation capability. Such results have been produced by relying on a carefully curated set of RESTful services and on state-of-the-art LLMs so as to investigate how well these LLMs derive the maturity level of these services and how precise they are in identifying respective issues and fixes. These results seem quite promising and highlight certain directions for further improving our API's maturity level generation capability.

The rest of this paper is organized as follows. Section 2 reviews related work. Section 3 analyzes our RESTful API and showcases its main architecture. Section 4

---

[2] https://swagger.io/specification/.

describes the experiments made and presents the respective results produced. Finally, Sect. 5 concludes the paper and draws directions for further research.

2 Related Work

As our paper focuses mainly on our API's maturity level derivation capability, we consider as related work to ours maturity models for RESTful services as well as tools or prototypes able to compute a RESTful service's maturity level or knowledge that can contribute/assist to/in this computation.

2.1 Maturity Models

The most known and well adopted maturity model for RESTful services is the one proposed by Richardson [3]. In this model, 4 basic maturity levels exist:

- *Level 0 (The Swamp of POX)*: the RESTful service exposes a single endpoint via which any kind of request can be made and does not consistently use HTTP methods (often only exclusively GET or POST is used even, e.g., for resource deletion)
- *Level 1 (Resources)*: the RESTful service now exposes resource-oriented endpoints (e.g., /books & /authors) but still does not consistently use HTTP methods
- *Level 2 (HTTP verbs)*: apart from resource-oriented endpoints, the RESTful service now properly uses HTTP verbs (e.g., GET, POST, UPDATE, DELETE for CRUD) and makes consistent use of HTTP status codes and other HTTP features
- *Level 3 (Hypermedia Controls - HATEOAS)*: the RESTful service includes suitable links (e.g., links to the authors of a specific book as the represented resource in the response) in its responses in order to dynamically guide the client in its proper use. This makes the service self-discoverable and more flexible

Another known maturity model, called Web API Design Maturity Model, has been proposed by Amundsen [4]. This model does not focus just on the RESTful service documentation but on the overall maturity of a whole API ecosystem within an organization with an emphasis on service adoption, governance and automation. This model comprises six main levels. However, it must be highlighted that due to its focus on API ecosystems, this maturity model is more difficult to derive than the one proposed by Richardson, especially with the limited knowledge of just an OpenAPI specification, as it is the case with our API.

A last API/service maturity model has been proposed by we-archers[3]. This model focuses mainly on the ability of an organization to apply API architecture, design, development, testing and devops practices in projects based on well-defined strategic objectives. This model, similarly to the one of Amundsen, also comprises 6 levels and is obviously difficult to assess based on e.g. a single OpenAPI specification.

Based on our analysis, only the Richarson's maturity model can be derived easily from OpenAPI specifications. The other two maturity models require specialized knowledge that might not be available within a service registry or be difficult or impossible to be supplied by service providers.

---

[3] https://we-archers.com/blog/api-maturity-model-A-step-by-step-approach.

In the quest to derive the Richardson's maturity model, there are particular baselines that can be mentioned. First, we have the formal OpenAPI Specification[4] itself that outlines the structure and content that an OpenAPI description of a RESTful service must have. Second, we have the book titled "REST API Design RuleBook" [5], which categorizes and specifies a set of rules that an OpenAPI description should adhere to. This ruleset aims at evaluating the design quality of an OpenAPI description. It has been constructed by following best design practices that conform to the REST architectural style. Some of these rules have an impact on the maturity level that an OpenAPI description has with respect to the Richardson's maturity model. For example, the rule about resource modelling enforces resource-orientation in the design of the OpenAPI description. So, if it is violated, then the OpenAPI description of a RESTful service conforms to Level 0 of the Richardson's maturity model.

2.2 Tools and Prototypes for Maturity Level Computation

Apart from validation tools for OpenAPI descriptions that include, for example, the open-source Swagger-Parser project[5], there exist some tools and prototypes that attempt to identify issues not strictly related to the OpenAPI specification syntax. Spectral[6] is one of such tools that takes the form of a linter for OpenAPI descriptions. This tool relies on specific rulesets[7] to apply its linting functionality. In particular, it has constructed a ruleset per each version of the OpenAPI Specification as well as a ruleset that maps to multiple versions. The linting functionality encompasses the enforcement of syntax-based rules as well as rules that attempt to identify missing elements (that could e.g., enhance discoverability) or more complete and consistent ways to specify many elements in the OpenAPI Specification.

A sophisticated approach in detecting design issues and the respective Richardon's maturity level for RESTful services has been proposed in [6]. This approach relies on a set of heuristics to evaluate whether a specific RESTful service conforms to best practices like those referred to by the aforemenetioned book [5]. Then upon the detection of the violation of one or more of the heuristics, the approach relies on their mapping to Richardson's maturity levels to infer the actual maturity level of the examined service. While this approach is sophisticated, it includes a medium-sized set of heuristics compared to the amount of issues that state-of-the-art LLMs can produce as indicated in our API's experimental analysis in Sect. 4. Further, it does not rely on the availability of an OpenAPI description for the examined service but a history of calls to that service, which is usually not available, especially in the auspices of a service registry.

The work of Palma et al. [7] attempts to identify design patterns and anti-patterns for RESTful services based on the services' OpenAPI descriptions and invocation history. However, as indicated above, a service's invocation history is usually unavailable. Further, that work infers anti-patterns but does not correlate them to a specific level of the Richardson's maturity model.

---

[4] https://swagger.io/specification/.

[5] https://github.com/swagger-api/swagger-parser.

[6] https://github.com/stoplightio/spectral.

[7] https://docs.stoplight.io/docs/spectral/4dec24461f3af-open-api-rules.

Based on the above analysis, only one prototype is able to infer the Richardson's maturity level of a RESTful service. However, this prototype is limited in its scope as it relies on the invocation history of a service, usually unavailable, so as to produce a corresponding set of rules/heuristics that can infer issues that lead to a certain Richardson maturity level. In this respect, it is not able to identify other issues that might be detected upon examining an OpenAPI specification that could impact the maturity level of the examined service. On the contrary, our API relies solely on the usually available OpenAPI specification of a RESTful service and is able to identify a magnitude of issues (see Sect. 4), some of which directly impact a service's maturity level. As such, it has the potential to better identify a service's actual maturity level.

3   RESTful API Development

3.1   Development Process

Our RESTful API is still under heavy development. Once it is released, it will be available as an open-source project in Github. We follow an iterative method for its development. Starting with an outline of its main requirements, which were drawn by conducting a respective literature review, we have produced its overall architecture and we now itera-tively design and implement it feature-wise in terms of increments. The first increment has focused on the core API functionality in terms of CRUD operations on OpenAPI spec-ifications. The second increment focused on supporting IR-based matching of RESTful services and the automatic generation of OpenAPI specifications from source code. The third increment, which is ongoing, focuses on the automatic derivation of the maturity level of RESTful services. In particular, we have developed a preliminary version of the capability that we have then evaluated. Based on the evaluation results and the obser-vations derived (see Sect. 4), we will complete this capability in order to finalize this increment. Finally, the next increments will focus on the planned future work directions that are described in Sect. 5.

- The outline of the main requirements produced for our RESTful API is as follows:
- Fully support the CRUD-based manipulation of OpenAPI specifications
- Exhibit the capability to produce automatically the OpenAPI specification of a RESTful service based on its source code and the use of LLMs
- Enhance through the use of LLMs (and other techniques) the OpenAPI specifications stored for RESTful services

  - Infer the maturity level of OpenAPI specification/RESTful service
  - Automatically map a RESTful service's I/O parameters to semantic concepts
  - Automatically categorize RESTful services
  - Automatically infer the quality and security level of RESTful services
  - Place any kind of inference/mapping/categorization within the respective Ope-nAPI specification as a custom annotation with the x-* mechanism

- Exhibit a service matching functionality that takes into consideration semantics (e.g., embeddings vectors and/or ontological concepts) plus both the functional and non-functional aspect

- Exhibit a service ranking functionality that takes into account the quality and security level of the RESTful services and respective requirements and preferences coming from the user

3.2   API Architecture

The architecture of our RESTful API, see Fig. 1, has relied on an extension of the well-known Model-View-Controller (MVC) pattern with the addition of the Service and Repository layers for better separation of concerns and maintainability. In particular, the Controller-Service- Repository architectural pattern (CSR) has been followed.

The *Controller* component exposes our API and handles the received HTTP requests. It also hands over the business logic in request processing to the service layer.

Due to the various distinct functionalities that need to be in place for the main business logic realization, the service layer is separated into multiple service components. The *BusinessLogicService* is responsible for realizing our API's main methods. The *LLMService* is responsible for interacting with the LLM with which our API is configured. In particular, it generates appropriate prompts and conducts requests over an LLM and then it parses the response received and produces the output to be given back to the *BusinessLogicService*. The *OpenAPIService* is responsible for loading, validating and updating OpenAPI specifications. The *IRService* covers the production of the TF-IDF vectors from OpenAPI specifications and user requests as well as the computation of the similarity between two TF-IDF vectors based on different similarity measures.

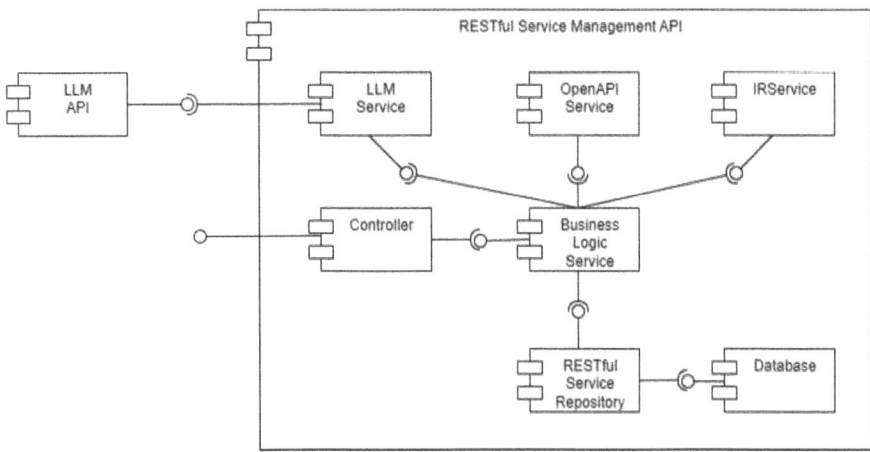

Fig. 1. The architecture of our RESTful Service Management API

At the repository layer, we have the *RESTfulServiceRepository* component, which is responsible for the manipulation of *RESTfulService*(s) and their storage in the underlying database through exploiting an Object-Relational-Mapping (ORM) mechanism. Please note that a *RESTfulService* is a class that encapsulates all appropriate information for a RESTful service manipulated by our API like its id, name, OpenAPI specification and its IR/embeddings vector. However, the central source of service features is mainly the service's OpenAPI specification, which includes not only the core specification elements but also the annotations derived through our API.

Finally, a last component in our architecture is the *Database* itself, responsible for the direct storage, retrieval and updating of our API's main entities.

Please note that our API's architecture is tentative and may be extended depending on the way our API's future increments will be designed and implemented.

3.3   Implementation Details

Our RESTful API for RESTful service/OpenAPI specification management has been developed in Java as a Spring Boot[8] application by extending the MVC pattern as indicated in the previous Subsect. 3.2. To support OpenAPI specifications manipulation, we have relied on the swagger-parser and the swagger-models libraries from the aforementioned open-source Swagger Parser project. ORM was realized by using Hibernate[9]. The underlying database is PostgreSQL[10], a relational database (DB) that also supports the manipulation of vectors, like embedding ones, as well as JSON data (like OpenAPI specifications). To interact with the LLMs, we have utilized the Hugging Face platform's API[11]. This platform provides access to thousands of LLMs, including state-of-the-art ones. The access to this API relies on the *RestTemplate* class in the spring-boot-starter-web library, a class enabling the access to any RESTful API/service as a client. Finally, we have relied on the Smile[12] library in order to support the computation of the IR vectors of OpenAPI specifications and user textual requests and their matching based on the different similarity measure that are available in this library.

The RESTful API source code can be compiled into a Docker[13] image by using a certain Dockerfile. As such, the whole API can be deployed as an orchestration of different containers (one for the API core and one for the PostgreSQL DB) via Docker Compose[14] by following the API's docker-compose.yaml file. This makes our API platform independent as well as a cloud-native application that can be deployed and scaled in cloud environments.

Please note that our API is quite flexible by offering multiple configuration points, including the API key for the Hugging Face platform, the URL in that platform of the LLM to be exploited and the similarity measure to use for matching RESTful services.

4   Experimental Evaluation

The conducted experiment intended to examine our API's capability to automatically derive the maturity level of a RESTful service. It relied on the set of 19 existing RESTful services, which was collected in the form of a benchmark called EMB[15] to support the

---

[8] https://spring.io/projects/spring-boot.

[9] https://hibernate.org/

[10] https://www.postgresql.org/.

[11] https://huggingface.co/docs/api-inference/index.

[12] https://haifengl.github.io/.

[13] https://www.docker.com/.

[14] https://docs.docker.com/compose/.

[15] https://github.com/WebFuzzing/EMB.

evaluation of Evo Master [8]. This set/benchmark includes both the source code as well as the OpenAPI/Swagger specifications of all these services. In this respect, it seems ideal for the evaluation of the maturity level derivation capability of our API.

To evaluate this capability, we relied on 4 state-of-the-art LLMs, namely GPT 4.0, DeepSeek R1, Claude 3.5 Sonnet and Mistral 7B v0.2, which have been extensively evaluated and showcased by many researchers in multiple tasks, even similar to the one examined here.

To realise the examined capability, we relied on a particular prompt that is indicated below. This prompt relies on the Persona (i.e., role) and Template (i.e., format) patterns [9]. It requires the LLM to play the role of an experienced OpenAPI maturity level evaluator plus produce the derivation result in a JSON like format that includes the maturity level derived, the respective maturity issues identified, cases within the examined OpenAPI specification that witness each issue plus fixes for addressing this issue.

"Act as an expert in evaluating OpenAPI specification maturity level and follow best practices for OpenAPI 3.0.0 compliance. Please infer the Richardson maturity level of the following OpenAPI specification and explain the main issues discovered, all the cases in the specification that witness these issues and fixes to these cases/issues. Please group all respective cases in each issue and provide a fix for all of them. Please provide your response in JSON-like structure without comments before or afterwards."

Based on the above analysis, the experiment was conducted 4 times, one per each LLM used. Each time, our API was configured with the right LLM to use and was utilized to examine the maturity level of the 19 RESTful services in the EMB benchmark. The respective results generated by our API per each service and LLM were collected in order to perform the subsequent analysis and synthesis. For each result, we examined the accuracy of the maturity level derived and of all the issues reported. This was conducted based on our own expertise and our convenience to examine also the source code of the respective RESTful service, especially in cases where the accuracy of some issues was not easy to infer based solely on the service's OpenAPI specification and its limited (textual) documentation. Please consider that the latter convenience was not available to the LLMs examined. It must be also highlighted that this human expert evaluation was conducted in two rounds: (a) in the first round, each expert supplied his own judgement over the maturity level and issues concerning a specific OpenAPI and (b) in the second round, judgement deviations were discussed and resolved.

The results analysis has generated various interesting conclusions that we intend to present in the following. We begin the presentation with the supply of some statistics about the performance of the considered LLMs in the form of the following table. As it can be seen, Mistral was a clear winner with an accuracy of 70% and the highest number of issues (6.82) and cases per issue (16.05). It was followed by GPT in terms of accuracy (55%) and Claude in terms of the number of reported issues (6.07). Please note that DeepSeek came second in terms of cases per issue (6.02). Further, please consider that the accuracy of LLMs was computed in terms of the number of correct maturity level predictions divided by the total number of predictions. On the other hand, the number of issues and cases per issue were averaged across all the OpenAPI specifications for which an LLM was able to produce a result.

Some interesting observations from the collected results in terms of the LLM performance were the following:

- In few cases (3), Mistral was able to produce the correct maturity level while the respective issue that downgraded an OpenAPI specification to that level was not included in the reported issues in the JSON response produced by Mistral.
- In one case, GPT did not supply a proper justification for the maturity level derived.
- In some cases, DeepSeek (5) and GPT (1), while they found a respective downgrading issue, did not report a precise maturity level. So, there was a problem in their final reasoning over the maturity level while they had the right ingredients to precisely generate it.
- In very few cases (3), all LLMs were wrong in terms of the derived maturity level.
- In few cases (5), all LLMs were correct about the actual maturity level. But this concerns, in some of those cases, only those LLMs able to generate a response.
- Some OpenAPI specifications were too long to be processed by some LLMs. We had two winners here with respect to this issue, the usual suspect Mistral and DeepSeek, as they were able to process 17 out of 19 specifications (89%). Second came Claude, able to process 14 out of 19 specifications (73%).

Table 1. Statistics about the performance of LLMs in terms of maturity level derivation.

LLMs	Accuracy	Number of issues	Number of Cases / Issue
GPT 4.0	55%	5.6	4.85
DeepSeek R1	47%	4.82	6.02
Claude 3.5 Sonnet	35%	6.07	2.32
Mistral 7B v0.2	70%	6.82	16.05

Apart from the LLMs performance, we also focused on the collected issues that were reported to identify the unique ones, their number and those LLMs that seem to excel in some of these issues. As such, we identified 42 unique issues out of which 7 were downgrading ones (downgrade an OpenAPI specification to a certain maturity level), 22 were issues affecting how well a maturity level is respected and the rest were presentation/styling/versioning/security issues (but also including, e.g., the issue of neglecting textual descriptions of elements like input parameters that plays a significant role in service discovery). The next table shows in three parts the downgrading, affecting and presentation issues where particular LLMs excel with high confidence (percentage of OpenAPI specifications reported with respect to those that have the issue), respectively (Table 1).

Table 2. Downgrading/affecting issues where particular LLMs excel.

Issue	LLMs	Confidence
Lack of Hypermedia Controls (HATEOAS)	DeepSeek R1	14/15
Missing HTTP method diversity	DeepSeek R1, Claude 3.5 Sonnet	3/6
Inconsistent use of HTTP methods	DeepSeek R1	6/9
Missing or incomplete response schemas	Claude 3.5 Sonnet	8/12
Lack of detailed error schemas	DeepSeek R1	13/15
Inconsistent use of response content / media types	Mistral 7B v0.2	8/9
Missing media types in responses	Claude 3.5 Sonnet, Mistral 7B v0.2	3/5
Inconsistent use of HTTP status codes	GPT 4.0	6/9
Inconsistent parameter naming (in paths)	Claude 3.5 Sonnet	4/4
Missing field validations in schemas	Claude 3.5 Sonnet	3/3
Inconsistent parameter descriptions / requirements	Mistral 7B v0.2	13/14
Inconsistent response descriptions	Mistral 7B v0.2	6/9
Lack of request body validation	Mistral 7B v0.2	2/2
Inconsistent use of path and query parameters	DeepSeek R1	3/6
Inconsistent use of data types	Claude 3.5 Sonnet	2/3
Missing API documentation information	Claude 3.5 Sonnet	4/6
Improper or missing security definition	Claude 3.5 Sonnet, Mistral 7B v0.2	6/13
Lack of pagination and filtering support	DeepSeek R1	3/3
Using lower OpenAPI version than 3.0	Mistral 7B v0.2	12/12
Missing operation descriptions and summaries	Mistral 7B v0.2	4/7
Lack of versioning information in the API	DeepSeek R1	4/4
Insecure HTTP schema	Claude 3.5 Sonnet	2/2

As it can be seen, DeepSeek excels in 6 out of 7 downgrading issues so it can be considered as an important/critical source for these issues and for inferring the correct maturity level of an OpenAPI specification. On the other hand, in terms of the affecting issues, the situation is rather mixed. In particular, Claude and Mistral excel each in 5 out of the 12 issues while DeepSeek only in 2 out of the 12. The same situation occurs for presentation/versioning/security issues where Claude and Mistral excel each in 3 out of 7 issues and DeepSeek in 2 out of 7. The above observations indicate that DeepSeek should be advocated as a source for inferring the maturity level while multiple LLMs must be combined to identify affecting and presentation/security issues.

Please note that we do not report in Table 2 issues affecting just 1 OpenAPI specification from the 19 or issues where the confidence of the LLM that excels is below 30%.

From the above analysis, we can conclude that there is no LLM that prevails in all aspects concerning maturity level derivation. On the contrary, it seems that there is a need to combine multiple LLMs to generate all possible maturity issues. This is one possible future research direction we intend to follow. In particular, we intend to utilize and collect all issues reported by many LLMs and then derive the actual maturity level of an OpenAPI specification by checking the existence of downgrading issues.

Further, we have observed that in some cases the source of imprecision in terms of maturity level inference is the lack of proper OpenAPI (textual) documentation. In particular, in some cases, we have discovered that this lack as well as the syntactic checking of OpenAPI specifications by the LLMs lead to wrongly identifying issues and thus imprecisely inferring the respective maturity level. As such, a semantic checking of the OpenAPI specifications is missing. Such a semantic checking can be conducted by considering the source code of the RESTful service. In this respect, another direction of work for improving our API's maturity level inference capability is to consult an LLM with the issues collected and the source code of a respective RESTful service in order to properly infer semantically the correct maturity level of this service. This indicates that we follow the direction of consulting one LLM to evaluate the responses given by other LLMs (or even the same).

Finally, in order to alleviate the issue of OpenAPI specifications that are too long to be processed by LLMs, we plan to process them in chunks. However, this needs to be carefully conducted in order not to influence the final maturity level derivation result. One initial thought is to conduct the chunking based on the exposed paths. This can lead to producing almost evenly sized chunks and can avoid issues where wrong maturity levels are produced as different chunks have different parts of the same path.

5 Conclusions and Future Work

This paper has presented a novel RESTful API for the management of RESTful services based on their API specification that intends to play the role of an open global or organizational service registry. This API not only allows the publishing and discovery of RESTful services but also exhibits some additional, innovative capabilities that are backed up through the use of LLMs. These capabilities concern the automatic generation of the OpenAPI specification of a RESTful service based on its source code and the derivation of its maturity level. Such capabilities pave the way for a more accurate service discovery as they enable including additional textual descriptions and elements in the OpenAPI specification for a RESTful service. Further, they witness how well a RESTful service conforms to REST and how easy it is to integrate it in a certain application. In addition to presenting our API, the paper also showcases an experimental evaluation of the API's maturity level generation capability that has resulted in quite promising results and interesting observations.

Apart from the mentioned improvements in the previous section, the following directions for further work are planned. First, we intend to enhance the automatic generation of OpenAPI specifications such that more complete specifications are produced. Second, we plan to support the automatic categorization of the published RESTful services such that the publisher does not require to manually create and select the categories that his/her services map to. Third, we intend to make service discovery more semantic by exploring and evaluating two alternative ways to achieve that: (a) the use of embeddings vectors for IR-based similarity and (b) the mapping of service I/O to ontology concepts for semantic I/O matchmaking. Again, the role of LLMs will be crucial to support both sub-directions. Finally, we plan to enhance service discovery by also covering the non-functional aspect by, e.g., automatically deriving the quality and security level of a RESTful service's source code.

References

1. Hou, X., et al.: Large language models for software engineering: a systematic literature review. ACM Trans. Softw. Eng. Methodol. **33**, 1–79 (2024). https://doi.org/10.1145/3695988
2. Vidgof, M., Bachhofner, S., Mendling, J.: Large language models for business process management: opportunities and challenges. In: Di Francescomarino, C., Burattin, A., Janiesch, C.,Sadiq, S. (eds.) Business Process Management Forum, LNCS, pp. 107–123. Springer Nature Switzerland, Cham (2023). https://doi.org/10.1007/978-3-031-41623-1_7
3. Martin Fowler: Richardson Maturity Model: steps toward the glory of REST. https://martinfowler.com/articles/richardsonMaturityModel.html
4. Mike Amundsen: The Web API Design Maturity Model (WADM). WS-REST 2016. , Lugano, Switzerland (2016)
5. Massé, M.H., Massé, M.: REST API design rulebook: designing consistent RESTful Web Service Interfaces. O'Reilly, Beijing, Köln (2012)
6. Rodríguez, C., et al.: REST APIs: a large-scale analysis of compliance with principles and best practices. In: Bozzon, A., Cudre-Maroux, P., Pautasso, C. (eds.) Web Engineering. ICWE 2016. LNCS, vol. 9671, pp. 21–39. Springer, Cham (2016). https://doi.org/10.1007/978-3-319-38791-8_2
7. Palma, F., Gonzalez-Huerta, J., Moha, N., Guéhéneuc, Y.G., Tremblay, G.: Are RESTful APIs well-designed? Detection of their linguistic (anti)patterns. In: Barros, A., Grigori, D., Narendra, N., Dam, H. (eds.) Service-Oriented Computing. ICSOC 2015. LNCS, vol. 9435, pp. 171–187. Springer, Berlin, Heidelberg (2015). https://doi.org/10.1007/978-3-662-48616-0_11
8. Arcuri, A.: RESTful API automated test case generation with EvoMaster. ACM Trans. Softw. Eng. Methodol. **28**, 1–37 (2019). https://doi.org/10.1145/3293455
9. White, J., et al.: A Prompt Pattern Catalog to Enhance Prompt Engineering with ChatGPT (2023). https://arxiv.org/abs/2302.11382, https://doi.org/10.48550/ARXIV.2302.11382

Improving Content-Based Data Product Retrieval in Federated Environments with LLM and Sampling

Matteo Falconi$^{(\boxtimes)}$ and Pierluigi Plebani

Politecnico di Milano, Milan, Italy
{matteo.falconi,pierluigi.plebani}@polimi.it

Abstract. Data products have emerged as a powerful paradigm for managing data in both intra-enterprise and federated environments, providing structured data assets that include not only the data itself but also services, metadata, and access policies. However, a key challenge in federated environments is the discovery of relevant data products. Traditional discovery mechanisms are heavily dependent on metadata, which is often inconsistent, incomplete, or not standardized across organizations. This lack of metadata quality significantly limits the effectiveness of discovery, making it difficult for consumers to identify and retrieve the data they need. To address this challenge, we propose a content-based discovery framework that shifts the focus from metadata to the actual content of data products. Our approach uses sampling techniques to extract meaningful data representations and a tabular retrieval model for natural language queries. Directly interacting with data improves discovery accuracy, enabling effective data access in federated environments.

Keywords: Data Product · Federated Data Sharing · Content-based Discovery

1 Introduction

The advent of data products is modifying the way organizations manage and share information [10]. Introduced within the data mesh framework [5], in this concept, data related to a specific domain is managed by a specialized team that deals, like a product, with its entire lifecycle, from collection to preparation for consumption [7]. The Data Space Support Center [3] has adopted the concept of data products as data sharing units that contain not only data and services but also metadata that describe resources and associated licensing agreements. These metadata are usually used to drive the *discovery* of data product, but they are often inconsistent and incomplete [6], and the data discovery is also worsened by diverse governance and a lack of standards.

© The Author(s), under exclusive license to Springer Nature Switzerland AG 2025
J. Grabis and Y. Wautelet (Eds.): CAiSE 2025 Workshops, LNBIP 556, pp. 289–297, 2025.
https://doi.org/10.1007/978-3-031-94931-9_23

To improve the efficacy of discovery, our work proposes an innovative framework based on a *content-based discovery* approach that directly exploits the data content rather than relying on metadata. Specifically, the proposed method assumes that the data involved is structured data, so the framework extracts a significant sample from the data of each data product and leverages a tabular retriever model to perform content-based queries across all the data products of the federation, thus overcoming the limitations imposed by different governance policies and lack of metadata quality.

The paper is organized as follows. After the discussion on relevant work in the literature presented in Sect. 2, Sect. 3 presents the proposed LLM-based data product discovery process architecture. and Sect. 4 analyses the data product sampling problem. An evaluation of the proposed approach is discussed in Sect. 5 and Sect. 6 concludes the paper outlining possible future directions.

2   Related Works

In federated data architectures, data discovery [11] is often hindered by metadata that is inconsistent, incomplete, or lacks a common standard [6]. This is confirmed by a recent study [12] stating the few dataset are described leveraging metadata standards.

Although still at an early stage [1], content-based discovery techniques promise to improve the accuracy of results by exploiting the content of data, for instance, by leveraging embedding and vector-based retrieval. Due to the growth in the size of datasets, generating embeddings for the entire content is often unfeasibly expensive. The challenge of small context windows in Large Language Models has been extensively studied in the literature through various approaches [2]. However, an interesting alternative to overcome this limitation is the use of sampling and clustering techniques to extract significant data samples that are then fed into the LLMs to bypass the context window constraint.

Various sampling approaches, including random, systematic, and stratified sampling [13], provide computationally efficient solutions but do not always effectively capture the information characteristics of the data. To improve the significance of the samples, clustering-based methods can be used: e.g., mixed-attributes such as k-means [8] or k-medoids [9], the latter more robust to outliers than k-means. In addition, clustering methods such as DBSCAN and the improved version K-DBSCAN have been widely used to detect clusters of arbitrary shape in the data, starting from regions of data with high density.

3   General Architecture

The proposed LLM-based data product discovery process (see Fig. 1) is conceived as a federation service that is offered, for instance, to all members of a given data space. Considering the definition proposed by the DSSC [4], a federation service is a service that enables secure and regulated data sharing by managing

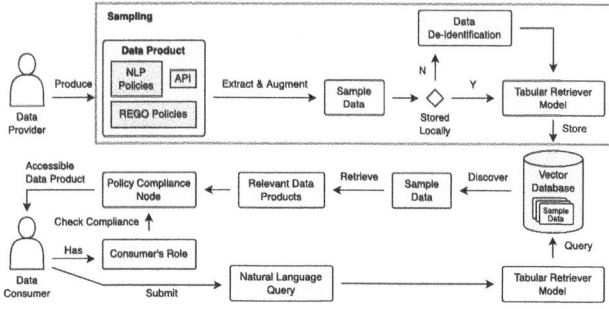

Fig. 1. Overview of the proposed Framework

various aspects, including but not limited to policy compliance, access control, and discoverability, while ensuring compliance with relevant regulations.

In this context, the end user of the framework is a data consumer who wants to discover specific data within the federation of which they are a participant. The objective of the framework is to facilitate the discovery of only those data that are relevant to their query and to which they actually have a right of access[1].

The content-based discovery process starts with the data producer, who has created a properly structured data product according to the organization's and federation's data governance policies. A valid data product must include the data, the APIs for accessing the data, and a set of access policies that define how and by whom the data can be used.

With the APIs, the framework extracts data from the data product. Through augmentation and sampling, a representative subset of the original data, called sample data, is generated. This *sample data* is essential for enabling efficient discovery, as it captures the key characteristics of the data product while being much smaller in size.

When working in a federated setting, some organizations may prefer, or may be required, not to store their data outside a given region unless it has been anonymized. For instance, an organization collecting sensitive data regulated by the European GDPR may only store that data outside the European Union if it has first been anonymized. These restrictions are usually expressed in the policies attached to the data products. To address these constraints, our content-based data product discovery framework includes an optional de-identification step when policies or the vector database's location require anonymizing generated sample data before storage.

After this optional de-identification process, an *embedding* is generated from the sample data using a table retrieval model, which will be stored in a vector database containing the embeddings of all data products in the federation.

The content-based discovery process continues when the data consumer, interacts with it. Each data consumer is part of an organization and has a specific

---

[1] It is worth highlighting that in this paper, the issues related to the access authorization are not covered. It will be the objective of future work.

role within said organization that determines its data access permissions. Data consumers aim to find relevant information within the federation by submitting natural language queries. This allows them to search for data products that meet their needs while adhering to organizational policies and access restrictions. By leveraging the same tabular retriever model used to generate the sample data embeddings, an embedding of the query is generated, and the vector database is queried.

The vector database returns a list of sample data satisfying the query, together with a relevance score. A relevance metric and a distance metric are calculated to select only the best performing samples data. The data products whose sample data have been selected are then forwarded, together with the role of the data consumer, to the policy compliance node. The policy compliance node is a complex component of the frameworks that is responsible for ensuring compliance with the policies. In fact, the policy compliance node encapsulates a policy compliance engine, which is able to read the policies of a data product and the identity of the data consumer, i.e., their role and organization. Given these information, the objective of this component is to generate a tailored version of the gathered data products that contains only the subset of data that the data consumer has the right to access based on their identity. The generated data products are then finally given to the data consumers.

By leveraging these components, the proposed framework greatly simplifies the process of data discovery and access in a federated data product architecture. At the same time, the framework ensures that access to data is highly granular by strictly complying with the access policies defined by the data producers.

4 Data Product Sampling

Within the framework presented in Sect. 3, this paper focuses on the process of sample data generation and data retrieval. The goal is to extract a meaningful sample of the content of the data product and use it for content-based discovery, overcoming the limitations of metadata, and to discover relevant data via a natural language query. The need for sample data arises from the limitations imposed by the context window of artificial intelligence models, i.e., the maximum input size that a model can process.

4.1 Generating a Sample Data

The process of generating sample data involves the use of a sampling algorithm, an LLM generative model, and a tabular retrieval model to support content-based discovery based on sample data effectively. The red rectangle in Fig. 1 encloses the main steps. Having obtained the data from the data product exploiting the offered API, two different sampling methods have been considered.

The first is the *Random* sampling that, as the name suggests, randomly chooses a subset of records in the data product, and it is leveraged as a baseline in the discovery process. A second method is based on *DBSCAN with an augmentation phase* that utilizes the DBSCAN algorithm to generate a sample data and leverages a generative LLM model, specifically GPT-4o mini, to augment the column descriptions. The DBSCAN clustering algorithm identifies patterns in the data based on density and is used to divide the data into distinct homogeneous groups. Since data products can contain both categorical and numerical data, the distance matrix for the DBSCAN clustering algorithm is calculated utilizing the Gower distance [14], which is often used for the similarity analysis of mixed data. Gower distance is defined as a measure that calculates the similarity between two elements. It normalizes each variable to compare them equally and then averages the differences between the values. The purpose of the augmentation step is to improve the quality of the descriptive columns of the sample data, making them more representative of the original content and thus optimizing the effectiveness of the content-based discovery. The generative LLM model produces a new list of descriptors which, after being cleansed, replaces the original one, creating an *augmented sample data.*

From the generated clusters, a *sample data* of 150 elements is selected with a distribution proportional to the density of the clusters, ensuring that the sample data remains representative of the original data product. The size of the sample data is constrained by the limited context window of the tabular retriever model. At the same time, from the data extracted from the data product, leveraging a random sampling algorithm, we generate *random sample data.* If the data product contains fewer than 150 elements, sampling is not required, and all data are included in both the sample data and the random sample data.

As per Fig. 1, a sample day may undergo a de-identification process if it is required due to the content of the data. Next, both sample data are converted into the appropriate format and passed to a table retriever model, such as mpnet-base-v2-table[2], which generates the embeddings of the sample data. These embeddings are finally stored in a vector database, making the framework ready for content-based searching.

4.2 Discovering a Data Product

The process of discovering sample data begins with the query of a data consumer and follows the workflow illustrated in Fig. 2.

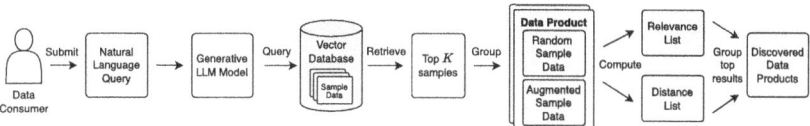

Fig. 2. Process of discovering data products

---

[2] https://huggingface.co/deepset/all-mpnet-base-v2-table.

Initially, the query is processed by the same tabular retriever model that embedded the sample data. The vector database is then queried, and the data consumer can choose how many data products to retrieve; for instance, let's consider only the top 20 results. These results are transformed into a list that contains the location of each data product along with a score that reflects he relevance of the sample data, and, by extension, the data product, to the query.

It is expected that both types of sample data will be retrieved from a given query due to the presence of both the augmented sample data and the random sample data in the vector database. The random sample data consists entirely of randomly selected samples from the data product, whereas the augmented sample data provides a density-based representation with augmented data columns that more accurately reflect the content of the product. Therefore, the two sample types produce different results. By comparing these scores, it is possible to calculate the following two metrics.

Relevance Metric. $Rel(Q, DP) \in [0..1]$. Calculate how pertinent a data product DP is to the query Q, where 0 means not and 1 very relevant to the query. For each retrieved sample data, the relevance metric is calculated as the mean of the scores. If only a single sample from a data product is retrieved, the relevance metric corresponds to that sample's score.

$$Rel = (Score_{Random} + Score_{Augmented})/2 \tag{1}$$

Distance Metric. $Dis(Q, DS) \in [0..1]$. It measures the precision of the query in relation to the data product's content. Thus, a sample data containing mostly only the data requested in the query will have a distance close to 1. The distance metric is evaluated using the following sigmoid function:

$$Dis = (1 + e^{-(\alpha x + \beta)})^{-1} \tag{2}$$

where α and β are parameters that place the curve within a range of 0 to 0.5, representing the minimum and maximum possible values for the input, corresponding to 20 and -2, respectively.

A higher relevance metric indicates a more relevant data product; at the same time, a higher distance metric signifies a more precise query. In fact, where the query closely matches the data product, the augmented data sample tends to perform better than the random data sample. On the other hand, if the query is contextually relevant but not precisely matched to the stored data, both metrics will typically receive a similar score and thus produce a lower distance metric.

5   Evaluation

The validation of the approach is based on datasets from Kaggle that could be seen as representative of our data products. Specifically, they are grouped in four categories: sales (four datasets), environment (three datasets), lifestyle (four datasets), and entertainment (four datasets). These datasets were chosen

Table 1. Discovery Results for Query Q1   **Table 2.** Discovery Results for Query Q2

Sample Name	Sample Type	Score	Rel	Dis
Car_Price	Random Sample Data	0.59	0.545	0.46
	Augmented Sample Data	0.50		
E_Commerce	Augmented Sample Data	0.36	0.36	–
Synthetic_Sales	Augmented Sample Data	0.33	0.315	–
	Random Sample Data	0.30		
Daily_Nutrition	Augmented Sample Data	0.27	0.27	–

Sample Name	Sample Type	Score	Rel	Dis
CO2_Emissions	Random Data Sample	0.48	0.46	0.27
	Augmented Data Sample	0.44		
Rainfall	Augmented Data Sample	0.30	0.30	–
Nutrition	Augmented Data Sample	0.29	0.29	–
E-commerce	Random Data Sample	0.28	0.28	–
Car_Price	Random Data Sample	0.26	0.26	–

to ensure a heterogeneous set of data while maintaining some degree of similarity to evaluate the effectiveness of the approach.

We simulated a data consumer accessing the data by submitting queries to the vector database. Specifically, these queries were designed to evaluate whether the framework could identify the most relevant data products based on their content and the quality of the previously defined metrics. In order to evaluate the framework of the gathered data, we propose two test query, as presented in the next paragraphs. Each query has been studied to reflect the content of their context while targeting mainly one specific dataset.[3]

Q1: Dataset Containing Details about Car Models Sold. The objective of query *Q1* is to discover data on sold cars. However, since the vector database contains multiple sample data related to sales, this scenario provides an interesting test of our framework's performance. Table 1 presents the top six scores of the query with the *Rel* and *Dis* values, for the results within 20% of the higher relevance score. In this case, only the *Car_Price* dataset satisfies this constraint, and the distance metric is 0.46.

This outcome demonstrates that the framework effectively identifies the most relevant dataset in the database and that the query is quite accurate with respect to the content of the dataset. In fact, the *Car_Price* dataset contains data about car models, sold price, and additional attributes such as car brands and manufacturing years.

Q2: Dataset Containing CO^2 Emissions. Query *Q2* has been intentionally formulated vaguely, specifying only an interest in CO_2 emissions. The scores resulting from this query are listed in Table 2. Applying the same 20% relevance threshold, the output of query *Q2* is *CO2_Emissions* with a distance metric of 0.27. While this result indicates a relevant match, the query could be refined to better capture the dataset's content. By slightly augmenting the query to *Q2.2: Dataset containing data about CO2 emissions by continent*, the retrieved dataset remains the same with an unchanged relevance metric but with a significant improvement in the distance metric, going from 0.27 to 0.94. This improvement suggests that the refined query better aligns with the dataset's content, demonstrating the impact of query specificity on retrieval accuracy.

---

[3] For a complete description of the selected datasets and additional queries considered in the validation, refer to https://github.com/TheFalco/Complete-Evaluation.

6   Conclusion and Future Work

The solution proposed in this paper enables the generation of representative samples of data products and the use of a tabular retrieval model to support the content-based user's queries, thus facilitating the discovery of relevant data in federated environments. Our framework has two metrics to evaluate discovered data. They identify relevant data products and indicate the query's relevance to their content. This metric allows data consumers to improve their queries by adding or removing details to discover more relevant data products.

In future work, we aim to further explore the definition and implementation of the policy compliance node, with a focus on automatic access control management. This aspect is critical to ensure that access to data products is regulated in a secure manner that complies with the policies defined by the data providers. The integration of access control mechanisms will further refine the granularity of permissions and improve the overall security of the framework.

Acknowledgments. This work has been funded by the European Union (TEADAL, 101070186).

References

1. Chapman, A., et al.: Dataset search: a survey. VLDB J. **29**(1), 251–272 (2020). https://doi.org/10.1007/S00778-019-00564-X
2. Chen, S., Wong, S., Chen, L., Tian, Y.: Extending context window of large language models via positional interpolation. ArXiv (2023). https://doi.org/10.48550/arXiv.2306.15595
3. Data Space Support Center: DSSC - Blueprint v1.5 (October 2024). https://dssc.eu/space/bv15e/766065053/Data+Product
4. Data Space Support Center: DSSC key concepts of data spaces-services (October 2024)
5. Dehghani, Z.: Data mesh principles and logical architecture (December 2020). https://martinfowler.com/articles/data-mesh-principles.html
6. Edwards, P.N., et al.: Science friction: data, metadata, and collaboration. Soc. Stud. Sci. **41**(5), 667–690 (2011)
7. Goedegebuure, A., et al.: Data mesh: a systematic gray literature review. ACM Comput. Surv. **57**(1) (2024). https://doi.org/10.1145/3687301
8. Huang, Z.: Extensions to the k-means algorithm for clustering large data sets with categorical values. Data Min. Knowl. Discov. **2**(3), 283–304 (1998). https://doi.org/10.1023/A:1009769707641
9. Lund, B., Ma, J.: A review of cluster analysis techniques and their uses in library and information science research: k-means and k-medoids clustering. Perform. Meas. Metrics **22**(3), 161–173 (2021)
10. Machado, I.A., Costa, C., Santos, M.Y.: Data mesh: concepts and principles of a paradigm shift in data architectures. Procedia Comput. Sci. **196**, 263–271 (2022). https://doi.org/10.1016/j.procs.2021.12.013
11. Paton, N.W., Chen, J., Wu, Z.: Dataset discovery and exploration: a survey. ACM Comput. Surv. **56**(4) (2023). https://doi.org/10.1145/3626521

12. Tenopir, C., et al.: Changes in data sharing and data reuse practices and perceptions among scientists worldwide. PLoS ONE **10**(8), e0134826 (2015)
13. Turner, D.P.: Sampling methods in research design. Headache **60**(1), 8–12 (2020)
14. Yoo, J., An, Y., Kim, Y.M.: Density-based spatial clustering of applications with noise using gower distance. J. Korean Data Inf. Sci. Soc. **32**(5), 1121–1133 (2021)

Leveraging LLMs and RAG for Enhanced Football Talent Scouting

Felice Antonio Martire and Davide Ragazzi[(✉)]

Kama.Sport Srl, Via Luigi Suardo 18/C, 24067 Paratico, Italy
{felice.martire,davide.ragazzi}@kama.sport

Abstract. In the world of professional football, the ongoing search for new talents is of paramount importance. Each club relies on scouts, who produce thousands of players' reports every year. As a result, scout managers are faced with an overwhelming volume of data, primarily in the form of unstructured text. To explore and analyze such data, Large Language Models (LLMs) have recently emerged as promising tools, offering new possibilities for handling and interpreting these vast amounts of data. In this paper, we propose an LLM-based approach to assist scout managers in exploring players' reports textual data. The approach leverages a Retrieval-Augmented Generation (RAG) architecture, wherein LLMs are employed for multiple tasks: (i) summarizing and extracting key information from players' reports; (ii) interpreting scout managers' input queries; (iii) generating the final response based on scout managers' queries and on summarized players' reports, the latter extracted from a vector database. The approach has been implemented within a service-oriented ecosystem, and validated in the scope of a real-world talent scouting use case, demonstrating its benefits in providing insights from unstructured players' reports.

Keywords: Retrieval-Augmented Generation · Large Language Models · Football Scouting · Talent Discovery · Sports Analytics

1 Introduction

In the realm of professional football, the talent scouting process plays a pivotal role in shaping recruitment decisions, squad development, and long-term competitiveness [2]. As part of this process, vast amounts of unstructured textual data are generated in the form of players' reports, by football talent scouts, to be reviewed and inspected by club management. These reports typically combine qualitative assessments of a player's abilities with quantitative data to help clubs and scout managers identify new talents, reduce transfer risks, and make informed decisions. Nevertheless, efficiently managing this data presents significant challenges, creating a strong demand for advanced techniques to extract actionable insights.

To explore and analyse such data, Large Language Models (LLMs) have recently emerged as promising tools to streamline and enhance sports analytics,

J. Grabis and Y. Wautelet (Eds.): CAiSE 2025 Workshops, LNBIP 556, pp. 298–309, 2025.
https://doi.org/10.1007/978-3-031-94931-9_24

including football scouting data [12]. However, despite the impressive capabilities of LLMs, they are prone to generating so-called *hallucinations* (i.e., inaccurate or unverified outputs) when operating without a well-defined context. To address poor contexts issues, Retrieval-Augmented Generation (RAG) has proven to be an effective strategy [4]. Roughly speaking, RAG integrates a LLM with a retrieval mechanism that grounds the generation process on a curated context, typically drawn from a vector database (renowned to ensure efficient storage and faster retrieval), thereby improving the reliability of the output while avoiding the computational and economic expenses associated with an extensive LLM fine-tuning.

In this paper, we propose an approach that combines LLMs with a RAG-based architecture to support scout managers in their analysis of players' reports. Our approach not only leverages the advanced natural language processing capabilities of LLMs for summarization and key information extraction from players' reports, but also provides a robust mechanism for query interpretation and result generation. In fact, within the RAG-based architecture, LLMs are employed for multiple tasks: (i) summarizing and extracting key information from players' reports; (ii) interpreting scout managers' input queries; (iii) generating the final response based on scout managers' queries and on summarized players' reports, the latter extracted from a vector database. Moreover, the whole RAG-based architecture is integrated into a service-oriented ecosystem, enabling seamless interaction through REST APIs and ensuring easy deployment in real-world settings.

The remainder of this paper is organized as follows. Section 2 reviews related works, highlighting existing applications of LLMs and RAG within the football domain. Section 3 outlines the motivations behind our approach and the specific challenges addressed. Section 4 delves into the details of the system architecture and its components. Section 5 presents a preliminary evaluation of the LLM-based approach, to test its effectiveness in a real-world talent scouting scenario. Finally, Sect. 6 offers a discussion on the strengths and limitations of the approach, as well as on potential future research streams.

2   Related Work

The continuous advancement of Artificial Intelligence has opened new frontiers in football data analysis, enabling innovative methods to extract valuable insights from diverse data, including match events, player performance, and scouting reports. Building on these advancements, several studies have explored AI-driven solutions for football data analysis, proposing rigorous methodologies for analyzing match events and players data [5,8]. Additionally, some research efforts have highlighted both the potential and the challenges of integrating AI into talent scouting workflows, addressing issues such as data sparsity and contextual ambiguity [1,7]. Recently, the rise of LLMs has further boosted the application of Generative AI in football data analysis, particularly through the use of RAG architectures. These solutions enhance football analysis by combining efficient data retrieval with precise, context-aware responses, improving accuracy and overcoming challenges related to extracting information from large volumes of textual data [9,10].

Novel Contributions. While the approaches mentioned earlier are compelling, they have two major limitations: (i) only a few of them are focused on football talent scouting and on processing unstructured textual data; (ii) they primarily depend on publicly available numerical data, overlooking the personalized, club-specific aspects of scouting, such as the unique structures and strategic goals of individual football clubs. In contrast, our approach strives to combine the transformative power of LLMs with a RAG architecture, to process unstructured textual data from club-specific scouting reports. In particular, it fully harnesses the capabilities of LLMs to extract key insights from scouting reports, which are crucial for scout managers and tailored to the specific needs of modern scouting operations. Furthermore, unlike the aforementioned approaches, which have not yet been implemented in real-world scenarios, our LLM-based solution has already been successfully deployed in a service-oriented ecosystem, and it is currently serving a group of Italian football clubs.

3   Motivating Scenario

In the landscape of professional football, clubs and federations, such as the Italian Football Federation[1] (in brief, FIGC), routinely employ specialized scouting teams dedicated to identifying emerging talents, often focusing on players under the age of 18. These scouts observe matches and training sessions, meticulously documenting their evaluations in textual reports.

Scouts Reports. Figure 1 illustrates an example of a scout report. Typically, a scout report consists of two sections. The first section details the *player's personal data*, including age, nationality, playing position (e.g., defender, midfielder, forward, goalkeeper), and a potential rating assigned by the scout on a five-point scale. The second section comprises a *textual note*, written by the scout either during or shortly after observing the player's performance. This text encapsulates the core expertise of the scout, as it embeds *key attributes* (e.g., technical and tactical attributes such as ball control, shooting, passing accuracy, off-ball movement) and nuanced evaluations that extend beyond the basic player's personal data. Clearly, this important information is inherently subject to the individual scout's writing style and the form in which they choose to express their evaluations. Although different scout teams might adopt alternative formats, with variations in the number or structure of attributes and even the inclusion of multiple notes, this two-sections format reflects a common structural pattern for reports, in the vast majority of cases.

Challenges. Notably, a top-tier club (for instance, one competing in *Serie A*, which is the top football league in Italy) may generate over 10,000 scouting reports per year, encompassing evaluations of approximately 5,000 players, ranging from established professionals to promising youth prospects. These assessments, produced by a plethora of individual scouts, underscore the magnitude

---

[1] https://www.figc.it/en/home/.

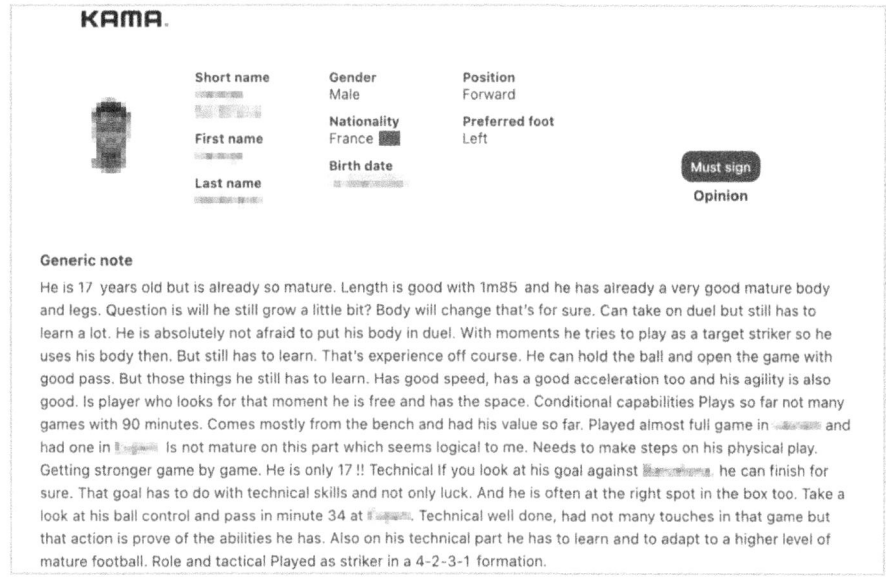

Fig. 1. Example report generated by a top-tier club scout. The report features structured information (e.g., date of birth, nationality) alongside an extensive unstructured textual note. All sensitive information has been censored for privacy reasons. Data source provided by Kama.Sport.

and complexity of modern scouting operations. All these scouting reports are typically stored and managed within a centralized system, to which scout managers have access for query and consultation purposes. However, since the key attributes encapsulating the scout's expertise are concealed within unstructured textual notes, managers encounter significant challenges in performing advanced queries to find relevant talents, categorizing observations, and identifying similarities among players with analogous attributes. The absence of structured data formats complicates the extraction of meaningful insights, limiting the effectiveness of traditional analytical methods. Consequently, valuable information remains underexplored, undermining both strategic decision-making and the continuous refinement of scouting methodologies. To overcome these limitations, we propose to foster a LLM-based solution designed to effectively extract and use these key attributes, paving the way for a more systematic and scalable approach to talent evaluation, streamlining the query process for scout managers.

4   LLM-Based Architecture with RAG Integration

The proposed architecture integrates LLMs with RAG techniques in a scalable and modular Web-based service-oriented ecosystem. An illustration of the proposed architecture is shown in Fig. 2. The architecture is composed of two services: (i) **Data Ingestion and Processing**, a service dedicated to the inges-

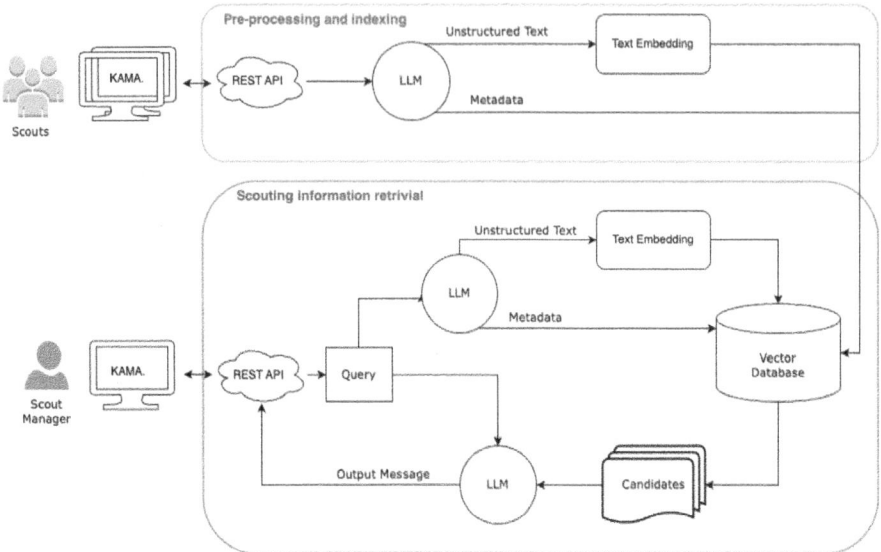

Fig. 2. High-level RAG-based architecture illustrating the two services: (i) pre-processing and indexing of data and (ii) scouting information retrieval and response generation, which uses a vector database and LLM-based query processing. Both services communicate with the Kama platform through REST APIs for data ingestion and response generation.

tion, pre-processing, and indexing of the reports produced by the scouts team into a vector database; (ii) **Scouting Information Retrieval and Response Generation**, a service dedicated to leveraging indexed data in combination with LLM capabilities to generate context-aware responses to scout manager requests. These services are implemented in Python using a Web framework, specifically FastAPI[2], and are hosted on an Amazon Elastic Container Service (Amazon ECS) cluster. Such services are capable of invoking LLMs, such as those provided through OpenAI APIs. Indexing and storage of players' reports are managed with the support of a Qdrant vector database[3], hosted in a cloud-based cluster. Both services are accessible through the Kama ecosystem[4]. The Kama platform features a Web-based front-end that collects and displays information, communicating with the two services through REST APIs. This integration ensures a cohesive service-oriented ecosystem that is both scalable and flexible, aligning with the demands of scientific application scenarios.

---

[2] https://fastapi.tiangolo.com/m.
[3] https://qdrant.tech/.
[4] https://kama.sport/en/home/.

4.1   Data Ingestion and Processing

In this section, we explain how the original unstructured texts from the input scouts reports are processed and stored in a vector database. This phase is crucial because raw reports, in their original form, may contain inconsistent formatting, ambiguous terminology, or redundant information. We implemented a pipeline using a Python script that reads the input report (in JSON format) through a REST API and processes it, to produce a summarized version of the report. In this respect, each report is summarized with an emphasis on key terms representing scouts' expertise, ensuring that essential insights are captured and presented in a consistent format. The summarization is performed by calling the OpenAI API, specifying the `gpt-4o-mini` LLM. In these API calls, we provide the report text within a prompt for the LLM, containing also specific instructions to extract and categorize information according to the following five predefined scouts' expertise attributes categories:

- *Technical Attributes* (e.g., ball control, passing accuracy, shooting).
- *Tactical Attributes* (e.g., off-ball movement, first press, linking play).
- *Physical Attributes* (e.g., height, overall build, speed, agility).
- *Psychological Attributes* (e.g., determination, maturity, leadership, altruism).
- *Future Potential and Evaluation* (e.g., suitability level, projected development).

An example of a summarized report is shown in Fig. 3. After the summarization phase, each report is transformed into a dense vector representation, also known as *embedding*. An embedding is a numerical encoding of text that captures semantic relationships, enabling more nuanced comparisons than traditional keyword-based searches [3]. The summarized text is embedded using the `text-embedding-3-small` model via OpenAI APIs [6]. These vectors are stored in the Qdrant vector database in a collection (i.e., an organisational unit to group embeddings and associated metadata), by specifying the cosine distance metric as a default similarity metric to be used for the retrieval phase, and a vector size of 1536 (it is the length of the vector used to represent the text of each report.). In addition to storing the embeddings, they are also tagged with the essential player's personal data attributes presented in Sect. 3 (e.g., nationality, playing position). The latter serve as metadata for embeddings, to enable a preliminary filtering, thus pre-selecting relevant reports during the retrieval phase, as described in the following section.

4.2   Scouting Information Retrieval and Response Generation

In this section, we provide a concise overview of the modules composing the second service, thus outlining the workflow that processes a scout manager's query and produces a structured and well-formatted response, containing the summarized reports. To this aim, as for the previously described service, we implemented a pipeline using a Python script. When a scout manager submits a request, the LLM (specifically, the `gpt-4o` OpenAI model) performs the following two key operations.

LLM processed:
Standard build, 1.84 m tall, hypertrophic structure, robust, physical strength, power, muscular elasticity, quick in tight spaces, good progression in wide areas, left-footed, decent fundamentals, frenetic management, good at shielding the ball, effective on the flanks, less so in linking play, good command when driving in the open field, comes on in the 60th minute, deployed as an attacking forward, makes runs in behind, goal-oriented, needs to improve in team play, does not hold back in duels, active pressing

Fig. 3. Example of summarized report, after LLM processing. All sensitive information has been censored for privacy reasons. Data source provided by Kama.Sport.

(1) *Parsing* – The LLM first determines whether the query is genuinely requesting player information based on football-related attributes. If the query lacks valid player attributes or is otherwise irrelevant, the LLM either requests clarification from the user or falls back to a predefined query template.
(2) *Attributes extraction* – The LLM is instructed to extract key information such as: (i) descriptive traits resembling the key attributes associated with scouts' expertise (e.g., technical and tactical features), rephrasing them to align with the format used for storing players' data in the vector database; (ii) player's personal data attributes, such as age (numeric), nationality (string), positional role (defender, midfielder, forward, goalkeeper), and rating (numeric).

This entire process is facilitated by the *function-calling* feature of the OpenAI API, implemented through a dedicated Python script, which allows LLMs to call external functions, APIs, or tools to retrieve structured data and perform specific tasks in a dynamic way.

Once the preliminary steps (1) and (2) of the retrieval workflow have been performed, the key attributes extracted in (2) – regarding technical and tactical features, physical and psychological attitudes and so forth – are embedded using the `text-embedding-3-small` OpenAI model. The resulting dense vector is then compared, through a similarity search, with the a subset of vector embeddings contained in the Qdrant vector database (such subset is determined by filtering embeddings in the vector database using the player's personal data extracted in step (2), which are employed to tag vector embeddings in the data ingestion and processing phase, as explained in Sect. 4.1). The similarity search is apt to identify the scouting reports that best match the user's request [11]. Noteworthy, the similarity search is achieved with cosine similarity, which measures the angle between vectors rather than their magnitude, which is particularly well-suited for text embedding comparisons.

The outcome of the similarity search is a ranked list of k candidate reports, sorted by descending similarity scores. The number k of retrieved reports is a tunable service parameter (by default, it is set to 5). Finally, the original query and the top-k list of scouting reports are passed to a second instance of the LLM, the OpenAI `gpt-4o-mini`. This model consolidates all relevant information and synthesizes insights into a coherent narrative that directly addresses the user's request. When the number k of retrieved results is greater than 5, the LLM helps producing an aggregated summary that highlights common patterns across multiple talent candidates. This consolidated output is returned as a structured JSON object, forming the response of the REST API invocation. We remark that setting a value of k too high (in this scenario, above 10) reduces diversity in the retrieved reports, causing the LLM to incur in the so-called *long-context issue* [13], which leads the LLM to focus on less relevant reports.

5   Preliminary Evaluation

We conducted a preliminary evaluation to assess the potential of our solution. First, the service dedicated to *Data Ingestion and Processing*, presented in Sect. 4.1, was employed to process, index and store approximately 5,000 scouting reports. These reports were written by various scouts from top-tier football teams. The test involved assessing, using both **quantitative** metrics and **qualitative** evaluations, the output generated by the service dedicated to *Scouting Information Retrieval and Response Generation*, as described in Sect. 4.2.

   In the talent scouting context, domain expertise is essential. Hence, to assess the quality of the responses generated by our service, we adopted a *human-based evaluation*. According to this evaluation strategy, domain experts were asked to assess the LLM-generated text produced downstream the *Scouting Information Retrieval and Response Generation* service, assigning scores to various criteria based on their specialized knowledge apt to capture the quality aspects of the generated content. Five individuals with extensive experience in football scouting were recruited for this study. Each participant was asked to submit to the LLM-based system a set of twenty predefined queries, focusing on different scouting-related attributes and having different levels of specificity (i.e., ranging from broad and general queries to highly detailed and precise queries). The testers interacted with the LLM-based system through the front-end interface provided by the Kama platform. An example of a request submitted via the text prompt, along with the corresponding displayed results, is shown in Fig. 4. For each query, domain experts were asked to: (i) provide a rating on a 1-to-5 Likert scale reflecting their agreement or disagreement with specific criteria, and (ii) supply an accompanying textual judgment. The evaluation criteria chosen for this preliminary evaluation are enlisted below.

- *Correctness.* The response must accurately reflect both the original query and the data retrieved, ensuring that interpretations and outputs are free of errors.
- *Completeness.* The answer should fully address every aspect of the query, incorporating all relevant data without omitting crucial details.
- *Clarity.* The final output must be well-organized and easily understandable, using precise language to convey the necessary information.

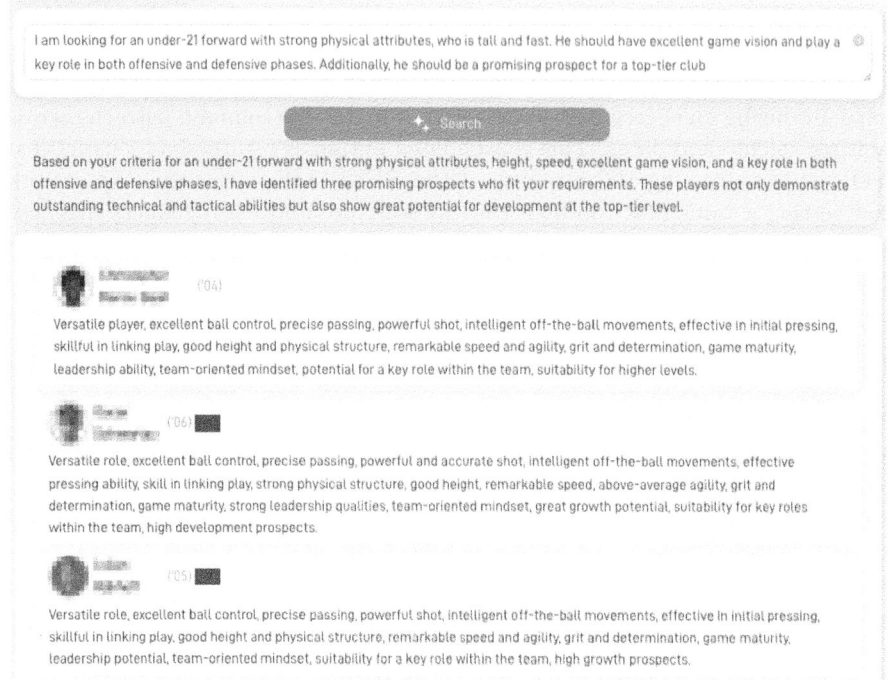

I am looking for an under-21 forward with strong physical attributes, who is tall and fast. He should have excellent game vision and play a ⊚
key role in both offensive and defensive phases. Additionally, he should be a promising prospect for a top-tier club

⌕ Search

Based on your criteria for an under-21 forward with strong physical attributes, height, speed, excellent game vision, and a key role in both
offensive and defensive phases, I have identified three promising prospects who fit your requirements. These players not only demonstrate
outstanding technical and tactical abilities but also show great potential for development at the top-tier level.

('04)

Versatile player, excellent ball control, precise passing, powerful shot, intelligent off-the-ball movements, effective in initial pressing,
skillful in linking play, good height and physical structure, remarkable speed and agility, grit and determination, game maturity,
leadership ability, team-oriented mindset, potential for a key role within the team, suitability for higher levels.

('06)

Versatile role, excellent ball control, precise passing, powerful and accurate shot, intelligent off-the-ball movements, effective
pressing ability, skill in linking play, strong physical structure, good height, remarkable speed, above-average agility, grit and
determination, game maturity, strong leadership qualities, team-oriented mindset, great growth potential, suitability for key roles
within the team, high development prospects.

('05)

Versatile role, excellent ball control, precise passing, powerful shot, intelligent off-the-ball movements, effective in initial pressing,
skillful in linking play, good height and physical structure, remarkable speed and agility, grit and determination, game maturity,
leadership potential, team-oriented mindset, suitability for a key role within the team, high growth prospects.

Fig. 4. Front-end interface enabling searches. All sensitive information has been censured for privacy reasons. Data source provided by Kama.Sport.

– *Truthfulness.* The response must be factually accurate and derived from real scout reports, avoiding *hallucinations.*

Quantitative Evaluation. We collected the ratings for each query across the various categories and aggregated the values from different participants. For each tester, we then computed the mean, median, and standard deviation, with the results displayed graphically in Fig. 5. We obtained an overall mean (median) of 3.8 (3.7). In particular, the mean (median) ratings were 3.5 (3.6) for Correctness, 3.0 (3.0) for Completeness, 4.4 (4.4) for Clarity, and 4.2 (4.1) for Truthfulness. The standard deviation values ranged from 0.7 for Clarity to 1.6 for Correctness. These numerical evaluations indicate that the best results were obtained for Clarity, followed by Truthfulness and Completeness, while Correctness received the lowest score. Future efforts will be devoted to investigate the potential reasons behind the lower scores for Correctness and, especially, Completeness, aiming to identify specific areas for improvement. This may include refining data ingestion processes, enhancing query interpretation mechanisms, or providing additional contextual information to improve response accuracy.

Qualitative Evaluation. From a qualitative perspective, feedbacks from the five experienced users revealed the following insights. The responses from the

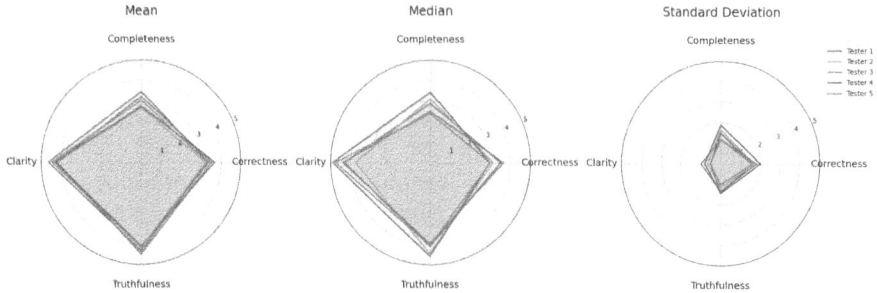

Fig. 5. Evaluation of the quality of the response over a set of predefined queries: Mean, Median, and Standard Deviation values for the four criteria assessed by the five evaluators.

LLM-based system were generally clear, largely due to the organized presentation of player profiles, with clarity being frequently cited as the system primary strength. The answers were also deemed truthful and reliable, as there were only isolated episodes of hallucinated responses or deviations from the reported profiles. In particular, testers noted that the system consistently provided accurate responses when queries included precise descriptions of technical, tactical, and physical attributes, using the specialized terminology common in scouting. Conversely, when the input queries were more generic or imprecise, the results were sometimes less aligned with the initial request, which impacted the evaluations of correctness and completeness. Overall, the testers' feedback converge on similar points. The findings underscore the system strengths in handling structured, domain-specific inquiries, while suggesting the need for further improvement in addressing less specific queries.

6   Discussion and Conclusions

In this paper, we proposed an LLM-based approach based on a RAG architecture, leveraging two services. One service is devoted to extract and index key attributes associated with scouts' expertise from textual players' reports, while the other assists scout managers in exploring the textual data concerning players' reports. By combining LLM capabilities with vector database technologies, the system efficiently captures, retrieves, and synthesizes scouting reports.

6.1   Strengths and Limitations

The proposed approach demonstrates several advantages. One prominent strength is its *versatility*, as the LLM-based system can assess a wide range of players' attributes, from physical and technical to psychological, and can be expanded to include additional players' attributes as needed. It is also highly *scalable*, capable of handling a significant corpus of thousands of evaluations.

Moreover, leveraging players' reports representation as dense vectors ensures compatibility with multilingual contexts, remaining unaffected by the language in which the original scouting reports were written (which is typically Italian or English).

Nevertheless, certain limitations persist. For instance, outdated evaluations stored in the vector database may not accurately reflect a player's current abilities, creating a need for a weighting mechanism that accounts for the time sensitivity of each report. Additionally, because all scouting data sources are presently treated equally, implementing a more refined method to assess data reliability would likely enhance overall precision. Indeed, players often accumulate multiple evaluations over different years and from various observers, and an LLM-based system capable of aggregating and reconciling these assessments would offer substantial improvements in predictive accuracy.

6.2   Future Developments

Despite the focus of this work on identifying promising young talents based on specific attributes, its potential applications extend far beyond this scope. These applications could include transfer market analytics, performance tracking over multiple seasons, or even injury and rehabilitation monitoring.

One direction we are currently exploring involves shifting from an attribute-based approach to an example-based approach, where the LLM-based system extracts the defining characteristics of a reference player and subsequently identifies other players with similar traits. This methodology would allow scouts and coaching staff to find "like-for-like" replacements or complementary squad additions with greater precision.

Another avenue for advancement lies in enhancing the metadata used to tag players' reports embeddings when they are stored in the vector database. Incorporating additional physical attributes, such as precise height measurements (e.g., above 180 cm) or detailed positional data (e.g., left-footed central midfielder), could refine the retrieval process. Likewise, capturing contextual information about the clubs or leagues in which these players currently compete would provide deeper insights into experience level and potential adaptability to new environments.

Regardless of the two aforementioned directions, we plan also to further expand the experimentation by investigating and exploring the usage of different LLMs (e.g., Open Source LLMs from the Ollama library[5]) and embedding models (e.g., from the HuggingFace platform hub[6]). Lastly, we will experiment the use of techniques to move towards automatic output evaluation. For instance, using the recently proposed *LLM-as-judge evaluation strategy* [14], thus assessing the output of an LLM (referred to as *evaluated LLM*), adopting an *evaluator LLM* (different from the evaluated LLM and offering superior inference performance), whose aim is to score the output of the evaluated LLM.

---

[5] https://ollama.com/.
[6] https://huggingface.co/.

References

1. Lacan, S.: Stacking-based deep neural network for player scouting in football. arXiv preprint arXiv:2403.08835 (2024). https://arxiv.org/abs/2403.08835
2. Lazarević, S., Lukić, J., Mirković, V.: Role of football scouts in player transformation process: From talented to elite athlete. Sport-Nauka I Praksa **10**, 65–79 (2020)
3. Lewis, P., et al.: Retrieval-augmented generation for knowledge-intensive nlp tasks. In: Advances in Neural Information Processing Systems (NeurIPS 2020) (2020)
4. Lewis, P., et al.: Retrieval-augmented generation for knowledge-intensive nlp tasks (2021). https://arxiv.org/abs/2005.11401
5. Liu, G., Luo, Y., Schulte, O., Kharrat, T.: Deep soccer analytics: learning an action-value function for evaluating soccer players. Data Min. Knowl. Disc. **34**(5), 1531–1559 (2020). https://doi.org/10.1007/s10618-020-00705-9
6. Pan, J.J., Wang, J., Li, G.: Survey of vector database management systems. arXiv preprint arXiv:2310.14021 (2023). under review, available at https://arxiv.org/abs/2310.14021
7. Pavitt, J., Braines, D., Tomsett, R.: Cognitive analysis in sports: supporting match analysis and scouting through artificial intelligence. Appl. AI Lett. **2** (2021). https://doi.org/10.1002/ail2.21
8. Schilling, A., et al.: Querying Football Matches for Event Data: Towards Using Large Language Models, pp. 216–227 (September 2024). https://doi.org/10.1007/978-3-031-69073-0_19
9. Sepasdar, Z., Gautam, S., Midoglu, C., Riegler, M., Halvorsen, P.: Enhancing structured-data retrieval with graphrag: soccer data case study (September 2024). https://doi.org/10.48550/arXiv.2409.17580
10. Strand, A., Gautam, S., Midoglu, C., Halvorsen, P.: Soccerrag: multimodal soccer information retrieval via natural queries (June 2024). https://doi.org/10.48550/arXiv.2406.01273
11. Wang, J., et al.: Milvus: a purpose-built vector data management system. In: Proceedings of the 2021 ACM SIGMOD International Conference on Management of Data (SIGMOD '21) (2021). https://doi.org/10.1145/3448016.3457550
12. Xia, H., et al.: Language and multimodal models in sports: a survey of datasets and applications. arXiv preprint arXiv:2406.12252 (2024)
13. Xu, P., et al.: Retrieval meets long context large language models. In: The Twelfth International Conference on Learning Representations (2023)
14. Zheng, L., et al.: Judging LLM-as-a-judge with MT-bench and chatbot arena. Adv. Neural Inf. Process. Syst. **36**, 46595–46623 (2023)

On the Maturity of LLMOps Services Computing: An Industrial Study

Nemania Borovits[1]([envelope]), Damian A. Tamburri[1],
and Willem-Jan van den Heuvel[2]

[1] Eindhoven University of Technology, JADS, Eindhoven, The Netherlands
{n.borovits,d.a.tamburri}@tue.nl
[2] Tilburg University, JADS, Tilburg, The Netherlands
W.J.A.M.v.d.Heuvel@jads.nl

Abstract. The way in which data-driven services are rendered and operated at industrial scale often assumes the connotation of *LLMOps*, or large-language model (LLM) operations, specifically, service operations stemming from data-driven, LLM-instrumented business processes. At the same time, a general understanding over the principles of DevOps services computing is still lacking. To gain such a generalisable understanding, In this study we perform mixed-method research using in-depth interviews in the largest service provider—a logistics service provider industry also active around the EU—of the Netherlands combined with an online survey to assess the relevance, challenges, and best practices of LLMOps services computing in industry. Our findings show that, on the one hand the literature has provided so far valuable insights into many practical lessons already applied in action, but, on the other hand, not all such practicalities have equal application to various services computing scenarios in the same way. In conclusion the study shows that the assessment of LLMOps in industry is considerable but its level of maturity—intended as the established way to employ its benefits while minimising the risks connected to its use—is still very low. We conclude recommending a careful evaluation of the principles and goals emerging from our study.

Keywords: LLMOps · Data Services · Industrial Empirical Studies

1 Introduction

The demand for data-driven decision making and data in general has increased rapidly over the past years, especially so in large-scale services operations, as part of a model typically referred to as *LLMOps* [1]. On the one hand, Data Operations applied on Large-Language Models—LLMOps for short—is a set of practices, processes and technologies that enables automated continuous deployment from a process-oriented perspective on LLM data, while guaranteeing privacy, security, quality and the possibility of cross-functional collaboration [4] in service organisations. Despite its industrial penetration, evidence around LLMOps

J. Grabis and Y. Wautelet (Eds.): CAiSE 2025 Workshops, LNBIP 556, pp. 310–317, 2025.
https://doi.org/10.1007/978-3-031-94931-9_25

is limited, and what little we know shows only that for many organisations these investments do not receive the expected return on investment [6].

From this premise, we initiated a mixed-methods industrial study to determine the state of practice around LLMOps services computing at scale, with the end objective to address the following research question: *What are implications of applying LLMOps goals and principles in the industry-grade service operations?* the study provides substantial evidence for the desired features of a LLMOps framework to be deployed in production within organisations, stemming from the experience and practice of a large-scale data-driven organisation in The Netherlands. Thus, this study indicates whether there is consensus between the principles and goals delineated in literature and related domains as well as the industry. The support is be obtained via both an in-depth qualitative research in the largest logistics service provider in the Netherlands via ethnographic research [8] as well as confirmatory quantitative research in the overall industrial scenario via a survey study tailored from previous work [15].

2   Research Materials and Methods

2.1   Research Approach

First, a survey was used to to obtain the software and automation requirements perceived by practitioners to design and deploy a LLMOps framework [13]. An overview of this process is illustrated in Fig. 1.

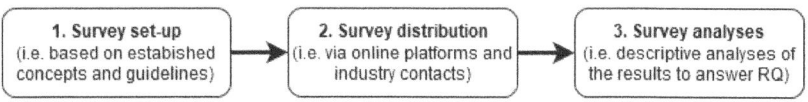

Fig. 1. Process of the taken steps during the study.

2.2   Survey Setup

For the set-up of the survey, the following steps were sequentially executed: 1) extracting the information from the interviews and literature, 2) constructing the survey, 3) evaluating the survey and 4) updating the survey before it was distributed [14]. The survey was initially set-up based on the principles and goals delineated by Ereth [6] and the outline of the survey executed by Tamburri et al. [15]. Moreover, in order to create precise, understandable, and unambiguous questions the guidelines designed by Kitchenham [14] were followed. The majority of the questions were closed, because closed questions are easier to analyse [14]. For the response to the questions measuring importance of the principles and goals a 5-point Likert evaluation scale was used [14]. The answers consisted of the following options: 1) Unimportant, 2) Moderately Important, 3) Important, 4) Very Important and 5) Paramount. Neutral answers such as: don't know or a neutral option was not given in the survey. However, respondents could choose not to respond to a question. For all principles and goals multiple questions were used in order to improve reliability (i.e. covering for measurement error) [16].

2.3 Survey Distribution

The survey was distributed to a targeted practitioner sample whose diverse backgrounds and broad responses reflect the varied application of LLMOps principles across roles, including data analysts, data scientists, engineers, and business end users. To mitigate potential response bias, the survey was posted at different times across multiple platforms—LinkedIn, Reddit (in data-related threads), Twitter, Medium, and relevant Facebook and LinkedIn groups. After two weeks, it was also shared via contacts at two randomly selected academic institutions in the Netherlands, and one month later through industry contacts at Company X, a major logistics service provider. The survey remained open for 51 days, yielding 58 responses. Submissions containing only comments without completed questions were discarded [14], resulting in 55 valid responses. For items with one or two missing answers, the mean was imputed; for those with higher non-response, only completed responses were analyzed.

2.4 Analysis and Inter-rater Reliability Assessment

The principles and goals were measured via multi-item indicators. In case of some of the statements the scale had to be re-coded as the statement was stated as a negation. The usage of the negation was to ensure the quality of the survey, thus in case the respondents were filling the survey without thought this was noticed. Due to the usage of multi-item indicators for the LLMOps principles and goals there was a need to assess the reliability of these indicators. For this the well-known Cronbach was used [17]. The formula used to calculate the Cronbach is: $\alpha = \frac{k}{k-1}(1 - \frac{\sum s_i^2}{s_T^2})$. From a theoretical perspective, the closer the Cronbach is to one the better, however an acceptable cutoff value is $>> 0.7$ [18]. In order to improve the internal consistency some items were removed. The identification of the items to be removed was executed via an analysis based on correlation. Based upon these results the items Automation, Integrated end-to-end thinking, Testing, Monitoring and Data-driven improvement were taken out of the set, because they were not measured in a reliable manner. These steps and corresponding results are illustrated in Table 1. At the end of the survey analyses, the survey was analysed similarly to the methodology applied by Lismont et al. [12] (i.e. the descriptive results of the survey were outlined to indicate the natural setting of the researched phenomena).

3   Results

3.1 Statistical Representativeness

The survey responses represented a variety of 16 different industries, such as technology, financial sector, logistics, oil and gas, consumer services etc. However, most respondents were from either the financial (16.3%) or applied technology (24.5%) industry. Furthermore, regarding the distribution of the size of the companies in which the respondents work was as following: the majority of

Table 1. Evaluation of the multi-scale items of the survey.

Principle or goal	Cronbach α	#Deleted	Cronbach α Var.
Reuse of artifacts	0.16	3	0.70
Automation	0.37	3	0.60
Integrated end-to-end thinking	-0.16	3	0.25
Short cycles and incremental change	0.49	3	0.81
Analytics as code	0.89	-	0.89
Testing	0.33	3	0.50
Monitoring	0.37	1	0.60
Data-driven improvement	-0.16	3	0.39
Process-oriented data pipelines	0.27	3	0.79
Continuous improvement	0.59	3	0.89
Orchestration	0.51	3	0.79
Empowerment of citizen users	0.74	-	0.74
Agility and speed	0.48	3	0.77
Collaboration and trust	0.57	2	0.76

the responses were from respondents working at companies with 10,001–100,000 employees (34.5%). Afterwards companies with a size between 501–2,000 employees (25.5%) and companies with 6–20 employees (14.5%) were represented the most. Moreover, 52% of respondents work in a team with a size of 6–20 employees, followed by teams containing 1–5 employees (38%). About 8% of the respondents indicated that they work in teams of 21–100 employees and only 2% of respondents works in teams of 100+ employees. Considering the employment function of the respondents, 45.5% of respondents are active as a data scientist or data analyst, 23.6% are data engineer, 10.9% are active as business end-users of data and further the respondents are cloud engineer, design engineer, data architect or manager.

3.2 LLMOps as an Industrial Context

Considering the context (see Fig. 2), most respondents indicated to use data for marketing services (54.5%), process optimization services (76%), business services development (67.3%), service/product optimization (67.3%) and service commercialisation and sales (49.1%). Besides, the data infrastructure is in 65.5% of the cases marked as centralised and in 34.5% of the cases as decentralised. Other control questions considered the time it takes to answer data related questions and how frequent these questions occur. 63.0% of the respondents indicated that they need less than a week to answer data related questions and in 22.2% of the cases this is even less than a day. Considering the frequency of these data related questions, in 72.2% of the cases data related questions occur

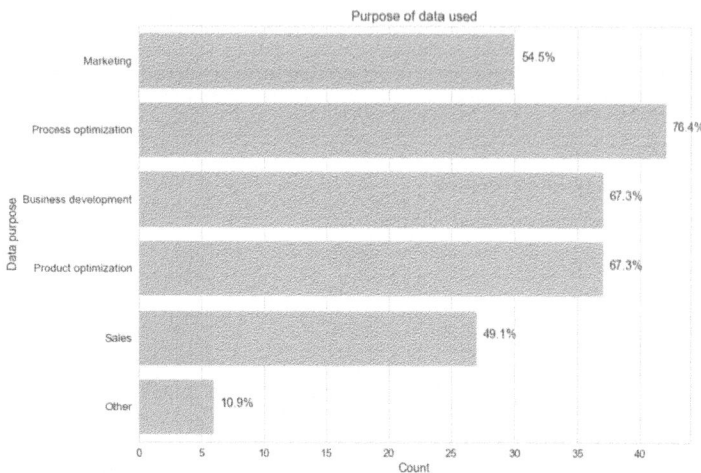

Fig. 2. Contexts of service operations rotating around data usage across our sample.

on a daily basis, for 13.0% twice a week, 7.4% once a week and respectively 1.9% and 5.6% monthly or sporadically.

3.3 LLMOps Data Provisioning Services

In addition, the ways in which data is obtained and shared was asked to the respondents. About 51.9% of the respondents multiple data sources are combined. Further more, for about 20.4% of the respondents the data (insights) are obtained via analytical programs such as Python or R. For 14.8% of the respondents the data (insights) are obtained via data exports, 11.1% of the respondents do this via dashboards and for 1.9% of the respondents they do this via a database management system. Moreover, it is shown that 49.1% of the respondents share their data (insights) via dashboards, 20.8% does this via data exports and 15.1% via analytical programs. Only 5.7% of the population uses multiple tools for sharing, 3.8% via a database management system, and 1.9% of the population uses reports, PowerPoint or enterprise software.

3.4 LLMOps Services Computing Maturity

In light of the measured multi-item indicators regarding the principles and goals the assessed importance per principle or goal is indicated in Table 2. In Table 2 the responses were re-coded from the values *Not important* to *Paramount* to a scale from 0 to 4 for purposes of analyses. Considering the principles all items are on average evaluated above 2, which aligns with the values between *Important* and *Very important* or simply as *Very important*. The goals are rated similarly, only the mean value of orchestration is merely rated as 1.7 which aligns with the value less than *Important*. To be noted is that the standard deviation over the principles and goals are relatively low. Most of the items have a standard deviation of $\ll 1$. Though, to be noted, the response rate to the goals is much lower than the response rate to the principles. The lowest response rate is to the item empowerment of citizen users with only 21 complete responses compared to the 55 responses for all the discussed principles.

Table 2. Descriptive statistics measured goals and principles

Principle or goal	Count	Mean	Standard Deviation
Reuse of artifacts	55	2.34	0.93
Short cycles and incremental change	55	2.67	0.97
Analytics as code	55	3.05	0.85
Process-oriented data pipelines	55	2.33	1.08
Continuous improvement	28	2.29	1.11
Orchestration	27	1.70	1.01
Empowerment of citizen users	21	2.51	0.90
Agility and speed	31	2.56	0.83
Collaboration and trust	27	2.85	0.89

4 Discussion

In this section the results per research question, limitations and future research are discussed.

4.1 Ops Data Services Reuse Still at Large Vs. LLMs Adotion

Ereth [6] considered only the principles 1) reuse of artifacts, 2) testing and 3) monitoring, and the goals: 1) continuous improvement and 2) agility and speed to be relevant. Considering this in light to the results, the emphasis of importance was mostly put on the principles 1) short cycles and incremental change and 2) analytics as code. However, the principles 1) reuse of artifacts and 2) process-oriented data pipelines were also more skewed between *Important* and *Very important* when mapped to LLMOps in our survey and its results. It should be mentioned that the sample was very diverse in terms of background of industry, function and size of company, department and team enabling a better motivated generalization. At the same time, whether service reuse still reflects an established and valuable practice with the onset of more and more automated orchestration and service continuity remains to be seen. Perhaps further work on the matter might shed light on whether the practice still reflects quality rather than churn.

4.2 Enterprise-Level LLM Goals Often Linger

Remarkable to the results was the low response rate to the items considering the goals. Due to the closed character of the survey it is difficult to assert with certainty what was the reason for the low response rate. However, there are two likely explanations for this phenomenon. The first one is a problem with the survey itself. It was a relatively long survey and it might be the case that the respondents thought it was too much. Although, this would not explain the high response rate on the next section, namely measures of success. A second explanation might have to do with the maturity level of the companies at which the respondents work. Within the literature it is asserted that companies (often smaller companies) at a lower level of maturity in the field of data analytics are less concerned with topics such as enterprise wide data strategy, collaboration and an orchestrated system [1,12].

5 Conclusions

This study assessed the principles and goals of LLMOps in the industry from a high level. For future research it would be interesting to discuss these principles, goals and performance measures based upon the evaluation of an implemented framework. Moreover, due to the limited amount of scientific research in the field of practical and scalable LLMOps services computing it would also be interesting to design and evaluate more of such architectures in different industries and with different service operations' configuration. Another possible future research direction would be a similar research with a re- evaluation of the methods and a larger sample for both the qualitative and quantitative study. Going into this direction it would also be recommended to make adjustments to the survey to enable measurement of all the defined principles. Another direction would be to go deeper into the measures of success and failure. From that part it would be interesting to understand the value of the measurements and what the application of those measurements would be in such company. It would also be interesting to create measurements to concretely measure the degree to which an architecture is compliant to the LLMOps principles and goals. These possible directions fit into the defined lacunae by [6], which were also mentioned. In addition, it could also be argued that these suggestions for future research shape the broadly defined lacunae even further. Finally, future validation of this study will be pursued within the COMFORTage[1] project, where multiple sources of data and knowledge on dementia and frailty will be leveraged in thirteen real-world scenarios.

Acknowledgements. The research leading to the results presented in this paper has received funding from the European Union's Horizon Europe research and innovation program under grant agreement no 101137301 and is supported by the Innovative UK under grant agreement no 10103541.

---

[1] https://ec.europa.eu/info/funding-tenders/opportunities/portal/screen/how-to-par ticipate/org-details/952657953/project/101137301/program/43108390/details.

References

1. Thusoo, A.: Practical DataOps: Delivering Agile Data Science at Scale. Apress (2019)
2. Atwal, H.: Creating a Data-Driven Enterprise with DataOps: Insights from Facebook, Uber, LinkedIn, Twitter, and EBay. O'Reilly Media (2017)
3. Zahid, H., Mahmood, T., Ikram, N.: Enhancing Dependability in Big Data Analytics Enterprise Pipelines. Springer (2018)
4. Patterson, P., DataOps: modernizing BI with DevOps for data analytics. Big Data Quart. **5**(2), 21–26. (2019). https://search.proquest.com/docview/2248170750?accountid=27128
5. Sahoo, P.R., Premchand, A.: DataOps in manufacturing and utilities industries (2019)
6. Ereth, J.: DataOps - towards a definition. CEUR Workshop Proc. **2191**, 104–112 (2018)
7. Hevner, A.R., March, S.T., Park, J., Ram, S., Design science in information systems research. MIS Quart., 75–105. JSTOR (2004)
8. Hammersley, M., Atkinson, P.: Ethnography. Routledge, London (2003)
9. Swanson, E.B., Information systems innovation among organizations. Manage. Sci. **40**, 1069–1092. INFORMS (1994)
10. Lwakatare, L.E., Kuvaja, P., Oivo, M., Dimensions of DevOps. In: International Conference on Agile Software Development, pp. 212–217. Springer (2015)
11. Cosic, R., shanks, G., Maynard, S., Towards a business analytics capability maturity model. ACIS 2012: Location, Location, Location: Proceedings of the 23rd Australasian Conference on Information Systems 2012, ACIS, pp. 1–11 (2012)
12. Lismont, J., Vanthienen, J., Baesens, B., Lemahieu, W., Defining analytics maturity indicators: a survey approach. Int. J. Inf. Manage. **37**(3), 114–124. Elsevier (2017)
13. Singer, J., Sim, S.E., Lethbridge, T.C.: Software engineering data collection for field studies. In: Guide to Advanced Empirical Software Engineering, pp. 9–34. Springer (2008)
14. Kitchenham, B.A., Pfleeger, S.L., Personal opinion surveys. In: Guide to Advanced Empirical Software Engineering, pp. 63–92. Springer (2008)
15. Tamburri, D.A., Miglierina, M., Di Nitto, E.: Cloud applications monitoring: an industrial study. Manage. Sci. **43**, 1-26. Elsevier (2020)
16. Gliem, J.A., Gliem, R.R.: Calculating, interpreting, and reporting Cronbach's alpha reliability coefficient for Likert-type scales. In: Midwest Research-to-Practice Conference in Adult, Continuing, and Community Education (2003)
17. Bland, J.M., Altman, D.G., Statistics notes: Cronbach's alpha. BMJ **314**(7080), 572. British Medical journal Publishing Group (1997)
18. Santos, J., Reynaldo, A.: Cronbach's alpha: a tool for assessing the reliability of scales. J. Extension **37**(2), 1–5 (1999)
19. Wolff, E.: A Practical Guide to Continuous Delivery. Addison-Wesley, Boston (2017). 978-0-13-469147-3

Automated Newsrooms and Enhanced Editorial Processes Through Large Language Models

Dario Pellegrini and Davide Ragazzi[(✉)]

Stark Technology Partner Srl, Via Luigi Suardo 18/C, 24067 Sarnico, Italy
{dario.pellegrini,davide.ragazzi}@starktechnologypartner.com

Abstract. In today's hyperconnected world, news sources are widely accessible, yet challenges persist in managing redundancy, retrieval efficiency, and content personalization. This paper presents a modular automated newsroom leveraging Large Language Models (LLMs) to streamline news processing and enhance editorial workflows. The system employs a structured pipeline of LLM-powered agents, each performing specialized tasks in sequence to transform raw news data from multiple sources into enriched, structured content. This content is stored in a database, making it accessible via API-driven services for editorial applications. By integrating Retrieval-Augmented Generation (RAG), the framework enables semantic search, intelligent content retrieval, and real-time editorial automation, enhancing discoverability and efficiency within a scalable, Service-Oriented Architecture.

Keywords: automated newsrooms · large language models · news generation pipeline · AI-powered journalism · retrieval-augmented generation · editorial automation · natural language processing · service-oriented architecture

1 Introduction

The digital age has made news widely accessible across online platforms, where content is gathered, reshaped, and distributed to fit various objectives [11]. Recent advances like Retrieval-Augmented Generation (RAG) have improved semantic search and information retrieval [5]. This paper presents a Service-Oriented Architecture for an automated newsroom that generates and distributes personalized news content at scale using LLM-powered automation. The system ensures editorial control, stylistic consistency, and personalization, while enriching articles with metadata such as sentiment, geospatial tags, and vector embeddings to support retrieval and categorization. RAG integration further enhances semantic retrieval, duplicate detection, and AI-driven query responses. Its modular design supports seamless deployment in editorial environments. The proposed framework consists of three core components: (i) a modular pipeline that transforms raw data into structured, coherent articles, enriched with metadata such

J. Grabis and Y. Wautelet (Eds.): CAiSE 2025 Workshops, LNBIP 556, pp. 318–325, 2025.
https://doi.org/10.1007/978-3-031-94931-9_26

as sentiment, geolocation, and vector representations to support semantic search and classification; (ii) an integration of Retrieval-Augmented Generation (RAG) with vector databases to enable real-time semantic search, enhance content relevance, and power AI-driven editorial tools; (iii) a scalable and interoperable Service-Oriented Architecture (SOA) designed to integrate seamlessly with editorial systems, applications, and distribution channels, facilitating dynamic and personalized news delivery. The rest of the paper is organized as follows: Sect. 2 outlines key challenges; Sect. 3 details the generation pipeline; Sect. 4 focuses on RAG-based retrieval; Sect. 5 describes the SOA framework; Sect. 6 presents evaluations; Sect. 7 reviews related work; and Sect. 8 concludes the paper, sketching future research directions.

2   Motivating Example: Addressing Real-World Challenges

Despite notable advancements in AI-driven news automation, significant challenges remain in ensuring content quality, retrieval efficiency, and editorial adaptability. To ground these issues in practical settings, we draw insights from two real-world applications: *Italy Nowadays* and *Odeum*, both of which have implemented key aspects of the proposed system. These platforms reveal a shared set of core challenges:

- Efficient retrieval and clustering of news content based on thematic relevance, geographic focus, and user interests required scalable and semantically rich methods.
- Automated synthesis needed to preserve the nuance and integrity of the original articles while avoiding loss of key information.
- Traditional keyword based search was insufficient, highlighting the need for semantic search capabilities that could understand context and support more relevant, personalized content discovery.
- Generated outputs, whether textual or audio, had to maintain logical coherence and factual consistency, especially when aggregating content from multiple heterogeneous sources.
- Delivering content in customizable formats, tones, and languages called for flexible personalization mechanisms tailored to individual user preferences.

By addressing these interconnected challenges, *Italy Nowadays* and *Odeum* demonstrate how AI-driven automation can be adapted to meet the evolving demands of modern newsrooms, providing structured, high-quality, and efficiently retrievable content across modalities.

3   Generation Pipeline with LLM Models and Metadata

The news generation system, reported in Fig. 1, operates as a structured pipeline composed of three main sequential steps: raw data retrieval, news generation, and news metadata enrichment.

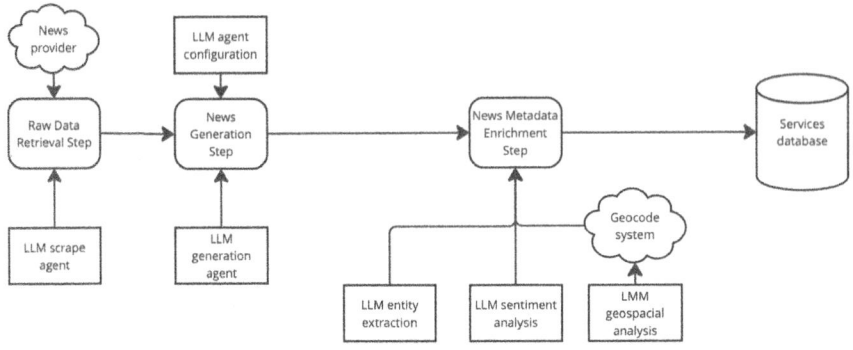

Fig. 1. Generation pipeline architecture.

3.1   Raw Data Retrieval Step

News articles are sourced from various providers, each supplying key attributes: (i) a unique identifier, (ii) full text, and (iii) publication date. Leveraging multiple providers improves coverage and reduces bias. Content is retrieved programmatically via two main methods: (1) structured sources such as APIs, web services, and RSS feeds (e.g., Google Cloud News API, Mediastack [3]) that support pull or push updates; and (2) unstructured websites, where a large language model (LLM) agent extracts and normalizes headlines, body text, publication dates, and metadata [4]. After retrieval phase, all content is standardized and stored in an intermediate database to reduce redundancy and enable efficient access.

3.2   News Generation Step

> **Example 3.1: Generated news**
>
> **Title** - Stock Market: Hong Kong surges at the opening, up 2.16%
>
> **Excerpt** - Shanghai opens at +0.25%, Shenzhen at +0.31%. BYD stock soars.
>
> **Body** - Hong Kong stocks opened higher, led by tech. The Hang Seng rose 2.16%, with the Tech index up nearly 3%. Alibaba and Tencent advanced, while BYD jumped 6.03% after unveiling a charging platform twice as powerful as Tesla's V4. Shanghai and Shenzhen indexes rose 0.25% and 0.31%, respectively.

Standardized data feeds into the LLM Configuration Agent, which generates articles using structured prompts aligned with editorial guidelines. The agent controls key attributes such as language, tone, and style to ensure consistency and audience alignment; article length, ranging from summaries to full reports; and bias control, factual accuracy, and source attribution to maintain neutrality and credibility. The model outputs multiple articles per dataset, each covering different angles to enhance depth and avoid oversimplification. Example 3.1 illustrates a sample centered on economic arguments.

3.3   News Metadata Enrichment Step

LLM powered agents enrich generated articles to boost discoverability and categorization:

- **Entity Extraction:** Identifies people, organizations, and keywords for better searchability.
- **Sentiment Analysis:** Assigns sentiment scores indicating emotional tone (range: -1 to 1) and magnitude (range: 0 upward), reflecting intensity. These scales are configurable based on user needs. For instance, a sentiment score of 0.8 with a magnitude of 5.0 suggests strongly positive, emotionally rich content.
- **Geospatial Analysis:** Extracts locations using geocoding (e.g., OpenStreetMap) for localized content.

Enriched articles (see Example 3.2) are stored in the Services database for retrieval and distribution through frontends or other consumers.

Example 3.2: Metadata Enriched Components

Places: Hong Kong (China), Shanghai (China), Guangdong (China)

Sentiment: Score: 0.8 - Magnitude: 5.0

Tags: Markets; Stock Exchanges, Economic Indicators, Stock Activities

---

4   News Retrieval Enhancement with RAG Technology

This section presents the application of Retrieval-Augmented Generation (RAG) technology within an automated newsroom to enhance news search and retrieval efficiency (see Fig. 2). RAG significantly improves question answering (Q&A) and duplicate detection, crucial for maintaining content quality and user satisfaction.

4.1   Embedding Phase

Each generated news article is processed to populate the newsroom's vector database. Essential information stored includes: (i) title and subtitles; (ii) Abstract or content; (iii) Categories or tags. Metadata, such as unique identifiers and publication dates, is stored alongside the vector representation in databases like Qdrant, enabling efficient retrieval and recency-based filtering. Each article is converted into an embedding using models like *text-embedding-3-small* [6], facilitating efficient semantic search.

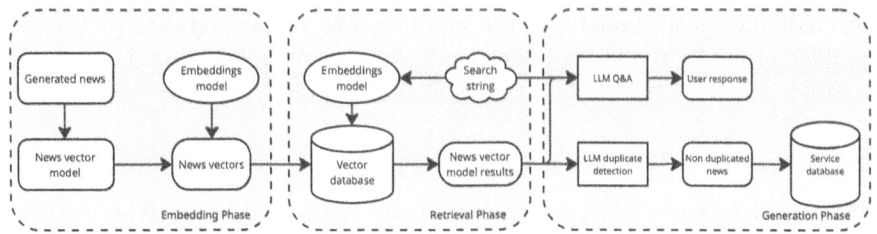

Fig. 2. News RAG retrieval architecture.

4.2 Retrieval Phase

Vector search is fundamental for retrieving contextually relevant articles based on semantic similarity. The retrieval process involves:

1. **Query Input**: Users submit queries as plain text.
2. **Embedding Generation**: Queries are embedded using AI models [7].
3. **Vector Search Execution**: database performs nearest neighbour searches.
4. **Document Retrieval**: A ranked list of semantically relevant documents is provided as result.

This semantic retrieval approach boosts search accuracy and enables advanced features such as Q&A and duplicate detection.

4.3 Generation Phase

Retrieved data supports various newsroom functionalities, notably:

Q&A - Contextual vector search retrieves relevant articles to support user queries. An LLM then generates accurate, grounded answers by leveraging the retrieved content.

Duplicate Detection - Content duplication across providers can degrade user experience and system efficiency. To mitigate this, the system uses vector-based semantic similarity search with a defined similarity threshold. Articles exceeding this threshold are considered duplicates and filtered accordingly, ensuring content uniqueness and reducing redundancy. Once detected, duplicates are handled through one of three strategies:

- **Arbitrary Exclusion**: Near-identical articles are removed entirely, including from the vector database.
- **LLM Based Exclusion**: For highly similar content, the most reliable and clearly written version is retained.
- **Semantic Merging via LLM**: For partially overlapping articles, key information from each source is merged into a single, enriched version that preserves complementary content. This is achieved using an LLM guided by structured prompts tailored to identify and consolidate non redundant elements.

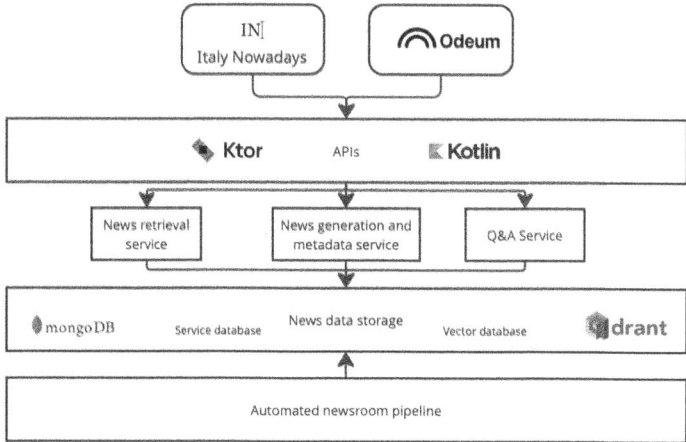

Fig. 3. Service-Oriented Architecture.

This approach ensures a high quality, streamlined news corpus with minimal redundancy while preserving valuable source variations. Deduplication results are stored in the service database, enabling the API to deliver clean content to both front-end and external systems (Fig. 3).

5   Service-Oriented Architecture

The architecture presented above can be aggregated to offer services that can be consumed by different types of systems, such as live APIs, web applications, or mobile apps. Here are some proposed services that could be implemented with the architecture just presented.

Generated News Publication - The architecture allows to publish news from the database where they are stored and made accessible to any type of consumer interested in them.

Branded News Generation with Configuration - The news generation system can be used in real-time to provide a personalized configuration based on frontend input or user-provided information, resulting in personalized news specifically tailored for that user. Examples of this include a news summary, a news synthesis, or the extraction of specific information.

Question and Answer Service - With a Retrieval-Augmented Generation (RAG) implementation, it is possible to create a service that accepts a structured or unstructured question as input and returns a list of relevant news articles related to the query. Additionally, using an LLM model, the system can generate a direct answer based on the retrieved news articles (Fig. 4).

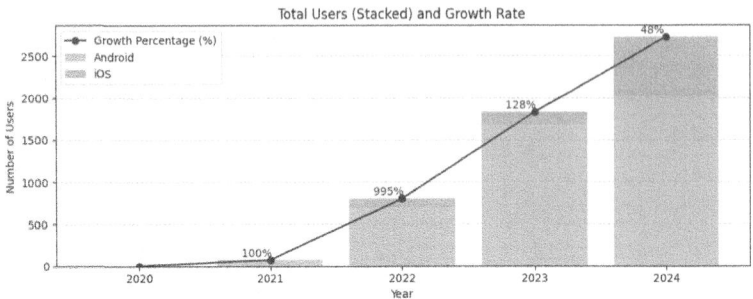

Fig. 4. Stores Statistics.

6 Implementation and Experimental Evaluation

To ensure efficiency and scalability, our system is built on a robust Service-Oriented Architecture using advanced models and technologies. We selected LLAMA3.3-70B-Versatile for fast text generation, speech synthesis, and structured data handling, and text-embedding-3-small for efficient, accurate, and cost-effective embeddings. Qdrant serves as the vector database for scalable, metadata-rich semantic search, while MongoDB manages structured, multi-source data. The back-end is powered by Kotlin Ktor for secure, multithreaded API handling. Native mobile performance is achieved through Swift (iOS) and Kotlin (Android), enabling seamless UX and integration with notifications and geolocation. The deployed application (Sect. 2), available on the App Store and Play Store, has demonstrated strong adoption. Downloads increased significantly in 2022 with the integration of metadata-based NLP, and again in 2024 after introducing LLM and metadata enhancements. The system processed **509,407** articles, enriched **494,102** with location data, and analysed **93,422** for sentiment. It also generated **10,180** podcasts, with average processing times of **3.3 s** for articles and **1.8 s** for metadata.

7 Related Works

AI has advanced digital journalism through summarization, generation, and retrieval. Just-in-Time News [8] and AI-GlobalEvents [9] use chatbots and sentiment/entity analysis, while LeanContext [1] enables domain-specific QA with LLMs. These focus on user-driven interaction, not full newsroom automation. Our system builds on these by automating the editorial workflow with LLMs, RAG, and metadata enrichment (e.g., sentiment, geolocation, entities). Prior works like [2,5] explored personalization and semantic framing; we unify these in a context-aware pipeline. Recent work [10] emphasized scalable, modular AI for editorial use. We extend this with a Service-Oriented Architecture for cross-platform integration, enhancing discoverability and editorial efficiency.

8   Conclusions and Future Work

We proposed a scalable, SOA-based newsroom system powered by LLMs, combining RAG, modular pipelines, and metadata enrichment for personalized, multi-platform news delivery. Real-world use confirms its scalability and editorial value. SOA ensures API-driven integration; RAG improves retrieval and personalization. Together, they streamline content creation and distribution. Future work includes expanding user testing, enhancing retrieval with hybrid symbolic-neural models, supporting multilingual generation, reducing LLM bias, and scaling for real-time, customizable news delivery.

References

1. Arefeen, M.A., Debnath, B., Chakradhar, S.: LeanContext: cost-efficient domain-specific question answering using LLMS. Nat. Lang. Proc. J. **7**, 100065 (2024)
2. Alonso del Barrio, D., Gatica-Perez, D.: Framing the news: from human perception to large language model inferences. In: Proceedings of the 2023 ACM International Conference on Multimedia Retrieval, pp. 627–635 (2023)
3. Contributors, W.: RSS Wikipedia, the free encyclopedia (2024). https://it.wikipedia.org/wiki/RSS. Accessed 10 Mar 2024
4. JournalistsonHF: AI scraper. https://huggingface.co/spaces/JournalistsonHF/ai-scraper. Accessed 14 Mar 2025
5. Lewis, P., et al.: Retrieval-augmented generation for knowledge-intensive NLP tasks. In: Advances in Neural Information Processing Systems, vol. 33 (2020)
6. OpenAI: Getting started with Gdrant and OpenAI (2024). https://cookbook.openai.com/examples/vector_databases/qdrant/getting_started_with_qdrant_and_openai. Accessed 10 Mar 2024
7. OpenAI: OpenAI API documentation (2024). https://platform.openai.com/docs/api-reference/introduction. Accessed 10 Mar 2024
8. Sufi, F.: Just-in-time news: an AI chatbot for the modern information age. Pro Quest (11) (2025). https://www.proquest.com/openview/0007614fbe0470dae457ed121a941bad/1?pq-origsite=gscholar&cbl=5046920. Accessed 12 Mar 2025
9. Sufi, F.K.: AI-GlobalEvents: a software for analyzing, identifying and explaining global events with artificial intelligence. Softw. Impacts **11**, 100218 (2022)
10. Urbani, R., Ferreira, C., Lam, J.: Managerial framework for evaluating AI chatbot integration: Bridging organizational readiness and technological challenges. Bus. Horiz. **67**(5), 595–606 (2024)
11. Wu, C., Wu, F., Huang, Y., Xie, X.: Personalized news recommendation: methods and challenges. ACM Trans. Inf. Syst. **41**(1) (2023). https://doi.org/10.1145/3530257

Language Models for Legal NLP:
A Literature Review

Awais Abdul Khaliq(✉) and Stefano Montanelli

Università degli Studi di Milano, DI - Via Celoria, 18, 20135 Milan, Italy
{awais.abdul,stefano.montanelli}@unimi.it

Abstract. Legal NLP refers to the application of advanced techniques to processing and analysis of legal texts. In this paper, we present a review of the relevant literature on legal NLP, and we compare existing solutions on four main tasks, that are *document segmentation, information retrieval, document summarization*, and *knowledge extraction*. In the review, we focus on how language models are currently being employed for addressing NLP in the legal field, by also highlighting challenges where improvements are still possible.

Keywords: Language Models · Legal NLP · Literature Review

1 Introduction

The legal domain is known for its specialist language, domain-specific terms, and long documents. Legal texts often have archaic expressions, jargon, and precise language, in which minor differences can lead to very different meanings [2]. Legal documents range from laws and court judgments to legal contracts and play a vital role as a foundation for the smooth functioning of society, but legal documents are very hard to analyze due to domain-specific vocabulary, complex sentence structures, and domain-specific knowledge [1].

Transformer-based models and Natural Language Processing (NLP) are being increasingly employed in the law domain, with a special focus on tasks that aim to automate legal text processing and analysis as much as possible. Transformer-based architectures such as BERT and its variants are providing promising results in the law field, and preliminary contributions are now available in the literature (e.g. [3,5,12]). However, several issues that characterize legal documents are still open and language models can be used to further enhance the effectiveness of typical NLP tasks in this field. In Fig. 1, a summary diagram is provided, where common legal tasks are represented, as well as possible benefits derived from the adoption of NLP solutions, such as searching the case law, answering legal questions or finding the clause. The diagram also highlights challenges, innovations, and strengths in the field, including AI-powered legal chatbots and the use of data gleaned from past cases to predict unlawful court rulings. Advances in legal NLP promise to make legal research, compliance checks, and document management more efficient, faster, and cost-effective.

J. Grabis and Y. Wautelet (Eds.): CAiSE 2025 Workshops, LNBIP 556, pp. 326–337, 2025.
https://doi.org/10.1007/978-3-031-94931-9_27

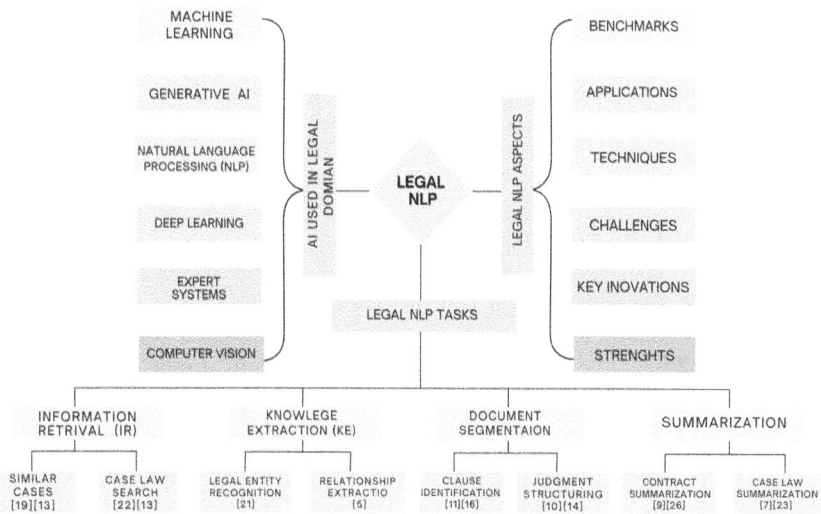

Fig. 1. Legal NLP tasks and aspects

In this paper, we present a review of the relevant literature on legal NLP, and we compare existing solutions on four main tasks, namely *document segmentation, information retrieval, document summarization*, and *knowledge extraction*. Document segmentation is about the division of a text into meaningful segments, that is particularly relevant in the legal field where official documents are characterized by predefined sections that are not explicitly delimited [8,9,14]. Information retrieval is about the capability to find relevant documents in a dataset that are about a target keyword(s) of interest, and it can be exploited in the legal field to collect suggestions for editing a new judgment by considering similar case-law decisions in a given repository of past court-cases [11,17,20]. Text summarization is about the creation of a short, synthetic description of a given text, and it is relevant in the legal field where complex and long documents with domain-specific vocabulary are usually considered [7,21,22]. Finally, knowledge extraction deals with the identification of entities/concepts with associated relationships that model a domain ontology over a set of considered documents, and it is relevant in the law field (as in other application domains) to enforce exploratory functionalities for expert and non-expert users (e.g., legal practitioners, judges, or simple citizens) [2,3,19].

Our work is motivated by the need to understand the degree of automation provided by NLP techniques to support the above tasks. In particular, in the review, we focus on how language models are currently being employed for addressing NLP in the legal field, by also highlighting challenges where improvements are still possible. A discussion is finally provided to illustrate future research direction.

The paper is organized as follows. Details and challenges about legal NLP tasks such as document segmentation, information retrieval, document summarization, and knowledge extraction are presented in Sects. 2, 3, 4, and 5, respectively. Discussion and future research directions are discussed in Sect. 6. Concluding remarks are finally provided in Sect. 7.

2   Document Segmentation

Legal document segmentation is the process of dividing legal documents into meaningful and coherent parts such as segments, headings, clauses, paragraphs or articles [7]. This task is a basis for the downstream applications including contract analysis, legal decision automation and document retrieval. Legal documents differ in structure between jurisdictions and document types, and are usually long and complex, which makes segmenting those documents a difficult but still very important task [8,9].

Methods used for document segmentation have varied from classical rule-based approaches to modern machine learning and transformer neural networks based techniques. Although rule-based techniques based on regular expressions, rules, and linguistic patterns perform well with structured documents, they lack robustness when applied to the diversity of legal text [10]. Despite the flexibility of these over rule-based methods, machine learning models (like Conditional Random Field - CRF, and Bidirectional Long short term memory networks - BiLSTM) have been widely analysed to make predictions on segment transitions. More advanced pre-trained models such as Generative Pre-trained Transformers (GPT) achieve state-of-the-art performance on various legal tasks, but depend on a large amount of labeled training data which is limited in the legal domain in general [12].

More recently, transformer-based models such as BERT, RoBERTa and Legal-BERT have been fine-tuned for segmentation tasks, reaching state-of-the-art results through contextual dependency - the relationship between the sentences in the text. In particular, advances of the transformer-based models at scale (e.g., GPT-4), have enabled adaptive segmentation using in-context learning, significantly reducing the need for labeled data usage for several downstream tasks [2,13,14].

However, document segmentation for legal users remains a major challenge. Unlike the standard documents used in some industries, legal documents have no unified format where you can always segment it in the same way. The variation in segment transitions with terms or phrases that can also signal section boundary ambiguity compounds the challenge. Secondly, legal documents are long, which are therefore expensive to process. Generalizability from one legal system to another, or from one language to another, is still a major challenge, as models trained in a particular jurisdiction or language do not usually generalize to another jurisdiction or language [8,9].

Large Language Models (LLMs) have been the game changer for solving these problems. Fine-tuning a pretrained transformer model on legal corpora, such as Legal-BERT, was shown to outperform other general pre-trained models such as BERT in segmentation tasks. GPT-like models can be used for zero-shot or few-shot rendition, as they benefit from contextual awareness to perform segmentation with few labeled examples. Furthermore, multimodal contexts that combine text with metadata or layout information (such as PDF structures) have improved the segmentation accuracy of complicated legal documents [13,14]. The performance of these models is typically benchmarked against standards such as COLIEE [11], LexGLUE [4] and LEDGAR, utilizing metrics such as F1 score, precision, and Intersection over Union (IoU) to guide the evaluation of segment boundary detection [10,12].

3   Information Retrieval

Information Retrieval (IR) in the legal field consists of retrieving pertinent legal documents or sections according to user queries. This is important for legal practitioners who must constantly access case law, statutes, contracts, or other legal text quickly. Legal documents tend to have highly complex and large volumes of content, so IR systems must properly balance precision and recall to ensure users find the most relevant information quickly and accurately [8,9].

A range of techniques have been proposed to address the task of legal IR, including traditional IR methods as well as advanced neural IR methods. Traditionally, IR methods such as Term Frequency-Inverse Document Frequency (TF-IDF) and BM25 rely on keyword matching and statistical relevance to retrieve documents. Given their computational efficiency in motivating queries of system information, these approaches are effective, but in that they struggle with the semantic complexity surrounding legal terms [10].

BERT-based retrievers provide a common solution to this limitation, resulting in various neural IR models [18]. The most relevant models, known as deep learning based encoder models, are capable of capturing semantic relevance between a query and documents, which has resulted in significant improvement in retrieval accuracy. Distance retrieval-based models such as Dense Passage Retrieval (DPR) which fine-tuned with legal dataset and represent queries as well as document in dense vector space to find more accurate matching yield better results [12,13].

However, legal IR has its own challenges. Legal queries are highly context-dependent, and systems must understand complex legal concepts and vocabulary. When a user enters, for example, "breach of contract", we should be able to augment this with words such as "contract violation" or "failure to perform".

The lack of labeled datasets thwarts the creation of IR models in the legal domain, as annotating legal documents involves a high cost in time as well as domain knowledge. This challenge becomes even greater when cross-jurisdictional retrieval is needed, as legal systems, terminologies, and languages differ across jurisdictions [8,15].

Recently, systems like GPT-4 and Legal-BERT further support query expansion, where the system generates additional relevant words or phrases to improve retrieval precision [2]. However, tuning retrieval models with different legal corpora allows dense retrieval models to use LLMs to more accurately match queries with appropriate documents. In addition to the law domain [13,14]. As an example, four benchmarks, such as CaseLaw and COLIEE [11], are used to evaluate the performance of these models, where the retrieval metrics consist of precision, recall, and mean average precision (MAP) [10,12].

4   Document Summarization

Legal text summarization is an important task, which is highly relevant to the legal domain, where legal practitioners need to understand the essentials of hundreds of pages, full of text, and also in a short period of time, as documents are large and can also be lengthy, and involves reading through judicial decisions, contracts, and legislation. Thus, in general, the task can be divided into two techniques in extractive summarization and abstractive summarization.

With extractive summarization, only fragments and phrases of the unique textual content are being decided. For this purpose,techniques like TextRank or BERT based models are commonly used. However, while these techniques work well to retrieve relevant information, they often struggle to provide coherent summaries and do not capture the subtlety of legal meaning. BERT based models have outperformed in finding important sentences but do not maintain the context in legal language that is very important when summarizing legal texts [8].

Early systems for summarizing legal documents include FLEXICON [20], which employed a keyword-based strategy. Subsequently, SALOMON and LetSum [27] utlized cosine similarity and cue-phrases, respectively. More recent approches include CaseSummarizer by Polsley et al. [21], which relies on TF-IDF scoring, and Zhong et al. [23] extractive system for PTSD legal cases based on CNN. Nguyen et al. [26] used reinforcement learning for legal summarization improvements, while Schraagen et al. [18] use BART and RL together to summarize brief legal documents.

Examples of extractive summarization include the graph-based ranking model proposed by Zhong [23], Moro et al.'s transfer learning using pre-trained model [22], Jain et al.'s hybrid sentence-scoring method [24], and Liu et al. Common Law Court Council Judgment Summarization (2024) [25]. The goal of these innovations is to improve the efficiency, accuracy, and scalability of legal summarization in diverse legal fields.

Moreover, legal documents often contain complicated, nested legal relationships that the extractive approaches may not be able to address adequately [9]. Although extractive summarization provides a simple and direct means of achieving this, it is not suitable for more complex interpretations, an area where the legal domain tends to ask of us.

Although BERT-based models have shown strong performance in identifying important sentences, they often struggle to preserve the nuanced context required in legal language [8]. This limitation further highlights the challenges of applying extractive techniques to legal texts, where maintaining the full legal meaning and coherence is crucial.

Unlike extractive summarization, which uses sentences from the original text, abstractive summarization creates new sentences that capture the essence of the original text content while making the summary more coherent and contextually enriched. Although requiring more computational power, this approach is better suited to legal language, as it can more effectively capture nuanced details within legal texts [10].

The models such as T5 and GPT are found to be particularly useful for abstractive summarization as they can generate summaries while maintaining the core legal meaning of the text while on the same time provide more flexibility in the output expression [12]. However, producing effective abstractive summaries requires large amounts of training examples, and these models can be very expensive to compute [13].Though both methods have their advantages, several key challenges exists for legal text summarisation. Legal documents can be long and have many types of dependencies between terms, clauses and conditions. With this, selection or generation of the salient aspects to compose a summary becomes much more challenging.

Legal professionals need very high accuracy summarization, as even the slightest misinterpretation can have significant legal repercussions [12]. In addition, large annotations of legal datasets that capture domain-specific features of the legal language are needed to build powerful summarization systems, and the unavailability of such data reduces the performance of the models [14]. Moreover, the existence of cross-jurisdictional variations in legal terminology and structure between different legal systems pose a significant challenge to developing a one-size-fits-all summarization model [16].

These advances, with the introduction of LLMs, such as GPT-4 and BART, that are trained to understand and generate coherent and high quality texts, allow these models to be used in the compliance text space. By retraining them on legal corpora, these models are now capable to generating summaries with both contextual accuracy, and legal significance [13].

Additionally, zero-shot summarization approach models create summary without training on task-specific data is also an important way for processing legal text [14]. This leads to significant improvements in performance for both GPT-4 and similar models, allowing them to generate legal summaries paired with attempts generating summaries with minimal annotated data, making them especially fitting for working on new or unseen legal texts.

Multi-task learning techniques, which train models on multiple related tasks in a parallel manner (document classification and summarization), provided an enhancement to legal summarization model performance. As the first layer is guided by an overarching goal given as external and previous tasks, models trained this way become aware of the overall context of legal documents and thus can produce accurate summaries from sets of query/document pairs [13]. Such models are usually evaluated with conventional metrics, such as ROUGE and BLEU metrics [15], measuring the overlap between the references of human-annotated and machine-generated summaries.

More recently, it has been shown that summarisation systems can benefit from using neural information retrieval methods. These systems, by enhancing the search and retrieval process for legal documents, can also produce more accurate summaries that capture the most pertinent aspects of the law domain [17].This is even more important when working on higher volumes of legal text, as it can help direct the models to the most relevant sections in a document summary will be generated. This is why the integration of neural IR methodologies into the legal text summarization systems adds flexibility to properly address documents belonging to different jurisdictions and legal systems [19].

5   Knowledge Extraction

Knowledge Extraction (KE) from legal documents means identifying and organizing important facts, such as entities (e.g. names of legal parties, statutes, dates) and relations (e.g. obligations, case outcomes, affiliations). This process allows raw legal text to become structured data so that it can be processed for advanced analytics and decision-making, or integrated into systems or databases of law. Legal texts can be long, dense, and specialized; therefore, unique approaches are further required to extract and present entities and the relationships among them.

In legal texts, Named Entity Recognition (NER) is a crucial task for knowledge extraction, focusing on discovering domain-specific entities (e.g. parties such as defendants and plaintiffs), legal terms (e.g. statutes, amendments) and event-related information such as trial dates and rulings. Typically, BiLSTM-CRF (Bidirectional Long Short-Term Memory with Conditional Random Fields) has been used to model sequence dependencies in text. More recent efforts have been directed toward adapting transformer-based architectures such as BERT to account for the intricacies of legal language.

While KE has promising prospects, there are multiple barriers to working with these technologies in the legal field. Legal languages differ significantly from general-purpose languages with respect to the specialized terminology and complex syntactic structures, which pose challenges for accurate entity / relationship identification. The lack of annotated datasets, required for training KE models, due to the specific knowledge necessary for the annotation of legal documents is another challenge. Additionally, the diverse legal domains have significant variability in systems and terminologies, making it very difficult to develop generalized KE models. Extracting knowledge from legal text is a challenging task, as ensuring the consistency and correctness of extracted knowledge is not easy due to inherent ambiguities and contradictions contained in a legal text. Such challenges indicate the necessity of solid and adaptable KE systems that are capable of addressing the inherent complexities of legal texts [10,12].

To overcome these challenges, LLM have played an integral role. Many pre-trained models such as BERT and GPT have been fine-tuned for NER and relation extraction, and they have shown state-of-the-art performance towards legal entities and relations extraction.

Additionally, LLMs can produce synthetic training data, thus eliminating the challenge of having limited annotated datasets in the legal field. For instance, Singh et al. [14] proposed prompt-based learning for relation extraction where the authors applied prompt-based learning for legal relation extraction and demonstrated the ability to generate complex relations between two legal entities.

A significant progress in this area, such as with the ASKE (Automatic System for Knowledge Extraction) method that enforces context-aware extraction of legal information. ASKE uses a three-phase extraction cycle, incorporating both context-aware embedding models and zero-shot learning techniques, in which concepts representative of the different meanings of terms found in chunks of legal documents are progressively extracted. The basic structure is a graph-based data structure known as the ASKE Conceptual Graph with iterative enrichments from newly classified document chunks, newly extracted terminology, and newly generated concepts. So far, ASKE has been quantitatively assessed against EurLex dataset and qualitatively applied in the context of a real case study of Italian case law decisions, with feedback from legal experts [3].

KE systems are evaluated using standard benchmarks and metrics. Benchmarks such as LexGLUE [4] and LEXTREME [6] provide datasets to evaluate the extraction of legal entities and relationships, and various metrics such as F1-score, precision, and recall are used to evaluate the quality of the knowledge extracted. Recent studies (Gupta et al. (2024)) investigate transformer-based models for knowledge extraction in law [19], as these models can capture the complex legal semantics and relationships. These benchmarks and metrics play a crucial role in advancing KE research by providing standardized evaluation frameworks and enabling comparisons between different methods.

6   Discussion and Future Research Directions

The comparative analysis of Legal NLP tasks presented in Table 1 highlights the diverse techniques, challenges, strengths, and innovations across four key areas: KE, Summarization, IR, and Document Segmentation. Each task plays a vital role in automating and streamlining the processing of legal documents, though they each face distinct challenges. For instance, KE benefits from advanced techniques like NER and relation extraction, but struggles with domain-specific terms and limited datasets, limiting its broader application. Summarization, on the other hand, has made significant improvements with abstractive methods like GPT and T5, but still faces challenges in preserving the technical legal meaning and managing lengthy documents. Similarly, IR systems, particularly BERT-based retrievers and Dense Passage Retrieval (DPR), excel at semantic understanding and cross-jurisdictional retrieval, yet must tackle issues like complex queries and semantic ambiguities. Document segmentation, which integrates rule-based, machine learning, and transformer-based methods, has shown promise in organizing and improving document readability but still contends with non-standard structures and ambiguous boundaries.

Table 1. Comparative Analysis of Legal NLP Tasks: Knowledge Extraction (KE), Summarization, Information Retrieval (IR), and Document Segmentation

Aspect	KE	Summarization	IR	Document Segmentation	References
Techniques	- NER - Relation extraction - Event extraction	- Extractive (TextRank, BERT) - Abstractive(T5, GPT)	- Traditional (TF-IDF, BM25) - Neural(BERT-based retrievers,DPR)	- Rule-based (regex, heuristics) - ML (CRF, BiLSTM) - Transformers (BERT)	[18] [13] [14] [19]
Challenges	- Domain-specific terms - Lack of datasets - Ambiguity	- Preserve legal meaning - Handle long docs - Lack of datasets	- Complex queries - Semantic understanding - Cross-jurisdictional issues	- Non-standard structures - Ambiguous boundaries - Long documents	[9] [10] [12]
Strengths	- Structured output - Legal reasoning - Broad applicability	- Concise overviews - Saves time - Improves accessibility	- Efficient search - Semantic understanding - Scalability	- Organizes docs - Improves readability - Supports downstream tasks	[9] [19]
Evaluation Metrics	- F1-score - Precision - Recall	- ROUGE - BLEU	- Precision - Recall - MAP	- F1-score - Accuracy - IoU	[9] [23] [13] [24] [19]
Benchmarks	- LexGLUE - LEXTREME	- BillSum - LexSum	- CaseLaw - COLIEE	- COLIEE - LEDGAR	[5] [6] [11] [4]
Applications	- Legal research - Contract analysis - Case law summarization	- Case law summaries - Contract summaries - Legislative summaries	- Legal doc search - Case law retrieval - Contract clause retrieval	- Contract analysis - Legal doc organization - Clause identification	[9] [13] [25] [19]
Key Innovations	- Context-aware embeddings - Zero-shot learning - Graph-based representations	- Abstractive methods - Zero-shot summarization - Multi-task learning	- Dense retrieval models - Query expansion - Cross-encoder architectures	- Transformer-based segmentation - Multi-modal approaches - Zero-shot	[9] [23] [13] [24] [19]

Key innovations in these tasks, such as zero-shot learning for KE, multi-task learning for summarization, and transformer-based segmentation, are pushing the boundaries of what Legal NLP can achieve. However, the scalability of these solutions remains a challenge, particularly when applied to different legal systems and jurisdictions with varying terminologies and document formats.

Given the difficulties encountered by legal professionals in dealing with complex documents and performing time-consuming research as a future direction, a single platform that incorporates a variety of Legal NLP techniques would be greatly beneficial. While legal texts across different domains have unique nuances, the platform can be customized to adapt to these variations, ensuring domain-specific accuracy. Bringing summarization (extractive and abstractive), document segmentation, IR and KE into a common single cohesive workflow would provide practitioners an encompassing solution to dealing with legal texts. It would simplify tasks like summarizing lengthy documents, searching for applicable case law, dividing complex legal documents into digestible parts and identifying important entities and events. By integrating both processes, it not only saves time but also improves the user experience, making legal research and document management more efficient and accurate. This unified system can further be improved through both multi-modal data and broader legal input, enabling it to better assist practitioners of all kinds in the field of law.

7   Concluding Remarks

Legal NLP has enabled significant advances in automating the processing of complex legal documents for tasks including segmentation, information retrieval, summarization, and knowledge extraction. The introduction of transformer-based and LLM has resulted in efficiency increase and lower dependence on labeled datasets. This review highlights the latest methods in legal NLP, discussing challenges and opportunities for future research. Our contribution emphasizes the need for an integrated platform that combines multiple NLP techniques, streamlining workflows for legal practitioners. Therefore, future research should focus on how to increase generalization ability, because legal texts in different domains may differ, also if domain-specificity is tried, multimodal approaches could potentially be used to enhance legal text processing performance even further.

Acknowledgments. This work was supported in part by project SERICS (PE00000014) under the NRRP MUR program funded by the EU - NGEU. Views and opinions expressed are however those of the authors only and do not necessarily reflect those of the European Union or the Italian MUR. Neither the European Union nor the Italian MUR can be held responsible for them.

References

1. Bommasani, R., et al.: On the opportunities and risks of foundation models. arXiv preprint: arXiv:2108.07258 (2021)
2. Chalkidis, I., Fergadiotis, M., Malakasiotis, P., Aletras, N., Androutsopoulos, I.: LEGALBERT: the Muppets straight out of law school. In: Findings of the Association for Computational Linguistics: EMNLP 2020, pp. 2898–2904. Association for Computational Linguistics (2020). https://doi.org/10.18653/v1/2020.findings-emnlp.261
3. Castano, S., et al.: Enforcing legal information extraction through context-aware techniques: The ASKE approach. Comput. Law Secur. Rev. **52**, 105903 (2024)
4. Chalkidis, I., Fergadiotis, M., Sætre, R., Malakasiotis, P., Androutsopoulos, I.: LexGLUE: a benchmark dataset for legal language understanding in English. In: Proceedings of the Conference on Empirical Methods in Natural Language Processing (EMNLP) (2021)
5. Shen, Z., Lo, K., Yu, L., Dahlberg, N., Schlanger, M., Downey, D.: Multi LexSum: real world summaries of civil rights lawsuits at multiple granularities. In: Koyejo, S., Mohamed, S., Agarwal, A., Belgrave, D., Cho, K., Oh, A. (eds.) Advances in Neural Information Processing Systems, vol. 35, pp. 13158–13173. Curran Associates, Inc (2022)
6. Niklaus, J., et al.: LEXTREME: a multi-lingual and multi-task benchmark for the legal domain. arXiv preprint: arXiv:2301.13126 (2023)
7. Ambedkar, K., Pal, S., Pamula, R.: Text summarization from legal documents: a survey. Artif. Intell. Rev. **51**, 371–402 (2019). https://doi.org/10.1007/s10462-017-9566-2

8. Xu, X., et al.: Legal document segmentation using transformer models. In: Proceedings of ACL 2023 (2023)

9. Zhang, Y., et al.: Deep learning approaches for legal clause segmentation. J. AI & Law (2022)

10. Kim, J., et al.: COLIEE 2023: advances in legal text processing. In: Legal AI Conference Proceedings (2023)

11. Goebel, R., et al.: Overview of benchmark datasets and methods for the legal information extraction/entailment competition (COLIEE) 2024. In: JSAI International Symposium on Artificial Intelligence. Springer Nature Singapore, Singapore (2024)

12. Li, H., et al.: Enhancing legal text understanding with transformer-based segmentation. ICLR (2024)

13. Patel, R., et al.: Adaptive legal document segmentation with large language models. AAAI (2025)

14. Singh, A., et al.: Zero-shot legal text segmentation using GPT-4. In: NeurIPS 2024 (2024)

15. Wang, L., et al.: Multi-modal legal document segmentation: combining text and layout features. In: Proceedings of EMNLP 2023 (2023)

16. Chen, T., et al.: Cross-jurisdictional legal text segmentation: challenges and solutions. J. Legal Inform. (2024)

17. Brown, M., et al.: neural information retrieval in legal texts: a comprehensive study. J. Artif. Intell. Res. (2023)

18. Devlin, J., Chang, M.W., Lee, K., Toutanova, K.: BERT: pre-training of deep bidirectional transformers for language understanding. In: Proceedings of the 2019 Conference of the North American Chapter of the Association for Computational Linguistics (NAACL-HLT), pp. 4171-4186. Association for Computational Linguistics (2019). arXiv:1810.04805

19. Gupta, R., et al.: Knowledge extraction from legal documents using transformers. J. Legal AI (2024)

20. Gelbart, D., Smith, J.C.: Flexicon, a new legal information retrieval system. Can. Law Libr. 16(9), 9 (1991)

21. Polsley, S., Jhunjhunwala, P., Huang, R.: CaseSummarizer: a system for automated summarization of legal texts. In: Proceedings of COLING 2016, the 26th International Conference on Computational Linguistics: System Demonstrations, Osaka, Japan, pp. 258-262. The COLING 2016 Organizing Committee, Osaka (2016). https://aclanthology.org/C16-2054

22. Moro, G., Piscaglia, N., Ragazzi, L., Italiani, P.: Multi-language transfer learning for low-resource legal case summarization. Artif. Intell. Law (2023). https://doi.org/10.1007/s10506-023-09373-8

23. Zhong, Y., Litman, D.: Computing and exploiting document structure to improve unsupervised extractive summarization of legal case decisions. In: Proceedings of the Natural Legal Language Processing Workshop 2022, Abu Dhabi, UAE (Hybrid), pp. 322–337 (2022)

24. Jain, D., Borah, M.D., Biswas, A.: A sentence is known by the company it keeps: improving legal document summarization using deep clustering. Artif. Intell. Law 32(1), 165–200 (2024)

25. Liu, S., Cao, J., Li, Y., Yang, R., Wen, Z.: Low-resource court judgment summarization for common law systems. Inf. Process. Manage. 61(5), 10379 (2024). https://doi.org/10.1016/j.ipm.2024.103796

26. Nguyen, D.-H., et al.: Robust deep reinforcement learning for extractive legal summarization. In: Mantoro, T., Lee, M., Ayu, M.A., Wong, K.W., Hidayanto, A.N.

(eds.) Neural Information Processing, pp. 597–604. Springer International Publishing, Berlin (2021)

27. Farzindar, A., Lapalme, G.: LetSum, an automatic legal text summarizing system. In: Gordon, T. (ed.) Legal Knowledge and Information Systems: JURIX 2004, the Seventeenth Annual Conference, pp. 11–18. IOS Press (2004)

Synthetic Data and Active Learning for Efficient Object Detection

Hooman Tavakoli Ghinani[1,2]([✉]), Nimesh Singh[1], Tatjana Legler[1,2], Achim Wagner[1,2], and Martin Ruskowski[1,2]

[1] University of Kaiserslautern-Landau, Kaiserslautern, Germany
hooman.tavakoli_ghinani@dfki.de
[2] German Research Center for Artificial Intelligence, Kaiserslautern, Germany

Abstract. With advancements in data availability and computational power, AI adoption has surged across science and technology. Vision-based methodologies have expanded, particularly in industrial applications, from assembly lines to human-robot interaction. Synthetic data generation in controlled environments enables dataset creation and mitigates challenges like labor-intensive labeling. While synthetic datasets are crucial for object detection training, the domain gap remains a key challenge. This paper explores a two-phase training strategy: first, pre-training with synthetic data, followed by fine-tuning using Active Learning (AL) with uncertainty sampling. We extensively evaluate this approach using well-established benchmarks and YOLOv11 as the detection framework. Additionally, we introduce an industrial Truck dataset, featuring CAD-generated and 3D-printed components of a Truck and Glue-gun. Our findings show that combining synthetic data with AL significantly reduces real data requirements while achieving superior precision, especially when real data is limited.

Keywords: Synthetic Data · Active Learning · Object Detection. · Uncertainty Sampling

1 Introduction

In the industrial domain, Object Detection (OD) plays a crucial role in various tasks, ranging from manual assembly to robotics [23]. For applications such as human-robot interaction and pick-and-place use cases (e.g., sorting scenarios), OD solutions are employed to identify target objects and localize them within camera frames [14], and [20]. The "You Only Look Once" (YOLO) framework, introduced by [15], quickly gained significant attention in the field of computer vision [2]. Data preparation is a critical phase requiring meticulous attention for OD. Acquiring and labeling data to train an OD model is often the most challenging and resource-intensive aspect of the process. Manual labeling is particularly time-consuming and prone to errors, with a high potential for ambiguity [8]. Real-world scenarios, such as target object occlusion and limited viewpoints, further complicate this phase of data preparation. Consequently, synthetic data has emerged as a key solution to address these challenges. Leveraging

© The Author(s), under exclusive license to Springer Nature Switzerland AG 2025
J. Grabis and Y. Wautelet (Eds.): CAiSE 2025 Workshops, LNBIP 556, pp. 338–350, 2025.
https://doi.org/10.1007/978-3-031-94931-9_28

visual environment-based synthetic data enables the generation of photo-realistic images with fine-grained control over various aspects, including the automatic labeling of each object in an image. This approach is faster, more efficient, and eliminates the errors associated with manual labeling. Additionally, synthetic dataset generation mitigates issues such as data bias and privacy concerns inherent in real-world data [19]. Thanks to the availability of Computer-Aided Design (CAD) models for objects and components in the industrial sector, visual environment-based synthetic dataset preparation has become an indispensable aspect of dataset creation. By utilizing these 3D models with domain randomization techniques, it is possible to generate ready-to-use datasets for OD training [25]. However, a significant challenge associated with synthetic data lies in the domain gap: the discrepancy between the synthetic data used for training and the real-world data on which the OD model is deployed [26]. This gap often results in poor OD performance in many use cases. To address this issue, we propose a two-phase training strategy. In the first phase, synthetic data is used for training the OD model to achieve initial precision, while in the second phase, the model is fine-tuned on real data to mitigate the domain gap. Uncertainty sampling of Active Learning (AL) is employed during this fine-tuning phase to label the most informative samples, rather than relying on random sampling of large datasets, thereby improving efficiency. This strategy is used because it prioritizes samples the model is least confident about, which are more likely to improve learning. In our work, we study this framework by extensively testing and generalizing it across multiple datasets of varying sizes.

Specifically, we employ the Truck dataset, which consists of inter-lockable components for manual assembly scenarios and contains separate synthetic and real datasets. We also incorporate COCO and KITTI as real datasets and GTA-V and SYNTHIA as corresponding synthetic datasets for the experiments. Our results show that this two-phase framework effectively bridges the domain gap between real and synthetic data, enhancing object detection precision, especially with limited dataset samples. Additionally, it significantly reduces data labeling effort and time while minimizing human error. This approach highlights the potential of combining synthetic data and AL techniques to enhance OD performance in industrial and other real-world applications.

2   Related Work

The use of synthetic data for OD has become a prominent area of research in recent years. Korakakis et al. [8] provided a comprehensive review of various studies on synthetic data across different vision-based AI tasks.

Seib et al. [19] analyzed approaches to enhancing model performance without requiring additional labeled real-world datasets, focusing on data augmentation techniques in synthetic data generation.

Tavakoli et al. [24] investigated synthetic data generation based on controlled visual environments for training OD models on breadboards and tiny objects. Tremblay et al. [25] addressed the issue of limited variation in appearance within synthetic datasets. They demonstrated that through domain randomization realistic photo-quality images are not necessary for effective OD training. While there are diverse methods for generating synthetic data, including GAN-based and visual environment techniques, Mumuni et al. [11] argued that 2D transformation approaches often lack semantic 3D information and fail to represent real-world variations accurately. They highlighted how 3D-to-2D transformations in graphical modeling address this limitation, enabling more representative data. Furthermore, Sevastopoulos et al. [22] noted that combining synthetic and real-world data can bridge gaps in capturing physical object attributes that synthetic data alone cannot fully replicate. Ljungqvist et al. [10] demonstrated that the largest differences between models trained on real and synthetic data are observed in the early layers of the network. A comprehensive survey by Tsirikoglou et al. [26] outlined key requirements for synthetic data generation for machine learning, including feature variation and coverage, domain realism, annotation quality, metadata inclusion, and scalability. Wrenninge et al. [28] introduced Synscapes, a synthetic dataset, and highlighted the impact of object distance and orientation relative to the camera on Intersection over Union (IoU) scores in OD. Perri et al. [13] introduced a two-phase training approach for object recognition, utilizing synthetic datasets in the initial phase and real-world scenario datasets in the subsequent phase.

Active Learning, also known as *query learning* or *optimal experimental design* is a subfield of machine learning that focuses on optimizing training data selection. By utilizing algorithms to choose the most informative samples, AL can significantly enhance performance while minimizing labeled data requirements [21]. AL approaches include uncertainty-based methods [3], diversity-based methods [1], and expected model change [6]. One prominent AL strategy is uncertainty sampling, which prioritizes labeling data points where the model's predictions are most uncertain, typically near decision boundaries. Roy et al. [18] demonstrated a DeepAL framework that efficiently selects a fraction of an OD dataset for labeling, proving effective in scenarios with costly annotation processes. Feng et al. [5] further showcased an AL method for autonomous driving, achieving up to a 60% reduction in labeling effort using various uncertainty estimation techniques.

The combination of synthetic data and active learning has also been explored in the context of surgical instrument segmentation by Haonan Peng et al. [12]. In their study, active learning is employed for labeling, followed by the use of a copy-and-paste approach to generate synthetic data based on these labeled images. Finally, Eversberg et al. [4] proposed a two-phase OD approach combining synthetic data and AL to optimize Faster R-CNN models for specific industrial use cases. Their study utilized uncertainty and diversity sampling methods in the second phase, outperforming random sampling approaches. For synthetic data generation, they employed a visual environment technique, incorporating variations in background imagery sourced from the COCO dataset to provide randomization and address the domain gap.

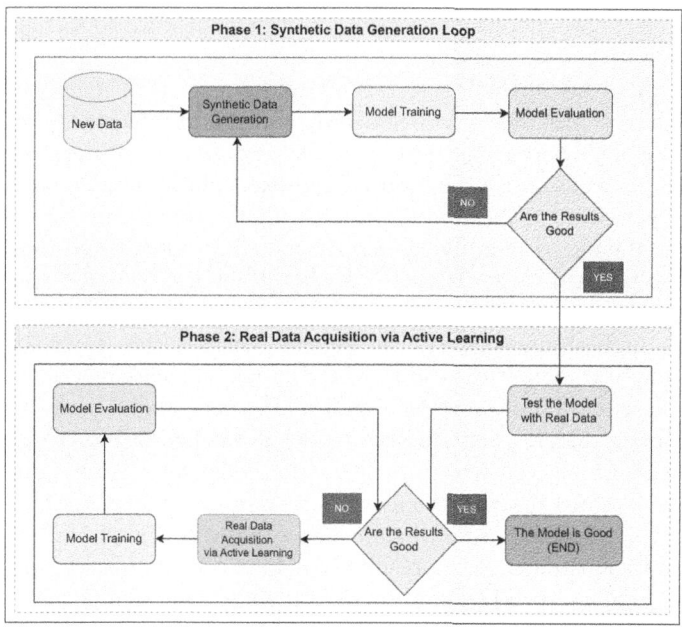

Fig. 1. The architecture of the proposed pipeline comprises two distinct phases: (1) generating synthetic data to enhance initial model training and (2) employing Active Learning techniques to identify and label the most informative real data samples.

3   Methodology

In this section, we detail the proposed approach and framework, which consists of two phases for OD training. The framework leverages synthetic data generation for the initial training and testing phase and subsequently fine-tunes the OD model trained on synthetic data using active learning with uncertainty-based approach on real data. The diagram of this pipeline is depicted in Fig. 1. The primary goal here is to achieve high average precision while minimizing reliance on extensive labeled datasets. The pipeline begins by introducing new data class(es) into the system as a CAD model of the target object(s). This model is then processed in the synthetic data generation block, simulating real environments to produce a high-fidelity dataset resembling real-world industrial data. The goal at this stage is to create a robust and diverse synthetic dataset for the initial training of the object detection model. By adjusting parameters such as rotation, lighting, and other factors, the dataset can be tailored to minimize biases in class distribution or attributes. Additionally, real-world backgrounds are randomly incorporated to reduce the domain gap between synthetic and real images. Once the synthetic dataset is prepared, it is used in the OD training phase, leveraging its diversity and fidelity to help the model learn meaningful patterns. The model is then evaluated on synthetic data to ensure it performs adequately and shows potential for generalization to real-world scenarios. If performance falls below the established threshold-indicating insufficient precision or generalization-the pipeline triggers an iterative process to generate additional synthetic samples, progressively refining the model until it meets the required criteria. If the model's performance using synthetic data alone is deemed sufficient, the pipeline proceeds to the real data acquisition phase, implemented through uncertainty sampling of AL approach. This phase strategically optimizes data selection for labeling by identifying only the most informative and representative samples from the real-world dataset. AL algorithms leverage uncertainty scores to nominate these critical samples. By focusing on instances where the model exhibits the highest uncertainty, the pipeline ensures that each labeled data point maximally contributes to improving the model's classification's precision and generalization. These selected samples are then labeled and incorporated into the training dataset, enabling the model to further shrink the domain gap between the synthetic and real-world scenario. Following the integration of real data into the training process, the model undergoes a final evaluation. This step assesses whether training on real data has successfully improved the model's precision and robustness. If the results remain below the desired performance criteria, the pipeline reverts to an iterative cycle of real data acquisition, labeling, and training in the second phase. This iterative refinement continues until the model consistently meets the requirements. Once the model achieves the desired level of accuracy and generalization, the pipeline is considered as the final ready-to-deploy model.

Phase 1: Synthetic Data Generation: Within our Truck dataset - an industrial dataset created for assembly line purposes that comprises eight distinct classes representing various truck's interlocked components and glue-gun - synthetic data generation is critical during this phase. In this work, the Unity Perception Package [27] has been chosen for its advanced capabilities in crafting realistic synthetic environments. Domain randomization for synthetic data generation involved initializing diverse randomization for parameters, including complex domain-specific backgrounds and simulation aspects such as object position, scale, rotation, lighting conditions, and the number of objects within the camera's field of view. In this study, the backgrounds are captured as 2D images from specific use cases relevant to the assembly line scenario, where detecting objects from the Truck dataset for assembly purpose through Hololens's World camera is required. By incorporating relevant and complex backgrounds, the OD model is guided to effectively differentiate the target object from other objects within the domain, enhancing its detection performance. Data generation for other general benchmark datasets is not utilized in this study.

Phase 2: Real Data Acquisition leveraging AL: In this phase, uncertainty sampling algorithms are employed to select the most informative samples from the real data points based on the classification precision scores generated by the OD model. Three approaches are utilized for this experiment: the sum of scores, the average of scores, and the maximum score. The top k candidates with the highest uncertainty scores are then selected for labeling and subsequently used to train the OD model in the second phase.

3.1 Experimental Setup

We conducted experiments on various datasets to validate and generalize our findings and solutions beyond an industrial dataset that is highly relevant for real-world use cases in the industrial domain. We extend our analysis to benchmarking datasets as following: **Dataset Combination 1:** GTA-V [16], and COCO [9]: GTA-V serves as the synthetic dataset, while COCO represents the real dataset. For this study, we focus on six shared classes: *Bike, Bird, Airplane, Car, Person,* and *Train.* **Dataset Combination 2:** SYNTHIA [17], and KITTI [7]: SYNTHIA is used as the synthetic dataset, while KITTI represents the real-world objects. We select three shared classes: *Bike, Car,* and *Person.* **Dataset Combination 3:** Truck Dataset: A fusion of synthetic and real datasets comprising eight classes of industrial interlocked truck components (e.g., *BlueLid, Cabin, Front Chassis,* and *Rear Chassis*) along with a *Glue-gun,* all generated from CAD models for synthetic version of the dataset.

The training process was performed using a standardized dataset split into training, validation, and testing subsets. The model was trained for a maximum of 100 epochs, with an early stopping criterion implemented to terminate training if the validation performance did not improve for 15 consecutive epochs. To enhance the reliability of our study and mitigate any potential bias toward specific classes, we trained the OD models from scratch. The training configuration included the following key hyperparameters: a batch size of 16, an input image size of 640 pixels, an initial learning rate of 0.01, and the use of the Stochastic Gradient Descent (SGD) optimizer.

4 Results and Discussion

Experiments and Dataset Combinations: We designed and evaluate three experimental setups with different datasets: **Experiment 1 (Exp1):** The hybrid approach integrating synthetic data with real data acquired via AL using uncertainty sampling. This evaluates whether synthetic data and selective acquisition of informative real samples enhance the precision of the model. **Experiment 2 (Exp2):** The hybrid approach integrating synthetic data with real data acquired through random sampling. This serves as a baseline to compare AL versus random sampling. **Experiment 3 (Exp3):** No synthetic data is used; real data is acquired exclusively via AL with uncertainty sampling. This setup assesses the effectiveness of AL without synthetic data set in the pretrained phase.

4.1 Discussion

The detailed results for the three dataset groups are presented in Tables 1, 2, and 3, respectively. These results indicate that Experiment 1 consistently outperforms the other two approaches in most iterations for the first and third

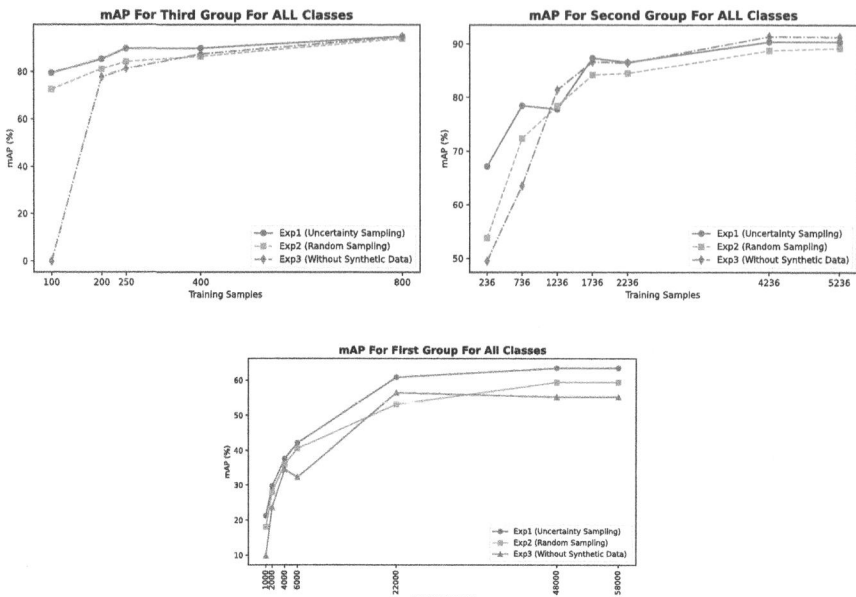

Fig. 2. The line chart illustrates the mAP results across three distinct dataset groups, evaluated over three experimental setups for all object classes.

Fig. 3. Comparison of the three experiments with training samples at 1K, 22K, and 58K for first group of dataset COCO and GTA-V. Each image contains the results of Experiment 1, Experiment 2, and Experiment 3, side by side.

Table 1. Comparison of mAP results on Dataset 1 (GTA-V as synthetic data and COCO as real data) using three different experiments. The table presents mAP values for various object classes with seven different numbers of training samples, ranging from 1,000 to 58,000.

Classes	Training Samples (Exp1)							Training Samples (Exp2)							Training Samples (Exp3)						
	1000	2000	4000	6000	22000	48000	58000	1000	2000	4000	6000	22000	48000	58000	1000	2000	4000	6000	22000	48000	58000
ALL	**21.3**	**29.7**	**37.7**	**42.2**	**60.9**	63.5	**63.5**	18.1	28.0	36.1	40.6	53.2	59.5	59.5	9.9	23.7	34.6	32.4	56.5	55.3	55.3
BIKE	17.9	29.1	34.2	35.2	56.8	59.5	59.5	10.3	23.0	31.5	34.7	49.3	55.9	55.9	3.5	16.4	22.1	20.5	50.8	48.7	48.7
BIRD	1.4	2.3	10.8	15.1	37.2	39.5	39.5	0.9	2.6	6.8	11.2	24.1	33.1	33.1	0.6	1.7	9.8	8.6	31.1	29.5	29.5
AIRPLANE	20.0	30.2	43.0	52.8	73.1	76.3	76.3	18.3	34.2	42.3	49.2	63.6	70.7	70.7	6.5	30.9	44.3	42.4	69.4	66.7	66.7
CAR	15.9	24.0	30.0	34.4	51.8	54.9	54.9	16.3	21.7	29.4	34.3	45.9	51.1	51.1	8.0	17.7	26.4	25.2	47.1	46.9	46.9
PERSON	42.3	50.6	55.8	58.4	71.8	74.2	74.2	42.4	50.9	57.6	61.4	69.0	72.3	72.3	35.7	49.1	54.1	52.6	67.9	68.1	68.1
TRAIN	30.5	42.2	52.5	57.4	74.6	76.7	76.7	20.3	35.7	49.3	52.8	67.5	73.9	73.9	5.2	26.3	51.0	45.5	72.9	71.6	71.6

Table 2. Comparison of mAP results on Dataset 2 (SYNTHIA as synthetic data and KITTI as real data) using different experiments. The table presents mAP values for various object classes with seven different numbers of training samples from 236 to 5236.

Classes	Training Samples (Exp1)							Training Samples (Exp2)							Training Samples (Exp3)						
	236	736	1236	1736	2236	4236	5236	236	736	1236	1736	2236	4236	5236	236	736	1236	1736	2236	4236	5236
ALL	**67.2**	**78.5**	77.8	**87.4**	**86.6**	90.4	90.4	53.8	72.4	78.4	84.2	84.5	88.8	89.2	49.5	63.6	**81.4**	86.7	86.5	**91.4**	91.3
CAR	89.3	93.1	93.8	96.1	96.1	97.7	97.7	87.5	92.1	93.9	95.2	95.5	97.0	97.2	72.1	84.1	91.8	94.9	95.3	98.0	97.9
PERSON	60.9	72.0	69.4	81.9	81.1	83.6	84.1	51.5	65.4	70.6	77.3	77.9	81.2	82.5	49.5	61.6	78.1	80.9	81.1	84.9	84.8
BIKE	51.2	70.4	70.3	84.3	82.6	89.9	89.5	22.4	59.8	70.8	80.0	80.0	88.0	87.7	26.8	45.2	74.2	84.3	83.1	91.3	91.2

dataset groups. In the second dataset group, while Experiment 1 shows superior performance in the early iterations, Experiment 3 surpasses it in the later stages, albeit with a marginal difference.

This section focuses on two key discussion points: (1) the behavior of different experiments during the initial iterations when real data is scarce and (2) the overall trend as more data is incrementally added. For the very first iterations, all three dataset groups demonstrate better performance with Experiment 1 compared to the other two. This trend is most pronounced in the Truck dataset, where, with just 100 samples, Experiment 3 achieves nearly zero Mean-Average-Precision (mAP), whereas Experiment 1 and Experiment 2 reach 79.6% and 72% mAP, respectively. A similar pattern is observed in the second dataset group, where for 236 and 736 samples, Experiment 1 outperforms the others. The same holds for the first dataset group, where Experiment 1 achieves a clear margin over the other two. This highlights the crucial role of synthetic data in the initial training phase when real data is limited. Moreover, Comparing Experiments 1 and 2 in these early iterations, Experiment 1 consistently outperforms Experiment 2. This suggests that the uncertainty sampling approach effectively selects informative samples, allowing the OD model to converge more efficiently. This trend is evident across all datasets. Additionally, when comparing Experiments 2 and 3, it is clear that in the early iterations-particularly in the Truck dataset-the synthetic dataset plays a vital role in achieving reliable OD precision. Similar behavior is observed in the first and second dataset groups. Examining model behavior in later iterations, as more data samples are added, we observe that

Table 3. Comparison of mAP results on Dataset 3 (Truck dataset) using three experiments. The table presents mAP values for various object classes with five different numbers of training samples from 100 to 800.

Classes	Training Samples (Exp1)					Training Samples (Exp2)					Training Samples (Exp3)				
	100	200	250	400	800	100	200	250	400	800	100	200	250	400	800
ALL	**79.6**	**85.6**	**90.1**	**90.1**	**95.2**	72.7	81.4	84.5	86.7	94.3	0.03	77.9	81.5	87.7	95.1
Blue_Lid	92.0	93.3	97.6	97.6	99.4	84.4	94.1	94.9	95.2	99.0	0.1	94.6	88.0	91.7	98.7
Blue_Trailer	94.2	96.5	98.6	98.8	99.1	90.3	95.3	96.7	98.4	99.0	0.0	91.0	86.6	93.3	98.7
Cabin	87.4	90.6	89.7	92.1	93.8	89.1	89.3	92.9	93.0	93.8	0.0	81.2	88.6	90.1	92.3
Front_Chassis	59.2	82.8	92.9	88.2	91.6	71.4	83.6	84.7	90.4	92.5	0.0	76.8	76.5	79.0	91.7
Rear_Chassis	58.1	77.8	87.0	85.9	90.2	67.0	78.6	83.1	83.2	92.3	0.0	79.7	81.4	77.7	88.9
Yellow_Lid	93.8	94.7	95.5	94.4	97.5	85.0	92.9	94.2	95.1	97.7	0.04	89.0	89.6	92.3	95.6
Yellow_Trailer	98.2	98.7	98.4	98.4	92.0	93.8	97.9	98.1	98.6	90.3	0.04	92.3	95.7	96.5	97.5
Glue_Gun	53.6	50.2	71.3	82.1	97.7	0.04	19.9	31.1	39.4	89.8	0.0	18.7	45.2	81.1	97.8

Experiment 1 continues to outperform Experiment 2 in the first and third dataset groups. However, in the second dataset group, at 1,236 samples, Experiment 2 outperforms Experiment 1 by a narrow margin. The difference becomes more pronounced in Experiment 3 for this dataset size. However, at 2,236 samples, even the third dataset group shows that Experiment 1 outperforms the other two approaches. Overall, these findings suggest that Experiment 1, which leverages the full two-phase pipeline, achieves the best results for mid-sized datasets. Furthermore, in the first and third dataset groups, Experiment 2 slightly outperforms Experiment 3 for mid-sized datasets. The line chart comparing all datasets groups is shown in Fig. 2.

When comparing performance with the complete dataset, we find that in the first dataset group, even with all available training data, combination of synthetic data and AL in Experiment 1 still surpasses Experiments 2 and 3. This suggests that selecting the most informative samples early in training leads to better convergence and higher mAP, compared to feeding the model the entire dataset randomly. In the Truck dataset, the performance difference is smaller. However, in the second dataset group, Experiment 3 outperforms the others, demonstrating the effectiveness of AL's uncertainty sampling strategy for semi-large datasets without synthetic data in this case. For the first and second dataset groups, Experiment 1 continues to yield better precision even with the full dataset. When comparing Experiment 2 and Experiment 3, Experiment 2 performs better in the first dataset group, but for the second and third groups, Experiment 3 generalizes the OD model more effectively. In the Truck dataset, we observe that even with half the available samples, the two-phase detection approach-combining synthetic data and AL-achieves a high precision of 90.1%. Although further improvements are achieved with the full dataset, this finding reinforces the effectiveness of synthetic data in training OD models with limited real samples. Furthermore, When categorizing datasets based on size-Group 1

Training Samples	Experiment 1	Experiment 2	Experiment 3
236			
1736			
5236			

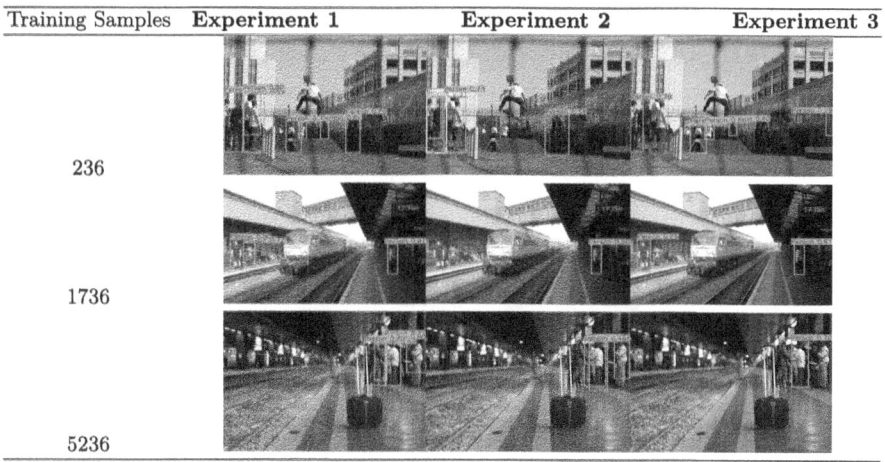

Fig. 4. Comparison of the three experiments with training samples at 236, 1736, and 5236 for second group of dataset KITTI and SYNTHIA. Each row corresponds to a different training sample size, and each row contains side-by-side results from Experiment 1, Experiment 2, and Experiment 3.

(large datasets), Group 2 (mid-sized datasets), and Group 3 (small datasets)-we observe that Experiment 1 consistently performs well across all three. In both large and small datasets, synthetic data plays a crucial role in enhancing detection performance, particularly across different data portions. However, for mid-sized datasets, Experiment 3 demonstrates a slight advantage over Experiment 1 when the full dataset is utilized. These trends are also illustrated in the line chart in Fig. 2.

Figures 5, 3, and 4 present sample detection results across different datasets, comparing the performance of three OD model experiments. In Fig. 3, for smaller datasets, such as the 1k sample size, Experiment 1 outperforms the others in detecting the Person class with higher precision. In contrast, Experiment 2 struggles with false negatives, particularly missing a person on the far right. In Fig. 3 additionally, in the 22k sample case, a truck is misclassified as an airplane, highlighting a clear false positive in second and third experiment. In Fig. 4, Experiment 1 consistently outperforms the other two approaches. For smaller dataset, false positives and false negatives are evident in Experiments 3 and 2, respectively. Finally, in Fig. 5, in the first row, with 200 training samples, the Glue-Gun in Experiment 1 is detected with higher precision. In the third row, the yellow trailer is correctly identified in Experiment 1, while Experiments 2 and 3 introduce false positives for a yellow lid that is not present in the image.

4.2   Conclusion

In this study, we extensively evaluated the two-phase pipeline, where synthetic data is used for pretraining in the first phase, followed by fine-tuning the OD

Training Samples	Experiment 1	Experiment 2	Experiment 3
200			
200			
250			

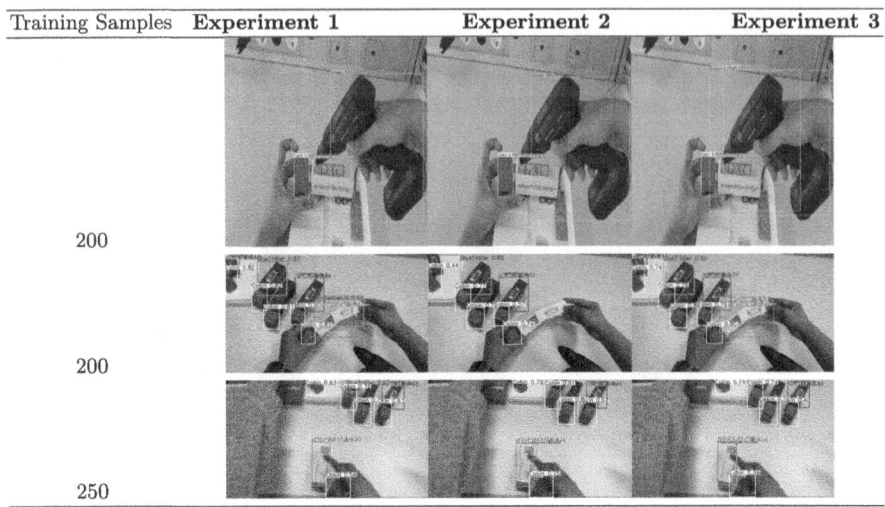

Fig. 5. Comparison of the three experiments with training samples at 200 for first two rows, and 250 as third row, for the third group of dataset Truck.

model with AL based on uncertainty sampling. Our findings demonstrate that this full pipeline plays a crucial role when dealing with limited data availability and restricted access to real data. Furthermore, we showed that even when the full dataset is used in the training loop for first group of dataset contain GTA-V and COCO, the two-phase approach offers significant advantages over other experimental setups that either lack synthetic data or do not incorporate uncertainty sampling. We observed that providing informative samples to the OD model earlier in the training process leads to improved precision.

References

1. Agarwal, S., Arora, H., Anand, S., Arora, C.: Contextual diversity for active learning. In: Vedaldi, A., Bischof, H., Brox, T., Frahm, J.-M. (eds.) ECCV 2020. LNCS, vol. 12361, pp. 137–153. Springer, Cham (2020). https://doi.org/10.1007/978-3-030-58517-4_9
2. Ahmad, T., Ma, Y., Yahya, M., Ahmad, B., Nazir, S., Haq, A.U.: Object detection through modified yolo neural network. Sci. Programm. **2020**(1), 8403262 (2020)
3. Beluch, W.H., Genewein, T., Nürnberger, A., Köhler, J.M.: The power of ensembles for active learning in image classification. In: Proceedings of the IEEE Conference on Computer Vision and Pattern Recognition, pp. 9368–9377 (2018)
4. Eversberg, L., Lambrecht, J.: Combining synthetic images and deep active learning: data-efficient training of an industrial object detection model. J. Imag. **10**(1) (2024)
5. Feng, D., Wei, X., Rosenbaum, L., Maki, A., Dietmayer, K.: Deep active learning for efficient training of a lidar 3D object detector. In: 2019 IEEE Intelligent Vehicles Symposium (IV), pp. 667–674. IEEE (2019)

6. Freytag, A., Rodner, E., Denzler, J.: Selecting influential examples: active learning with expected model output changes. In: Fleet, D., Pajdla, T., Schiele, B., Tuytelaars, T. (eds.) ECCV 2014. LNCS, vol. 8692, pp. 562–577. Springer, Cham (2014). https://doi.org/10.1007/978-3-319-10593-2_37

7. Geiger, A., Lenz, P., Urtasun, R.: Are we ready for autonomous driving? The KITTI vision benchmark suite. In: Conference on Computer Vision and Pattern Recognition (CVPR) (2012)

8. Korakakis, M., Mylonas, P., Spyrou, E.: A short survey on modern virtual environments that utilize AI and synthetic data (2018)

9. Lin, T.-Y., et al.: Microsoft COCO: common objects in context. In: Fleet, D., Pajdla, T., Schiele, B., Tuytelaars, T. (eds.) ECCV 2014. LNCS, vol. 8693, pp. 740–755. Springer, Cham (2014). https://doi.org/10.1007/978-3-319-10602-1_48

10. Ljungqvist, M.G., Nordander, O., Skans, M., Mildner, A., Liu, T., Nugues, P.: Object detector differences when using synthetic and real training data. SN Comput. Sci. **4**(3), 302 (2023)

11. Mumuni, A., Mumuni, F., Gerrar, N.K.: A survey of synthetic data augmentation methods in computer vision. arXiv preprint: arXiv:2403.10075 (2024)

12. Peng, H., et al.: Reducing annotating load: active learning with synthetic images in surgical instrument segmentation. Med. Image Anal. **97**, 103246 (2024)

13. Perri, D., Simonetti, M., Gervasi, O.: Synthetic data generation to speed-up the object recognition pipeline. Electronics **11**(1), 2 (2021)

14. Rakhimkul, S., Kim, A., Pazylbekov, A., Shintemirov, A.: Autonomous object detection and grasping using deep learning for design of an intelligent assistive robot manipulation system. In: 2019 IEEE International Conference on Systems, Man and Cybernetics (SMC), pp. 3962–3968 (2019)

15. Redmon, J.: You only look once: unified, real-time object detection. In: Proceedings of the IEEE Conference on Computer Vision and Pattern Recognition (2016)

16. Richter, S.R., Vineet, V., Roth, S., Koltun, V.: Playing for data: ground truth from computer games. In: Leibe, B., Matas, J., Sebe, N., Welling, M. (eds.) ECCV 2016. LNCS, vol. 9906, pp. 102–118. Springer, Cham (2016). https://doi.org/10.1007/978-3-319-46475-6_7

17. Ros, G., Sellart, L., Materzynska, J., Vazquez, D., Lopez, A.M.: The SYNTHIA dataset: a large collection of synthetic images for semantic segmentation of urban scenes. In: Proceedings of the IEEE Conference on Computer Vision and Pattern Recognition, pp. 3234–3243 (2016)

18. Roy, S., Unmesh, A., Namboodiri, V.P.: Deep active learning for object detection. In: BMVC, vol. 362, p. 91 (2018)

19. Seib, V., Lange, B., Wirtz, S.: Mixing real and synthetic data to enhance neural network training–a review of current approaches. arXiv preprint: arXiv:2007.08781 (2020)

20. Sekkat, H., Tigani, S., Saadane, R., Chehri, A.: Vision-based robotic arm control algorithm using deep reinforcement learning for autonomous objects grasping. Appl. Sci. **11**(17), 7917 (2021)

21. Settles, B.: Active learning literature survey (2009)

22. Sevastopoulos, C., Konstantopoulos, S., Balaji, K., Zaki Zadeh, M., Makedon, F.: A simulated environment for robot vision experiments. Technologies **10**(1), 7 (2022)

23. Surati, S., Hedaoo, S., Rotti, T., Ahuja, V., Patel, N.: Pick and place robotic arm: a review paper. Int. Res. J. Eng. Technol **8**(2), 2121–2129 (2021)

24. Tavakoli, H., Walunj, S., Pahlevannejad, P., Plociennik, C., Ruskowski, M.: Small object detection for near real-time egocentric perception in a manual assembly scenario. arXiv preprint: arXiv:2106.06403 (2021)

25. Tremblay, J., et al.: Training deep networks with synthetic data: bridging the reality gap by domain randomization. In: Proceedings of the IEEE Conference on Computer Vision and Pattern Recognition (CVPR) Workshops (2018)
26. Tsirikoglou, A., Eilertsen, G., Unger, J.: A survey of image synthesis methods for visual machine learning. In: Computer Graphics Forum, vol. 39, pp. 426–451. Wiley Online Library (2020)
27. Unity Technologies: Unity Perception package (2020)
28. Wrenninge, M., Unger, J.: Synscapes: a photorealistic synthetic dataset for street scene parsing. arXiv preprint: arXiv:1810.08705 (2018)

1st Workshop on Compliance in the Era of Artificial Intelligence (CAI)

1st Workshop on Compliance in the Era of Artificial Intelligence (CAI 2025)

The 1st Workshop on Compliance in the Era of Artificial Intelligence (CAI) explored the evolving role of compliance in business processes and information systems. As organizations face stringent regulatory requirements, such as GDPR, SOX, AML, and ISO standards, compliance is increasingly vital to operational strategy, helping organizations to avoid penalties, protect reputations, and remain competitive.

In addition to traditional methods such as control definition, risk assessment, compliance monitoring and reporting, CAI focuses on how emerging technologies, particularly Artificial Intelligence (AI) and Large Language Models (LLMs), can transform compliance management. These tools can automate repetitive tasks, process large datasets, enhance risk detection, and ensure real-time alignment with regulations, offering a more efficient and scalable approach.

The first edition of CAI received four submissions: three regular papers and one vision paper. Each submission underwent a thorough review process by three members of the Program Committee, ensuring high-quality feedback and selection. As a result, three papers were accepted for presentation, one regular paper and two vision papers, each contributing unique perspectives on the role of AI in compliance management. Only the regular paper is included in these proceedings. The papers were presented at the workshop, held in conjunction with the CAiSE conference in Vienna, Austria, and sparked engaging discussions among participants. In addition to the paper presentations, the workshop featured an outstanding keynote by Stefanie Rinderle-Ma, who shared insights on the transformative impact of AI in compliance management. The program concluded with an open discussion session, where attendees explored how emerging AI technologies could shape the future of compliance across various domains.

The three accepted papers encompassed a diverse range of compliance topics, including the potential of LLMs to augment violation explanations and propose remedial actions, the application of machine learning to predict compliance issues, and the compliance of the data/AI pipeline lifecycle itself:

In *Explaining the Compliance of Security Policies for GDPR in Business Processes*, *Cobo Ariza et al.* present an architecture that integrates business process management, security policy modeling, Complex Event Processing, and LLMs to enable real-time GDPR compliance monitoring. LLMs enhance explainability by clarifying violations and suggesting remedies, promoting transparency and accountability.

In *A Mashup-Based Approach for Predictive Compliance Monitoring*, *Romero-Flores et al.* propose a framework that integrates predictive process monitoring with compliance mashups to forecast rule compliance by composing multiple predictions. It also outlines future directions in predictive compliance monitoring.

In *DataPACT: Compliance by Design of Data/AI Operations and Pipelines*, *Roman et al.* present an overview of the DataPACT European initiative, focusing on its motivation, approach, and use cases. This initiative develops tools and methodologies to embed compliance, privacy, and sustainability into the design of data and AI pipelines. Data-PACT introduces a technical toolbox and a framework to support compliance-by-design across the data/AI pipeline lifecycle.

The organizers wish to thank all the authors who submitted papers to CAI 2025, the many participants creating fruitful discussions, Stefanie Rinderle-Ma for her excellent keynote, and the CAI 2025 Program Committee members for their valuable work in reviewing the submissions. We look forward to future editions of the workshop.

April 2025

Cristina Cabanillas
Andrea Marrella
Manuel Resinas
Karolin Winter

Organization

Organizing Committee

Cristina Cabanillas	University of Seville, Spain
Andrea Marrella	Sapienza University of Rome, Italy
Manuel Resinas	University of Seville, Spain
Karolin Winter	Eindhoven University of Technology, The Netherlands

Program Committee

Simone Agostinelli	Sapienza University of Rome, Italy
Chiara Di Francescomarino	University of Trento, Italy
Mohammadreza Fani Sani	Microsoft, Denmark
Walid Fdhila	University of Vienna, Austria
Pablo Fernandez	University of Seville, Spain
Laura Genga	Eindhoven University of Technology, The Netherlands
Guido Governatori	Central Queensland University, Australia
Hugo A. López	University of Copenhagen, Denmark
Fabrizio Maria Maggi	Free University of Bozen-Bolzano, Italy
Raimundas Matulevicius	University of Tartu, Estonia
Massimo Mecella	Sapienza Università di Roma, Italy
Luise Pufahl	TU Munich, Germany
Jana-Rebecca Rehse	University of Mannheim, Germany
Manfred Reichert	University of Ulm, Germany
Shazia Sadiq	University of Queensland, Australia
Emilio Sulis	University of Turin, Italy
Amy Van Looy	Ghent University, Belgium

Explaining the Compliance of Security Policies for GDPR in Business Processes

José Luis Cobo-Ariza$^{(\boxtimes)}$, Joaquín Arregui, Antonia M. Reina Quintero,
Ángel Jesús Varela-Vaca, and María Teresa Gómez-López

IDEA Research Group - Departamento de Lenguajes y Sistemas Informáticos i3US,
Instituto de Ingeniería Informática, Universidad de Sevilla, Sevilla, Spain
{jcobo,jarregui,reinaqu,ajvarela,maytegomez}@us.es
https://www.idea.us.es/

Abstract. Achieving compliance with the General Data Protection Regulation (GDPR) presents significant challenges to organisations, requiring substantial adaptations to business processes and the implementation of robust technical measures. This paper addresses the critical need to integrate security policies into business process management systems to enhance data protection. We propose an innovative architecture for access and usage control, aligned with GDPR's technical measures. This architecture integrates a business process management system, security policy modelling, a Complex Event Processing (CEP) engine, and Large Language Models (LLMs). This integration enables real-time detection of security policy violations, a capability that is crucial to maintaining compliance and mitigating risks. LLMs help bridge the gap between security policy definitions and the explainability of policy violations. They identify the reasons behind compliance breaches and suggest potential solutions. By leveraging their capabilities, we aim to simplify complex violation diagnoses into accessible insights. Thereby, this approach improves transparency and accountability, facilitating GDPR compliance.

Keywords: GDPR · Explainability · Security policies · Compliance · Business Process Models

1   Introduction

Implementing the General Data Protection Regulation (GDPR) is a legal obligation for organisations, but implementing it in practice is a complex task. Interpreting the regulation often presents additional challenges [1], and this complexity can result in inconsistent application of security practices and expose organisations to critical vulnerabilities. Furthermore, non-compliance with GDPR requirements can lead to significant fines imposed by European Data Protection Authorities[1]. In this context, correct compliance with the GDPR requires

---

[1]   https://www.enforcementtracker.com/.

© The Author(s), under exclusive license to Springer Nature Switzerland AG 2025
J. Grabis and Y. Wautelet (Eds.): CAiSE 2025 Workshops, LNBIP 556, pp. 355–367, 2025.
https://doi.org/10.1007/978-3-031-94931-9_29

significant adaptations of business processes (BP), as well as the definition and implementation of organisational and technical measures [2]. Consequently, data controllers - responsible for ensuring compliance with the GDPR - must identify and implement appropriate technical and organisational measures that ensure a level of security corresponding to known risks, as outlined in Article 32 of the GDPR.

Processing of personal data is at the core of the GDPR, which requires organisations to adopt technical measures to control both access and usage of such data [3]. On the one hand, access control [4] is a fundamental technical measure required to ensure the confidentiality and security of personal data. Organisations can significantly mitigate the risk of unauthorised data exposure by limiting access exclusively to authorised individuals. These practices align with the GDPR's principle of data minimisation, ensuring that only individuals whose job functions require access to specific data are granted these permissions. This approach not only reduces the risk of data breaches, but also reinforces organisational accountability by maintaining a controlled and auditable access management framework. On the other hand, usage control [5] complements access control by focussing on the appropriate use and processing of personal data in accordance with GDPR requirements. Establishing clear policies and mechanisms to monitor how data is accessed, used, and processed ensures that it is handled strictly for legitimate and predefined purposes. This includes implementing systems for monitoring data usage, conducting access audits, and integrating alerting mechanisms to detect potential misuse or unauthorised activities. These measures uphold the principles of integrity and confidentiality of the GDPR by safeguarding data against inappropriate or illicit processing. Furthermore, these controls foster transparency and enable organisations to demonstrate compliance through verifiable logs and audit trails.

An important part of the compliance process is the effective functioning of the organisational and technical measures that have been implemented. Specifically, the definition, implementation, and continuous monitoring of security policies are crucial to ensure compliance, because security policy violations can lead to non-compliance systems [6]. However, despite the need to incorporate security policies into business process models [7], a significant gap exists between the definition of security policies and their verification and diagnosis at runtime, as highlighted by Leitner&Rinderle-Ma in [8]. That work provided a complete analysis of the state-of-the-art and identified major unsolved research challenges regarding security in BPs, including monitoring, testing, evaluation, and the detection of security items. Although current research on secure BPM and its practice provides theoretical results on certain aspects, it often does not provide practical, technological solutions that explain whether (and why) the regulation is being satisfied in real-time operations.

Recently, LLMs have demonstrated their applicability in the field of BPM [9]. However, their application has been outside the scope of security-related use cases. In this article, we address the challenge of applying LLMs not only to explain why policy rules have been violated, but also to provide valuable insights on how such a situation can be solved. To overcome this challenge, we present XSecBPMN, a solution that: 1) includes an architecture to enforce GDPR compliance through security policies in business processes; 2) integrates a BP management system, security policies, and a Complex Event Processing (CEP) engine to detect security policy violations at runtime; and 3) incorporates LLMs enabling a user-friendly analysis of security policy violations by explaining why compliance is violated.

The remainder of this paper is structured as follows. Section 2 introduces the XSecBPMN framework, while Sect. 3 explains the detection of security violations. In Sect. 4 we discuss how LLMs enhance the explainability of policy rule violations. Section 5 validates the proposed approach through a real-world use case, which includes violation analysis and explanations aligned with GDPR compliance. Section 6 reviews related work. Finally, Sect. 7 summarises the key findings and outlines potential directions for future research.

2   XSecBPMN in a Nutshell

The XSecBPMN architecture (cf. Fig. 1) integrates a set of coordinated modules designed to achieve the objectives mentioned above. Essentially, XSecBPMN includes a BPM Modeller, which extends Camunda^{TM}, to allow experts to specify BP models and their associated security policies. These policies are specified directly in the BP model by using annotations. To support this, XSecBPMN provides a lightweight extension to the BPMN language, by adding new elements and attributes that captures both role-based and use-control access control models [10].

Once the security rules are specified, they are automatically transformed into Complex Event Processing (CEP) rules and stored in a ruleset. To implement this transformation, we have defined a set of *rule patterns* that allows us to transform all security rules into CEP rules written in an EPL. These patterns are then sent to the CEP Engine[2] to form a *ruleset*.

XSecBPMN also integrates a BPM Engine which generates a stream of events during BP model executions, some of which may violate defined policy rules. Using the security policies, *Create rules for Policy Violations module* generates the rules injected into the CEP Engine.

To improve the explainability of security rule violations, we have included an *Explain Policy Violation (LLM) module*, comprising three different LLM agents. This module uses the CEP Engine's output, the BP model, and the security policy rules as input and generates enriched information about violations, including explanations regarding GDPR compliance and suggestions for fixes. Section 3 provides a detailed explanation of security policies and how to detect policy violations.

---

[2] Esper: https://www.espertech.com/esper/.

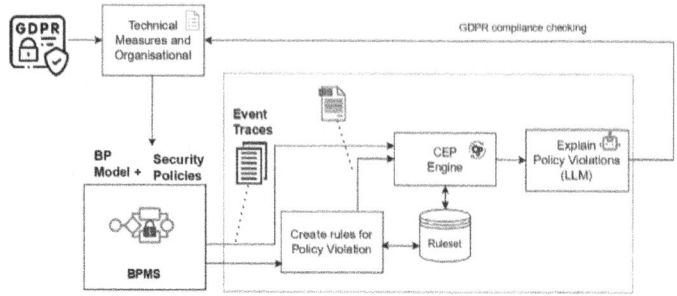

Fig. 1. XSecBPMN architecture schema.

3   Security Policy Description and Detecting Violations

To effectively detect policy rule violations, BP models should be annotated with usage and access control rules, as detailed in Subsect. 3.1. These rules are the foundation for automated compliance monitoring. The detection and verification of such violations during process execution are handled through the CEP engine, as detailed in Subsect. 3.2.

3.1   Usage and Access Control Policies in Business Process Models

Several studies have explored the importance of incorporating security artefacts into process models [8]. We propose the annotation of BPMN including the most common security policies related to the enforcement of authorisation and usage of control constraints to comply with the GDPR. The types of security policies supported by XSecBPMN are the following:

- **Separation of duty (SoD)** [11] represents a constraint that requires two or more different roles or users to complete a task. SoD is crucial for data integrity and confidentiality. By requiring critical tasks to be performed by different people or roles, the risk of fraud, abuse, or unauthorised access to personal data is reduced. This practice is aligned with the GDPR principle of integrity and confidentiality, as it prevents a single person from having full control over the data, thereby minimising the risk of manipulation or improper disclosure. In addition, SoD also supports the principle of proactive accountability, as it implements controls to demonstrate that measures are taken to protect information.
- **Binding of Duty (BoD)** [12] represents a constraint that requires that certain activities in the process be performed by the same user or role. This constraint is relevant to the GDPR in situations where it is necessary for the same user or role to perform related tasks to ensure data consistency and accuracy. For example, if a user initiates a data update, that same person might need to complete it to avoid inconsistencies. In this context, BoD aligns with the principles of accuracy and data minimisation, as it avoids

the need to transfer information between multiple users, which could lead to errors. Violating this BoD constraint (i.e., no single user or role performs the bound tasks), could lead to breaches of the principles of accuracy and data minimisation (GDPR Arts. 5, 24, 32, and 33).

-   **Usage of Control (UoC)** [5] controls the maximum number of accesses to a resource (cardinality) or the obligation to delete local copies of a data item after accessing and using these data. This control is directly relevant to the GDPR, as it focusses on enforcing the use and processing of personal data. By establishing conditions on how data can be accessed and used, UoC ensures compliance with the GDPR principles of purpose limitation, data minimisation, integrity, and confidentiality. For example, by limiting the number of accesses to a personal data file, the risk of misuse or unauthorised access is reduced. Furthermore, the obligation to delete local copies is directly related to the principle of storage limitation. Violating UoC constraints relates directly to the GDPR regulations on data minimisation and storage limitation, specifically outlined in GDPR Arts. 5, 24, 32, and 33. Non-compliance with these constraints would constitute a violation of these GDPR provisions.

3.2   Create Rules for Policy Violations

To detect violations during the execution of the BP, we chose CEP technology. This decision is driven by the need to analyse a large volume of events to identify when a policy rule is violated, something that CEP is particularly well suited for.

For each security policy, we have created a corresponding CEP rule. These rules are designed to detect specific data patterns (that is, event conditions) that trigger alerts for potential violations. By analysing event traces of the process model execution and matching them against CEP rules, we can detect any violation of security policies. When a violation occurs, an entry is made in the policy violation log detailing the data involved, which includes a timestamp, lane IDs, role or user IDs, task IDs, and the specific policy that was violated.

4   Explainability of Policy Violations Using LLMs

CEP engines detect rule violations but do not explain how they can be solved or their implications for GDPR compliance. To address this gap, we propose the integration of Large Language Models (LLMs). LLMs are highly advanced computational models characterised by large parameter sizes, robust learning capabilities, and the ability to understand and generate human language [13]. By providing a conversational interface, LLMs enable users with limited expertise in query languages (e.g., SQL) or specific domains (e.g., process optimisation) to interact with data more intuitively. This allows them to harness advanced functionalities without requiring specialised training or prior knowledge. However, LLMs may struggle to handle domain-specific or highly specialised queries beyond their training data [14]. To improve the precision and relevance of the responses generated, the Retrieval-Augmented Generation (RAG) approach suggests supplementing the LLMs with external data sources, which serve as contextual references for data retrieval and response generation [14].

Moreover, LLM output can be refined through prompting, a technique that involves providing textual inputs, such as instructions or examples that guide the model response format and content [15]. Prompts play a crucial role in shaping the behaviour of the model, ensuring that its outputs align with the user's specific requirements [15]. However, given the text input limitations of LLMs, it is impossible to provide them with exhaustive GDPR-related content. As a result, the model's responses are constrained to the knowledge encoded in its training data. Despite this limitation, the integration of LLMs into business process modelling represents a transformative shift, minimising the reliance on manual effort and specialised expertise [16].

XSecBPMN provides the LLMs four key input parameters: the BP model, the defined security policy, the event traces, and the specific detected violated policy. The LLMs are first trained to understand the security policies and GDPR legislation and principles. To support the explanation of policy violations and improve the interpretation of GDPR compliance, XSecBPMN uses three state-of-the-art LLMs, each selected for its strengths, namely, GPT-4o [17], DeepSeek-R1 [18], and LLaMA (meta/llama-3.1-405b-instruct) [19].

GPT-4o, developed by OpenAI, is one of the great pioneers in this field. According to OpenAI's documentation[3], GPT-4o has great capabilities to understand the provided text and correctly evaluate the information. These capabilities make GPT-4o a good candidate for identifying the causes of security policy violations.

DeepSeek-R1, developed by DeepSeek, fits better to our requirements. Although it outperforms GPT-4o in areas such as programming, coding, mathematics, and logical reasoning, it falls short of text comprehension and generation. As a result, its performance in interpreting complex policy rules and suggesting improvements may be comparatively limited.

Lastly, LLaMA, an open-source family of LLMs developed by Meta AI, has been widely used in the business process domain [20]. It delivers excellent results in informing and providing highly relevant data to human workers in companies. However, its application in the context of applying security policies in business processes has not yet been explored, making its use in XSecBPMN a novel contribution to the field.

5   Validation

To validate XSecBPMN, we have used a real-world financial case study involving collaborative projects between private companies and research institutions. This scenario is based on the business process introduced in [21], which describes the

---

[3]   https://platform.openai.com/docs/.

workflow and interactions among these partnerships, as described in Fig. 2. The process model has been extended to include a set of security policies aligned with GDPR requirements, implemented as technical measures by the data controller to ensure compliance.

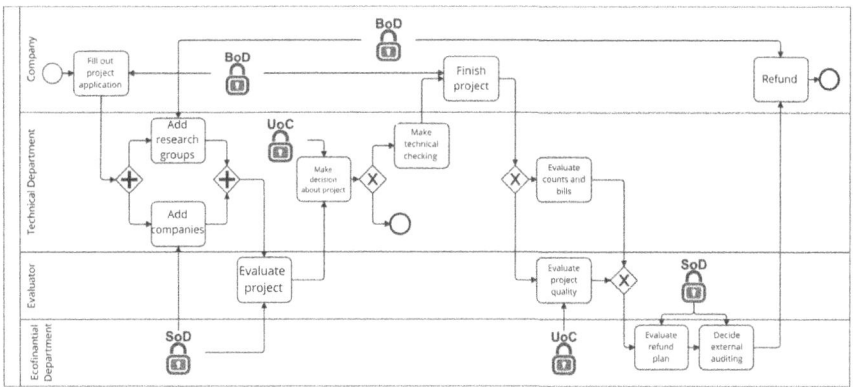

Fig. 2. Business Process Model with SoD, BoD and UoC policies.

Each of the LLMs has a predefined token size. For an input of 100 words, GPT-4o uses 286 tokens, DeepSeek-R1 uses 180 tokens, and LLaMA-3.1-405b uses 282 tokens. Once the token size is established, the price for 100K tokens is $0.0025 for GPT-4o, $0.00055 for DeepSeek-R1 and $0.0035 for LLaMA-3.1-405b. This analysis highlights not only variations in pricing, but also differences in tokenisation strategies, a factor that directly influences model performance. Tokenisation, particularly the segmentation of input into discrete units, can introduce significant inductive biases that influence tasks such as numerical reasoning. In this context, understanding the relationship between tokenisation strategies and their associated costs is essential to optimise their use in explainability processes.

To assess the practical effectiveness of the selected LLMs, we applied XSecBPMN to the defined business process and its associated security policies to identify policy violations. When policy violations are detected, we observed notable differences in the explanations and suggestions of the three LLMs. Next, we evaluate and compare the results of GPT-4o, DeepSeek-R1 and LLaMa-3.1-405b in terms of their ability to interpret violations.

– **GPT-4o** excels in analysing BP violations in-depth, offering comprehensive and highly detailed suggestions. It takes into account BPMN dependencies, providing specific solutions, such as changes in assignment logic, rule enforcement, or load balancing. It also provides relevant data on GDPR, highlighting and mentioning features such as the principle of accuracy, the principle of integrity, data minimisation, confidentiality, and storage limitation. Although its accuracy rate is moderate at 45% providing a suggested solution, it compensates with a thorough analysis, taking approximately 27.81 s per response. In complex process models, its suggestions can match those of other LLMs in accuracy, particularly due to its contextual understanding of violations within the BP. The evaluation with this LLM has been of 64,707 tokens at a price of 0.1617675 USD.

- **DeepSeek-R1** struggles to correctly interpret security policies and the given use case, often generating incorrect and contradictory suggestions. It demonstrates a poor understanding of GDPR, often confusing the most important terms of GDPR and misattributing these misconceptions to violations of security rules. With an accuracy of only 25% and the longest response time of 205 s, DeepSeek-R1 is not a reliable model to explain security policy compliance. Its inconsistencies and slow performance make it impractical for users who require accurate and efficient analysis of security policies. The evaluation involved 70132 tokens at a cost of 0.0385726 USD.
- **LLaMA-3.1-405b** performs well in analysing BPs, though it suggestions tend to be simpler and lower-level. while the suggestions are clear and easy to understand, they lack depth in addressing complex scenarios. It correctly understands the GDPR and interprets it well in simple BPs. However, as BP complexity increases, it fails to properly relate GDPR regulations to security policy violations. With the highest accuracy at 55% and a fast response time of 10.05 s, LLaMA-3.1-405b outperforms its peers in speed and precision. It excels in simpler BPs and simulations with fewer violations but becomes less precise when handling highly complex BP models. The evaluation with this LLM has been 68,190 tokens for 0.3634527 USD.

There are notable differences among the three LLMs in terms of their capabilities. DeepSeek-R1 performs the weakest, as it struggles to interpret the input correctly and shows inconsistency in its response. LLaMA-3.1-405b performs better, recognising the input data but providing ambiguous and imprecise responses. In contrast, GPT-4o is capable of understanding and giving the right suggestions, making it the most effective LLM in this evaluation.

The security policies are intentionally added to ensure compliance with GDPR. These policies relate tasks according to the principles of data minimisation, data access control, integrity, and confidentiality. In the following analysis, we examine one representative rule from each type of security policy, exploring the relationships between them and how each LLM responds to them.

- **Separation of Duty:** This rule is applied to the tasks "Evaluate refund plan" and "Decide external auditing", which must be carried out by two or more users to ensure the principles of integrity and confidentiality. The referenced GDPR articles vary by LLM: GPT-4o typically cites Article 5(1)(f) (Integrity and Confidentiality) and Article 5(2) (Accountability); DeepSeek adds Article 32 (Security of processing) to the ones mentioned before; while LLaMA refers to Article 5(1)(f)(Integrity and Confidentiality) and Article 24 (Proactive Accountability).

– **Binding of Duty:** This rule links the tasks "Fill out project application" and "Finish project", which requires a single role or user to complete both tasks to ensure the principle of accuracy and data minimisation under GDPR. All three LLMs refer to Article 5(1)(c) (Data Minimisation) and Article 5(1)(d) (Accuracy). DeepSeek sometimes refers to Article 32 (Security of processing).
– **Usage of Control:** This rule concerns the task "Evaluate project quality", where the number of users accessing data is limited to ensure compliance with the data minimisation regulation. GPT-4o and LLaMA both reference Articles 5(1)(b) (Purpose Limitation), 5(1)(c) (Data Minimisation), 5(1)(e) (Storage Limitation and Integrity) and 5(1)(f) (Confidentiality). DeepSeek references Articles 5(1)(b) (Purpose Limitation), 5(1)(c) (Data Minimisation), 5(1)(e) (Storage Limitation), 25 (Data Protection by Design and Default) and 32 (Security of processing).

In conclusion, the explanations given by the three LLMs provide the relevant articles that should be referenced. However, GPT-4o provides more consistent responses with a higher level of detail. While DeepSeek-R1 and LLaMA-3.1-405b remain within the general framework of the GDPR, their outputs are less comprehensive and precise.

XSecBPMN implementation, enriched BP model, EPL rules, event logs, LLM prompts, and detailed explanations for the use case are freely available in https://github.com/ajvarela/cai2025/.

6   Related Work

We consider related work in three different areas: business process compliance (BPC) for security, Event-Driven Business Process Management (EDBPM) for policy evaluation, and LLMs for business process models.

In the context of BP compliance, there are three different strategies for managing compliance in the literature: design-time, in which processes are assessed for non-compliance patterns at design time; runtime, in which compliance patterns are assessed while processes are being executed; and audit, in which the patterns are assessed in the logs produced by processes, in a post-mortem strategy. We consider that the approaches closest to ours are those that follow an audit strategy to manage compliance.

After conducting a systematic literature review on BP compliance, Hashimi et al. [22] found that 28% of the approaches surveyed adopt a design-time strategy to manage compliance, 32% use a run-time strategy, and only 10% rely on an audit strategy. They suggest that the low adoption of the audit strategy may be attributed to the regulatory pressure on companies to avoid non-compliance. The approaches that adopt an audit strategy usually employ process mining techniques and database technologies to detect non-compliance behaviour according to a given set of rules. Thus, van der Aalst and Medeiros [23] are some of the pioneers in using process mining techniques to analyse audit trails for security violations; concretely, they focus on intrusion detection. Bezerra et al. [24] also use process mining techniques to detect anomalies in traces. But the approaches most related to ours are those that audit violations of security constraints. In this sense, Alrahili [25] conducted a systematic literature review to study how process mining is being used for security analysis, specifically for Role-Based Access Control (RBAC). Table 1 summarises the approaches surveyed in that review that use an audit strategy.

Table 1. Approaches of business process security compliance that use an audit strategy.

Reference	Constraints	Formalism
[4]	SoD, BoD	LTL
[26]	Four-eyes principle	LTL
[27]	Role-based access control model, usage control, SoD, BoD, conflict of interest, and isolation	LTL
[28]	SoD	pattern-based, Markov Chains
[29]	SoD	control-flow alignment
[30]	BoD, SoD	LTL

In the field of Event-Driven Business Process Management, Amjad et al. [31] conducted a systematic literature review to examine Event-Driven Process Chain approaches for modelling and verifying business requirements. Among the 73 studies analysed, only two addressed complex events, and of these, only one, the proposed by Amjad et al. [32] focusses on verification. Furthermore, none of them deals with security requirements. In contrast, Sharifi et al. [33] proposed a CEP-based solution for business process monitoring, but their approach is based on a real-time strategy.

In the context of using LLMs for security auditing, Mothukuri et al. [34] employed GPT-4 to identify and fix vulnerabilities in smart contracts. However, unlike our approach, their work does not leverage LLMs for explainability, nor does it focus on security in BPs. To the best of our knowledge, although the potential of LLM in BPs has been explored [16,35], no proposal has yet used them to improve the explainability of security policy violations in the context of BPs.

7   Conclusions and Future Work

There exists a significant gap between GDPR compliance and how the violation of technical measures contributes to non-compliance. This paper introduces XSecBPMN, an architecture design to describe security policies in business processes as a response to technical measures for GDPR compliance. To achieve this, XSecBPMN integrates an engine to detect policy violations and a specific module to explain why these violations occur and how they relate to GDPR compliance. The architecture supports the full life cycle of security policy rules, which includes: the modelling of policy rules (SoD, BoD, and UoC) in a business process; the detection and diagnosis of security policy violation using CEP technologies; and an explanation of why the rules are violated and how to solve them using LLMs. Three state-of-the-art LLMs have been integrated to complete the explanation of why the policy rules are violated. Among them, GPT-4o demonstrated the highest performance, making it the most suitable for analysing policy rule violations in business processes.

In summary, XSecBPMN enables business experts to assign tasks to different roles and users within a business process, while embedding policy rules mandated as a technical measure of GDPR. These rules are validated in real-time using CEP, and LLMs contribute to explaining the origin of any violations and their relationship with GDPR compliance.

For future work, we identify two main areas for improvement: (1) Extending the types of policy rules, and (2) further exploring how LLMs can leverage the explanation capability, including their potential to prevent policy violations before they occur.

Acknowledgments. This work has been supported by the Grants KOSMOS-US PID2024-155363OB-C42, AETHER-US PID2020-112540RB-C44 and ALBA-US TED2021-130355B-C32 funded by MICIU/AEI/10.13039/501100011033 and by the "European Union NextGenerationEU/PRTR".

References

1. Almeida Teixeira, G., Mira da Silva, M., Pereira, R.: The critical success factors of GDPR implementation: a systematic literature review. Digit. Policy, Regul. Gov. **21**(4), 402–418 (2019)
2. Varela-Vaca, Á.J., Gómez-López, M.T., Zamora, Y.M., Gasca, R.M.: Business process models and simulation to enable GDPR compliance. Int. J. Inf. Secur. **24**(1), 1–21 (2025)
3. Basin, D., Debois, S., Hildebrandt, T.: On purpose and by necessity: compliance under the GDPR. In: Meiklejohn, S., Sako, K. (eds.) FC 2018. LNCS, vol. 10957, pp. 20–37. Springer, Heidelberg (2018). https://doi.org/10.1007/978-3-662-58387-6_2
4. Baumgrass, A., Baier, T., Mendling, J., Strembeck, M.: Conformance checking of RBAC policies in process-aware information systems. In: Business Process Management orkshops - BPM 2011 International Workshops, Clermont-Ferrand, France, August 29, 2011, Revised Selected Papers, Part II, volume 100 of Lecture Notes in Business Information Processing, pp. 435–446. Springer (2011)
5. Sandhu, R., Park, J.: Usage control: a vision for next generation access control. Comput. Netw. Secur., 17–31 (2003)
6. Brunel, J., Cuppens, F., Cuppens, N., Sans, T., Bodeveix, J.-P.: Security policy compliance with violation management. In: Proceedings of the 2007 ACM Workshop on Formal Methods in Security Engineering, pp. 31–40 (2007)

7. Müller, G., Accorsi, R.: Why are business processes not secure? In: Number Theory and Cryptography - Papers in Honor of Johannes Buchmann on the Occasion of His 60th Birthday, pp. 240–254 (2013)

8. Leitner, M., Rinderle-Ma, S.: A systematic review on security in process-aware information systems - constitution, challenges, and future directions. Inf. Softw. Technol. **56**(3), 273–293 (2014)

9. Vidgof, M., Bachhofner, S., Mendling, J.: Large language models for business process management: opportunities and challenges. In: Business Process Management Forum - BPM 2023, volume 490 of Lecture Notes in Business Information Processing, pp. 107–123. Springer (2023)

10. Quintero, A., Pérez, S.M., Varela-Vaca, Á.J., López, M., Cabot, J.: A domain-specific language for the specification of UCON policies. J. Inf. Secur. Appl. **64**, 103006 (2022)

11. Botha, R.A., Eloff, J.H.P.: Separation of duties for access control enforcement in workflow environments. IBM Syst. J. **40**(3), 666–682 (2001)

12. Koukovini, M., Papagiannakopoulou, E., Lioudakis, G.V., Dellas, N., Kaklamani, D.I., Venieris, I.S.: Privacy Compliance Requirements in Workflow Environments. In: Handbook of Research on Digital Crime, Cyberspace Security, and Information Assurance. IGI Global (2014)

13. Yupeng Chang, X., et al.: A survey on evaluation of large language models. ACM Trans. Intell. Syst. Technol. **15**(3), 1–45 (2024)

14. Lewis, P., et al.: Retrieval-augmented generation for knowledge-intensive NLP tasks. In: Proceedings of the 34th International Conference on Neural Information Processing Systems (NeurIPS 2020), pp. 9459–9474. Curran Associates, Inc. (2020)

15. Zamfirescu-Pereira, J.D., Wong, R.Y., Hartmann, B., Yang, Q.: Why johnny can't prompt: how non-AI experts try (and fail) to design LLM prompts. In: Proceedings of the 2023 CHI Conference on Human Factors in Computing Systems, CHI '23, pp. 1–21. ACM (2023)

16. Kourani, H., Berti, A., Schuster, D., van der Aalst, W.M.: Process modeling with large language models. In: Enterprise, Business-Process and Information Systems Modeling - 25th International Conference, BPMDS 2024, volume 511 of Lecture Notes in Business Information Processing, pp. 229–244. Springer (2024)

17. OpenAI. GPT-4 Technical Report, pp. 1–17. arXiv preprint: arXiv:2303.08774v6 (2024)

18. DeepSeek-AI. Deepseek-r1: Incentivizing reasoning capability in LLMS via reinforcement learning. In: Proceedings of the AIME 2024 Conference. arXiv (2025)

19. Touvron, H., et al.: Llama: open and efficient foundation language models (2023)

20. Bernardi, M. L., Casciani, A., Cimitile, M., Marrella, A.: Conversing with business process-aware large language models: the BPLLM framework. J. Intell. Inf. Syst. (2024)

21. Gomez-Lopez, M.T., Gasca, R.M., Rinderle-Ma, S.: Explaining the incorrect temporal events during business process monitoring by means of compliance rules and model-based diagnosis. In: 17th IEEE International Enterprise Distributed Object Computing Conference Workshops, EDOC Workshops, 2013, pp. 163–172 (2013)

22. Hashmi, M., Governatori, G., Lam, H.-P., Wynn, M.T.: Are we done with business process compliance: state of the art and challenges ahead. Knowl. Inf. Syst. **57**(1), 79–133 (2018). https://doi.org/10.1007/s10115-017-1142-1

23. Van der Aalst, W.M., de Medeiros, A.: Process mining and security: detecting anomalous process executions and checking process conformance. Electr. Notes Theor. Comput. Sci. **121**, 3–21 (2005)

24. Bezerra, F., Wainer, J., van der Aalst, W.: Anomaly detection using process mining. In: Halpin, T., Krogstie, J., Nurcan, S., Proper, E., Schmidt, R., Soffer, P., Ukor, R. (eds.) BPMDS/EMMSAD -2009. LNBIP, vol. 29, pp. 149–161. Springer, Heidelberg (2009). https://doi.org/10.1007/978-3-642-01862-6_13

25. Alrahili, R.: Towards employing process mining for role based access control analysis: a systematic literature review. In: Proceedings of the Future Technologies Conference (FTC) 2021, Volume 1, pp. 904–927. Springer International Publishing, Cham (2022)

26. Asare, E., Wang, L., Fang, X.: Conformance checking: workflow of hospitals and workflow of open-source EMRs. IEEE Access **8**, 139546–139566 (2020)

27. Accorsi, R., Stocker, T.: On the exploitation of process mining for security audits: the conformance checking case. In: Proceedings of the ACM Symposium on Applied Computing, SAC 2012, pp. 1709–1716. ACM (2012)

28. Zahoransky, R.M., Holderer, J., Lange, A., Brenig, C.: Process analysis as first step towards automated business security. In: 24th European Conference on Information Systems, ECIS 2016, Istanbul, Turkey, June 12-15, 2016 (2016)

29. Salnitri, M., Alizadeh, M., Giovanella, D., Zannone, N., Giorgini, P.: From security-by-design to the identification of security-critical deviations in process executions. In: Mendling, J., Mouratidis, H. (eds.) CAiSE 2018. LNBIP, vol. 317, pp. 218–234. Springer, Cham (2018). https://doi.org/10.1007/978-3-319-92901-9_19

30. Cabanillas, C., Ackermann, L., Schönig, S., Sturm, C., Mendling, J.: The RALph miner for automated discovery and verification of resource-aware process models. Softw. Syst. Model. **19**(6), 1415–1441 (2020). https://doi.org/10.1007/s10270-020-00820-7

31. Amjad, A., Azam, F., Anwar, M.W., Butt, W.H., Rashid, M.: Event-driven process chain for modeling and verification of business requirements-a systematic literature review. IEEE Access **6**, 9027–9048 (2018)

32. Amjad, A., Azam, F., Anwar, M.W., Butt, W.H.: Verification of event-driven process chain with timed automata and time petri nets. In: 2017 9th IEEE-GCC Conference and Exhibition (GCCCE), pp. 1–6 (2017)

33. Fardbastani, M.A., Allahdadi, F., Sharifi, M.: EDBPM: an event-driven business process monitoring mechanism. Int. J. Inf. Commun. Technol. Res., 10(2) (2018)

34. Mothukuri, V., Parizi, R.M., Massa, J.L.: LLMSmartSec: Smart contract security auditing with LLM and annotated control flow graph. In: IEEE International Conference on Blockchain, Blockchain, 2024, pp. 434–441. IEEE (2024)

35. Lashkevich, K., Milani, F., Avramenko, M., Dumas, M.: LLM-Assisted optimization of waiting time in business processes: A prompting method. In: Business Process Management - 22nd International Conference, BPM 2024, Krakow, Poland, September 1-6, 2024, Proceedings, volume 14940 of Lecture Notes in Computer Science, pp. 474–492. Springer (2024)

Author Index

© The Editor(s) (if applicable) and The Author(s), under exclusive license
to Springer Nature Switzerland AG 2025
J. Grabis and Y. Wautelet (Eds.): CAiSE 2025 Workshops, LNBIP 556, pp. 369–370, 2025.
https://doi.org/10.1007/978-3-031-94931-9

The manufacturer's authorised representative in the EU is Springer
Nature Customer Service Centre GmbH, Europaplatz 3, 69115 Heidelberg,
Germany. If you have any concerns regarding our products, please
contact ProductSafety@springernature.com

Printed and bound by CPI Group (UK) Ltd, Croydon, CR0 4YY

28/04/2026

02098521-0008